Fidelis Morgan has played major roles in plays from Beaumont & Fletcher to Brecht. She was for many years a leading actress with the Glasgow Citizens Company and has since worked at Nottingham and West Yorkshire Playhouses and in the West End production of Noël Coward's *The Vortex*. On television she played for three years in the children's series *Mr Majeika* as well as roles in *The Bill* and *Jeeves & Wooster*. Her other books include *A Misogynist's Source Book*, *The Female Tatler* and a novel, *My Dark Rosaleen*. She has also edited *The Female Wits: Women Playwrights of The Restoration* and *The Years Between: Plays by Women on the London Stage 1900–1950*. Fidelis Morgan lives in London.

WICKED

WOMEN'S WIT
AND HUMOUR
FROM ELIZABETH I
TO RUBY WAX

EDITED BY FIDELIS MORGAN

A *Virago* Book

Published by Virago Press 1996

First published in Great Britain by Virago Press 1995

This collection copyright © 1995 by Fidelis Morgan
Acknowledgements on pp. 355–56 constitute an extension of
this copyright page

A CIP catalogue record for this book
is available from the British Library.

ISBN 1 86049 166 9

Printed and bound in Great Britain by Clays Ltd, St Ives plc

Virago
A Division of
Little, Brown and Company (UK)
Brettenham House
Lancaster Place
London WC2E 7EN

CONTENTS

Preface by SUE TOWNSEND vii

THAT KIND OF WOMAN . . . THAT KIND OF MAN 1

VANITY, LIKE MURDER, WILL OUT 21

IS IT WORTH GETTING THERE? 39

IF LOVE IS THE ANSWER . . . 53

HOW WONDERFUL IT MUST HAVE BEEN 77

PLAT DU JOUR 93

TENNIS IS TOO VIOLENT A MOTION 111

GENERAL REVIEW OF THE SEX SITUATION 121

EVEN IF YOU WIN, YOU'RE STILL A RAT 133

DOWN THE GARDEN PATH 157

HERE COMES THE BRIDE 179

BITCHING AND WISECRACKING 213

ALL GOD'S CHILDREN 243

THE SINCEREST FORM OF FLATTERY 279

OCCUPATIONAL HAZARDS 299

GOD IS LOVE, BUT GET IT IN WRITING 319

TOTTERING TOWARDS THE TOMB 333

THE SERIOUS BIT: A MESSAGE FROM COMIC RELIEF 353

Acknowledgements 355
Index of Authors 357

PREFACE

I lost my sense of humour the other day. I was on a plane coming back from Australia, (I'd been on this plane for so long that by the time I got off I'd changed political opinions and forgotten what my children looked like). Anyway, I'm crammed into an economy-class seat, my ankles are puffing up and threatening to explode, and I have a wet, noisy and messy type of cold. The kind that makes you fall to your knees and thank science that paper handkerchiefs were invented.

I'm feverish and thirsty and the airline seems to be operating a quota system with the drinks: only when we pass a time zone do we get a fairy-acorn full of tepid orange juice. My poor dehydrated body is screaming for liquid. I moan audibly and the man next to me says, 'I will tell you some jokes to make you happy'. After a few dry runs, during which he mumbles the jokes to himself, he proceeds to tell me this *series* of incomprehensible Malaysian jokes. Perhaps if you're conversant with Malaysian politics or the names of Malaysian film stars or Malaysian football teams then his jokes were foot-stompingly funny. But I am not conversant with these things; the closest I've ever been to Malaysia is sitting in Dunkin Donuts at Khuala Lumpur Airport. Anyway, I think it was after the seventh joke that I lost my sense of humour. It went missing for about thirty-six hours, and I'm here to tell you that the world is a truly terrifying place without it. Men, for instance, are revealed as brutish hairy creatures who are totally incapable of simple tasks, such as plaiting a child's hair, or pressing the appropriate knobs on a washing machine. Children are fiends and my fellow workers tragic victims as they lugged their shopping bags about the place; or so it seemed to me during the long, humourless hours. My sense of humour was eventually found by a baggage handler at Heathrow Airport, the poor thing was cowering in the hold of the plane. On arrival at my house it was weak and in need of nourishment, so I fed it on this book, *Wicked*, and it was soon up and about and ringing its mate, Sense of Ridiculous, and arranging a get-together.

So, many thanks to all the contributors of *Wicked*. You restored me to health and happiness. I won't single anybody out for special praise; I was always the last girl to be chosen as a country dancing partner at school, so I embrace collectivism now. But I did laugh, long and hard. *Wicked* should be prescribed reading. Chemists should stock it. Who needs Prozac?

Sue Townsend, the car, Heathrow 1995

THAT KIND OF
WOMAN . . . THAT
KIND OF MAN

She's the kind of girl who climbed the ladder of success, wrong by wrong.

Mae West

Good women always think it is their fault when someone else is being offensive. Bad women never take the blame for anything.

Anita Brookner

From birth to eighteen a girl needs good parents. From eighteen to thirty-five, she needs good looks. From thirty-five to fifty-five, good personality. From fifty-five on, she needs good cash. I'm saving my money.

Sophie Tucker

Whatever women do they must do twice as well as men to
be thought half as good. Luckily, this is not difficult.

Charlotte Whitton

———

Female size especially brain size, has always been held to
explain their unfitness for this or that; whole nineteenth-
century theories were based on the smaller size of the brain
of women and 'inferior races' – until it was found that
elephants' brains were even larger than men's.

Katharine Whitehorn

———

The great and almost only comfort about being a woman is
that one can always pretend to be more stupid than one is
and no one is surprised.

Freya Stark

———

Committee

*The ladies are assembled in Mrs Hailestone's front room somewhere north of Birmingham. The
telly is full on. It is time to start the meeting.*

Well, let's get down to business, shall we?

Would you be so good as to turn off your telly, please, Mrs Hailestone?
Thank you. That's better. It's very good of you to let us use your front room.
I think we're all assembled. Mrs Brill, Miss Culch, Mrs Pell, Mrs Hailestone,
May and me. All right then, May, let's have the minutes of the last meeting.

Oh, May. You're supposed to have them in that little book I gave you.
I told you last time. You're supposed to write down everything we do and
say and then read it out at the next meeting, and I sign it.

I know we all know what we said and did, dear, but you have to write
it down. That's what minutes are for.

Don't cry, May, dear. Let's get on with the next item on the agenda.
Apologies for Absence. You read out the excuses. Oh, May. Well, you must
try and remember to bring your glasses next time. All right, I'll read them. Give
them here. Cheer up.

Mrs Slope is very sorry she's caught up. Can't come.

Miss Heddle's got her mother again. Can't come.

Lady Widmore sent a telegram: 'ALAS CANNOT BE WITH YOU DEVASTATED'. Can't come.

Well then. As you all know, this is *another* special meeting of the Ladies' Choral to talk about the forthcoming Festival and County Choral Competition. We know the date and we know the set song. Yes we do, May. It's in two parts for ladies' voices in E flat, 'My Bosom is a Nest'.

But of course what we are really here for tonight is this very important question of voices in the choir. Now, we don't want any unpleasantness. Friendly is what we are, and friendly is how we are going to go on. But it's no good beating about the bush, we all know there is *one* voice among the altos that did not ought to be there. And I think we all know to what I am referring.

Now, don't think that I don't like Mrs Codlin, because I do. Yes, she *is* a very nice woman. Look at how nice she is with her little car – giving us all lifts here and there. And she's a lovely lender – lends you her books, and her knitting patterns, recipes, anything. Lovely. Yes, she is a regular churchgoer *and* a most generous donator to the fund. But she just has this one fault: she does not blend.

May, dear, would you be so kind as to slip out and see if I left the lamp turned off on my bike? I don't want to waste the battery, and I can't remember if I did it. Thank you, May.

Ladies, I didn't like to say anything in front of May, but I must remind you that Mrs Codlin's voice is worse than what ever May's was; and you know what happened the last time we let May sing in the competition. We were disqualified. So you see it is very important and very serious.

Oh thank you, May, dear. Had I? I am a big silly, aren't I?

You see, it isn't as if Mrs Codlin had a voice you could ignore. I mean you can't drown her out. They can hear her all down the road, over the sopranos; yes, over your piano, Mrs Pell, over everything. You know, I was stood next to her at practice last week when we did 'The Wild Brown Bee is my Lover'. When we'd finished I said to her very tactfully, thinking she might like to take the hint, I said: 'I wonder who it is stands out so among the altos?' and she said she hadn't noticed. Hadn't noticed! Mrs Brill was on her other side and she said to me afterwards – didn't you, Mrs Brill? – she said the vibrations were so considerable they made her chest hum.

No, I know she doesn't do it on purpose, May.

No, of course she didn't ought to have been let in in the first place. It's ridiculous. It makes a nonsense of music. But the thing is, it was her idea, wasn't it? She founded the choir.

Do you think if anyone was to ask her very nicely not to sing it might stop her? I mean we could let her come and just stand there. Yes, Mrs Hailestone, she does *look* like a singer, I'll give her that. That's the annoying part.

Would anybody like to ask her? Well, has anybody got any suggestions? No, May, not anonymous letters. They aren't very nice.

May . . . ?

I wonder . . . May, one of your jobs as secretary is watching the handbags and the coats at competitions, isn't it? I mean you have to stay in the cloakroom all during the competitions, don't you? I thought so. Look, May; now don't think we don't appreciate you as secretary – we do, dear, don't we ladies? – But would you like to resign? Just say yes now, and I'll explain it all later. Lovely.

Well, we accept your resignation, and I would like to propose that we appoint Mrs Codlin secretary and handbag watcher for the next competition. Anybody second that? Thank you, Mrs Hailestone. Any against? Then that's passed unanimously. Lovely. Oh, I know it's not an order, Mrs Pell, but we haven't any minutes to prove it. May didn't have a pencil, did you, May?

Well, I think it's a very happy solution. We get rid of her and keep her at one and the same time.

What did you say, May? Can *you* sing if Mrs Codlin doesn't?

Oh, May, you've put us right back to square one.

Joyce Grenfell

Mlle du Plessis often honours us with her presence. She was saying yesterday that in Lower Brittany the food is admirable, and that at the wedding of her sister-in-law they ate twelve hundred chickens in one day. At this exaggeration we were all turned to stone. I plucked up my courage and said, 'Mademoiselle, think a moment, don't you mean twelve? Everyone makes mistakes sometimes.' 'No, Madame, it was twelve hundred, or eleven hundred. I won't

swear to you whether it was eleven or twelve, for fear of
telling a lie, but I am sure it was one or the other.' And she
repeated that a score of times, and wouldn't knock off a
single chicken. We felt that there must have been at least
three hundred dressers to prepare the birds with larding fat,
and that the scene must have been a big field in which
marquees had been set up, and that if they had numbered
only fifty they would have had to start a month in advance.
This table-talk was good and you would have enjoyed it.
Have you got some exaggerating female like that?

Madame de Sévigné

———

To be today's real woman, you need to have the physique
of Venus, the cunning of Cleopatra, the courage of Joan of
Arc, the wardrobe of Marie Antoinette, and the cleaning
ability of Ammonia D.

Joyce Jillson

———

The Perfectionist

Margot Fleming's father, whom Margot had greatly admired, had often said
to her, 'Anything worth doing is worth doing well.' Margot believed that
anything worth doing well was worth doing perfectly.

The Flemings' house and garden were at all times in perfect order.
Margot did all the gardening, though they could have afforded a gardener.
Even their Airedale, Rugger, slept only where he was supposed to sleep (on
a carpet in front of the fireplace), and never jumped on people to greet them,
only wagged his tail. The Flemings' only child, Rosamund, aged fourteen,
had perfect manners, and her only fault was that she was inclined to asthma.

If, in putting away a fork in the silverware drawer, Margot noticed an
incipient tarnish, she would get out the silver polish and clean the fork, and
this would lead, whatever the hour of day or night, to her cleaning the rest
of the silverware so it would all look equally nice. Then Margot would be
inspired to tackle the tea service, and then the cover for the meat platter,

and then there were the silver frames of photographs in the living-room, and the silver stamp box on the telephone table, and it might be dawn before Margot was finished. However, there was a housemaid, named Dolly, who came three times a week to do the major cleaning.

Margot seldom dared to prepare a meal for her own family, and never for guests. This, despite a kitchen equipped with every modern convenience, including a walk-in deep freezer, three blending machines, an electric tin-opener and an electric knife-sharpener, a huge stove with two glass-doored ovens in it, and cabinets around the walls full of pressure cookers, colanders, and pots and pans of all sizes. The Flemings almost never ate at home, because Margot was afraid her cooking would not be good enough. Something – maybe the soup, maybe the salad – might not be just right, Margot thought, so she ducked the whole business. The Flemings might ask their friends for drinks before dinner, but then they would all get into their cars and drive eight miles to the city for dinner at a restaurant, then perhaps drive back to the Flemings' for coffee and brandy.

Margot was a bit of a hypochondriac. She got up early every morning (if she was not still up after polishing silver or waxing furniture) to do her Yoga exercises, which were followed by a half hour of meditation. Then Margot weighed herself. If she had lost or gained a fraction of a kilo overnight, she would try to remedy this by the way she ate that day. Then she drank the juice of one lemon unsweetened. Twice a year she went for two weeks to a spa, and felt that she got rid of small aches and pains which had started in the preceding six months. At the spa, her diet was even simpler, and her slender face became a little more anxious, though she made an effort to maintain an intelligently pleasant expression, as this was part of the general perfection that she hoped to achieve.

'The So-and-sos are very informal,' her husband Harold would say sometimes. 'We don't have to give them a banquet, but it would be nice if we could ask them for dinner here.' No luck. Margot would say something like: 'I just don't think I can cope with it. A restaurant is so much simpler, Harold dear.'

Margot's expression would have become so pained, Harold could never bring himself to argue further. But he often thought, 'All that big kitchen, and we can't even ask our friends for an omelet!'

Thus it came as a staggering surprise to Harold when Margot announced one day in October, with the solemnity of a Crusader praying before battle: 'Harold, we're going to have a dinner party *here*.'

The occasion was a double-barrelled one: Harold's birthday was nine days off and fell on a Saturday. And he had just been promoted to vice-president of his bank with a rise in salary. That was enough to warrant a party, and Harold felt he owed it to his colleagues, but still – was Margot capable? 'There might be twenty people at least,' Harold said. 'Even I'd been thinking of a restaurant this time.'

But Margot plainly felt it was something she ought to do, to be a perfect wife. She sent out the invitations. She spent two days planning the menu with the aid of Larousse Gastronomique, typed it with two carbons, and made a shopping list with two carbons in case she mislaid one or two of them. This left seven days before the party. She decided that the living-room curtains looked faded, so she cruised the city in a taxi looking for the right material, then for just the right gold braid for the edges and the bottom. She made the new curtains herself. She hired an upholsterer to re-cover the sofa and four armchairs, and paid him extra for a rushed job. The already clean windows were washed again by Margot and Dolly, the already clean dinner service (for twenty–four people) washed again also. Margot was up all night the two nights preceding the birthday–promotion party, and of course she was busy during the days, too. She and Dolly made a trial batch of the complicated pudding that was to be the dessert, found it a success, and threw it away.

The big evening came, and twenty–two people arrived between 7.30 and 8 p.m. in a series of private cars and taxis. Margot and a hired butler and Dolly drifted out with trays of drinks and hot canapes and cheese dips. The dining table had been let out to its greatest length – a handsome field of white linen now, silver candelabra, and three vases of red carnations.

And all went well. The women praised the appearance of the table, praised the soup. The men pronounced the claret excellent. The president of Harold's bank proposed a toast to Margot. Then Margot began to feel ill. She had a second coffee, and accepted a second brandy which she didn't want, but one of Harold's senior colleagues had offered it. Then she ducked into her bedroom and took a benzedrine. She was not in the habit of taking pick-up pills, and had these only because she had promised not to abuse them. Ten minutes later, Margot felt up in the air, almost flying, and she became alarmed. She went back to her bedroom and took a mild sleeping pill. She drank another brandy, which someone pressed upon her. Harold proposed another toast, to his bank, and this was followed a few minutes later by a generally proposed toast to Harold, because it was his birthday.

Margot dutifully partook of all these toasts. In the last moments of the party, Margot felt she was walking in her sleep, as if she were a ghost or someone else. When the door closed after the last guest, she collapsed on the floor.

A doctor was summoned. Margot was rushed to hospital, and her stomach pumped. She was unconscious for many hours. 'Nothing to worry about, really,' the doctor said to Harold. 'It's exhaustion plus the fact that her nerves are upset by pills. It's just a matter of flushing out her system.' Water was being piped slowly down her throat. Margot regained consciousness, and at once experienced an agony of shame. She was sure she had done something *wrong* at the party, but just what she couldn't remember.

'Margot my dear, you did beautifully!' Harold said. 'Everyone said what a superb evening it was!'

But Margot was convinced she had passed out, and that their guests had thought she was drunk. Harold showed Margot appreciative notes he had received from several of their guests, but Margot interpreted them as polite merely.

Once home from the hospital, Margot took to knitting. She had always knitted a little. Now she undertook a vast enterprise: to knit coverlets for every bed in the house (eight counting the twin beds in the two guest rooms). Margot neglected her Yoga meditation, but not her exercises, as she knitted and knitted from 6 a.m. until nearly 2 a.m., hardly pausing to eat.

The doctor told Harold to consult a psychiatrist. The psychiatrist had a chat with Margot, then said to Harold, 'We must let her continue knitting, otherwise she may become worse. When she has got all the coverlets done, perhaps we can talk to her.'

But Harold suspected that the doctor was only trying to make *him* feel better. Things were worse than ever. Margot stopped Dolly from preparing dinner, saying that Dolly's cooking wasn't good enough. The three Flemings made hurried trips to restaurants, then went back home so Margot could resume her knitting.

Knit, knit, knit. And what will Margot think of to do next?

Patricia Highsmith

You Should Have Seen The Mess

I am now more than glad that I did not pass into the grammar school five years ago, although it was a disappointment at the time I was always good at English, but not so good at the other subjects!!

I am glad that I went to the secondary modern school, because it was only constructed the year before. Therefore, it was much more hygienic than the grammar school. The secondary modern was light and airy, and the walls were painted with a bright, washable gloss. One day, I was sent over to the grammar school, with a note for one of the teachers, and you should have seen the mess! The corridors were dusty, and I saw dust on the window ledges, which were chipped. I saw into one of the classrooms. It was very untidy in there.

I am also glad that I did not go to the grammar school, because of what it does to one's habits. This may appear to be a strange remark, at first sight. It is a good thing to have an education behind you, and I do not believe in ignorance, but I have had certain experiences, with educated people, since going out into the world.

I am seventeen years of age, and left school two years ago last month. I had my A certificate for typing, so got my first job, as a junior, in a solicitor's office. Mum was pleased at this, and Dad said it was a first-class start, as it was an old-established firm. I must say that when I went for the interview, I was surprised at the windows, and the stairs up to the offices were also far from clean. There was a little waiting-room, where some of the elements were missing from the gas fire, and the carpet on the floor was worn. However, Mr Heygate's office, into which I was shown for the interview, was better. The furniture was old, but it was polished, and there was a good carpet, I will say that. The glass of the bookcase was very clean.

I was to start on the Monday, so along I went. They took me to the general office, where there were two senior shorthand-typists, and a clerk, Mr Gresham, who was far from smart in appearance. You should have seen the mess!! There was no floor covering whatsoever, and so dusty everywhere. There were shelves all round the room, with old box files on them. The box files were falling to pieces, and all the old papers inside them were crumpled. The worst shock of all was the tea-cups. It was my duty to make tea, mornings and afternoons. Miss Bewlay showed me where everything was kept. It was kept in an old orange box, and the cups were all cracked. There were not enough saucers to go round, etc. I will not go into the facilities, but they were also far from hygienic. After three days, I told Mum, and she was upset, most of all about the cracked cups. We never keep a cracked cup, but throw it out, because those cracks can harbour germs. So Mum gave me my own cup to take to the office.

Then at the end of the week, when I got my salary, Mr Heygate said, 'Well, Lorna, what are you going to do with your first pay?' I did not like him saying this, and I nearly passed a comment, but I said, 'I don't know.' He said, 'What do you do in the evenings, Lorna? Do you watch telly?' I did take this as an insult, because we call it TV, and his remark made me out to be uneducated. I just stood, and did not answer, and he looked surprised. Next day, Saturday, I told Mum and Dad about the facilities, and we decided I should not go back to that job. Also, the desks in the general office were rickety. Dad was indignant, because Mr Heygate's concern was flourishing, and he had letters after his name.

Everyone admires our flat, because Mum keeps it spotless, and Dad keeps doing things to it. He has done it up all over, and got permission from the Council to re-modernize the kitchen. I well recall the Health Visitor, remarking to Mum, 'You could eat off your floor, Mrs Merrifield.' It is true that you could eat your lunch off Mum's floors, and any hour of the day or night you will find every corner spick and span.

Next, I was sent by the agency to a publisher's for an interview, because of being good at English. One look was enough!! My next interview was a success, and I am still at Low's Chemical Co. It is a modern block, with a quarter of an hour rest period, morning and afternoon. Mr Marwood is very smart in appearance. He is well spoken, although he has not got a university education behind him. There is special lighting over the desks, and the typewriters are the latest models.

So I am happy at Low's. But I have met other people, of an educated type, in the past year, and it has opened my eyes. It so happened that I had to go to the doctor's house, to fetch a prescription for my young brother, Trevor, when the epidemic was on. I rang the bell, and Mrs Darby came to the door. She was small, with fair hair, but too long, and a green maternity dress. But she was very nice to me. I had to wait in their living-room, and you should have seen the state it was in! There were broken toys on the carpet, and the ash trays were full up. There were contemporary pictures on the walls, but the furniture was not contemporary, but old-fashioned, with covers which were past standing up to another wash, I should say. To cut a long story short, Dr Darby and Mrs Darby have always been very kind to me, and they meant everything for the best. Dr Darby is also short and fair, and they have three children, a girl and a boy, and now a baby boy.

When I went that day for the prescription, Dr Darby said to me, 'You look pale, Lorna. It's the London atmosphere. Come on a picnic with us, in the car, on Saturday.' After that I went with the Darbys more and more. I liked them, but I did not like the mess, and it was a surprise. But I also kept in with them for the opportunity of meeting people, and Mum and Dad were pleased that I had made nice friends. So I did not say anything about the cracked lino, and the paintwork all chipped. The children's clothes were very shabby for a doctor, and she changed them out of their school clothes when they came home from school, into those worn-out garments. Mum always kept us spotless to go out to play, and I do not like to say it, but those Darby children frequently looked like the Leary family, which the Council evicted from our block, as they were far from houseproud.

One day, when I was there, Mavis (as I called Mrs Darby by then) put her head out of the window, and shouted to the boy, 'John, stop peeing over the cabbages at once. Pee on the lawn.' I did not know which way to look. Mum would never say a word like that from the window, and I know for a fact that Trevor would never pass water outside, not even bathing in the sea.

I went there usually at the week-ends, but sometimes on week-days, after supper. They had an idea to make a match for me with a chemist's assistant, whom they had taken up too. He was an orphan, and I do not say there was anything wrong with that. But he was not accustomed to those little extras that I was. He was a good-looking boy, I will say that. So I went once to a dance, and twice to films with him. To look at, he was quite clean in appearance. But there was only hot water at the week-end at his place, and he said that a bath once a week was sufficient. Jim (as I called Dr Darby by then) said it was sufficient also, and surprised me. He did not have much money, and I do not hold that against him. But there was no hurry for me, and I could wait for a man in a better position, so that I would not miss those little extras. So he started going out with a girl from the coffee bar, and did not come to the Darbys very much then.

There were plenty of boys at the office, but I will say this for the Darbys, they had lots of friends coming and going, and they had interesting conversation, although sometimes it gave me a surprise, and I did not know where to look. And sometimes they had people who were very down and out, although there is no need to be. But most of the guests were different, so it made a comparison with the boys at the office, who were not so educated in their conversation.

Now it was near the time for Mavis to have her baby, and I was to come in at the week-end, to keep an eye on the children, while the help had her day off. Mavis did not go away to have her baby, but would have it at home, in their double bed, as they did not have twin beds, although he was a doctor. A girl I knew, in our block, was engaged, but was let down, and even she had her baby in the labour ward. I was sure the bedroom was not hygienic for having a baby, but I did not mention it.

One day, after the baby boy came along, they took me in the car to the country, to see Jim's mother. The baby was put in a carry-cot at the back of the car. He began to cry, and without a word of a lie, Jim said to him over his shoulder, 'Oh shut your gob, you little bastard.' I did not know what to do, and Mavis was smoking a cigarette. Dad would not dream of saying such a thing to Trevor or I. When we arrived at Jim's mother's place, Jim said, 'It's a fourteenth-century cottage, Lorna.' I could well believe it. It was very cracked and old, and it made one wonder how Jim could let his old mother live in this tumble-down cottage, as he was so good to everyone else. So Mavis knocked at the door, and the old lady came. There was not much anyone could do to the inside. Mavis said, 'Isn't it charming, Lorna?' If that was a joke, it was going too far. I said to the old Mrs Darby, 'Are you going to be re-housed?' but she did not understand this, and I explained how you have to apply to the Council, and keep at them. But it was funny that the Council had not done something already, when they go round condemning. Then old Darby said, 'My dear, I shall be re-housed in the Grave.' I did not know where to look.

There was a carpet hanging on the wall, which I think was there to hide a damp spot. She had a good TV set, I will say that. But some of the walls were bare brick, and the facilities were outside, through the garden. The furniture was far from new.

One Saturday afternoon, as I happened to go to the Darbys, they were just going off to a film and they took me too. It was the Curzon, and afterwards we went to a flat in Curzon Street. It was a very clean block, I will say that, and there were good carpets at the entrance. The couple there had contemporary furniture, and they also spoke about music. It was a nice place, but there was no Welfare Centre to the flats, where people could go for social intercourse, advice, and guidance. But they were well-spoken and I met Willy Morley, who was an artist. Willy sat beside me, and we had a drink. He was young, dark, with a dark shirt, so one could not see right away if he was clean. Soon after this, Jim said to me, 'Willy wants to paint you, Lorna. But you'd better ask your Mum.' Mum said it was all right if he was a friend of the Darbys.

I can honestly say that Willy's place was the most unhygienic place I have seen in my life. He said I had an unusual type of beauty, which he must capture. This was when we came back to his place from the restaurant. The light was very dim, but I could see the bed had not been made, and the sheets were far from clean. He said he must paint me, but I told Mavis I did not like to go back there. 'Don't you like Willy?' she asked. I could not deny that I liked Willy, in a way. There was something about him, I will say that. Mavis said, 'I hope he hasn't been making a pass at you, Lorna.' I said he had not done so, which was almost true, because he did not attempt to go to the full extent. It was always unhygienic when I went to Willy's place, and I told him so once, but he said, 'Lorna, you are a joy.' He had a nice way, and he took me out in his car, which was a good one, but dirty inside, like his place. Jim said one day, 'He has pots of money, Lorna,' and Mavis said, 'You might make a man of him, as he is keen on you.' They always said Willy came from a good family.

But I saw that one could not do anything with him. He would not change his shirt very often, or get clothes, but he went round like a tramp, lending people money, as I have seen with my own eyes. His place was in a terrible mess, with the empty bottles, and laundry in the corner. He gave me several gifts over the period, which I took as he would have only given them away, but he never tried to go to the full extent. He never painted my portrait, as he was painting fruit on a table all that time, and they said his pictures were marvellous, and thought Willy and I were getting married.

One night, when I went home, I was upset as usual, after Willy's place. Mum and Dad had gone to bed, and I looked round our kitchen which is done in primrose and white. Then I went into the living-room, where Dad has done one wall in a patterned paper, deep rose and white, and the other walls pale rose, with white woodwork. The suite is new, and Mum keeps everything beautiful. So it came to me, all of a sudden, what a fool I was, going with Willy. I agree to equality, but as to me marrying Willy, as I said to Mavis, when I recall his place, and the good carpet gone greasy, not to mention the paint oozing out of the tubes, I think it would break my heart to sink so low.

Muriel Spark

[In a letter to Thomas Carlyle, husband:] I am not at all the
sort of person you and I took me for.

Jane Carlyle

———

A woman is like a teabag – only in hot water do you realise
how strong she is.

Nancy Reagan

———

No matter how old a mother is she watches her middle-
aged children for signs of improvement.

Florida Scott-Maxwell

———

The works of women are symbolical.
We sew, sew, prick our fingers, dull our sight,
Producing what? A pair of slippers, sir,
To put on when you're weary.

Elizabeth Barrett Browning

———

Woman's virtue is man's greatest invention.

Cornelia Otis Skinner

———

Our opposers usually miscall our quickness of thought,
fancy and flash, and christen their own heaviness by the
specious names of judgement and solidity; but it is easy to
retort upon them the reproachful ones of dullness and
stupidity.

Mary Astell

———

Some of us are becoming the men we wanted to marry.

Gloria Steinem

——

Show me a woman who doesn't feel guilty, and I'll show you a man.

Erica Jong

——

[To Edward de Vere, Earl of Oxford, returning from seven years self-imposed exile after breaking wind in the royal presence:] My Lord, I had forgot the fart.

Elizabeth I

——

It might be marvellous to be a man – then I could stop worrying about what's fair to women and just cheerfully assume I was superior, and that they had all been born to iron my shirts. Better still I could be an Irish man – then I would have all the privileges of being male without giving up the right to be wayward, temperamental and an appealing minority.

Katharine Whitehorn

——

A man in the house is worth two in the street.

Mae West

——

I require only three things of a man. He must be handsome, ruthless and stupid.

Dorothy Parker

——

Women want mediocre men, and men are working hard to be as mediocre as possible.

Margaret Mead

———

Most women set out to try to change a man, and when they have changed him they do not like him.

Marlene Deitrich

———

Powerful men often succeed through the help of their wives. Powerful women only succeed in spite of their husbands.

Linda Lee Potter

———

The minute you walked in the joint,
I could see you were a man of distinction,
A real big spender.
Good looking, so refined,
Say, wouldn't you like to know what's going on in my mind?
So let me get right to the point.
I don't pop my cork for every guy I see.
Hey! big spender, spend a little time with me.

Dorothy Fields

———

An archaeologist is the best husband any woman can have: the older she gets the more he is interested in her.

Agatha Christie

———

The Jungle Husband

Dearest Evelyn, I often think of you
Out with the guns in the jungle stew
Yesterday I hittapotamus
I put the measurements down for you but they got lost in the fuss
It's not a good thing to drink out here
You know, I've practically given it up dear.
Tomorrow I am going alone a long way
Into the jungle. It is all gray
But green on top
Only sometimes when a tree has fallen
The sun comes down plop, it is quite appalling.
You never want to go in a jungle pool
In the hot sun, it would be the act of a fool
Because it's always full of anacondas, Evelyn, not looking ill-fed
I'll say. So no more now, from your loving husband, Wilfred.

Stevie Smith

———

The legend of the jungle heritage and the evolution of man
as a hunting carnivore has taken root in man's mind . . . He
may even believe that equal pay will do something terrible
to his gonads.

Elaine Morgan

———

Il n'y a point de héros pour son valet de chambre.
No man is a hero to his valet.

Madame Cornuel

———

My husband is a jolly good sort, one of those hearty men.
He wears plus-fours, smokes a long pipe, and talks about
nothing but beer and rugby football. My nerves won't stand
much more of it.

**Wife giving evidence at Tottenham
Police Court**

A husband is what is left of a lover, after the nerve has been extracted.

Helen Rowland

———

No nice men are good at getting taxis.

Katharine Whitehorn

———

Give a man a free hand and he'll run it all over you.

Mae West

———

He who loves and runs away may live to love another day.

Carolyn Wells

———

The follies which a man regrets most, in his life, are those which he didn't commit when he had the opportunity.

Helen Rowland

———

If men could get pregnant, abortion would be a sacrament.

Florynce Kennedy

———

It is well within the order of things
That man should listen when his mate sings;
But the true male never yet walked
Who liked to listen when his mate talked.

Anna Wickham

———

Never trust a husband too far, nor a bachelor too near.

Helen Rowland

———

Men

They hail you as their morning star
Because you are the way you are.
If you return the sentiment,
They'll try to make you different;
And once they have you, safe and sound,
They want to change you all around.
Your moods and ways they put a curse on;
They'd make of you another person.
They cannot let you go your gait;
They influence and educate.
They'd alter all that they admired.
They make me sick, they make me tired.

Dorothy Parker

———

Somehow a bachelor never quite gets over the idea that he
is a thing of beauty and a boy for ever.

Helen Rowland

———

Macho does not prove mucho.

Zsa Zsa Gabor

———

VANITY, LIKE

MURDER, WILL OUT

When a tall, thin, gorgeous blonde walks into a room your first thought is unlikely to be: 'I bet she's got some A levels.'

Jenny Lecoat

———

Do I look different today? I just spent the entire day at the beauty shop. They really dolled me up. They worked on my hair, not the color because I happen to be a natural blond. True, the roots are black, but that's just because my hair grows faster than my color. When they finished with me, I looked great. They gave me fake fingernails, false eyelashes, a wig, and a padded bra. For once I felt like the real me. When I got home, Edgar took me in his arms and kissed me and made love to me like never before. Then he drew me close and whispered, "You better get out of here before Joan comes home."

Joan Rivers

The feminine vanity case is the grave of masculine illusions.

Helen Rowland

———

Since man with that inconstancy was born,
To love the absent, and the present scorn,
Why do we deck, why do we dress
For such a short-lived happiness?
Why do we put attraction on,
Since either way 'tis we must be undone?

Aphra Behn

———

I'm tired of all this nonsense about beauty being only skin-deep. That's deep enough. What do you want – an adorable pancreas?

Jean Kerr

———

If you want to have a real good time,
If you want to have a figure just like mine,
You must do
What I tell you to.
If you want to exercise your bust
Pay attention, friends, to me, you really must.
Take my tips,
For those Rubens hips.
You may cry, 'What is it I lack?
Is it fame or fortune?'
'No!', I answer back.

Beauty Beauty,
To have it is everyone's duty.
Every girl can get good looks,
With the aid of one of our sixpenny books,
Beauty Beauty,

Just try a diet that's fruity,
Full many a man has wooed a maid
On radishes and orangeade,
With nuts to help him make the grade.
Three cheers for beauty.

Healthy healthy!
I'd sooner be healthy than wealthy.
What is the good of pearls in rows
If you're quite unable to touch your toes?
Healthy healthy!
Really my footwork is filthy!
That's not the way to catch a man.
Remember that our two-year plan
Turns weak Miss Can't into strong Miss Can.
Three cheers for beauty.

Dainty dainty!
Don't go all swoony and fainty.
To fall on your back is simply grand
If you fall on the proper word of command.
Dainty dainty!
A man's only human now, ain't he?
Take my advice, you'll find it wise,
He's made like that, so realize
He likes a girl who takes exercise.
Three cheers for beauty.
Hearty hearty
The life and soul of the party.
You'll never long for a prune or a fig
If you join the health and beauty league.
Hearty hearty!
I'd rather be hearty than tarty.
For virtue brings its own reward
And many a girl who's not been pawed
Has ended up with a real live Lord!
Three cheers for beauty.

Hermione Gingold

If beauty is truth, why don't women go to the library to get their hair done?

Lily Tomlin

———

Vanity, like murder, will out.

Hannah Cowley

———

Any girl can be glamorous: all you have to do is stand still and look stupid.

Hedy Lamarr

———

[Asked if she really had nothing on in the calendar photograph, Marilyn, her blue eyes wide, purred]: I had the radio on.

Marilyn Monroe

———

A woman can look both moral and exciting – if she also looks as if it was quite a struggle.

Edna Ferber

———

They used to photograph Shirley Temple through gauze. They should photograph me through linoleum.

Tallulah Bankhead

———

Fashion Expert

TV AM set – large sofa. Jennifer is the interviewer, Dawn the 'expert'.

JENNIFER   So, today I'm joined by Dawn French, top fashion expert to the stars and the high street. So tell me, Dawn, what can we expect to see in the shops this year?

DAWN   Clothes, mostly . . . and some hats and some shoes.

JENNIFER   I see, so what's really 'in' this year?

DAWN   Fabric is 'in', we'll be seeing jackets, skirts, trousers, blouses,
           bras, underwear, maxis, minis, midis, etc., tops and coats in
           fabric and certain textiles.

JENNIFER   So anything goes fabric-wise. And what about this year's
           colours? Purple?

DAWN   Yes.

JENNIFER   Green?

DAWN   Yes.

JENNIFER   Yellow?

DAWN   Yes, and red and brown.

JENNIFER   Ah, so *not* blue then?

DAWN   Yes, blue . . . and black or white . . . and lilac.

JENNIFER   And shapes?

DAWN   Well, some shapes I know are circles, squares, rectangles,
           triangles.

JENNIFER   Dodecahedrons?

DAWN   Inevitably, there will be some, yes.

JENNIFER   Hats?

DAWN   Do you mean for the head?

JENNIFER   Yes, indeed.

DAWN   Only if you want to wear them, you don't *have* to. We at the
           top of the fashion business are leaving it up to the people to
           decide if they want to wear a hat or not.

JENNIFER   Of course it depends if one is inside or outside. And have we
           got time for a fashion tip. – Yes, I think we have.

DAWN   Right, a fashion tip, always carry one of these in case of rain.
           (*Takes out piece of plastic.*) You put it on your head, or anywhere
           rain might land, you see!

JENNIFER   So, to sum up . . . what can we expect to see on the catwalk?

DAWN   Some cats.

JENNIFER   Thank you very much. Illuminating as always.

Dawn French and Jennifer Saunders

———

Hats divide generally into three classes: offensive hats, defensive hats, and shrapnel . . . I have recently acquired a new hat of such ferocity that it has been running my whole life for me. I wake up in the morning thinking 'Who shall I wear my hat at today?'

Katharine Whitehorn

———

Englishwomen's shoes look as if they had been made by someone who had often heard shoes described but had never seen any.

Margaret Halsey

———

DIGNITARY   If you will turn your head ever so slightly, Lady Peel, I will fasten this necklace.
MILADY   Righto, buster. Now then, may I see a coronet, please?
DIGNITARY   Oh, I'm so sorry, Lady Peel, but we don't have a coronet at this time.
MILADY   No? Well, it doesn't matter really. In any case, I don't know how to play one.

Beatrice Lillie

———

Ne porte jamais de bijoux artistiques, ça déconsidère complètement une femme.
Don't ever wear artistic jewellery; it wrecks a woman's reputation.

Colette

———

While clothes with pictures and/or writing on them are not entirely an invention of the modern age, they are an unpleasant indication of the general state of things . . .
I mean, be realistic. If people don't want to listen to *you* what makes you think they want to hear from your sweater.

Fran Lebowitz

from The Female Spectator

I believe that if the ladies would retrench a yard or two of those extended hoops they now wear, they would be much less liable to many embarrassments one frequently beholds them in walking the streets. How often do the angular corners of such immense machines, as we sometimes see, though held up almost to the armpits, catch hold of those little poles that support the numerous stalls with which this populous city abounds, and throw down, or at least endanger the whole fabric, to the great damage of the fruiterer, fishmonger, comb and buckle sellers and others of these small chapmen.

Many very ugly accidents of this kind have lately happened, but I was an eye witness from my window of one which may serve as a warning to my sex either to take chair or coach or to leave their enormous hoops at home, whenever they have occasion to go out on a Monday or Friday, especially in the morning.

It was on the former of those unhappy days, that a young creature, who, I dare answer, had no occasion to leave anyone at home to look after her best clothes, came tripping by with one of those mischief-making hoops, which spread itself from the steps of my door quite to the posts placed to keep off the coaches and carts. A large flock of sheep were that instant driving to the slaughter house, and an old ram, who was the foremost, being put out of his way by some accident, ran full-butt into the footway, where his horns were immediately entangled in the hoop of this fine lady, as she was holding it up on one side, as the genteel fashion is, and as the make of it requires. In her fright she let it fall down, which still more encumbered him, as it fixed upon his neck. She attempted to run, he to disengage himself, which neither of them were able to do. She shrieked, he baa'd, the rest of the sheep echoed the cry, and the dog who followed the flock barked so that all together made a most hideous sound. Down fell the lady, unable to sustain the forcible efforts the ram made to obtain his liberty. A crowd of mob, who were gathered in an instant, shouted. At last the driver, who was at a good distance behind, came up and assisted in setting free his beast and raising the lady; but never was finery so demolished. The late rains had made the place so excessive dirty, that her gown and petticoat, which before were yellow, the colour so revered in *Hanover*, and so much the mode in *England* at present, were now most barbarously painted with a filthy brown; her gauze cap, half off her head in the scuffle, and her *tête de mouton* hanging down on one shoulder. The rude populace, instead of pitying, insulted her misfortune, and continued their shouts till she got into a chair and was quite out of sight.

Eliza Haywood

Notes on Black

This has been my wardrobe for say ten years: black shirts, black jeans, black dresses, black trousers, black bras, black panties, black stockings, black jewelry, black coat, black shoes, gray gloves. I don't know why the gray gloves.

Now the honeymoon is over.

Contrary to popular opinion, clothes are not for warmth, not for modesty. If we didn't have clothes, we'd have to wear signboards saying, say, 'Hello, I'm a radical lesbian mother with a Stalinist streak,' or 'Hello, I prefer you to think I'm athletic.' But clothes take care of this: Each item screams to the world our innermost dreams and fears. Thus when we notice a girl with a Peter Pan collar on the bus, we can sadly shake our heads at the thought of father fixations.

Wearing constant black used to mean: 'Hello, I get a nosebleed above Twenty-third Street, and I will never tell you to "have a nice day." I believe nothing on television. Sure, I'll talk about Zydeco music. I cried when Dali died. Don't try to tell me about Julian Schnabel. Barbara Walters is foul Roseanne Barr, who cares? I was a dweeb in high school: I write, or maybe I paint. I have criminally low self-esteem, body flaws that I think hideous, and never go to bed until dawn. Leave me alone.'

Black, the most magical of colors! Black is cynicism and beyond. Black is for people who inanely believe there is a counterculture. Black is the grandchild of beatnik. Black loves truth and beauty, but hates the American Way.

Used to be, if you went to a party wearing all black and saw someone else, a total stranger, wearing all black, you could go up to him and say, 'Let's get outa here.'

You'd go to the Pyramid to hear some weird band and find out on the way that your boyfriend before last was his best friend in high school and that you were both at that party at Max's where Patti Smith ran amok.

Now the riffraff are wearing it.

My friend Jake goes to parties. 'Who was there?' I keep asking him. 'Oh, you know,' he answers, 'a bunch of people wearing black.'

The girl at the Alaia shop on Mercer Street was complaining the other day about black-wearers in Texas. 'They go to nightclubs wearing black, but it's the wrong black, it's like black Laura Ashley or something. It looks really stupid.'

I went to a New Year's Eve party where every single person, no exceptions, was in solid black. Except the hostess – she was in a dreamy pale green Angel Estrada.

Lawyers now wear black. Wall Streeters wear black. People who think, 'The hell with the dolphins, I have to worry about my accessories career' wear black. People who send their children to prep schools wear black. People who desperately want to know the Kennedys wear black. People who liked Cats wear black. Everyone at every Spy magazine party wears black. People who know what 'leveraged buy-out' means wear black.

Wearing black has lost its intrinsic meaning.

The obvious, most practical remedy would be to establish a city agency, a board of directors who would issue permits. We'd all have to bring in portfolios, manuscripts, or tapes to establish artistic credentials, letters from our shrinks to prove we are utterly and irredeemably bonkers, punch in at some time clock at four a.m. to prove we're still awake. We would have to fail tests in money management. Every Kennedy in the world would have to swear we'd never tried to corner him at a cocktail party. We would have to provide photographs of us either a) passed out in a pool of vomit at The World, b) marching on Washington, or c) flirting with a salesperson at Patricia Field.

Then, if an interloper were caught by the Fashion Police wearing black without a permit, she would be fined one black article of clothing for the first offense, her entire wardrobe would be seized for the second offense, and she would be forced to actually purchase and wear only Adolfo clothes for a year as the third offense.

Elitist? I don't think so. More like truth in advertising.

But we can't expect our city government to take the enlightened view. We will have to form our own vigilante groups and prowl the streets. The minute we find a perpetrator wearing black without the proper and correct attitude, we must surround him and point and laugh. This will work.

But even more important, we ourselves must stop wearing black. I do not have to tell you the obvious substitute colors – you already know in your hearts. For some demented reason, the artistic, the decadent, and the severely deranged are considered fashionable in Manhattan and therefore the country. They will copy us, they will stop wearing black.

Then we start again.

Cynthia Heimel

———

Bombazine would have shown a deeper sense of her loss.

Elizabeth Gaskell

———

At one early, glittering dinner party at Buckingham Palace, the trembling hand of a nervous waiter spilled a spoonful of decidedly hot soup down my neck. How could I manage to ease his mind and turn his embarrassed apologies into a smile, except to put on a pretended frown and say, without thinking: 'Never darken my Dior again!'

Beatrice Lillie

———

Warren Street

Nan had had another god-awful day. Nobody seemed to use any under-arm deodorant any more. She had been wincing from whiffs of sweat all day, as people flung off their garments to try on her designs.

That maddening Mrs Fine had, of course, noticed the seam that wasn't exactly right; while that stupid, stupid woman – who apparently worked in some important position in an estate agent's – had forgotten again what she wanted made out of the woollen material but was absolutely certain that it wasn't the poncho that Nan had cut out for her.

'Why would I have said a poncho, when I have one already?' she asked wide-eyed.

'That's what I asked you at the time,' hissed Nan.

But the thing that was making Nan's heart leaden was that she had had a row with Shirley.

Now nobody had rows with Shirley. She had a face so like the rising sun you expected rays to stick out from her head like in a child's drawing. If Nan had rowed with her, it had to have been Nan's fault and that was that.

Shirley had been coming to Nan for two years now, ordering maybe five garments a year. Nan remembered the first day she came she had been pressing her nose against the window rather wistfully, looking at a little bolero and skirt outfit on display. The skirt wouldn't have gone over Shirley's head, let alone made it to her waist.

Nan pulled back the curtain and waved her inside – she still wondered why she did it. Normally she never encouraged customers. She had enough enquiries she couldn't deal with, and this was obviously not a fashion-conscious girl whom it would be a pleasure to dress.

Shirley's great, happy face and bouncing, bulging body arrived in Nan's little shop.

'I think I have the wrong place,' she began. 'Lola who works with me and who's eight months pregnant said she got her smocks here, and I was wondering if you have any more smocks. I mean, they might fit me, even though I'm not pregnant.'

Nan had liked her cheerful face so much she'd encouraged her.

'Sit down. I'll go and see. I've very few things really – I mainly make clothes up for people you see.'

'Oh, are you a designer?' asked Shirley innocently.

She had touched on something very near to Nan's heart. She would have liked to think of herself as a designer and she had a flair for ideas and style. She sold things to classy boutiques from time to time. But something about Shirley's face made her answer, to her own surprise: 'No, more a dress-maker.'

'Oh, that's great,' Shirley had said. 'I thought that they'd disappeared. I wonder, would you be able to make me a smock . . . ?' She broke off, seeing a refusal beginning to form itself on Nan's face.

'Oh, please, please do!' she said. 'I can't find anything in the shops that doesn't have white collars or tiny, thoughtful, mum-to-be prints on it.'

'It's just that I'm very busy . . . ' Nan began.

'It would be very easy to do,' said Shirley. 'You wouldn't have to put any shape in it, and you wouldn't have to waste time wondering if the fit was right.' She grinned encouragingly, and that did it. Nan couldn't bear her to go around the world as vulnerable as that, and indeed, as badly dressed in that hideous, diagonally-striped garment she had on.

'You win,' Nan had said, and they spent a happy half hour planning what Shirley would wear for the winter.

Away went the belted grey army issue-type coats – the only one that fitted Shirley – and on came a cape. Away, too, the men's warm sweaters and on with a rosy red dress and a warm pink one.

Nan also made her a multicoloured evening dress, which had all the shades of the rainbow in it. It was, she thought, a pleasure to design a dress for Shirley. She was so grateful, so touched and happy when it was finished. Sometimes she would whirl around in it in front of the mirror, her fat little hands clasped excitedly like a child.

Shirley was one of the few clients who didn't seem to have a list of complaints and personal problems, which was another bonus. Nan thought of Mrs Fine, always running down her husband. Shirley never complained about men at all.

Miss Harris was always bitching about traffic or work, or how you couldn't get a taxi or a waiter who spoke English, or proper wholemeal bread. Shirley never seemed in the least upset by such deprivations.

In fact, Nan knew little of Shirley's life, except that she fancied her boss in an advertising agency. Or maybe she didn't – Shirley was always so jokey. The last garment she had made Shirley was a really lovely dress. Nan had spent hours on the very fine wool, with its embroidery, ruffs and frills, its soft blues and yellows. Shirley looked like an enormous, beautiful baby.

It was for some gala evening and Shirley had said: 'If he doesn't tear the clothes off me when he sees me like this, he never will.'

Nan worked on a system of appointments that meant you had to come and see her on the hour, and she only saw eight people a day. That way, she said, the job was manageable. People didn't stay longer than twenty minutes at the most. The rest of the hour Nan worked away with her quiet, little machinist burring on in the background.

She would never be rich, never be famous, but it was a living. She couldn't see a life where she would be finishing buttonholes at three a.m. for a show next day. Her own life and her own lover were far too precious for that. Colin and she had lived together happily for ages and often thought of getting married but they'd never actually got the details organized.

That's what they said. The truth was that Colin would have disappeared very sharply if Nan had suggested marriage. She didn't mind much; although sometimes she felt he had it all ways since they both worked. She did the housework and paid the rent, but then it was her place, and he did share the bills.

And he loved the fact that she worked downstairs. Sometimes if he had a day off he would come in and give her a rose in the workroom, and on one never-to-be-forgotten occasion he had asked the machinist to go for a walk, locked the door and made love to her there and then, to the accompaniment of Miss Harris pounding on the door.

One day Colin had seen Shirley leaving with a finished dress. 'Who on earth was the beach ball bouncing out a minute ago?' he asked. Shirley wasn't the usual mould of Nan's clients.

'That's our Shirl whom I talk about sometimes,' Nan said.

'You never told me she looked like a technicoloured Moby Dick,' said Colin. Nan was annoyed. True, Shirley was enormous; true, she was dressed extremely brightly – mainly at Nan's insistence. But because she had such a lovely face, she looked well in colourful clothes and Nan didn't like Colin's joke.

'That's a bit uncalled for, isn't it?' she said sharply. Colin was amazed.

'Sorry to tease her – let me hold out my hand for a smack,' he mocked. 'Yes it was very uncalled for, teacher, nobody called for it at all.'

Nan retorted: 'It's cruel to laugh at somebody's shape.'

'Aw, come on, come on,' said Colin reasonably. 'You're always saying someone's like a car aerial or the Michelin Man or whatever. It was just a remark, just a joke.'

Nan forgave him. 'It's just that I feel, I don't know, a bit protective about her. She's so bloody nice compared with almost anyone who comes in here, and she's literally so soft – in every way. I just feel she'd melt into a little pool if she heard anyone making a remark like that about her, honestly.'

'She was halfway down the street before I opened my mouth,' said Colin.

'I know – I suppose I just hope that nobody says such things whether she hears them or not,' said Nan.

That conversation had been a few months ago, Nan reflected, as she sat, head in hands. Funny that it all came back to her now. She did remember exactly how protective she had felt, as if Shirley had been her favourite sister and their mother had entrusted Nan with the care of seeing that nobody ever laughed at the fat girl.

Nan could hardly believe that, not half an hour ago, Shirley had banged out of the door and shouted from the street that she would never come back. It was like a nightmare where people behave completely out of character.

Shirley had come along for a final fitting for the wedding outfit. Her best friend was getting married and Shirley and Nan had been through reams of ideas before settling on the emerald green dress and matching hat.

Nan had been delighted with it and Shirley's face was a picture of happiness as they both looked at the outfit in the mirror: the tall, slim, slightly wary-looking dressmaker in her elegant grey wool tunic and the short, mountainous client in her metres and metres of glittering emerald.

'You'll need green eye-shadow, not blue,' said Nan. 'I'll lend you some for the wedding if you like.' She looked around for her bag. 'Do you know, I was running out of some, and then I thought of you and this colour, so I asked Colin to get me some. He's in the trade, you know, so it's a little perk. I can't find the wretched thing anywhere.' As she hunted for the parcel which wasn't in her handbag after all, Nan felt a strange, unnatural, silence descend behind her.

'Is that it?' asked Shirley, holding up an envelope that was on a table. The envelope had writing on it. It said 'Green eye-shadow for burly Shirley'.

The two women looked at the inscription in silence for what must have been only four seconds or so, but seemed never-ending. Nan could think of only one thing to say.

When it was obvious that Shirley was going to say nothing either, she tried, but her voice only came out like a squeak. What she had been going to say was, 'I didn't write that', and that didn't seem a very helpful thing to say at that moment.

She thought she would kill Colin. She would physically hurt him and bruise him for this. She would never forgive him.

Shirley's face had turned pink. Her fat neck had gone pink too, which didn't go very well with the emerald.

'Is that what you call me: "Burly Shirley"? Well I suppose it has the advantage of rhyming,' she said. She was so hurt she was almost bleeding.

Nan found her words finally. 'Colin has rude, destructive nicknames for all my clients. It amuses him – it's childish, immature and senseless,' she snapped fiercely.

'How does he know I'm . . . burly? He's never met me,' said Shirley.

'Well, you see he makes up these nicknames without knowing who people are. You do see that it's not an insult and it's not a comment. He could have written anything.' Nan nearly laughed with relief. How marvellous to get out of it in this way. But Shirley was looking at her oddly.

'So I expect he just chose the word because it rhymes with your name. If you had been called Dotty he might have said Spotty.' Nan was very pleased with herself, at the unknown powers of invention that were suddenly welling up within her.

Shirley just looked.

'So now that's cleared up, why don't you take the eye-shadow and put a little on to see how it looks with the outfit?' urged Nan.

Shirley politely started to put it on, and Nan released her breath and foolishly didn't leave well, or nearly well, alone.

'I mean it's not as if anyone would deliberately make a joke about being fat to anyone, not that you are very fat or anything, but one wouldn't mention it even if you were.'

'Why not?' asked Shirley.

'Why? Well, you know why – it would be rude and hurtful to tell someone they were fat. Like saying they were ugly or . . . you know . . . '

'I didn't think being fat was on the same level as being ugly, did you?'

Desperately Nan tried to get back to the comparatively happy level they had just clawed their way to a few moments ago.

'No, of course I don't think being fat is the same as being ugly, but you know what I mean – nobody wants to be either if they can possibly avoid it.'

'I haven't hated being fat,' said Shirley. 'But I wouldn't like to think it was on a par with being ugly – something that would revolt people and make them want to turn away.'

'You're not very fat, Shirley,' Nan cried desperately.

'Oh but I am, I am very fat. I am very short and weigh sixteen stone, and no normal clothes will fit me. I am very, very fat, actually,' said Shirley.

'Yes, but you're not really fat; you're not fat like . . . ' Nan's inventive streak gave out and she stopped.

'I'm the fattest person you know, right? Right. I thought it didn't matter so much because I sort of felt I had a pretty face.'

'Well, you do have a very pretty face.'

'You gave me the courage to wear all these bright clothes instead of the blacks and browns . . . '

'You look lovely in . . . '

'And I didn't worry about looking a bit ridiculous; but you know, ridiculous was the worst I thought I ever looked. I didn't think it was ugly . . .'

'It isn't, you misunderstood . . .'

'It's always disappointing when you discover that someone hasn't been sincere, and has just been having a bit of fun, that she's just been pitying you.'

'I don't pity you . . . I wasn't . . .'

'But thanks anyway, for the outfit.' Shirley started to leave. 'It's lovely and I'm really very grateful. But I won't take the eye-shadow, if you don't mind.'

'Shirley will you sit down . . .?'

'The cheque is here – that *is* the right price, by the way? You're not doing it cheaply just for me, I hope.'

'Please, listen . . .'

'No, I'm off now. The life has gone out of it here, now that you pity me. I suppose it's just silly pride on my part, but I wouldn't enjoy it any more.'

'Shirley, let me say something. I regard you as my most valued customer. I know that sounds like something out of a book, but I mean it. I looked forward to your coming here. Compared with most of the others you're a joy – like a friend, a breath of fresh air. I enjoyed the days that you'd been. Now don't make me go down on my knees. Don't be touchy . . .'

'You've always been very friendly and helpful . . .'

'Friendly . . . helpful . . . I regard you as some kind of kid sister or daughter. I had a fight with Colin about you not three months ago, when he said you looked like Moby Dick with stripes or something.'

'Oh yes.'

'Oh God.'

Shirley had gone. The bang of the door nearly took the pictures off the walls.

'I'll miss her dreadfully,' thought Nan. 'She was the only one with any warmth or life. The rest are just bodies for the clothes.' To hell with it. She would telephone Lola, the friend who had sent Shirley to her in the first place.

'Listen, Lola, this sounds trivial but you know that nice Shirley who worked with you . . .'

'Shirley Green? Yeah, what about her?'

'No, her name is Kent, Shirley Kent.'

'I know it used to be till she married Alan Green.'

'Married?'

'Nan, do you feel OK? You made her wedding dress for her, about a year ago.'

'She never told me she got married. Who's Alan Green? Her husband?'

'Well, he's my boss, and was hers. Nan, what is this?'

'Why do you think she didn't tell me she got married?'

'Nan, I haven't an idea in the whole wide world why she didn't tell you. Is this what you rang up to ask me?'

'Well have a guess. Think why she mightn't have told me.'

'It might have been because you and Colin weren't getting married. She's very sensitive, old Shirl, and she wouldn't want to let you think she was pitying you or anything.'

'No, I suppose not.'

'Anyway, it was the most smashing wedding dress – all that ruffle stuff and all those lovely blues and lace embroidery. I thought it was the nicest thing you've ever made.'

                                                          Maeve Binchy

———

The Fat Black Woman Goes Shopping

Shopping in London winter
is a real drag for the fat black woman
going from store to store
in search of accommodating clothes
and de weather so cold

Look at the frozen thin mannequins
fixing her with grin
and de pretty face salesgals
exchanging slimming glances
thinking she don't notice

Lord is aggravating

Nothing soft and bright and billowing
to flow like breezy sunlight
when she is walking

The fat black woman curses in Swahili/Yoruba
and nation language under her breathing
all this journeying and journeying

The fat black woman could only conclude
that when it comes to fashion
the choice is lean

Nothing much beyond size 14

Grace Nichols

IS IT WORTH

GETTING THERE?

Now, nature, as I am only too well aware, has her
enthusiasts, but on the whole, I am not to be counted
among them. To put it rather bluntly, I am not the type
who wants to get back to the land; I am the type who
wants to get back to the hotel.

Fran Lebowitz

———

I dislike being in the country in August, because my legs
get so bitten by barristers.

Lydia Lopokova

———

The great and recurrent question about abroad is, is it
worth getting there?

Rose Macaulay

———

*Florence, a sprightly housemaid, who, in the inscrutable wanderings of the
sketch's plot, got to telling a startled visitor about an imaginary trip to
Africa.*

FLORENCE   Oh, yes we had quite a safari – *quite* a safari! We shot a lot of
elephants, tigers, lions, canteloupe and rats. We shot a lot
of rats – really! Pardon my rumbling – rambling.

VISITOR   Did you get a big bag?

FLORENCE   How did that go again?

VISITOR   I said, did you get a *big bag*?

FLORENCE   Natu*rally*. We had to – to put the elephants in. We wouldn't
want to drag them through the jungle by their tusks, you
know, so they had to go in the bag.

VISITOR   Did you get a bison?

FLORENCE   *Comment*? I beg your pardon.

VISITOR   I said, did you get a bison?

FLORENCE   A bison? Oh, good Lord, no! We had to wash in a bucket.
We roughed it out there. D'you know, I didn't see a bison the
whole time we were out there? Nothing but buckets.

Beatrice Lillie

———

Travelling is the ruin of all happiness! There's no looking
at a building here after seeing Italy.

Fanny Burney

———

One has no great hopes from Birmingham. I always say
there is something direful in the sound.

Jane Austen

———

[Advice to Clara Butt:] So you're going to Australia!
Well, I made twenty thousand pounds on my tour there,
but of course that will never be done again. Still, it's a
wonderful country, and you'll have a good time. What are
you going to sing? All I can say is – sing 'em muck! It's all
they can understand!

Nellie Melba

———

When it's three o'clock in New York, it's still 1938 in
London.

Bette Midler

———

When I was in England I was so cold I almost got married . . .

Shelley Winters

———

England's not a bad country – it's just a mean, cold, ugly,
divided, tired, clapped-out, post-imperial, post-industrial,
slag-heap covered in polystyrene hamburger cartons.

Margaret Drabble

———

from Life and Other Punctures

The fourth croissant and one thick white china cup of coffee were taken
very early indeed next morning in the company of two wine-quaffing
workmen in a small café in Trouville. Their lugubrious dialogue sounded
wonderfully sane. It was almost too early. I had gone to bed just as soon
as I had eaten my orange, determined that I should be up and away before
anyone was astir. I was up at the crack, dressed in a trice and with my bags
packed ready for stowing before I realised that I could not after all simply
leave – I had to pay my bill. And of course there was no one to pay, no
sign of Greta at that hour, let alone Monsieur Ix. Heaven knows where his

wild fancy had led them all last night after dinner – Paris, Monte Carlo, Dijon. . . . I hung about for an hour and a half before at last a bleary waiter appeared. Reluctant though he was – and rightly as it turned out – to accept any responsibility, I persuaded him of my urgent need to settle my bill. Money changed hands. I was free to go. After a whole day of near inertia there was a moment of disbelief before my muscles came to themselves and then we almost flew up that craggy drive, Moulton, muscles and I. The lanes were narrow and twisting and felt like English lanes. Trees and bushes dripped into puddles. Everywhere was wet; but the rain had stopped and the air had a freshness that did not carry the smell of more rain. My relief was boundless. I did not tempt fortune by crossing the narrow divide to Deauville. I was afraid I might come across Monsieur Ix recovering from yet another night on the tiles, stranded like a great whale on the Promenade des Planches.

My diary laconically postpones recording my sojourn on the cliffs:

Caen, 10 Sept.

'2 days in Honfleur – to be written . . . ';

and continues more happily,
'Now lovely Caen.

Village le Chaos à 8km
Houlgate
Trouville coffee: two men in berets talking about a man who had hanged himself. Great relief in leaving Y.
Picnic at Merville
Slowly into Caen.
Walked about a lot looking, after hotel – lovely (what a difference).
Place Royale. Happy supper. Terribly tired [almost illegible].
Can't make up my mind over tomorrow to Bayeux and back or stay there or what. Weather forecast is discouraging.

I felt completely and instantly at home in Caen. There used to be a guidebook for American tourists which, among many other ratings, occasionally awarded to deserving townships a 'J' for *joie de vivre*. At the time I read it, before Swinging London, there was only one town in the whole of the British Isles which was thought to deserve this accolade and that was Torquay. Well, if I had been a scout for Fielding's France, I should have roundly and unhesitatingly recommended a treble 'J' for Caen. I don't think it was only that I arrived at the best moment, with the new term just beginning; the moment just after August, with its heaviness and reaping and final fruits, when everything starts up again. January 1 for New Year has always seemed to me arbitrary and wrong; and spring alarms me with its buds. I like best this cool hiatus between summer and autumn, post-ploughing, pre-sowing, when all things seem possible.

It was not only the new term, nor the city contrast with the docile seaside towns and the countryside I had just cycled through that made Caen seem so alive. Nor do all towns that have been smashed and rebuilt sustain such a positive mood. This was not hasty, shallow reconstruction that goes to seed within a few minutes and which time can blacken and begrime but does not mellow. Here there were relics preserved and lovingly, spaciously reset among gardens, space and light and the honey colour of the walls, and stronger than the walls, an awareness of survival, a feeling of gratefulness and of pride.

I found a real hotel, I think it was the Hotel Bristol (I wish I knew why there is a Hotel Bristol in every town in every country I have ever visited) – a large comfortable room with dark polished wood fittings. I settled in and walked out to explore a little before it got dark, found a fish and vegetable and fruit market close to antique streets and old churches, and then went back to the bustle of the main streets, big stores and bookshops, cinemas and neon lights and students and working people leaving offices and gathering in cafés before going off home.

At the hotel I made my ritual reverse-Dracula transformation from black to multicolour and set out again for supper. It was some wonderful fish dish as I recall, in a bright bouncy restaurant where I was treated like an old friend. How different from the previous evening, I reflected rosily. But this comparison led me to make another, moments later, as I was paying my bill. It struck me that in fact the bill I had paid that morning had been remarkably low for two nights, with a breakfast and two dinners. I had the hotel bill with me and took it out. Sure enough, my morning waiter had been right to fret about assuming so much responsibility: he had charged me for one night only. Far from being filled with glee at this twist I became very uneasy. Monsieur Ix had at one point invited me to stay on as his guest, but I could not suppose that he would have repeated that invitation the following day and I had no desire to enjoy his inadvertent hospitality. What is more I should not have put it past him to set the police on me for evasion of payment, and suspicious behaviour, if not for actually being a spy.

I foresaw a second night of hammerings at the door, with harsher voices demanding to be let in.

By the time I got back to the Bristol I was all of a jitter. No one tried to stop me as I entered. The welcoming smiles seemed sincere enough. I raced upstairs and sat on the bed, breathing hard. After less than enough thought I found the hotel number in Michelin and lifted the telephone. Monsieur Ix was eventually found, dragged no doubt from the middle of some anecdote about looping the loop with M. Anouilh. I explained that I was afraid there had been some mistake about my bill.

'I do not occupy myself with those things there,' he said with hauteur. 'I pass you my receptionist.'

And he did. She was amazed by my call – whose full daftness even I can now see – but I persevered, promising to send a cheque for the equivalent amount as soon as I got back to England. (England! How long ago, how far away!) So call your men off, I might have added, had my German been up to it. And that was that, I thought, and settled down to write my journal.

I did decide on Bayeux although, according to the entry of 11 September: 'Woke this morning feeling incapable, aching, weary. How to go on. BUT.' I did go on. The sun was shining and the spell of Caen was cast beyond its immediate perimeters and over all the environs. 'Not pushing hard any more, or my legs are getting used to it or the wind's a little less. A happy trip along a great main road straight and thundering lorries pass me – brief respite from the wind – reluctantly leaving Caen, full of love for it. Cheered myself by deciding to go back, circularly, the sea route, and then probably on to Paris.'

My mood was great. I sang as I pushed along and made up fragmentary poems.

> Quel Sens?
> Regarde-moi donc
> *Oh! Look at those*
> ces grands nuages
> *big black clouds!*
> majestueux
> et sombres.
>
> Le temps souffle
> *Don't worry –*
> autant que le vent;

they'll blow away
ils s'en iront.
soon.
Oui.
Yes . . .
Mais dans quel sens?
But will they blow
from left to right or from
right to left?

Eleanor Bron

Once when Beerbohm Tree came home from a holiday in
Paris [Lady Tree] asked him if he had enjoyed himself. 'Oh
yes, I did, but Paris was thronged with hundreds of
appalling Cook's tourists.' 'Ah,' she said, 'I suppose too
many Cooks spoiled the brothels.'

Lady Maude Warrender

---

from Gentlemen Prefer Blondes

April 27th
Paris is devine. I mean Dorothy and I got to Paris yesterday, and it really is
devine. Because the French are devine. Because when we were coming off
the boat, and we were coming through the customs, it was quite hot and it
seemed to smell quite a lot and all the French gentlemen in the customs were
squealing quite a lot. So I looked around and I picked out a French gentleman who was really in a very gorgeous uniform and he seemed to be a very,
very important gentleman and I gave him twenty francs worth of French
money and he was very very gallant and he knocked everybody else down
and took our bags right through the custom. Because I really think that
twenty francs is quite cheap for a gentleman that has got on at least $100
worth of gold braid on his coat alone, to speak nothing of his trousers.

I mean the French gentlemen always seem to be squealing quite a lot,
especially taxi drivers when they only get a small size yellow dime called a

'fifty santeems' for a tip. But the good thing about French gentlemen is that every time a French gentleman starts in to squeal, you can always stop him with five francs, no matter who he is. I mean it is so refreshing to listen to a French gentleman stop squeaking, that it would really be quite a bargain even for ten francs.

So we came to the Ritz Hotel and the Ritz Hotel is devine. Because when a girl can sit in a delightful bar and have delicious champagne cocktails and look at all the important French people in Paris, I think it is devine. I mean when a girl can sit there and look at the Dolly sisters and Pearl White and Maybelle Gilman Corey, and Mrs Nash, it is beyond worlds. Because when a girl looks at Mrs Nash and realizes what Mrs Nash has got out of gentlemen, it really makes a girl hold her breath.

And when a girl walks around and reads all of the signs with all of the famous historical names it really makes you hold your breath. Because when Dorothy and I went on a walk, we only walked a few blocks but in only a few blocks we read all of the famous historical names, like Coty and Cartier and I knew we were seeing something educational at last and our whole trip was not a failure. I mean I really try to make Dorothy get educated and have reverance. So when we stood at the corner of a place called the Place Vendome, if you turn your back on a monument they have in the middle and look up, you can see none other than Coty's sign. So I said to Dorothy, does it not really give you a thrill to realize that that is the historical spot where Mr Coty makes all the perfume? So then Dorothy said that she supposed Mr Coty came to Paris and he smelled Paris and he realized that something had to be done. So Dorothy will really never have any reverance.

So then we saw a jewelry store and we saw some jewelry in the window and it really seemed to be a very very great bargain but the price marks all had francs on them and Dorothy and I do not seem to be mathematical enough to tell how much francs is in money. So we went in and asked and it seems it was only 20 dollars and it seems it is not diamonds but it is a thing called 'paste' which is the name of a word which means imitations. So Dorothy said 'paste' is the name of the word a girl ought to do to a gentleman that handed her one. I mean I would really be embarrassed, but the gentleman did not seem to understand Dorothy's English.

So it really makes a girl feel depressed to think a girl could not tell that it was nothing but an imitation. I mean a gentleman could deceeve a girl because he could give her a present and it would only be worth 20 dollars. So when Mr Eisman comes to Paris next week, if he wants to make me a present I will make him take me along with him because he is really quite an inveteran bargain hunter at heart. So the gentleman at the jewelry store said that quite a lot of famous girls in Paris had imitations of all their jewelry and they put the jewelry in the safe and they really wore the imitations, so they could wear it and have a good time. But I told him I thought that any girl who was a lady would not even think of having such a good time that she did not remember to hang on to her jewelry.

So then we went back to the Ritz and unpacked our trunks with the aid of really a delightful waiter who brought us up some delicious luncheon and who is called Leon and who speaks english almost like an American and who Dorothy and I talk to quite a lot. So Leon said that we ought not to stay around the Ritz all of the time, but we really ought to see Paris. So Dorothy said she would go down in the lobby and meet some gentleman to show us Paris. So in a couple of minutes she called up on the telephone from the lobby and she said 'I have got a French bird down here who is a French title nobleman, who is called a veecount so come on down.' So I said 'How did a Frenchman get into the Ritz.' So Dorothy said 'He came in to get out of the rain and he has not noticed that it is stopped.' So I said 'I suppose you have picked up something without taxi fare as usual. Why did you not get an American gentleman who always have money?' So Dorothy said she thought a French gentleman had ought to know Paris better. So I said 'He does not even know it is not raining.' But I went down.

So the veecount was really delightful after all. So then we rode around and we saw Paris and we saw how devine it really is. I mean the Eyefull Tower is devine and it is much more educational than the London Tower, because you can not even see the London Tower if you happen to be two blocks away. But when a girl looks at the Eyefull Tower she really knows she is looking at something. And it would even be very difficult not to notice the Eyefull Tower. So then we went to a place called the Madrid to tea and it really was devine. I mean we saw the Dolly Sisters and Pearl White and Mrs Corey and Mrs Nash all over again.

So then we went to dinner and then we went to Momart and it really was devine because we saw them all over again. I mean in Momart they have genuine American jazz bands and quite a lot of New York people which we knew and you really would think you were in New York and it was devine. So we came back to the Ritz quite late. So Dorothy and I had quite a little quarrel because Dorothy said that when we were looking at Paris I asked the French veecount what was the name of the unknown soldier who is buried under quite a large monument. So I said I really did not mean to ask him, if I did, because what I did mean to ask him was, what was the name of his mother because it is always the mother of a dead soldier that I always seem to think about more than the dead soldier that has died.

So the French veecount is going to call up in the morning but I am not going to see him again. Because French gentlemen are really quite deceeving. I mean they take you to quite cute places and they make you feel quite good about yourself and you really seem to have a delightful time but when you get home and come to think it all over, all you have got is a fan that only cost 20 francs and a doll that they gave you away for nothing in a restaurant. I mean a girl has to look out in Paris, or she would have such a good time in Paris that she would not get anywheres. So I really think that American gentlemen are the best after all, because kissing your hand may make you feel very very good but a diamond and safire bracelet lasts forever. Besides, I do not think that I ought to go out with any gentlemen in Paris because Mr Eisman will be here next week and he told me that the only kind of gentlemen he wants me to go out with are intelectual gentlemen who are good for a girls brains. So I really do not seem to see many gentlemen around the Ritz who seem to look like they would be good for a girl's brains. So tomorrow we are going to go shopping and I suppose it would really be to much to expect to find a gentleman who would look to Mr Eisman like he was good for a girls brains and at the same time he would like to take us shopping.

*

May 2nd

So last night we went to the Foley Bergere and it really was devine. I mean it was very very artistic because it had girls in it that were in the nude. So one of the girls was a friend of Louie and he said that she was a very very nice girl, and that she was only 18 years of age. So Dorothy said, 'She is slipping it over on you Louie, because how could a girl get such dirty knees in only 18 years?' So Louie and Robber really laughed very very loud. I mean Dorothy was very unrefined at the Foley Bergere. But I always think that when girls are in the nude it is very artistic and if you have artistic thoughts you think it is beautiful and I really would not laugh in an artistic place like the Foley Bergere.

So I wore the imitation of a diamond tiara to the Foley Bergere. I mean it really would deceeve an expert and Louie and Robber could hardly take their eyes off of it. But they did not really annoy me because I had it tied on very very tight. I mean it would be fatal if they got the diamond tiara before Dorothy and I took them shopping a lot.

So we are all ready to go shopping this morning and Robber was here bright and early and he is in the parlor with Dorothy and we are waiting for Louie. So I left the diamond tiara on the table in the parlor so Robber could see how careless I really am with everything but Dorothy is keeping her eye on Robber. So I just heard Louie come in because I heard him kissing Robber. I mean Louie is always kissing Robber and Dorothy told Louie that if he did not stop kissing Robber, people would think that he painted batiks.

So now I must join the others and I will put the diamond tiara in my hand bag so that Louie and Robber will feel that it is always around and we will all go shopping. And I almost have to smile when I think of Lady Francis Beekman.

*

May 19th

Well yesterday Mr Spoffard and I and Dorothy got off the train at Munich to see all of the kunst in Munich, but you only call it Munich when you are on the train because as soon as you get off of the train they seem to call it Munchen. So you really would know that Munchen was full of kunst because in case you would not know it, they have painted the word 'kunst' in large size black letters on everything in Munchen, and you can not even see a boot black's stand in Munchen that is not full of kunst.

So Mr Spoffard said that we really ought to go to the theater in Munchen because even the theater in Munchen was full of kunst. So we looked at all of the bills of all of the theaters, with the aid of quite an intelectual hotel clerk who seemed to be able to read it and tell us what it said, because it really meant nothing to us. So it seems they were playing Kiki in Munchen, so I said, let us go and see Kiki because we have seen Lenore Ulric in New York and we would really know what it is all about even if they do not seem to talk the English landguage. So then we went to the Kunst theater. So it seems that Munchen is practically full of Germans and the lobby of the Kunst theater was really full of Germans who stand in the lobby and drink beer and eat quite a lot of Bermudian onions and garlick sausage and hard boiled eggs and beer before all of the acts. So I really had to ask Mr Spoffard if he thought we had come to the right theater because the lobby seemed to smell such a lot. I mean when the smell of beer gets to be anteek it gets to smell quite a lot. But Mr Spoffard seemed to think that the lobby of the Kunst theatre did not smell any worse than all of the other places in Munich. So then Dorothy spoke up and Dorothy said 'You can say what you want about the Germans being full of "kunst", but what they are really full of is delicatessen.'

So then we went into the Kunst theater. But the Kunst theater does not seem to smell so good as the lobby of the Kunst theater. And the Kunst theater seems to be decorated with quite a lot of what tripe would look like if it was pasted on the wall and gilded. Only you could not really see the gilding because it was covered with quite a lot of dust. So Dorothy looked around and Dorothy said, if this is 'kunst', the art center of the world is Union Hill New Jersey.

So then they started in to playing Kiki but it seems that it was not the same kind of a Kiki that we have in America, because it seemed to be all about a family of large size German people who seemed to keep getting in each others way. I mean when a stage is completely full of 2 or 3 German people who are quite large size, they really cannot help it if they seem to get in each others ways. So then Dorothy got to talking with a young gentleman who seemed to be a German gentleman who sat back of her, who she thought was applauding. But what he was really doing was he was cracking a hard boiled egg on the back of her chair. So he talked English with quite an accent that seemed to be quite a German accent. So Dorothy asked him if Kiki had come out on the stage yet. So he said no, but she was really a beautiful German actress who came clear from Berlin and he said we should really wait until she came out, even if we did not seem to understand it. So finally she came out. I mean we knew it was her because Dorothy's German gentleman friend nudged Dorothy with a sausage. So we looked at her, and we looked at her and Dorothy said, 'If Schuman Heinke still has a grandmother, we have dug her up in Munchen.' So we did not bother to see any more of Kiki because Dorothy said she would really have to know more about the foundations of that building before she would risk our lives to see Kiki do that famous scene where she faints in the last act. Because Dorothy said, if the foundations of that building were as anteek as the smell, there was going to be a catasterophy when Kiki hit the floor. So even Mr Spoffard was quite discouradged, but he was really glad because he said he was 100 per cent of an American and it served the Germans right for starting such a war against all we Americans.

*

May 20th

Well today Mr Spoffard is going to take me all around to all of the museums in Munchen, which are full of kunst that I really ought to look at, but

Dorothy said she had been punished for all of her sins last night, so now she is going to begin life all over again by going out with her German gentleman friend, who is going to take her to a house called the Half Brow house which is the worlds largest size of a Beer Hall. So Dorothy said I could be a high brow and get full of kunst, but she is satisfide to be a Half brow and get full of beer. But Dorothy will really never be full of anything else but unrefinement.

Anita Loos

IF LOVE IS THE

ANSWER . . .

Oh, life is a glorious cycle of song,
A medley of extemporanea;
And love is a thing that can never go wrong;
And I am Marie of Roumania.

Dorothy Parker

———

Oh, what a dear ravishing thing is the beginning of an
Amour!

Aphra Behn

———

How to Talk to a Hunter

When he says 'Skins or blankets?' it will take you a moment to realize that
he's asking which you want to sleep under. And in your hesitation he'll
decide that he wants to see your skin wrapped in the big black moose hide.
He carried it, he'll say, soaking wet and heavier than a dead man, across the

tundra for two – was it hours or days or weeks? But the payoff, now, will be to see it fall across one of your white breasts. It's December, and your skin is never really warm, so you will pull the bulk of it around you and pose for him, pose for his camera, without having to narrate this moose's death.

You will spend every night in this man's bed without asking yourself why he listens to top-forty country. Why he donated money to the Republican Party. Why he won't play back his messages while you are in the room. You are there so often the messages pile up. Once you noticed the bright green counter reading as high as fifteen.

He will have lured you here out of a careful independence that you spent months cultivating; though it will finally be winter, the dwindling daylight and the threat of Christmas, that makes you give in. Spending nights with this man means suffering the long face of your sheepdog, who likes to sleep on your bed, who worries when you don't come home. But the hunter's house is so much warmer than yours, and he'll give you a key, and just like a woman, you'll think that means something. It will snow hard for thirteen straight days. Then it will really get cold. When it is sixty below there will be no wind and no clouds, just still air and cold sunshine. The sun on the windows will lure you out of bed, but he'll pull you back under. The next two hours he'll devote to your body. With his hands, with his tongue, he'll express what will seem to you like the most eternal of loves. Like the house key, this is just another kind of lie. Even in bed; especially in bed, you and he cannot speak the same language. The machine will answer the incoming calls. From under an ocean of passion and hide and hair you'll hear a woman's muffled voice between the beeps.

Your best female friend will say, 'So what did you think? That a man who sleeps under a dead moose is capable of commitment?'

This is what you learned in college: A man desires the satisfaction of his desire; a woman desires the condition of desiring.

The hunter will talk about spring in Hawaii, summer in Alaska. The man who says he was always better at math will form the sentences so carefully it will be impossible to tell if you are included in these plans. When he asks you if you would like to open a small guest ranch way out in the country, understand that this is a rhetorical question. Label these conversations future perfect, but don't expect the present to catch up with them. Spring is an inconceivable distance from the December days that just keep getting shorter and gray.

He'll ask you if you've ever shot anything, if you'd like to, if you ever thought about teaching your dog to retrieve. Your dog will like him too much, will drop the stick at his feet every time, will roll over and let the hunter scratch his belly.

One day he'll leave you sleeping to go split wood or get the mail and his phone will ring again. You'll sit very still while a woman who calls herself something like Janie Coyote leaves a message on his machine: She's leaving work, she'll say, and the last thing she wanted to hear was the sound of his beautiful voice. Maybe she'll talk only in rhyme. Maybe the counter will change to sixteen. You'll look a question at the mule deer on the wall, and the dark spots on either side of his mouth will tell you he shares more with this hunter than you ever will. One night, drunk, the hunter told you he was sorry for taking that deer, that every now and then there's an animal that isn't meant to be taken, and he should have known that deer was one.

Your best male friend will say, 'No one who needs to call herself Janie Coyote can hold a candle to you, but why not let him sleep alone a few nights, just to make sure?'

The hunter will fill your freezer with elk burger, venison sausage, organic potatoes, fresh pecans. He'll tell you to wear your seat belt, to dress warmly, to drive safely. He'll say you are always on his mind, that you're the best thing that's ever happened to him, that you make him glad that he's a man.

Tell him it don't come easy, tell him freedom's just another word for nothing left to lose.

These are the things you'll know without asking: The coyote woman wears her hair in braids. She uses words like 'howdy.' She's man enough to shoot a deer.

A week before Christmas you'll rent *It's a Wonderful Life* and watch it together, curled on your couch, faces touching. Then you'll bring up the word 'monogamy.' He'll tell you how badly he was hurt by your predecessor. He'll tell you he couldn't be happier spending every night with you. He'll say there's just a few questions he doesn't have the answers for. He'll say he's just scared and confused. Of course this isn't exactly what he means. Tell him you understand. Tell him you are scared too. Tell him to take all the time he needs. Know that you could never shoot an animal, and be glad of it.

Your best female friend will say, 'You didn't tell him you loved him, did you?' Don't even tell her the truth. If you do you'll have to tell her that he said this: 'I feel exactly the same way.'

Your best male friend will say, 'Didn't you know what would happen when you said the word "commitment"?'

But that isn't the word that you said.

He'll say, 'Commitment, monogamy, it all means just one thing.'

The coyote woman will come from Montana with the heavier snows. The hunter will call you on the day of the solstice to say he has a friend in town and can't see you. He'll leave you hanging your Christmas lights; he'll give new meaning to the phrase 'longest night of the year.' The man who has said he's not so good with words will manage to say eight things about his friend without using a gender-determining pronoun. Get out of the house quickly. Call the most understanding person you know who will let you sleep in his bed.

Your best female friend will say, 'So what did you think? That he was capable of living outside his gender?'

When you get home in the morning there's a candy tin on your pillow. Santa, obese and grotesque, fondles two small children on the lid. The card will say something like 'From your not-so-secret admirer.' Open it. Examine each carefully made truffle. Feed them, one at a time, to the dog. Call the hunter's machine. Tell him you don't speak chocolate.

Your best female friend will say, 'At this point, what is it about him that you could possibly find appealing?'

Your best male friend will say, 'Can't you understand that this is a good sign? Can't you understand that this proves how deep he's in with you?' Hug your best male friend. Give him the truffles the dog wouldn't eat.

Of course the weather will cooperate with the coyote woman. The highways will close, she will stay another night. He'll tell her he's going to work so he can come and see you. He'll even leave her your number and write 'Me at Work' on the yellow pad of paper by his phone. Although you shouldn't, you'll have to be there. It will be you and your nauseous dog and your half-trimmed tree all waiting for him like a series of questions.

This is what you learned in graduate school: In every assumption is contained the possibility of its opposite.

In your kitchen he'll hug you like you might both die there. Sniff him for coyote. Don't hug him back.

He will say whatever he needs to to win. He'll say it's just an old friend. He'll say the visit was all the friend's idea. He'll say the night away from you has given him time to think about how much you mean to him. Realize that nothing short of sleeping alone will ever make him realize how much you mean to him. He'll say that if you can just be a little patient, some good will come out of this for the two of you after all. He still won't use a gender-specific pronoun.

Put your head in your hands. Think about what it means to be patient. Think about the beautiful, smart, strong, clever woman you thought he saw when he looked at you. Pull on your hair. Rock your body back and forth. Don't cry.

He'll say that after holding you it doesn't feel right holding anyone else. For 'holding,' substitute 'fucking.' Then take it as a compliment.

He will get frustrated and rise to leave. He may or may not be bluffing. Stall for time. Ask a question he can't immediately answer. Tell him you want to make love on the floor. When he tells you your body is beautiful say, 'I feel exactly the same way.' Don't, under any circumstances, stand in front of the door.

Your best female friend will say, 'They lie to us, they cheat on us, and we love them more for it.' She'll say, 'It's our fault; we raise them to be like that.'

Tell her it can't be your fault. You've never raised anything but dogs.

The hunter will say it's late and he has to go home to sleep. He'll emphasize the last word in the sentence. Give him one kiss that he'll remember while he's fucking the coyote woman. Give him one kiss that ought to make him cry if he's capable of it, but don't notice when he does. Tell him to have a good night.

Your best male friend will say, 'We all do it. We can't help it. We're self-destructive. It's the old bad-boy routine. You have a male dog, don't you?'

The next day the sun will be out and the coyote woman will leave. Think about how easy it must be for a coyote woman and a man who listens to top-forty country. The coyote woman would never use a word like 'monogamy'; the coyote woman will stay gentle on his mind.

If you can, let him sleep alone for at least one night. If you can't, invite him over to finish trimming your Christmas tree. When he asks how you are, tell him you think it's a good idea to keep your sense of humor during the holidays.

Plan to be breezy and aloof and full of interesting anecdotes about all the other men you've ever known. Plan to be hotter than ever before in bed, and a little cold out of it. Remember that necessity is the mother of invention. Be flexible.

First, he will find the faulty bulb that's been keeping all the others from lighting. He will explain, in great detail, the most elementary electrical principles. You will take turns placing the ornaments you and other men, he and other women have spent years carefully choosing. Under the circumstances, try to let this be a comforting thought.

He will thin the clusters of tinsel you put on the tree. He'll say something ambiguous like 'Next year you should string popcorn and cranberries.' Finally, his arm will stretch just high enough to place the angel on the top of the tree.

Your best female friend will say, 'Why can't you ever fall in love with a man who will be your friend?'

Your best male friend will say, 'You ought to know this by now: Men always cheat on the best women.'

This is what you learned in the pop psychology book: Love means letting go of fear.

Play Willie Nelson's 'Pretty Paper.' He'll ask you to dance, and before you can answer he'll be spinning you around your wood stove, he'll be humming in your ear. Before the song ends he'll be taking off your clothes, setting you lightly under the tree, hovering above you with tinsel in his hair. Through the spread of the branches the all-white lights you insisted on will shudder and blur, outlining the ornaments he brought: a pheasant, a snow goose, a deer.

The record will end. Above the crackle of the wood stove and the rasp of the hunter's breathing you'll hear one long low howl break the quiet of the frozen night: your dog, chained and lonely and cold. You'll wonder if he knows enough to stay in his doghouse. You'll wonder if he knows that the nights are getting shorter now.

                                                                    Pam Houston

———

After all, my erstwhile dear,
My no longer cherished,
Need we say it was not love,
Now that love is perished?
                    Edna St Vincent Millay

———

The Singing Lesson

With despair – cold, sharp despair – buried deep in her heart like a wicked knife, Miss Meadows, in cap and gown and carrying a little baton, trod the cold corridors that led to the music hall. Girls of all ages, rosy from the air, and bubbling over with that gleeful excitement that comes from running to school on a fine autumn morning, hurried, skipped, fluttered by; from the hollow classrooms came a quick drumming of voices; a bell rang, a voice like a bird cried, 'Muriel'. And then there came from the staircase a tremendous knock-knock, knocking. Someone had dropped her dumbbells.

The Science Mistress stopped Miss Meadows.

'Good mor-ning,' she cried, in her sweet, affected drawl. 'Isn't it cold? It might be win-ter.'

Miss Meadows, hugging the knife, stared in hatred at the Science Mistress. Everything about her was sweet, pale, like honey. You would not have been surprised to see a bee caught in the tangles of that yellow hair.

'It is rather sharp,' said Miss Meadows, grimly.

The other smiled her sugary smile.

'You look fro-zen,' said she. Her blue eyes opened wide; there came a mocking light in them. (Had she noticed anything?)

'Oh, not quite as bad as that,' said Miss Meadows, and she gave the Science Mistress, in exchange for her smile, a quick grimace and passed on. . . .

Forms Four, Five and Six were assembled in the music hall. The noise was deafening. On the platform, by the piano, stood Mary Beazley, Miss Meadows' favourite, who played accompaniments. She was turning the music stool. When she saw Miss Meadows she gave a loud warning, 'Sh-sh! girls!' and Miss Meadows, her hands thrust in her sleeves, the baton under her arm, strode down the centre aisle, mounted the steps, turned sharply, seized the brass music stand, planted it in front of her, and gave two sharp taps with her baton for silence.

'Silence, please! Immediately!' and, looking at nobody, her glance swept over that sea of coloured flannel blouses, with bobbing pink faces and hands, quivering butterfly hair-bows, and music-books outspread. She knew perfectly well what they were thinking. 'Meady is in a wax.' Well, let them think it! Her eyelids quivered; she tossed her head, defying them. What could the thoughts of those creatures matter to someone who stood there bleeding to death, pierced to the heart, to the heart, by such a letter –

. . . 'I feel more and more strongly that our marriage would be a mistake. Not that I do not love you. I love you as much as it is possible for me to love any woman, but, truth to tell, I have come to the conclusion that I am not a marrying man, and the idea of settling down fills me with nothing but – ' and the word 'disgust' was scratched out lightly and 'regret' written over the top.

Basil! Miss Meadows stalked over to the piano. And Mary Beazley, who was waiting for this moment, bent forward; her curls fell over her cheeks while she breathed, 'Good morning, Miss Meadows', and she motioned towards rather than handed to her mistress a beautiful yellow chrysanthemum. This little ritual of the flower had been gone through for ages and ages, quite a term and a half. It was as much part of the lesson as opening the piano. But this morning, instead of taking it up, instead of tucking it into her belt while she leant over Mary and said, 'Thank you, Mary. How very nice! Turn to page thirty-two', what was Mary's horror when Miss Meadows totally ignored the chrysanthemum, made no reply to her greeting, but said in a voice of ice, 'Page fourteen please, and mark the accents well.'

Staggering moment! Mary blushed until the tears stood in her eyes, but Miss Meadows was gone back to the music stand; her voice rang through the music hall.

'Page fourteen. We will begin with page fourteen. "A Lament". Now, girls, you ought to know it by this time. We shall take it all together; not in parts, all together. And without expression. Sing it, though, quite simply, beating time with the left hand.'

She raised the baton; she tapped the music stand twice. Down came Mary on the opening chord; down came all those left hands, beating the air, and in chimed those young, mournful voices:

> Fast! Ah, too Fast Fade the Ro-o-ses of Pleasure;
> Soon Autumn yields unto Wi-i-nter Drear.
> Fleetly! Ah, Fleetly Mu-u-sic's Gay Measure
> Passes away from the Listening Ear.

Good Heavens, what could be more tragic than that lament! Every note was a sigh, a sob, a groan of awful mournfulness. Miss Meadows lifted her arms in the wide gown and began conducting with both hands. ' . . . I feel more and more strongly that our marriage would be a mistake . . . ' she beat. And the voices cried: Fleetly! Ah, Fleetly. What could have possessed him to write such a letter! What could have led up to it! It came out of nothing.

His last letter had been all about a fumed-oak bookcase he had bought for 'our' books, and a 'natty little hall stand' he had seen, 'a very neat affair with a carved owl on a bracket, holding three hat-brushes in its claws'. How she had smiled at that! So like a man to think one needed three hat-brushes! *From the Listening Ear*, sang the voices.

'Once again,' said Miss Meadows. 'But this time in parts. Still without expression.' *Fast! Ah, too Fast.* With the gloom of the contraltos added, one could scarcely help shuddering. *Fade the Roses of Pleasure.* Last time he had come to see her, Basil had worn a rose in his buttonhole. How handsome he had looked in that bright blue suit, with that dark red rose! And he knew it, too. He couldn't help knowing it. First he stroked his hair, then his moustache; his teeth gleamed when he smiled.

'The headmaster's wife keeps on asking me to dinner. It's a perfect nuisance. I never get an evening to myself in that place.'

'But can't you refuse?'

'Oh, well, it doesn't do for a man in my position to be unpopular.'

Music's Gay Measure, wailed the voices. The willow trees, outside the high, narrow windows, waved in the wind. They had lost half their leaves. The tiny ones that clung wriggled like fishes caught on a line. ' . . . I am not a marrying man . . . ' The voices were silent; the piano waited.

'Quite good,' said Miss Meadows, but still in such a strange, stony tone that the younger girls began to feel positively frightened. 'But now that we know it, we shall take it with expression. As much expression as you can put into it. Think of the words, girls. Use your imaginations. *Fast! Ah, too Fast,*' cried Miss Meadows. 'That ought to break out – a loud, strong *forte* – a lament. And then in the second line, *Winter Drear*, make that *Drear* sound as if a cold wind were blowing through it. *Dre-ear!*' said she so awfully that Mary Beazley, on the music stool, wriggled her spine. 'The third line should be one crescendo. *Fleetly! Ah, Fleetly Music's Gay Measure.* Breaking on the first word of the last line, *Passes.* And then on the word, *Away*, you must begin to die . . . to fade . . . until *the Listening Ear* is nothing more than a faint whisper . . . You can slow down as much as you like almost on the last line. Now, please.'

Again the two light taps; she lifted her arms again. *Fast! Ah, too Fast.* ' . . . and the idea of settling down fills me with nothing but disgust – ' Disgust was what he had written. That was as good as to say their engagement was definitely broken off. Broken off! Their engagement! People had been surprised enough that she had got engaged. The Science Mistress would not believe it at first. But nobody had been as surprised as she. She was thirty.

Basil was twenty-five. It had been a miracle, simply a miracle, to hear him say, as they walked home from church that very dark night, 'You know, somehow or other, I've got fond of you.' And he had taken hold of the end of her ostrich feather boa. *Passes away from the Listening Ear.*

'Repeat! Repeat!' said Miss Meadows. 'More expression, girls! Once more!'

Fast! Ah, too Fast. The older girls were crimson, some of the younger ones began to cry. Big spots of rain blew against the windows, and one could hear the willows whispering, ' . . . not that I do not love you . . . '

'But, my darling, if you love me,' thought Miss Meadows, 'I don't mind how much it is. Love me as little as you like.' But she knew he didn't love her. Not to have cared enough to scratch out that 'disgust', so that she couldn't read it! *Soon Autumn yields unto Winter Drear.* She would have to leave the school, too. She could never face the Science Mistress or the girls after it got known. She would have to disappear somewhere. *Passes away.* The voices began to die, to fade, to whisper . . . to vanish . . .

Suddenly the door opened. A little girl in blue walked fussily up the aisle, hanging her head, biting her lips, and twisting the silver bangle on her red little wrist. She came up the steps and stood before Miss Meadows.

'Well, Monica, what is it?'

'Oh, if you please, Miss Meadows,' said the little girl, gasping, 'Miss Wyatt wants to see you in the mistresses' room.'

'Very well,' said Miss Meadows. And she called to the girls, 'I shall put you on your honour to talk quietly while I am away.' But they were too subdued to do anything else. Most of them were blowing their noses.

The corridors were silent and cold; they echoed to Miss Meadows' steps. The Head Mistress sat at her desk. For a moment she did not look up. She was as usual disentangling her eyeglasses, which had got caught in her lace tie. 'Sit down, Miss Meadows,' she said very kindly. And then she picked up a pink envelope from the blotting-pad. 'I sent for you just now because this telegram has come for you.'

'A telegram for me, Miss Wyatt?'

Basil! He had committed suicide, decided Miss Meadows. Her hand flew out, but Miss Wyatt held the telegram back a moment. 'I hope it's not bad news,' she said, no more than kindly. And Miss Meadows tore it open.

'Pay no attention to letter must have been mad bought hat stand today Basil,' she read. She couldn't take her eyes off the telegram.

'I do hope it's nothing very serious,' said Miss Wyatt, leaning forward.

'Oh, no, thank you, Miss Wyatt,' blushed Miss Meadows. 'It's nothing bad at all. It's' – and she gave an apologetic little laugh – 'it's from my *fiancé* saying that . . . saying that – ' There was a pause. 'I *see*,' said Miss Wyatt. And another pause. Then – 'You've fifteen minutes more of your class, Miss Meadows, haven't you?'

'Yes, Miss Wyatt.' She got up. She half ran towards the door.

'Oh, just a minute, Miss Meadows,' said Miss Wyatt. 'I must say I don't approve of my teachers having telegrams sent to them in school hours, unless in case of very bad news, such as death,' explained Miss Wyatt, 'or a very serious accident or something to that effect. Good news, Miss Meadows, will always keep, you know.'

On the wings of hope, of love, of joy, Miss Meadows sped back to the music hall, up the aisle, up the steps, over to the piano.

'Page thirty-two, Mary,' she said, 'page thirty-two,' and, picking up the yellow chrysanthemum, she held it to her lips to hide her smile. Then she turned to the girls, rapped with her baton: 'Page thirty-two, girls. Page thirty-two.'

> *We come here Today with Flowers o'erladen,*
> *With Baskets of Fruit and Ribbons to boot,*
> *To-oo Congratulate . . .*

'Stop! Stop!' cried Miss Meadows. 'This is awful. This is dreadful.' And she beamed at her girls. 'What's the matter with you all? Think, girls, think of what you're singing. Use your imaginations. *With Flowers o'erladen. Baskets of Fruit and Ribbons to boot.* And *Congratulate.*' Miss Meadows broke off. 'Don't look so doleful, girls. It ought to sound warm, joyful, eager. *Congratulate.* Once more. Quickly. All together. Now then!'

And this time Miss Meadows' voice sounded over all the other voices – full, deep, glowing with expression.

Katherine Mansfield

––––

No Answer

I waited
For the phone
To ring

And when at last
It didn't,
I knew it was you.

Eleanor Bron

———

I loved Kirk so much, I would have skied down Mount
Everest in the nude with a carnation up my nose.

Joyce McKinney giving evidence at
Epsom Magistrates Court

———

Indian Summer

In youth, it was a way I had
  To do my best to please,
And change, with every passing lad,
  To suit his theories.

But now I know the things I know,
  And do the things I do;
And if you do not like me so,
  To hell, my love, with you!

Dorothy Parker

———

The Lady's Yes

'Yes,' I answered you last night;
'No,' this morning, sir, I say.
Colours seen by candle-light
Will not look the same by day.

Elizabeth Barrett Browning

———

A Gay Call

I tell you what Ethel said Bernard Clark about a week later we might go and pay a call on my pal the Earl of Clincham.

Oh do lets cried Ethel who was game for any new adventure I would dearly love to meet his lordship.

Bernard gave a frown of jellousy at her rarther mere words.

Well dress in your best he muttered.

Ethel skipped into her bedroom and arrayd herself in a grass green muslin of decent cut a lace scarf long faun colored kid gloves and a muslin hat to correspond. She carried a parasole in one hand also a green silk bag containing a few stray hair pins a clean handkerchief five shillings and a pot of ruge in case. She looked a dainty vishen with her fair hair waving in the breeze and Bernard bit his lips rarther hard for he could hardly contain himself and felt he must marry Ethel soon. He looked a handsome sight himself in some exquisite white trousers with a silk shirt and a pale blue blazer belt and cap. He wore this in honour of the earl who had been to Cambridge in his youth and so had Bernard Clark.

At last they found themselves in the entrance hall of the Crystale palace and speedily made their way to the privite compartments. Edward Procurio was walking up and down the passage looking dark and mystearious as usual.

Is His Lordship at home cried Bernard Clark cheerily.

Which one asked Procurio many lords live here he said scornfully.

Well I mean the Earl of Clincham said Bernard.

Oh yes he is in responded Procurio and to the best of my belief giving a party.

Indeed ejaculated Bernard we have come in the nick of time Ethel he added. Yes said Ethel in an excited tone.

Then they pealed on the bell and the door flew open. Sounds of laughter and comic songs issued from the abode and in a second they were in the crowded drawing room. It was packed with all the Elite and a stout duchess with a good natured face was singing a lively song and causing much merriment. The earl strode forward at sight of two new comers. Hullo Bernard old boy he cried this is a pleasure and who have you got with you he added glancing at Ethel.

Oh this is Miss Monticue said Bernard shall I introduce you –

If you will be so good said the earl in an affable tone and Bernard hastily performed the right. Ethel began a bright conversatiun while Bernard stroled off to see if he could find any friends amid the throng.

What plesant compartments you have cried Ethel in rarther a socierty tone.

Fairly so so responded the earl do you live in London he added in a loud tone as someone was playing a very difficult piece on the piano.

Well no I dont said Ethel my home is really in Northumberland but I am at present stopping with Mr Clark at the Gaierty Hotel she continud in a somewhat showing off tone.

Oh I see said the earl well shall I introduce you to a few of my friends.

Oh please do said Ethel with a dainty blow at her nose.

The earl disserppeard into the madding crowd and presently came back with a middle aged gentleman. This is Lord Hyssops he said my friend Miss Monticue he added genially.

Ethel turned a dull yellaw. Lord Hyssops she said in a faint voice why it is Mr Salteena I know him well.

Hush cried the earl it is a title bestowed recently by my friend the Prince of Wales.

Yes indeed murmered Mr Salteena deeply flabbergasted by the ready wit of the earl.

Oh indeed said Ethel in a peevish tone well how do you come to be here.

I am stopping with his Lordship said Mr Salteena and have a set of compartments in the basement so there.

I dont care said huffy Ethel I am in handsome rooms at the Gaierty.

Nothing could be nicer I am sure struck in the earl what do you say Hyssops eh.

Doubtless it is charming said Mr Salteena who was wanting peace tell me Ethel how did you leave Bernard.

I have not left him said Ethel in an annoying voice I am stopping with him at the Gaierty and we have been to lots of theaters and dances.

Well I am glad you are enjoying yourself said Mr Salteena kindly you had been looking pale of late.

No wonder in your stuffy domain cried Ethel well have you got any more friends she added turning to the earl.

Well I will see said the obliging earl and he once more disapeared.

I dont know why you should turn against me Ethel said Mr Salteena in a low tone.

Ethel patted her hair and looked very sneery. Well I call it very mystearious you going off and getting a title said Ethel and I think our friendship had better stop as no doubt you will soon be marrying a duchess or something.

Not at all said Mr Salteena you must know Ethel he said blushing a deep red I always wished to marry you some fine day.

This is news to me cried Ethel still peevish.

But not to me murmered Mr Salteena and his voice trembled in his chest. I may add that I have always loved you and now I seem to do so madly he added passionately.

But I dont love you responded Ethel.

But if you married me you might get to said Mr Salteena.

I think not replied Ethel and all the same it is very kind of you to ask me and she smiled more nicely at him.

This is agony cried Mr Salteena clutching hold of a table my life will be sour grapes and ashes without you.

Be a man said Ethel in a gentle whisper and I shall always think of you in a warm manner.

Well half a loaf is better than no bread responded Mr Salteena in a gloomy voice and just then the earl reappeard with a very brisk lady in a tight silk dress whose name was called Lady Gay Finchling and her husband was a General but had been dead a few years. So this is Miss Monticue she began in a rarther high voice. Oh yes said Ethel and Mr Salteena wiped the foaming dew from his forehead. Little did Lady Gay Finchling guess she had just disturbed a proposal of marriage.

The earl chimed into the conversation now and again and Lady Gay Finchling told several rarther witty stories to enliven the party. Then Bernard Clark came up and said they had better be going.

Well goodbye Clincham he said I must say I have enjoyed this party most rechauffie I call it dont you Ethel.

Most cried Ethel I suppose you often come she added in a tone of envy to Lady Gay Finchling.

Pretty often said Lady G. F. well goodbye as I see you are in a hurry to
be off and she dashed off towards the refreshment place.

Goodbye Ethel said poor Mr Salteena in a spasam and he seized hold
of her hand you will one day rue your wicked words farewell he repeated
emphatically.

Oh well goodbye said Ethel in a vage tone and then turning to the earl
she said I have enjoyed myself very much thankyou.

Please dont mention it cried the earl well goodbye Bernard he added I
shall look you up some day at your hotel.

Yes do muttered Bernard always welcome Clincham old boy he
added placing his blue crickit cap on his head and so saying he and
Ethel left the gay scene and once more oozed forth into the streets of
London.

Daisy Ashford

Love, a child, is ever crying:
Please him and he straight is flying,
Give him, he the more is craving,
Never satisfied with having.

Lady Mary Wroth

------

from Love and Friendship
LETTER 4TH. *Laura to Marianne*

Our neighbourhood was small, for it consisted only of your mother. She may
probably have already told you that, being left by her parents in indigent
circumstances, she had retired into Wales on economical motives. There it
was our friendship first commenced. Isabel was then one and twenty. Though
pleasing both in her person and manners, between ourselves she never
possessed the hundredth part of my beauty or accomplishments. Isabel had
seen the world. She had passed two years at one of the first boarding schools
in London, had spent a fortnight in Bath, and had supped one night in
Southampton.

'Beware, my Laura,' she would often say, 'beware of the insipid vanities and idle dissipations of the Metropolis of England; beware of the unmeaning luxuries of Bath and of the stinking fish of Southampton.'

'Alas!' exclaimed I, 'how am I to avoid those evils I shall never be exposed to? What probability is there of my ever tasting the dissipations of London, the luxuries of Bath, or the stinking fish of Southampton? I, who am doomed to waste my days of youth and beauty in an humble cottage in the Vale of Usk.'

Ah! little did I then think I was ordained so soon to quit that humble cottage for the deceitful pleasures of the world.

Adieu,
Laura

LETTER 5TH. *Laura to Marianne*

One evening in December, as my father, my mother, and myself were arranged in social converse round our fireside, we were on a sudden greatly astonished by hearing a violent knocking on the outward door of our rustic cot.

My father started – 'What noise is that?' said he. 'It sounds like a loud rapping at the door,' replied my mother. 'It does indeed,' cried I. 'I am of your opinion,' said my father, 'it certainly does appear to proceed from some uncommon violence exerted against our unoffending door.' 'Yes,' exclaimed I, 'I cannot help thinking it must be somebody who knocks for admittance.'

'That is another point,' replied he. 'We must not pretend to determine on what motive the person may knock – though that someone *does* rap at the door, I am partly convinced.'

Here, a second tremendous rap interrupted my father in his speech and somewhat alarmed my mother and me.

'Had we not better go and see who it is?' said she. 'The servants are out.' 'I think we had,' replied I. 'Certainly,' added my father, 'by all means.' 'Shall we go now?' said my mother. 'The sooner the better,' answered he. 'Oh! let no time be lost,' cried I.

A third more violent rap than ever again assaulted our ears. 'I am certain there is somebody knocking at the door,' said my mother. 'I think there must,' replied my father. 'I fancy the servants are returned,' said I; 'I think I hear Mary going to the door.' 'I'm glad of it,' cried my father, 'for I long to know who it is.'

I was right in my conjecture; for Mary instantly entering the room informed us that a young gentleman and his servant were at the door, who had lost their way, were very cold, and begged leave to warm themselves by our fire.

'Won't you admit them?' said I. 'You have no objection, my dear?' said my father. 'None in the world,' replied my mother.

Mary, without waiting for any further commands, immediately left the room and quickly returned, introducing the most beauteous and amiable youth I had ever beheld. The servant she kept to herself.

My natural sensibility had already been greatly affected by the sufferings of the unfortunate stranger, and no sooner did I first behold him, than I felt that on him the happiness or misery of my future life must depend.

Adieu,
Laura

LETTER 6TH. *Laura to Marianne*

The noble youth informed us that his name was Lindsay – for particular reasons however I shall conceal it under that of Talbot. He told us that he was the son of an English baronet, that his mother had been many years no more and that he had a sister of the middle size. 'My father,' he continued, 'is a mean and mercenary wretch – it is only to such particular friends as this dear party that I would thus betray his failings. Your virtues, my amiable Polydore (addressing himself to my father), yours, dear Claudia, and yours, my charming Laura, call on me to repose in you my confidence.' We bowed. 'My father, seduced by the false glare of fortune and the deluding pomp of title, insisted on my giving my hand to Lady Dorothea. "No, never!" exclaimed I. "Lady Dorothea is lovely and engaging; I prefer no woman to her; but know, sir, that I scorn to marry her in compliance with your wishes. No! never shall it be said that I obliged my father."'

We all admired the noble manliness of his reply. He continued.

'Sir Edward was surprised; he had perhaps little expected to meet with so spirited an opposition to his will. "Where, Edward, in the name of wonder," said he, "did you pick up this unmeaning gibberish? You have been studying novels, I suspect." I scorned to answer: it would have been beneath my dignity. I mounted my horse, and followed by my faithful William set forwards for my aunt's.

'My father's house is situated in Bedfordshire, my aunt's in Middlesex, and though I flatter myself with being a tolerable proficient in geography, I know not how it happened, but I found myself entering this beautiful vale which I find is in South Wales, when I had expected to have reached my aunt's.

'After having wandered some time on the banks of the Usk without knowing which way to go, I began to lament my cruel destiny in the bitterest and most pathetic manner. It was now perfectly dark, not a single star was there to direct my steps, and I know not what might have befallen me had I not at length discerned, through the solemn gloom that surrounded me, a distant light, which, as I approached it, I discovered to be the cheerful blaze of your fire. Impelled by the combination of misfortunes under which I laboured, namely fear, cold, and hunger, I hesitated not to ask admittance, which at length I have gained; and now, my adorable Laura,' continued he, taking my hand, 'when may I hope to receive that reward of all the painful sufferings I have undergone during the course of my attachment to you, to which I have ever aspired? Oh! when will you reward me with yourself?'

'This instant, dear and amiable Edward,' replied I. We were immediately united by my father, who, though he had never taken orders, had been bred to the church.

Adieu,
Laura

LETTER 7TH. *Laura to Marianne*

We remained but a few days after our marriage in the Vale of Usk. After taking an affecting farewell of my father, my mother, and my Isabel, I accompanied Edward to his aunt's in Middlesex. Philippa received us both with every expression of affectionate love. My arrival was indeed a most agreable surprise to her as she had not only been totally ignorant of my marriage with her nephew, but had never even had the slightest idea of there being such a person in the world.

Augusta, the sister of Edward, was on a visit to her when we arrived. I found her exactly what her brother had described her to be – of the middle size. She received me with equal surprise, though not with equal cordiality, as Philippa. There was a disagreable coldness and forbidding reserve in her reception of me which was equally distressing and unexpected: none of that interesting sensibility or amiable sympathy in her manners and address to me which should have distinguished our introduction to each other. Her language was neither warm, nor affectionate, her expressions of regard were neither animated nor cordial; her arms were not opened to receive me to her heart, though my own were extended to press her to mine.

A short conversation between Augusta and her brother, which I accidentally overheard, increased my dislike to her, and convinced me that her heart was no more formed for the soft ties of love than for the endearing intercourse of friendship.

'But do you think that my father will ever be reconciled to this imprudent connection?' said Augusta.

'Augusta,' replied the noble youth, 'I thought you had a better opinion of me than to imagine I would so abjectly degrade myself as to consider my father's concurrence in any of my affairs either of consequence or concern to me. Tell me, Augusta, tell me with sincerity; did you ever know me consult his inclinations or follow his advice in the least trifling particular since the age of fifteen?'

'Edward,' replied she, 'you are surely too diffident in your own praise. Since you were fifteen only! – My dear brother, since you were five years old, I entirely acquit you of ever having willingly contributed to the satisfaction of your father. But still I am not without apprehensions of your being shortly obliged to degrade yourself in your own eyes by seeking a support for your wife in the generosity of Sir Edward.'

'Never, never, Augusta, will I so demean myself,' said Edward. 'Support! what support will Laura want which she can receive from him?'

'Only those very insignificant ones of victuals and drink,' answered she.

'Victuals and drink!' replied my husband in a most nobly contemptuous manner, 'and dost thou then imagine that there is no other support for an exalted mind such as is my Laura's than the mean and indelicate employment of eating and drinking?'

'None that I know of so efficacious,' returned Augusta.

'And did you then never feel the pleasing pangs of love, Augusta?' replied my Edward. 'Does it appear impossible to your vile and corrupted palate to exist on love? Can you not conceive the luxury of living in every distress that poverty can inflict, with the object of your tenderest affection?'

'You are too ridiculous,' said Augusta, 'to argue with; perhaps, however, you may in time be convinced that . . .'

Here I was prevented from hearing the remainder of her speech by the appearance of a very handsome young woman, who was ushered into the room at the door of which I had been listening. On hearing her announced by the name of Lady Dorothea, I instantly quitted my post and followed her into the parlour, for I well remembered that she was the lady proposed as a wife for my Edward by the cruel and unrelenting baronet.

Although Lady Dorothea's visit was nominally to Philippa and Augusta, yet I have some reason to imagine that (acquainted with the marriage and arrival of Edward) to see me was a principal motive to it.

I soon perceived that, though lovely and elegant in her person, and though easy and polite in her address, she was of that inferior order of beings with regard to delicate feelings, tender sentiments, and refined sensibility, of which Augusta was one.

She stayed but half an hour, and neither in the course of her visit confided to me any of her secret thoughts, nor requested me to confide in her any of mine. You will easily imagine therefore, my dear Marianne, that I could not feel any ardent affection or very sincere attachment for Lady Dorothea.

Adieu,
Laura

LETTER 8TH. *Laura to Marianne, in continuation*

Lady Dorothea had not left us long before another visitor, as unexpected a one as her ladyship, was announced. It was Sir Edward, who, informed by Augusta of her brother's marriage, came doubtless to reproach him for having dared to unite himself to me without his knowledge. But Edward, foreseeing his design, approached him with heroic fortitude as soon as he entered the room, and addressed him in the following manner.

'Sir Edward, I know the motive of your journey here. You come with the base design of reproaching me for having entered into an indissoluble engagement with my Laura without your consent. But sir, I glory in the act – . It is my greatest boast that I have incurred the displeasure of my father!'

So saying, he took my hand, and whilst Sir Edward, Philippa, and Augusta were doubtless reflecting with admiration on his undaunted bravery, led me from the parlour to his father's carriage, which yet remained at the door and in which we were instantly conveyed from the pursuit of Sir Edward.

The postilions had at first received orders only to take the London road; as soon as we had sufficiently reflected, however, we ordered them to drive to M—, the seat of Edward's most particular friend, which was but a few miles distant.

At M—, we arrived in a few hours; and on sending in our names, were immediately admitted to Sophia, the wife of Edward's friend. After having been deprived during the course of three weeks of a real friend (for such I term your mother), imagine my transports at beholding one most truly worthy of the name. Sophia was rather above the middle size; most elegantly formed. A soft languor spread over her lovely features, but increased their beauty. It was the characteristic of her mind: she was all sensibility and feeling. We flew into each other's arms, and after having exchanged vows of mutual friendship for the rest of our lives, instantly unfolded to each other the most inward secrets of our hearts – . We were interrupted in this delightful employment by the entrance of Augustus (Edward's friend), who was just returned from a solitary ramble.

Never did I see such an affecting scene as was the meeting of Edward and Augustus.

'My life! My soul!' exclaimed the former. 'My adorable angel!' replied the latter, as they flew into each other's arms. It was too pathetic for the feelings of Sophia and myself. We fainted alternately on a sofa.

Adieu,
Laura

Jane Austen

———

Love, by whom I was beguiled,
Grant I may not bear a child.

Edna St Vincent Millay

———

Loss
The day he moved out was terrible –
That evening she went through hell.
His absence wasn't a problem
But the corkscrew had gone as well.

Wendy Cope

———

Love ceases to be a pleasure, when it ceases to be a secret.

Aphra Behn

———

Love Song

My own dear love, he is strong and bold
　And he cares not what comes after.
His words ring sweet as a chime of gold,
　And his eyes are lit with laughter.
He is jubilant as a flag unfurled –
　Oh, a girl, she'd not forget him.
My own dear love, he is all my world –
　And I wish I'd never met him.

My love, he's mad, and my love, he's fleet,
　And a wild young wood-thing bore him!
The ways are fair to his roaming feet,
　And the skies are sunlit for him.
As sharply sweet to my heart he seems
　As the fragrance of acacia.
My own dear love, he is all my dreams –
　And I wish he were in Asia.

My love runs by like a day in June,
　And he makes no friends of sorrows.
He'll tread his galloping rigadoon
　In the pathway of the morrows.
He'll live his days where the sunbeams start,
　Nor could storm or wind uproot him.
My own dear love, he is all my heart –
　And I wish somebody'd shoot him.

Dorothy Parker

———

If love is the answer, could you please rephrase the
question?

Lily Tomlin

———

HOW WONDERFUL IT

MUST HAVE BEEN

'How wonderful it must have been for the Ancient Britons,' my mother said once, 'when the Romans arrived and they could have a Hot Bath.'

Katharine Whitehorn

———

Tenuous and Precarious

Tenuous and Precarious
Were my guardians,
Precarious and Tenuous,
Two Romans.

My father was Hazardous,
Hazardous,
Dear old man,
Three Romans.

There was my brother Spurious,
Spurious Posthumous,
Spurious was spurious
Was four Romans.

My husband was Perfidious,
He was perfidious,
Five Romans.

Surreptitious, our son,
Was surreptitious,
He was six Romans.

Our cat Tedious
Still lives,
Count not Tedious
Yet.

My name is Finis,
Finis, Finis;
I am Finis,
Six, five, four, three, two,
One Roman,
Finis.

Stevie Smith

———

from History of England

HENRY IV

Henry the 4th ascended the throne of England much to his own satisfaction
in the year 1399, after having prevailed on his cousin and predecessor Richard
the 2nd, to resign it to him, and to retire for the rest of his life to Pomfret
Castle, where he happened to be murdered. It is to be supposed that Henry
was married, since he had certainly four sons, but it is not in my power to
inform the Reader who was his wife. Be this as it may, he did not live for ever,

but falling ill, his son the Prince of Wales came and took away the crown; whereupon the King made a long speech, for which I must refer the Reader to Shakespear's Plays, and the Prince made a still longer. Things being thus settled between them the King died, and was succeeded by his son Henry.

HENRY V

This prince after he succeeded to the throne grew quite reformed and amiable, forsaking all his dissipated companions. His Majesty then returned his thoughts to France, where he went and fought the famous Battle of Agincourt. He afterwards married the King's daughter Catherine, a very agreeable woman by Shakespear's account. In spite of all this however he died, and was succeeded by his son Henry.

HENRY VI

I cannot say much for this Monarch's sense. Nor would I if I could, for he was a Lancastrian. I suppose you know all about the Wars between him and the Duke of York who was of the right side; if you do not, you had better read some other History, for I shall not be very diffuse in this, meaning by it only to vent my spleen against, and shew my Hatred to all those people whose parties or principles do not suit with mine, and not to give information. This King married Margaret of Anjou, a Woman whose distresses and misfortunes were so great as almost to make me who hate her, pity her. It was in this reign that Joan of Arc lived and made such a row among the English. They should not have burnt her – but they did. There were several Battles between the Yorkists and Lancastrians in which the former (as they ought) usually conquered. At length they were entirely overcome; the King was murdered – The Queen was sent home – and Edward the 4th ascended the Throne.

EDWARD V

This unfortunate Prince lived so little a while that nobody had him to draw his picture. He was murdered by his Uncle's Contrivance, whose name was Richard the 3rd.

RICHARD III

The Character of this Prince has been in general very severely treated by Historians, but as he was a York, I am rather inclined to suppose him a very respectable Man. It has indeed been confidently asserted that he killed his two Nephews and his Wife, but it has also been declared that he did not kill his two Nephews, which I am inclined to believe true; and if this is the case, it may also be affirmed that he did not kill his Wife, for if Perkin Warbeck was really the Duke of York, why might not Lambert Simnel be the Widow of Richard. Whether innocent or guilty, he did not reign long in peace, for Henry Tudor E. of Richmond as great a villain as ever lived, made a great fuss about getting the Crown and having killed the King at the battle of Bosworth, he succeeded to it.

HENRY VII

This Monarch soon after his accession married the Princess Elizabeth of York, by which alliance he plainly proved that he thought his own right inferior to hers, tho' he pretended to the contrary. By this Marriage he had two sons and two daughters, the elder of which Daughters was married to the King of Scotland and had the happiness of being grandmother to one of the first Characters in the World. But of her, I shall have occasion to speak more at large in future. The youngest, Mary, married first the King of France and secondly D. of Suffolk, by whom she had one daughter, afterwards the Mother of Lady Jane Grey, who tho' inferior to her lovely Cousin the Queen of Scots, was yet an amiable young woman and famous for reading Greek while other people were hunting. It was in the reign of Henry the 7th that Perkin Warbeck and Lambert Simnel before mentioned made their appearance, the former of whom was set in the stocks, took shelter in Beaulieu Abbey, and was beheaded with the Earl of Warwick, and the latter was taken into the King's kitchen. His Majesty died and was succeeded by his son Henry whose only merit was his not being quite so bad as his daughter Elizabeth.

MARY I

This woman had the good luck of being advanced to the throne of England, in spite of superior pretensions, Merit and Beauty of her cousins Mary Queen of Scotland and Jane Grey. Nor can I pity the Kingdom for the misfortunes they experienced during her Reign, since they fully deserved them, for having allowed her to succeed her Brother – which was a double piece of folly, since they might have foreseen that as she died without children, she would be succeeded by that disgrace to humanity, that pest of society, Elizabeth. Many were the people who fell martyrs to the protestant Religion during her reign; I suppose not fewer than a dozen. She married Philip King of Spain who in her sister's reign was famous for building Armadas. She died without issue, and then the dreadful moment came in which the destroyer of all comfort, the deceitful Betrayer of trust reposed in her, and the Murderess of her Cousin succeeded to the Throne.

ELIZABETH I

It was the peculiar misfortune of this Woman to have bad Ministers – Since wicked as she herself was, she could not have committed such extensive mischief, had not these vile and abandoned Men connived at, and encouraged her in her Crimes. I know that it has by many people been asserted and beleived that Lord Burleigh, Sir Francis Walsingham, and the rest of those who filled the cheif offices of State were deserving, experienced, and able Ministers. But oh! how blinded such writers and such Readers must be to true Merit, to Merit despised, neglected and defamed; if they can persist in such opinions when they reflect that these men, these boasted men were such scandals to their Country and their sex as to allow and assist their Queen in confining for the space of nineteen years, a Woman who if the claims of Relationship and Merit were of no avail, yet as a Queen and as one who condescended to place confidence in her, had every reason to expect assistance and protection; and at length in allowing Elizabeth to bring this amiable Woman to an untimely, unmerited, and scandalous Death.

JAMES I

Though this King had some faults, on the while I cannot help liking him.

As I am myself partial to the roman catholic religion, it is with infinite regret that I am obliged to blame the Behaviour of any Member of it: yet Truth being I think very excusable in an Historian, I am necessitated to say that in this reign the roman catholics of England did not behave like Gentlemen to the protestants.

Jane Austen

Song of One of the Girls

Here in my heart I am Helen;
  I'm Aspasia and Hero, at least.
I'm Judith and Jael, and Madame de Staël;
  I'm Salome, moon of the East.

Here in my soul I am Sappho;
  Lady Hamilton am I, as well.
In me Recamier vies with Kitty O'Shea,
  With Dido, and Eve and poor Nell.

I'm of the glamorous ladies
  At whose beckoning history shook.
But you are a man, and see only my pan,
  So I stay at home with a book.

                    Dorothy Parker

———

Why did Napoleon behave in the way he did? First of all,
by all accounts, he was a bit of a short-arse and you know
what they say about small men. They only come up to your
Adam's apples and don't like it so they have to compensate
by becoming Emperor of France.

                    Jo Brand

———

from The Provincial Lady in Wartime

Remain on duty till 12.30, and have brief passage of arms with Red Cross
nurse who complains that I have *not* given her two-pennyworth of
marmalade. Explain that the amount of marmalade bestowed upon her in
return for her twopence is decided by a higher authority than my own, then
think this sounds ecclesiastical and slightly profane and add that I only mean
the head cook, at which the Red Cross nurse looks astounded and simply
reiterates that two-pennyworth of marmalade should reach to the *rim* of the
jar, and not just below it. Can see by her expression that she means to
contest the point from now until the Day of Judgment if necessary, and that

I shall save much wear and tear by yielding at once. Do so, and feel that I am wholly lacking in strength of mind – but not the first time that this has been borne in on me, and cannot permit it to overshadow evening's activities.

Mock air-raid takes place at midnight, just as I am preparing to leave, and I decide to stay on and witness it, which I do, and am privileged to see Commandant racing up and down, smoking like a volcano, and directing all operations with great efficiency but, as usual, extreme high-handedness.

Stand at entrance to the underworld, with very heavy coat on over trousers and overall, and embark on abstract speculation as to women's fitness or otherwise for positions of authority and think how much better I myself could cope with it than the majority, combining common sense with civility, and have just got to rather impressive quotation – *Suaviter in modo fortiter in re* – when ambulance-man roars at me to Move out of the way or I shall get run over, and stretcher-bearing party at the same moment urges me to Keep that Gangway clear for Gawd's sake.

I go home shortly afterwards.

Gas-mask still missing, have only got temporary Registration Card, and find I have neglected to get new battery for electric torch.

Go to bed to the reflection that if Hitler should select to-night for long-awaited major attack on London by air, my chances of survival are not good. Decide that in the circumstances I shall feel justified in awaiting the end in comparative comfort of my bed.

November 17th Last night *not* selected by Hitler. Serena appears at which seems to me like dawn and discusses proposed party for to-night with enthusiasm. She is going home to get some sleep and talk to Refugee sandwich-expert, and get out the sherry. Will I collect flowers, cigarettes and more sherry, and lend her all the ash trays I have?

Agree to everything and point out that we must also expend some time in inviting guests, which Serena admits she has forgotten. Shall she, she asks madly, ring some of them up at once?

No, eight o'clock in the morning not at all a good time, and I propose to take her out for some breakfast instead. Lyons' coffee much better than mine. (Serena agrees to this more heartily than I think necessary.)

Proceed to Lyons and am a good deal struck by extraordinary colour of Serena's face, reminding me of nothing so much as the sea at Brighton. Implore her to spend the morning in sleep and leave all preparations to me, and once again suggest that she might employ her time to more purpose than in sitting about in the underworld, where she is wrecking her health and at present doing nothing particularly useful.

Serena only says that the war has got to be won *somehow*, by someone.

Can think of several answers but make none of them, as Serena, for twopence, would have hysterics in the Strand.

We separate after breakfast and I make a great number of telephone calls, on behalf of myself and Serena, inviting our friends and acquaintances to drink sherry – *not* a party – and eat sandwiches – Refugee, ex-Legation, a genius with sandwiches – in Hampstead – flat one minute's walk from bus-stop.

Humphrey Holloway accepts change of *locale* without a murmur, Rose declares that she will be delighted to come – she has, ha-ha-ha, nothing whatever to do and sees no prospect of getting anything.

The Weatherbys also thank me, thank Serena, whom they don't yet know, and will turn up if Mr W. can possibly leave his office in time. He hopes to be able to – believes that he will – but after all, anything may happen, at any moment, any-where – and if it does, I shall of course understand that he will be Tied. Absolutely Tied.

Reply that I do, and refuse to dwell on foolish and flippant fancy of Agrippa, fastened up by stout cords, dealing with national emergency from his office desk.

Ring up Uncle A's flat, answered by Mrs Mouse, and request her to take a message to Uncle A. which I give her in full, and beg her to ascertain reply whilst I hold on. Within about two seconds Uncle A. has arrived at the telephone in person and embarked on long and sprightly conversation in the course of which he assures me that nothing could give him greater pleasure than to accept my young friend's very civil invitation, and I am to present his compliments and assure her that he will not fail to put in an appearance. Frail attempt to give Uncle A. precise instructions as to how he is to find the scene of the entertainment in the black-out proves a failure, as he simply tells me that he will be able to manage very well indeed between the public conveyance (bus from Kensington High Street?) and Shanks' mare.

He further adds recommendation to me to be very careful as the streets nowadays are – no doubt properly – uncommonly dark, and says that he looks forward to meeting me and my young friend. Affairs in Germany, in Uncle A.'s opinion, are rapidly approaching a crisis and that unhappy fellow is in what is vulgarly known – (though surely only to Uncle A.?) – as The

Mulligatawny. Express my gratification in words that I hope are suitable, and Uncle A. rings off.

Later in the morning case arrives – which I have great difficulty in opening, owing to absence of any tools except small hammer, and have to ask if caretaker's husband will very kindly Step Up – and proves to contain half-dozen bottles of sherry with affectionately-inscribed card from Uncle A.

Am deeply touched and ring up again, but Mrs M. replies that Uncle A. has gone out for his walk and announced his intentions of lunching at the Club and playing Bridge afterwards.

Lady Blowfield, also invited, is grateful, but dejected as ever and feels quite unequal to Society at present. Assure her that this *isn't* Society, or anything in the least like it, but she remains unconvinced and only repeats that, what with one thing and another, neither she nor Archie can bear the thought of being anywhere but at home just now, waiting for whatever Fate may send. (Implication here that Fate is preparing something that will be unpleasant at best, and fatal at worst. Probably bombs.)

Assure Lady Blowfield untruthfully that I know exactly what she means, but am very sorry not to be seeing her and, naturally, Sir Archibald. *How* kind I am, returns Lady Blowfield – voice indicates that she is evidently nearly in tears – she can only hope that in happier times, if such are one day vouchsafed to this disordered world, we may achieve another meeting.

Tell her that I hope so too, and am rather shocked at hearing myself adopt most aggressively cheerful accents. Cannot suppose that these will really encourage Lady Blowfield to brighter frame of mind, but rather the contrary.

Final invitation is to Literary Agent, who much regrets that he is already engaged and would like to know how my new novel is getting on.

Well, it isn't very far on *yet*, I reply – as though another week would see it halfway to completion at least.

No? repeats Literary Agent, in tone of distressed surprise. Still, no doubt I realise that now – if ever – is the time when books are going to be *read*, and of course, whilst there are so few places of entertainment open, and people go out so little in the evenings, they will really be almost *forced* to take to books

Am left wondering how many more people are going to dangle this encouraging reflection before me, and why they should suppose it to be a source of inspiration.

Review my wardrobe and can see nothing I should wish to wear for sherry-party. Decide that my Blue is less unbearable than my Black, but that both are out-of-date, unbecoming and in need of pressing, and that I shall wear no hat at all as none of mine are endurable and can never now afford to buy others. Ring at the bell interrupts very gloomy train of thought – Lady Blowfield outdone – and am startled at seeing familiar, but for an instant unrecognisable, figure at the door.

Turns out to be old school friend Cissie Crabbe, now presenting martial, and yet at the same time rather bulging, figure in khaki uniform.

Cissie assures me that she couldn't pass the door without looking in on me, but that she hasn't a moment to call her own, and that she expects to be sent Behind the Line any time now. Can only congratulate her, and say that I wish I was making myself equally useful. Suggestion from Cissie that I can sign on for four years or the duration, if I like, is allowed to pass unheeded.

Enquire what she has done with her cats, which are the only items I can ever remember in her life, and Cissie says that one Dear old Pussy passed away just after Munich – as though he *knew* – another one has been evacuated to the Isle of Wight, which Cissie feels to be far safer than Norwich for her – and the third one, a very, very individual temperament indeed and could never have survived for even a day if separated from Cissie – had to be Put to Sleep.

Consecrate a moment of reverent silence to this announcement, and then Cissie says that she can't possibly stop, but she felt she had to get a glimpse of me, she never forgets dear old days in the Fifth Form and do I remember reciting 'The Assyrian Came Down like a Wolf on the Fold' and breaking down in the third verse?

No, I don't, but feel it would be unsympathetic to say so crudely, and merely reply that we've all *changed* a good deal since then, with which contribution to original contemporary thought we exchange farewells.

Watch Cissie walking at unnaturally smart pace towards the Strand and decide once and for all that women, especially when over forty, do not look their best in uniform.

Remainder of the morning goes in the purchase of cigarettes – very expensive – and flowers – so cheap that I ask for explanation and shop-man informs me gloomily that nobody is buying them at all and he would be glad to *give* away carnations, roses and gardenias. He does not, however, offer to do so, and I content myself with chrysanthemums and anemones, for which I pay.

Pause in front of alluring window of small dress-shop has perfectly fatal result, as I am completely carried away by navy-blue siren suit, with zip fastener – persuade myself that it is not only practical, warm and inexpensive – which it is – but indispensable as well, and go straight in and buy it for Serena's party.

Cannot regret this outburst when I put it on again before the glass in flat, and find the result becoming. Moreover, telephone call from Serena ensues later, for the express purpose of asking (a) How many men have I raked up? she's only got four, and five women not counting ourselves and the Refugees, and (b) What do I mean to Wear?

On hearing of siren suit she shrieks and says she's got one *too*, and it was meant to surprise me, and we shall both look too marvellous.

Hope she may be right.

Do the best I can with my appearance, but am obliged to rely on final half hour before Serena's mirror as I start early for Hampstead, heavily laden with flowers and cigarettes. Am halfway to Charing Cross before I remember Uncle A.'s case of sherry, when nothing is left for it but to take a taxi, go back and collect case, and start out all over again. Appearance by now much disordered but am delighted at having excellent excuse for taxi, and only regret that no such consideration will obtain on return journey.

Youngest and most elegant of Serena's Refugees opens the door to me – she is now disguised in charming pink check, frills and pleated apron, exactly like stage soubrette, and equally well made-up – we shake hands and she says Please! – takes all the packages from me, and when I thank her says Please! again – case of sherry is deposited by taxi-driver, to whom soubrette repeats Please, please! with very engaging smiles – and she then shows me into Serena's sitting-room, on the threshold of which we finally exchange Thank you and Please!

Serena is clad in claret-coloured siren suit and delighted with herself – quite justifiably – and we compliment one another.

Strenuous half hour follows, in the course of which Serena moves small bowl of anemones from window-sill to bookcase and back again not less than five several times.

Sherry is decanted – Serena has difficulties with corkscrew and begs soubrette to fetch her the scissors, but soubrette rightly declines, and takes corkscrew and all the bottles away, and presently returns two of them, uncorked, and says that her grandfather will open the others as required.

Is the oldest Refugee her grandfather, I enquire.

Serena – looks rather worried – says that they all seem to be related but she doesn't quite know how, anyway it's perfectly all *right*.

Accept this without hesitation and presently Serena's Refugees come in more or less *en bloc* and we all shake hands, Serena pours out sherry and we drink one another's healths, and glasses are then rushed away by the soubrette, washed and returned.

Serena puts on Six O'clock News – nothing sensational has transpired and we assure one another that, what with one thing and another, the Hitler régime is on the verge of a smash, but, says Serena in tones of preternatural wisdom, we must beware at all costs of wishful thinking. The German Reich *will* collapse, but not immediately, and anything may happen meanwhile. We have got to be prepared.

Assure her that I am prepared – except for loss of gas-mask, which has not yet been replaced – and that, so far as I know, the whole of the British Empire has been prepared for weeks and weeks, and hasn't had its morale in the least impaired by curious and unprecedented nature of Hitler's War of Nerves.

Serena, rather absent-mindedly, says Rule, Britannia, moves small pink crystal ash tray from one table to another, and studies the effect with her head on one side.

Diversion is occasioned by the soubrette, who comes in bearing succession of plates with sandwiches, tiny little sausages on sticks, and exotic and unfamiliar looking odds-and-ends at which Serena and I simultaneously shriek with excitement.

Very shortly afterwards Serena's guests begin to arrive – J.L. amongst the earliest, and my opinion of him goes up when I see him in earnest discussion with grandfather-presumptive Refugee, I think about the Nature of Eternity, to which both have evidently given a good deal of thought.

Mrs Peacock comes, as expected, with Mr Peacock, who is pale and wears pince-nez and is immediately introduced by Serena to pretty A.R.P. worker, Muriel, with whom she thinks he may like to talk about air-raids. They at once begin to discuss Radio-stars Flotsam and Jetsam, and are evidently witty on the subject as both go into fits of laughter.

Party is now going with a swing and second glass of sherry causes me, as usual, to think myself really excellent conversationalist and my neighbours almost equally well worth hearing.

This agreeable frame of mind probably all to the good, as severe shock is inflicted by totally unexpected vision of old Mrs Winter-Gammon, in rakish-looking toque and small fur cape over bottle-green wool.

Shall never believe that Serena really invited her.

She waves small claw at me from a distance and is presently to be seen perched on arm of large chair – toes unable to touch the floor – in animated conversation with three men at once.

Am much annoyed and only slightly restored when Rose arrives, looking very distinguished as usual, and informs me – quite pale with astonishment – that she thinks she has got a very interesting job, with a reasonable salary attached, at Children's Clinic in the North of England. Congratulate her warmly and introduce Mr Weatherby, whom I very nearly – but not quite – refer to as Tall Agrippa. Hope this *rapprochement* will prove a success as I hear them shortly afterwards talking about Queen Wilhelmina of Holland, and both sound full of approval.

Uncle A. – more like distinguished diplomat than ever – arrives early and stays late, and assures me that he has little or no difficulty in finding his way about in black-out. He takes optimistic view of international situation, says that it will take probably years to establish satisfactory peace terms but he has no doubt that eventually – say in ten or fifteen years' time – we shall see a very different Europe – free, he trusts and believes, from bloodshed and tyranny. Am glad to see that Uncle A. has every intention of assisting personally at this world-wide regeneration and feel confident that his expectation of doing so will be realised.

He seems much taken with Serena, and they sit in a corner and embark on a long *tête-à-tête*, while J.L and I hand round Serena's refreshments. (J.L. inclined to be rather dejected, and when I refer to Plato – which I do solely with a view to encouraging him – he only says in reply that he has, of late, been reading Tolstoy. In the French translation, of course, he adds. Look him straight in the eye and answer, Of course, but he is evidently not taken in by this for one instant.)

Humphrey Holloway – original *raison d'être* for entire gathering – never turns up at all, but telephones to say that he is very sorry he can't manage it.

Am quite unable to feel particularly regretful about this – but find myself wishing several times that Robert could be here, or even Aunt Blanche.

Similar idea, to my great fury, has evidently come over Granny Bo-Peep, and she communicates it to me very shrilly above general noise, which has now reached riotous dimensions.

What a pity that dear, good man of mine isn't here! she cries – she knows very well that I should feel much happier if he were. She can read it in my face. (At this I instinctively do something with my face designed to make it look quite different, and have no doubt that I succeed – but probably at cost of appearance, as Mrs W.-G. sympathetically enquires whether I bit on a tooth.)

And poor dear Blanche! *What* a lot of good it would do dear old Blanche to be taken out of herself, and made to meet people. Mrs W.-G. doesn't want to say anything about herself – (since when?) – but friends have told her over and over again: Pussy – you *are* the party. Where you are, with your wonderful vitality and your ridiculous trick of making people laugh, and that absurd way you have of getting on with everybody – *there* is the party. How well she remembers her great friend, the late Bishop of London, saying those very words to her – and she at once told him he mustn't talk nonsense. She could say anything she liked to the Bishop – anything. He always declared that she was as good as a glass of champagne.

Think this Episcopal pronouncement quite unsuitable, and have serious thoughts of saying so – but Mrs W.-G. gives me no time.

She has heard, she says, that dear Blanche's eldest brother is here and wishes to meet him. Is that him over there, talking to Serena?

It is, and can plainly see that if I do not perform introduction instantly, Mrs W.-G. will do it for herself.

Can only conform to her wishes, and she supplants Serena at Uncle A.'s side.

Serena makes long, hissing speech in an undertone of which I can only make out that she thinks the party is going well, and is her face purple, she *feels* as though it were, and whatever happens I'm not to go.

Had had no thought of going.

Everybody talks about the war, and general opinion is that it can't last long – Rose goes so far as to say Over by February, but J.L. tells her that the whole thing is going to be held up till the spring begins – at which I murmur to myself: Air-raid by air-raid the spring begins, and hopes that nobody hears me – and then, says J.L., although short, it will be appalling. Hitler is a desperate man, and will launch a fearful attack in every direction at once. His main objective will be London.

J.L. states this so authoritatively that general impression prevails that he has received his information direct from Berlin, and must know what he is talking about.

Mrs Weatherby alone rallies very slightly and points out that an air-raid over London would be followed instantly by reprisals, and she doubts whether the morale of the German people would survive it. She believes them to be on the brink of revolution already, and the Czechs and the Austrians are actually *over* the brink.

She adds that she wouldn't break up the party for anything – none of us are to stir – but she must go.

She does go, and we all do stir, and party is broken up – but can quite feel that it has been a success.

Serena, the Refugees and I, see everybody off into depths of blackness unlit by single gleam of light anywhere at all, and Serena says they'll be lucky if they don't all end up with broken legs, and if they do, heaven knows where they'll go as no patients allowed in any of the Hospitals.

One of her Refugees informs her, surprisingly, that the black-out is nothing – nothing at all. Vienna has always been as dark as this, every night, for years – darker, if anything.

Serena and I and the Refugees finish such sandwiches as are left, she presses cigarettes on them and in return they carry away all the plates and glasses and insist that they will wash them and put them away – please – and Serena and I are not to do anything but rest ourselves – please, please.

Thank you, thank you.

Please.

November 21st Am startled as never before on receiving notification that my services as a writer are required, and may even take me abroad.

Am unable to judge whether activities will permit of my continuing a diary but prefer to suppose that they will be of too important a nature.

Ask myself whether war, as term has hitherto been understood, can be going to begin at last. Reply, of sorts, supplied by Sir Auckland Geddes over the wireless.

Sir A.G. finds himself obliged to condemn the now general practice of running out into the street in order to view aircraft activities when engaged with the enemy overhead.

Can only hope that Hitler may come to hear of this remarkable reaction to his efforts, on the part of the British.

                                                    E. M. Delafield

During the last few weeks I have felt that the Suez Canal
was flowing through my drawing-room.

Lady Clarissa Eden

———

Cogito Ergo Boom

Susan Sontag

———

PLAT DU JOUR

Your recipe is enclosed.

This particular dish is our most spectacular and popular, and requires great skill. We suggest you do not attempt it until you are fully confident of success. Once you have mastered it you will find it is requested of you again and again,

> WARNING: This will affect your statutory rights.

ESSENTIAL EQUIPMENT
1 ripe man
1 ripe woman
A glass or two of good wine
A little oil
A generous handful of time
A flat surface for rolling out on
A few sweet words for decoration

METHOD
Pour wine into two glasses. Drink a little from time to time.
Remove outer garments from the man and woman carefully.

Set aside. Check the skin for any remaining undergarments,
remove slowly assessing each area uncovered for damage.

Any damage may be removed at this stage with careful
application of lips to the area.

Place undergarments with outer garments for use later.

Feel remaining flesh all over for less obvious signs of
damage.

If whole and unbruised, rub all over generously with oil,
then lay out flat.

Wait for the man to rise fully.

The man and the woman are now ready.

Let them prove themselves, turning occasionally.

Judge when they are done by how they feel. They
should be very hot and very damp.

Sprinkle with sweet words.

Leave to rest before returning to original under and outer
garments.

Mavis Cheek

Sweets to the Sweet

In these drab and dreary war-time days it is pleasant indeed to let the mind
dwell on the gay, colourful, almost fairy-tale quality of sweets.

I have always craved beauty in any form, as men crave heady wine. In
early nursery days Mipsie and I would lie, like two lawless poachers, regardless of exposure and discomfort, on the pile carpet of the top landing at
home, watching with breathless interest the brilliant and gracious guests go
down to dinner four floors below. Shimmering satin and sparkling jewels!

'Aren't they beautiful, Mipsie?' I whispered to her once.

'Yes, lovely, Blanchie,' she replied, 'especially the ones with long
moustaches.' I had been looking at the women, she at the men!

Later in life, when I was shown my new governess, I am told I shrieked
out, 'Take her away, take her away, she's ugly!' Mama then took me aside and
gently explained that governesses had to be plain, for reasons which she said
I should understand later. But I digress.

What sweets they were in those wonderful old days! Great towering edifices of the pastry cook's art, sometimes several feet high. There was one occasion, I recall, when my father permitted his coronet to be modelled (with two detectives standing by in case of accidents) in puff pastry and wine-coloured ice-cream. Another time when the chef whom I mentioned earlier in these pages had set his heart on an exact replica of the Eiffel Tower in angelica, filled with bon-bons, for some special occasion. Being an artist to his fingertips, he told my mother that he must be sent over to Paris for the week-end in order to refresh his memory. 'Nonsense,' my father said to Mama, when told of the plan. 'You can't possibly spare him, dear. I will go to Paris instead of chef and bring back a faithful description of the Eiffel Tower.' I tell this little anecdote to show how my father, martinet though we sometimes thought him, yet had his gentle and considerate side.

Indeed, I have reason to remember that visit to Paris for another reason, and one that further shows Papa's loving disposition, which was hidden so deeply under the aristocrat's iron reserve. Shortly after he returned, the butler entered the drawing-room with a small package, which he had found in a coat pocket when unpacking; a package which proved to be – the most beautiful sapphire bracelet imaginable. Inside the case was a slip of paper bearing these words: '*à Mademoiselle Blanche, avec mille remerciements de son ami devoué,* COOT.'

Needless to say I jumped up, clapping my hands, and seized on my treasure. I remember crying. 'But Papa, why a present to *me* suddenly, and why call me Mademoiselle and not sign yourself Papa, and why write in French, and *thank* me, and why not give me the present before?' But Papa only pinched my cheek and told me not to ask so many questions but to make the most of my luck, which I certainly did. Papa seemed, truth to tell, really put out that the existence of the bracelet had slipped his memory till that moment. What beautiful manners from a father to a daughter!

To return to sweets, I have always said that the menu is half the battle. Read that you are eating Zabaglione, and you will expect Zabaglione. That is why I stick to menus – though for paper economy I cut up sugar cartons and stick them in our lovely silver holders – and that is why I was able proudly to announce on it the other day 'Banana Melba with whipped cream'. Let me tell you how it was done. For my banana, I cut out a turnip in *precisely* the same shape, covered it in custard, and made an exquisite 'top dressing' consisting of a pint of dried milk, sweetened with saccharine, to which I added a tube of one of the best and purest makes of toothpaste, which whipped like a dream, and tasted faintly of peppermint, an added advantage as it disguised the fact that the turnip did not taste of banana. What could be simpler?

Another useful and harmless deception is Blackcurrant Charlotte – which to the initiated is really Sago Charlotte, made with stale bread and sago died with very strong cochineal. If you want to complete the picture you can scatter in a few finely chopped flower stalks which look like the stalks of the blackcurrants and deceive any but the most discerning eye. Unluckily, my evacuees all possess that sharp intelligence which is so often found in the dear old Cockney folk.

One last piece of advice, touching pastry. It is always wisest to have not only a very sharp knife, but a bread saw as well when serving. Sometimes, however, I find a pastry is still stubborn and resists all efforts. When this occurs try this recipe.

Grate the hard remains and soak them overnight in the rinsing water from a used jam or marmalade jar. Next day, take your pastry pulp and work it into a flan shape, which you fill with any remnants handy. Some cereals, the end of a pudding, a piece of stale cake or crumpet perhaps. Sweeten a white sauce with sugar beet, pour over the top and bake quickly. The result is really very tasty, considering, and extremely economical. I call it White Elephant Flan, and intend to present one to our Salute the Soldier Fête, of which I shall tell you more next week.

Mary Dunn

She did not so much cook as assassinate food.

Storm Jameson

Beautiful Soup

You have a love for soup – I share it,
You declare it
The work of subtle minds.
There are so many different kinds.
Gazpacho bisque garbure and minestrone
Borscht vichyssoise purée avgolemono . . .

But the hardest soup of all to make – really well – they say,
Is consommé.

Our love is in the soup.
Sometimes
I wonder whether
We ever
Shall make consommé
Together.

Eleanor Bron

———

from The Soul of Kindness

Percy and Ba went for a day or two to Brighton after the wedding. They had often been there before, especially in the early years of knowing one another. Flora had tried to persuade them to be more venturesome, but her suggestions had set Percy off on one of his arraignments. 'I can't stand people who go abroad,' he declared. 'They come back and talk the hind legs off a donkey about riding on a camel. That Geoffrey Pringle fellow the other night at your place, Flora. Boasting about the cheap hotels he stays in in Spain. The highlight of his holiday is being taken into a filthy hovel to eat some bony old fish with one of the locals. If you can't organise yourself better than that abroad, I say you'll be better off staying at home.'

So they went to Brighton as usual, and to the same hotel. Ba even wore the same wedding-ring.

'This place begins to give me a sense of guilt,' she said, looking round the bedroom before she unpacked: and for the first time, she was embarrassed at being alone with him. Their relationship had been set on a different basis – more private. Yes, she thought, we are a part of society now. Before, they had been secret (more or less), anonymous, selfish. She hoped he did not feel that just because they were married she would expect him to make love to her. About that, at least, she thought they should be allowed to please themselves. There was no one, after all, to know what they did, or did not do.

Percy grumbled a great deal to begin with. His sole, at dinner, was not done in the way he had set his heart on – a mistake arising from the menu's being in French. He made his usual speech about that, and Ba seemed to find it as amusing as ever.

He was still muttering about the sole as he got ready for bed. 'If there's one thing I can't stand, it's cheese – cooked cheese. It lies on my gut all night.'

'It was what you asked for, honey.'

'You shouldn't have let me. You know I can't talk Frog language. How can I tell that *Mornay* stands for cheese? I like things to be plain. Very plain.'

'We may be on our honeymoon, but I think I know by now how you like your food.'

'No *sauces*. Just plain fish. The way you do it.'

'Thank you, my angel.'

She had creamed her face clean, was as sallow as an icon.

'I'd rather have the bed nearest to the window,' he said.

'Yes, dear, I know.'

He tied the cord of his pyjamas, which were broad blue and white striped, like a schoolboy's. 'But you can have it, if you want,' he said, hesitating.

She shook her head, and at once he got into bed and pulled the bed-clothes over his shoulder. Ba liked to read a little before she went to sleep, and she tilted the lamp nearer to her and opened her book. Her pale face glistened, and there were dark half-circles under her eyes. Her hair was plaited into a thin pigtail.

'Sorry about causing all that fuss, old girl,' Percy said drowsily into his pillow.

'What fuss?'

'About that bloody awful fish.'

'Oh, the fish! I shouldn't worry.'

'I'm afraid being meek and mild's not my strong suit.'

'No, honey.'

Peacefully, she turned a page. In a short time, he began to snore.

Elizabeth Taylor

––––

from Jade Junkies

She could do anything with a knife.
Gut shrimp
with a single slice
dice
an onion before a tear
could slide
. . .
Some say she was cut deep
when her G.I. split
and left her
in the middle of America.
She couldn't go back home
in disgrace
so carved out a place,
her one counter cafe
long before sushi
became fashionable
to jade junkies
. . .
Yea, they'd stand in line
to see her magic
with a knife
scale,   skin
   slice
dice,
   chop

And they'd always ask,
Do you orientals
do everything
so neatly?

Janice Mirikitani

Poisson d'Avril

The atmosphere of the waiting-room set at naught at a single glance the theory that there can be no smoke without fire. The station-master, when remonstrated with, stated, as an incontrovertible fact, that any chimney in the world would smoke in a south-easterly wind, and further, said there wasn't a poker, and that if you poked the fire the grate would fall out. He was, however, sympathetic, and went on his knees before the smouldering mound of slack, endeavouring to charm it to a smile by subtle proddings with the handle of the ticket-punch. Finally, he took me to his own kitchen fire and talked politics and salmon-fishing, the former with judicious attention to my presumed point of view, and careful suppression of his own, the latter with no less tactful regard for my admission that for three days I had not caught a fish, while the steam rose from my wet boots, in witness of the ten miles of rain through which an outside car had carried me.

Before the train was signalled I realized for the hundredth time the magnificent superiority of the Irish mind to the trammels of officialdom, and the inveterate supremacy in Ireland of the Personal Element.

'You might get a foot-warmer at Carrig Junction,' said a species of lay porter in a knitted jersey, ramming my suitcase upside down under the seat. 'Sometimes they're in it, and more times they're not.'

The train dragged itself rheumatically from the station, and a cold spring rain – the time was the middle of a most inclement April – smote it in flank as it came into the open. I pulled up both windows and began to smoke; there is, at least, a semblance of warmth in a thoroughly vitiated atmosphere.

It is my wife's habit to assert that I do not read her letters, and being now on my way to join her and my family in Gloucestershire, it seemed a sound thing to study again her latest letter of instructions.

'I am starting to-day, as Alice wrote to say we must be there two days before the wedding, so as to have a rehearsal for the pages. Their dresses have come, and they look too delicious in them – '

(I here omit profuse particulars not pertinent to this tale.)

'It is sickening for you to have had such bad sport. If the worst comes to the worst couldn't you buy one? – '

I smote my hand upon my knee. I had forgotten the infernal salmon! What a score for Philippa! If these contretemps would only teach her that I was not to be relied upon, they would have their uses, but experience is wasted upon her; I have no objection to being called an idiot, but, that being so, I ought to be allowed the privileges and exemptions proper to idiots.

Philippa had, no doubt, written to Alice Hervey, and assured her that Sinclair would be only too delighted to bring her a salmon, and Alice Hervey, who was rich enough to find much enjoyment in saving money, would reckon upon it, to its final fin in mayonnaise.

Plunged in morose meditations, I progressed through a country parcelled out by shaky and crooked walls into a patchwood of hazel scrub and rocky fields, veiled in rain. About every six miles there was a station, wet and windswept; at one the sole occurrence was the presentation of a newspaper to the guard by the station-master; at the next the guard read aloud some choice excerpts from the same to the porter. The Personal Element was potent on this branch of the Munster and Connaught Railway. Routine, abhorrent to all artistic minds, was sheathed in conversation; even the engine-driver, a functionary ordinarily as aloof as the Mikado, alleviated his enforced isolation by sociable shrieks to every level crossing, while the long row of public houses that formed, as far as I could judge, the town of Carrig, receiving a special and, as it seemed, humorous salutation.

The time-table decreed that we were to spend ten minutes at Carrig Junction; it was fifteen before the crowd of market people on the platform had been assimilated; finally, the window of a neighbouring carriage was flung open, and a wrathful English voice asked how much longer the train was going to wait. The station-master, who was at the moment engrossed in conversation with the guard and a man who was carrying a long parcel wrapped in newspaper, looked round, and said gravely: 'Well now, that's a mystery!'

The man with the parcel turned away, and convulsively studied a poster. The guard put his hand over his mouth.

The voice, still more wrathfully, demanded the earliest hour at which its owner could get to Belfast.

'Ye'll be asking me next when I take me Breakfast,' replied the station-master, without haste or palpable annoyance.

The window went up again with a bang, the man with the parcel dug the guard in the ribs with his elbow, and the parcel slipped from under his arm and fell on the platform.

'Oh my! oh my! Me fish!' exclaimed the man, solicitously picking up a remarkable good-looking salmon that had slipped from its wrapping of newspaper.

Inspiration came to me, and I, in my turn, opened my window and summoned the station-master.

Would his friend sell me the salmon? The station-master entered upon the mission with ardour, but without success.

No; the gentleman was only just after running down to the town for it in the delay, but why wouldn't I run down and get one for myself? There was half a dozen more of them below at Coffey's, selling cheap; there would be time enough, the mail wasn't signalled yet.

I jumped from the carriage and doubled out of the station at top speed, followed by an assurance from the guard that he would not forget me.

Congratulating myself on the ascendancy of the Personal Element, I sped through the soapy limestone mud towards the public houses. En route I met a heated man carrying yet another salmon, who, without preamble, informed me that there were three or four more good fish in it, and that he was after running down from the train himself.

'Ye have whips o' time!' he called after me. 'It's the first house that's not a public house. Ye'll see boots in the window – she'll give them for tenpence a pound if ye're stiff with her!'

I ran past the public houses.

'Tenpence a pound!' I exclaimed inwardly, 'at this time of year! That's good enough.'

Here I perceived the house with boots in the window, and dived into its dark doorway.

A cobbler was at work behind a low counter. He mumbled something about Herself, through lengths of waxed thread that hung across his mouth, a fat woman appeared at an inner door, and at that moment I heard, appallingly near, the whistle of the incoming mail. The fat woman grasped the situation in an instant, and with what appeared but one movement, snatched a large fish from the floor of the room behind her and flung a newspaper round it.

'Eight pound weight!' she said swiftly. 'Ten shillings!'

A convulsive effort of mental arithmetic assured me that this was more than tenpence a pound, but it was not the moment for stiffness. I shoved a half-sovereign into her fishy hand, clasped my salmon in my arms, and ran.

Needless to say it was uphill, and at the steepest gradient another whistle stabbed me like a spur; above the station roof successive and advancing puffs of steam warned me that the worst had probably happened, but still I ran. When I gained the platform my train was already clear of it, but the Personal Element held good. Every soul in the station, or so it seemed to me, lifted up his voice and yelled. The station-master put his fingers in his mouth and sent after the departing train an unearthly whistle, with a high trajectory and a serrated edge. It took effect; the train slackened, I plunged from the platform and followed it up the rails, and every window in both trains blossomed with the heads of deeply interested spectators. The guard met me on the line, very apologetic and primed with an explanation that the gentleman going for the boat-train wouldn't let him wait any longer, while from our rear came an exultant cry from the station-master.

'Ye *told* him ye wouldn't forget him!'

'There's a few countrywomen in your carriage, sir,' said the guard, ignoring the taunt, as he shoved me and my salmon up the side of the train, 'but they'll be getting out in a couple of stations. There wasn't another seat in the train for them!'

My sensational return to my carriage was viewed with the utmost sympathy by no less than seven shawled and cloaked countrywomen. In order to make room for me, one of them seated herself on the floor with her basket in her lap, another, on the seat opposite to me, squeezed herself under the central elbow flap that had been turned up to make room. The aromas of wet cloaks, turf smoke, and salt fish formed a potent blend. I was excessively hot, and the eyes of the seven women were fastened upon me with intense and unwearying interest.

'Move west a small piece, Mary Jack, if you please,' said a voluminous matron in the corner, 'I declare we're as throng as three in a bed this minute!'

'Why then, Julia Casey, there's little throubling yourself,' grumbled the woman under the flap. 'Look at the way meself is! I wonder is it to be putting humps on themselves the gentry has them things down on top o' them! I'd sooner be carrying a basket of turnips on me back than to be scrooged this way!'

The woman on the floor at my feet rolled up at me a glance of compassionate amusement at this rustic ignorance, and tactfully changed the conversation by supposing it was at Coffey's I got the salmon.

I said it was.

There was a silence, during which it was obvious that one question burnt in every heart.

'I'll go bail she axed him tinpence!' said the woman under the flap, as one who touches the limits of absurdity.

'It's a beautiful fish!' I said defiantly. 'Eight pounds weight. I gave her ten shillings for it.'

What is described in newspapers as 'sensation in court' greeted this confession.

'Look!' said the woman under the flap, darting her head out of the hood of her cloak, like a tortoise, ''tis what it is, ye haven't as much roguery in your heart as'd make ye a match for her!'

'Divil blow the ha'penny Eliza Coffey paid for that fish!' burst out the fat woman in the corner. 'Thim lads o' hers had a creel full o' thim snatched this morning before it was making day!'

'How would the gentleman be a match for her?' shouted the woman on the floor through a long-drawn whistle that told of a coming station. 'Sure a Turk itself wouldn't be a match for her! That one has a tongue that'd clip a hedge!'

At the station they climbed out laboriously, and with groaning. I handed down to them their monster baskets, laden, apparently, with ingots of lead; they told me in return that I was a fine *grauver* man, and it was a pity there weren't more like me; they wished, finally, that my journey might well thrive with me, and passed from my ken, bequeathing to me, after the agreeable manner of their kind, a certain comfort-able mental sleekness that reason cannot immediately dispel. They also left me in possession of the fact that I was about to present the irreproachable Alice Hervey with a contraband salmon.

The afternoon passed cheerlessly into evening, and my journey did not conspicuously thrive with me. Somewhere in the dripping twilight I changed trains, and again later on, and at each change the salmon moulted some more of its damp raiment of newspaper, and I debated seriously the idea of interring it, regardless of consequences, in my portmanteau. A lamp was banged into the roof of my carriage, half an inch of orange flame, poised in a large glass globe, like a gold-fish, and of about as much use as an illuminant. Here also was handed in the dinner basket that I had wired for, and its contents, arid though they were, enabled me to achieve at least some measure of mechanical distension, followed by a dreary lethargy that was not far from drowsiness.

At the next station we paused long; nothing whatever occurred, and the rain drummed patiently upon the roof. Two nuns and some schoolgirls were in the carriage next door, and their voices came plaintively and in snatches through the partition: after a long period of apparent collapse, during which I closed my eyes to evade the cold gaze of the salmon through the netting, a voice in the next carriage said resourcefully: 'Oh, girls, I'll tell you what we'll do! We'll say the Rosary!'

'Oh, that will be lovely!' said another voice. 'Well, who'll give it out? Theresa Condon, you'll give it out.'

Theresa Condon gave it out, in a not unmelodious monotone, interspersed with the responses, always in a lower cadence; the words were indistinguishable, but the rise and fall of the western voices was lulling as the hum of bees. I fell asleep.

I awoke in total darkness; the train was motionless, and complete and profound silence reigned. We were at a station, that much I discerned by the light of a dim lamp at the far end of a platform glistening with wet. I struck a match and ascertained that it was eleven o'clock, precisely the hour at which I was to board the mail train. I jumped out and ran down the platform; there was no one in the train; there was no one even on the engine, which was forlornly hissing to itself in the silence. There was not a human being anywhere. Every door was closed, and all was dark. The name-board of the station was faintly visible; with a lighted match I went along it letter by letter. It seemed as if the whole alphabet were in it, and by the time I got to the end I had forgotten the beginning. One fact I had, however, mastered, that it was not the junction at which I was to catch the mail.

I was undoubtedly awake, but for a moment I was inclined to entertain the idea that there had been an accident, and that I had entered upon existence in another world. Once more I assailed the station-house and the appurtenances thereof, the ticket-office, the waiting-room, finally, and at some distance, the goods store, outside which the single lamp of the station commented feebly on the drizzle and the darkness. As I approached it a crack of light under the door became perceptible, and a voice was suddenly uplifted within.

'Your best now agin that. Throw down your Jack!'

I opened the door with pardonable violence, and found the guard, the station-master, the driver, and the stoker, seated on barrels round a packing case, on which they were playing a game of cards.

To have too egregiously the best of a situation is not, to a generous mind, a source of strength. In the perfection of their overthrow I permitted the driver and stoker to wither from their places, and to fade away into the outer darkness without any suitable send-off; with the guard and the station-master I dealt more faithfully, but the pleasure of throwing water on drowned rats is not a lasting one. I accepted the statements that they thought there wasn't a Christian in the train, that a few minutes here or there wouldn't signify, that they would have me at the junction in twenty minutes, and it was often the mail was late.

Fired by this hope I hurried back to my carriage, preceded at an emulous gallop by the officials. The guard thrust in with me the lantern from the card table, and fled to his van.

'Mind the goods, Tim!' shouted the station-master, as he slammed my door, 'she might be coming any time now!'

The answer travelled magnificently back from the engine.

'Let her come! She'll meet her match!' A war-whoop upon the steam whistle fittingly closed the speech, and the train sprang into action.

We had about fifteen miles to go, and we banged and bucketed over it in what was, I should imagine, record time. The carriage felt as if it were galloping on four wooden legs, my teeth chattered in my head, and the salmon slowly churned its way forth from its newspaper, and moved along the netting with dreadful stealth.

All was of no avail.

'Well,' said the guard, as I stepped forth on to the deserted platform of Loughranny, 'that owld Limited Mail's th' unpunctualest thrain in Ireland! If you're a minute late she's gone from you, and maybe if you were early you might be half an hour waiting for her!'

On the whole the guard was a gentleman. He said he would show me the best hotel in the town, though he feared I would be hard set to get a bed anywhere because of the *Feis* (a *Feis*, I should explain, is a Festival, devoted to competitions in Irish songs and dances). He shouldered my portmanteau, he even grappled successfully with the salmon, and, as we traversed the empty streets, he explained to me how easily I could catch the morning boat from Rosslare, and how it was, as a matter of fact, quite the act of Providence that my original scheme had been frustrated.

All was dark at the uninviting portals of the hotel favoured by the guard. For a full five minutes we waited at them, ringing hard: I suggested that we should try elsewhere.

'He'll come,' said the guard, with the confidence of the Pied Piper of Hamelin, retaining an implacable thumb upon the button of the electric bell. 'He'll come. Sure it rings in his room!'

The victim came, half awake, half dressed, and with an inch of dripping candle in his fingers. There was not a bed there, he said, nor in the town either.

I said I would sit in the dining-room till the time for the early train.

'Sure there's five beds in the dining-room,' replied the boots, 'and there's mostly two in every bed.'

His voice was firm, but there was a wavering look in his eye.

'What about the billiard-room, Mike?' said the guard, in wooing tones.

'Ah, God bless you! we have a mattress on the table this minute!' answered the boots, wearily, 'and the fellow that got the first prize for reels asleep on top of it!'

'Well, and can't ye put the palliasse on the floor under it, ye omadhawn?' said the guard, dumping my luggage and the salmon in the hall. 'Sure there's no snugger place in the house! I must run away home now, before Herself thinks I'm dead altogether!'

His retreating footsteps went lightly away down the empty street.

'Annything don't throuble *him*!' said the boots bitterly.

As for me, nothing save the Persónal Element stood between me and destitution.

It was in the dark of the early morning that I woke again to life and its troubles. A voice, dropping, as it were, over the edge of some smothering over-world, had awakened me. It was the voice of the first prize for reels, descending through a pocket of the billiard-table.

'I beg your pardon, sir, are ye going on the five to Cork?'

I grunted a negative.

'Well, if ye were, ye'd be late,' said the voice.

I received this useful information in indignant silence, and endeavoured to wrap myself again in the vanishing skirts of a dream.

'I'm going on the six-thirty meself,' proceeded the voice, 'and it's unknown to me how I'll put on me boots. Me feet is swelled the size o' three-pound loaves with the dint of the little dancing-shoes I had on me in the competition last night. Me feet's delicate that way, and I'm a great epicure about me boots.'

I snored aggressively, but the dream was gone. So, for all practical purposes, was the night.

The first prize for reels awoke, presenting an astonishing spectacle of grass-green breeches, a white shirt, and pearl-grey stockings, and accomplished a toilet that consisted of removing these and putting on ordinary garments, completed by the apparently excruciating act of getting into his boots. At any other hour of the day I might have been sorry for him. He then removed himself and his belongings to the hall, and there entered upon a resounding conversation with the boots, while I crawled forth from my lair to renew the strife with circumstances and to endeavour to compose a telegram to Alice Hervey of explanation and apology that should cost less than seven and sixpence. There was also the salmon to be dealt with.

Here the boots intervened, opportunely, with a cup of tea, and the intelligence that he had already done up the salmon in straw bottle-covers and brown paper, and that I could travel Europe with it if I liked. He further informed me that he would run up to the station with the luggage now, and that maybe I wouldn't mind carrying the fish myself; it was on the table in the hall.

My train went at six-fifteen. The boots had secured for me one of many empty carriages, and lingered conversationally till the train started; he regretted politely my bad night at the hotel, and assured me that only for Jimmy Durkan having a little drink taken – Jimmy Durkan was the first prize for reels – he would have turned him off the billiard-table for my benefit. He finally confided to me that Mr Durkan was engaged to his sister, and was a rising baker in the town of Limerick: 'indeed,' he said, 'any girl might be glad to get him. He dances like whalebone, and he makes grand bread!'

Here the train started.

It was late that night when, stiff, dirty, with tired eyes blinking in the dazzle of electric lights, I was conducted by the Herveys' beautiful footman into the Herveys' baronial hall, and was told by the Herveys' imperial butler that dinner was over, and the gentlemen had just gone into the drawing-room. I was in the act of hastily declining to join them there when a voice cried: 'Here he is!'

And Philippa, rustling and radiant, came forth into the hall, followed in shimmers of satin, and flutterings of lace, by Alice Hervey, by the bride-elect, and by the usual festive rout of exhilarated relatives, male and female, whose mission it is to keep things lively before a wedding.

'Is this a wedding present for me, Uncle Sinclair?' cried the bride-elect, through a deluge of questions and commiserations, and snatched from under my arm the brown-paper parcel that had remained there from force of direful habit.'

The bride-elect, with a shriek of disgust, and without an instant of hesitation, hurled it at her nearest neighbour, the head bridesmaid. The head bridesmaid, with an answering shriek, sprang to one side, and the parcel that I had cherished with a mother's care across two countries and a stormy channel, fell, with a crash, on the flagged floor.

Why did it crash?

'A salmon!' screamed Philippa, gazing at the parcel, round which a pool was forming. 'Why, that's whisky! Can't you smell it?'

The footman here respectfully interposed, and kneeling down, cautiously extracted from folds of brown paper a straw bottle-cover full of broken glass and dripping with whisky.

'I'm afraid the other things are rather spoiled, sir,' he said seriously, and drew forth, successively, a very large pair of high-low shoes, two long grey worsted stockings, and a pair of grass-green breeches.

They brought the house down, in a manner doubtless familiar to them when they shared the triumphs of Mr Jimmy Durkan, but they left Alice Hervey distinctly cold.

'You know, darling,' she said to Philippa afterwards, 'I don't think it was very clever of dear Sinclair to take the wrong parcel. I had counted on that salmon.'

E. Œ. Somerville and Martin Ross

———

SIR HERBERT BEERBOHM TREE   Let us give Shaw a beefsteak and put some red blood into him.

MRS PATRICK CAMPBELL   For heaven's sake, don't. He is bad enough as it is; but if you give him meat no woman in London will be safe.

———

Those magazine dieting stories always have the testimonial of a woman who wears a dress that could slipcover New Jersey in one photo and thirty days later looks like a well-dressed thermometer.

Erma Bombeck

———

Life, if you're fat, is a minefield – you have to pick your
way, otherwise you blow up.

Miriam Margoyles

I worry about scientists discovering that lettuce has been
fattening all along.

Erma Bombeck

Looks count! Forget 'inner beauty.' If a man wants inner
beauty, he'll take X rays.

Joan Rivers

TENNIS IS TOO

VIOLENT A MOTION

from Period Piece

We played the classic games to a certain extent, but we were not very good at them, and I myself was very bad indeed, especially at tennis. On the whole we thought them rather dull, and found it more amusing to invent new games of our own, such as Tennicroque, in which you had to move croquet balls about by throwing tennis balls at them. However, at school I managed to get into the hockey team; not by skill, but by a kind of terrified ferocity; and because I could run rather fast. I even broke a strange girl's nose in a match; at least, she skidded in the mud during a wild storm of rain, and fell gently forward, nose downwards, on to my stick; and I felt more guilty than if I had hacked her in the face on purpose. But such is guilt. And I won a race for a hundred yards at the school sports, and at last got my long-coveted book of Milton's *Poems* as a prize. I was not showing off in asking for it; I really wanted it.

The Bicycling craze came in when we were just about at the right age to enjoy it. At first even 'safety' bicycles were too dangerous and improper for ladies to ride, and they had to have tricycles. My mother had (I believe) the first female tricycle in Cambridge; and I had a little one, and we used to go out for family rides, all together; my father in front on a bicycle, and poor

Charles standing miserably on the bar behind my mother, holding on for all he was worth. I found it very hard work, pounding away on my hard tyres; a glorious, but not a pleasurable pastime.

Then, one day at lunch, my father said he had just seen a new kind of tyre, filled up with air, and he thought it might be a success. And soon after that everyone had bicycles, ladies and all; and bicycling became the smart thing in Society, and the lords and ladies had their pictures in the papers, riding along in the park, in straw boater hats. We were then promoted to wearing baggy knickerbockers under our frocks, and over our white frilly drawers. We thought this horridly improper, but rather grand; and when a lady (whom I didn't like anyhow) asked me, privately, to lift up my frock so that she might see the strange garments underneath, I thought what a dirty mind she had. I only once saw a woman (not, of course, a *lady*) in real bloomers.

My mother must have fallen off her bicycle pretty often, for I remember seeing, several times, the most appalling cuts and bruises on her legs. But she never complained, and always kept these mishaps to herself. However, the great Mrs Phillips, our cook, always knew all about them; as indeed she knew practically everything that ever happened. She used to draw us into the servants' hall to tell us privately: 'Her Ladyship had a nasty fall yesterday; she cut both her knees and sprained her wrist, and the front wheel of her bicycle is bent all crooked. But don't let her know I told you.' So we never dared say anything, even if we saw her Ladyship limping. Similar little contretemps used to occur when, at the age of nearly seventy, she insisted on learning to drive a car. She never mastered the art of reversing, and was in every way an unconventional and terrifying driver. Mrs Phillips used then to tell us, under the seal of secrecy: 'Her Ladyship ran into the back of a milk-cart yesterday; but it wasn't much hurt'; or 'A policeman stopped her Ladyship because she was on the wrong side of the road; but she said she didn't know what the white line on the road meant, so he explained and let her go on.' Mrs Phillips must have had an excellent Intelligence Service at her command, for the stories were always true enough. But though she was omniscient, she was always very discreet.

How my father did adore those bicycles! Such beautiful machines! They were as carefully tended as if they had been alive; every speck of dust or wet was wiped from them as soon as we came back from a ride; and at night they were all brought into the house, and slung up to the ceiling of the kitchen passage by a series of ingenious pulleys, for fear that the night air in the covered backyard might rust them. His heart would have bled to see the callous way in which we treat our humble necessary beasts of burden nowadays.

Sometimes, with friends, we used to harness four bicycles with ropes to a little four-wheeled wagon, and Margaret was obliged to be passenger in it. The brunt of the duties appertaining to the youngest always fell on Margaret, because Billy was really too small. Anyhow she had as yet no bicycle of her own, so she ought to have been very thankful to be allowed to be passenger. But she wasn't. The cart was too light; it upset if it were empty, and even with her weight in it, the back wheels banged up and down, in a very alarming way, when we went fast. Sometimes the four postilions quarrelled, and all went different ways, and the cart ran into the curb and upset; and sometimes the ropes all got tangled up and everyone fell off and the cart upset; and sometimes it just upset of its own accord; but Margaret was only terrified and never badly hurt, and after all one expects to pay something for the privilege of playing with older people.

Once the arrogance of the Upper Classes went too far, and the Lower Classes were driven into Red Revolution. We were playing soldiers in a pine-wood with the three Butler boys, and Margaret and the other young ones had been kept far too long on sentry duty, while the Generals (Jim and Charles and I) had been conferring in the tent; so Margaret suddenly mutinied in the most subversive manner, and said that she was going to run away, and would not be a soldier any more. We said, then she would be a Deserter; but when we tried to arrest her, she turned on us in a mad fury, and in the scrimmage *bit* Charles in the middle of his back, so fiercely that her teeth went right through his jacket and shirt and vest, and drew blood. (Biting is always the weapon of the weaker party.) We were absolutely stunned at her wickedness, and said, sanctimoniously, that we would never, NEVER, have anything to do with her again. She then ran away screaming, while the Butlers all watched in consternation. That was what made it so dreadful; that this family scandal should be seen by Jim and Gordon and Nevile. We were really ashamed of our treatment of her, though at the time we maintained that it was her own fault for contravening all the rules of military discipline. I went after her, and found her lying under a tree in a state of hysteria; I brought her firmly home and delivered her to Nana, who calmed her, and bathed Charles's back, and said nothing about the *fracas* to our parents. Neither the Butlers nor we ever referred to this shocking affair again, till many years later.

Gwen Raverat

Tennis . . . is too violent a motion for wholesome exercise,
for those that play much at tennis impair their health and
strength by wasting their vital spirits through much
sweating, and weaken their nerves by overstraining them.
Neither can tennis be a pastime, for it is too laborious for
pastime, which is only a recreation, and there can be no
recreation in sweaty labour.

Margaret Cavendish, Duchess of Newcastle

———

On Skating

It is my cross in life to be completely unathletic. At college I was a member
of the seventh hockey team. Hockey was compulsory; there were only seven
teams and the seventh rarely met, because there was no one bad enough to
meet them. The instructor who taught us fencing, after the first lesson,
advised me to take up folk dancing, and the night after I got over the horse
in gym, my class gave me a dinner. True, at school I was at the head of an
awkward squad that had to do deep-breathing exercises during the recess
period, but after a month a new athletic teacher decided we weren't worth
the trouble and turned us into a raw egg and Sanatogen list. Since that
remote time, no poet has ever sought the inspired word more avidly than I
the form of exercise I can pursue without looking like one of the Fratellini
brothers. I ought to realize that it is a fruitless quest, and stick to yeast and
vibrating machines; but now and again the urge re-awakens and I embrace
some new sport with desperate ambition, only to sink into a neurasthenia of
wondering if perhaps I'm not suffering from rickets. However, there seems
to be nothing wrong with me physically. My heart is the kind doctors
call in other doctors to listen to; my blood pressure is doing whatever
a blood pressure should, and, unless I attempt some set form of exercise, I
apparently co-ordinate.'

Elise listened to me with compassion. She too suffered from having a
spirit of the White Maid of Astolat imprisoned in the body of a great bouncing outdoor girl. Moreover, as she had been eating too well, she was losing
the bouncing quality and felt that something should be done about it. The
previous winter she had taken up golf at Wanamaker's and I had turned my
hand (or rather my ankle) at soft shoe dancing. But Elise found that the sub-

way gave her sinus trouble and my instructor told me that if only I'd started younger he'd have been able to 'place' me in burlesque, so we again found ourselves thrown on a sporting world without a muscle between us.

It was a cold day and we were walking in the Park. The long clean hiss of skates cutting new ice rose from the pond. It sounded fresh and wholesome above the roar and rumble of the Great City, as a milk churn would sound in a cocktail bar. A handful of people was gliding about the white surface below us in delicious cadence.

'Do you know how to skate?' asked Elise.

'Do you know how to walk a tight rope?' I replied. We admitted we neither of us knew how to do either but would like to learn and of the two pastimes skating seemed the more practical.

'It seems a lot to learn for so short a season,' I ventured.

'But think what a help it would be at St Moritz.'

The fact that neither Elise nor I can go abroad except in the middle of summer did not in the least dim our ardor.

'We might come here tomorrow,' I suggested.

'We'll have to take some indoor lessons first.' Elise appeared to know all about it.

'Where? At Ned Wayburn's?'

'No. One goes to a sort of academy and hires an instructor.' And we arranged to meet next day at the Palais de Glace or whatever our city's glorified ice-house calls itself.

After twenty-four hours I must admit the nap had a bit worn off (if there is a nap on ice). The marble approach to the skating edifice with its uniformed guard and gold paneled walls had more of a Roxy than a Hans Brinker atmosphere. I advanced to the 'guichet' and found myself asking for a seat on the parterre (a location, I ruefully reflected, in which I was only too likely and too frequently to be). Someone handed me a pink ticket and timidly I entered the chilly building.

An orchestra was playing the 'Blue Danube,' apparently assuming that stately river froze over every winter, and to its measure some two dozen couples were twirling swiftly and gracefully about a vast arena. Silent pairs glided around the outer edge, a wild youth was racing past them as if he'd been carrying the good news from Ghent to Aix and had lost the way, and in the center a little group of serious skaters were studying the intricacies of the figure eight, seemingly mistaking it for the Einstein theory. My heart was pounding with what I told myself was delight. 'What a sport! What a sport!'

I thought (or tried to), breathing deep of the ammonia-scented air and endeavoring to hear the music above the sudden roar of an elevated train. I was standing near the instructors. I knew they were instructors because their caps said so. Stalwart fellows they were, clad in uniforms of Lincoln green. They looked like Robin Hood's Merrie Men, except that they weren't especially merrie.

Elise arrived. She was going to a wedding later and was wearing a chiffon-velvet dress, a broadtail coat and white kid gloves. I asked her if she wasn't a little overdressed, but she said she thought not, and, as a concession to sport, changed the white kid gloves for a pair of gray mittens. We stood for a time uncertain what to do, until the kindly soul who kept the appointment book told us the young lady in the dressing-room would fit us to skates. A shudder went through me as if she had said thumbscrews.

The young lady in the dressing-room was colored and bored with life. Our entrance was an interruption to her perusal of a tabloid. She asked us resentfully what size skates we wore. (She might as well have asked what size diving bell I required.) After glancing scornfully at my foot she called to a hidden confederate, 'Marie! Send up a large pair!' Marie told her to come and get them, and she shambled away leaving me feeling like someone who, trying to purchase a dress in the misses' department, is told she will find what she wants at Lane Bryant. After a bit she impassively returned with two objects of torture – high laced shoes that I suspected had been left there by a Boston welfare worker, and fastened to their soles a glittering example of the steel-forger's art that weighed incredibly. After thrusting my feet into the boots she laced them so tightly I was about to scream when she took a buttonhook from her belt and pulled the laces until she'd made an excellent tourniquet at each ankle.

'Aren't you stopping the circulation?' I suggested.

'I guess so,' she replied and I thought what a pity I hadn't been bitten by a rattlesnake. 'You don't feel the cold, see,' she explained. She was right. After ten minutes I didn't feel anything.

The operation was repeated on Elise, who bore it bravely; after which the young lady returned to her tabloid and left us sitting helplessly on the bench.

'How do your new shoes hurt?' croaked Elise.

'Very well, thank you,' I replied. 'I suppose we'd better go on in.'

'How?' asked Elise. 'Do we coast down this wooden passageway?'

'No. We walk, of course.'

'Don't be funny. Someone will have to carry me.'

'You don't expect to be carried about the ice, do you?' I retorted. 'Come on, Elise, it isn't far.' And I sprang courageously to my feet, which turned out not to be where they usually were – a surprise that precipitated me back on to the bench.

'A well-equipped place like this ought to have wheelchairs,' I said savagely.

'Hold the wall,' came the tired voice of the young lady.

'How can you hold a wall!' snarled Elise. She had risen and was swaying like a helmsman in a gale.

'If worse comes to worst we can always crawl,' I said and wondered what one did in case of fire.

Lurching, clutching at benches and one another, we managed to progress down the passageway with the grace of trained bears and emerge near the group of instructors in Lincoln green. The appointment-book lady called out that someone named Kelly was to take Elise, and I saw her go away pale but gallant. There was some muttered conversation among the Merrie Men as to who was to take me. The chosen instructor apparently didn't feel adequate. At length a great creature, the Little John of the band, loomed up to me and said, 'I'll take you, lady,' as Hercules might have said, 'Allow me, Atlas.'

'I hate to bother you,' I murmured.

'It's a pleasure,' replied my gallant and steered me toward the ice. Here he paused, crossed my arms and, after doing the same with his own, seized my hands in a vice-like grip. I wondered if he wanted to play 'Wringing the dish-rag,' but with a swift spring he sailed on to the ice and yanked me after him irretrievably into the frozen waste. For a few moments things looked very bad indeed and the instructor and I looked even worse. We bent violently to one side, then to the other, then bowed forward several times like Moslems salaaming Mecca. Now I was ahead of my partner, now behind him; the next second found me wrapped about him like a drunkard about a lamp-post. He meantime was maintaining his equilibrium and murmuring 'Steady! Steady!' as if he thought I was Twenty Grand. At moments we were arm's length apart, only to come together in a passionate embrace that made me feel he ought to ask me to marry him. My ankles, meantime, were giving me all the support of india rubber. They bent and turned as I never knew they could and most of the time I was progressing on the side of my shoe.

'How is it you ain't never skated when you was a kid?' my Merrie Man panted. We had traversed the length of the room and were pausing for breath. For lack of a better excuse I said I had always lived in Cuba and wondered what I'd do if he started speaking to me in Spanish.

'Couldn't you let yourself go more?' he asked.

'Go where?' I inquired, but he didn't seem to know. There was an awkward pause. In an attempt to be chatty, I asked him what his name was. 'Call me M.,' he answered and I said I would, feeling that here indeed was an element of mystery.

'Come on,' said M. and we started the second lap. This was as spectacular as the first. Something seemed to be pulling my feet forward and my head backward and a mirror showed me the unfortunate image of myself executing a sort of Nordic cakewalk while the solicitous M. endeavored to divert my convulsions in the right direction. Once more we paused for breath. In the interval I caught sight of Elise. She was bending forward in the attitude of someone looking for a four-leaf clover and was daintily if uncertainly *walking*, lifting her foot a good six inches with every step. At times her arms, and consequently those of Mr Kelly, flew up in a manner that reminded one of the more animated figures of the Mazurka. This threw them at a perilous angle and I maliciously hoped the orchestra might play 'Slide, Kelly, Slide.' I called to her in what I considered a cheery tone but she gave me in reply only a dirty look.

'Shall we try again?' M. was saying, and once more we lurched forth. This time I managed to steer a straighter course. 'You'll do all right,' he said not unkindly.

'Oh, do you think so?' I simpered.

'Do you like to dance?' he asked abruptly.

'Yes,' I faltered. 'Do you?' And feeling that no price was too great to pay, I wondered if he were about to ask me to dinner at the Persian Room. But he only repeated, 'Then you'll do all right.'

Fired with ambition I started again. By now both of my feet had gone to sleep, and the calves of my legs were only half awake. I was quite numb all over and cheered myself with the thought that no fall could be more painful than the present state of my person. With the courage of despair I set forth at a swifter pace. Unfortunately that unseen force again pulled my head and feet in diametrically opposed directions and once more I was precipitated into the cakewalk, this time with such energy that I found myself going backward in time to the band which was rendering a lively foxtrot. M. too seemed to have caught the spirit of the dance, albeit un-willingly, and was backing with me at increasing speed, shouting 'Careful!' with as much efficacy as a Paris gendarme calls '*Attention!*' to the traffic.

Faster and faster we flew in a movement that must be difficult for even the most expert. I was aware of people stopping to watch, of flying bits of ice, of Elise's face blanched and horrified; then, in perfect unison, we struck the surface and landed, facing each other tailor-fashion, in the position of two people about to play 'Pease Porridge Hot!' Our manœuvre made a considerable stir and a small band of Merrie Men rushed out, as at the sound of Robin's horn, to our rescue. Firm hands seized and lifted me on to that completely uncontrollable part of my anatomy, my feet, and somebody said 'There you are!' as if I didn't know. Unfortunately no bones were broken, so I had to continue my lesson; but Elise, who had witnessed my tumbling act, suddenly remembered she had a date, waved a mitten at me and departed.

The remainder of the time passed uneventfully enough. M., that prince of diplomats, never once referring to our débâcle, patiently steered me, lurching, heaving, now waving my arms as if semaphoring, now bowing as a sovereign to my subjects. I tried the theory of mental images. I thought of Charlotte, of beautiful mad Tartars skimming over the ice of whatever mad Tartars skim over the ice of, of Rear-Admiral Byrd sailing over the Pole; but my power of imagination was defeated by my lack of co-ordination and the reflection of myself in passing mirrors. After half an hour that seemed interminable, M. expressed the opinion that I had done enough for the day. Surely the day had done more than enough for me, and I was only too relieved to be shoved to the edge and deposited on the wooden runway. Thence I made my way in a quaint and somewhat primitive rhythm to the dressing-room.

The colored young lady sighed deeply and unlaced the Iron Maidens. Tales of Northern exposure and frozen members that drop off assailed me and I half expected her to remove my feet with the boots. They appeared, however, still to be attached, though completely paralyzed and bearing across each instep curious markings that made them look like waffles. This interesting design showed plainly through my chiffon hose and lasted most of the day, but I was lucky to have escaped with no further injury.

Since then, Elise and I have returned a few times to the strong arms of M. and Kelly. We have not, however, as yet come into our own – though we have succeeded in coming into everything and everybody in the ice palace. I feel there is too much of the Latin in me to excel in so Nordic a sport, although M. keeps assuring me that if I can dance I ought to do – do what, he doesn't say; and, what's more, I have an idea he is entertaining the petty suspicion that I don't even dance. Elise and I have lately discussed taking up some sport that doesn't hurt so, to re-establish our self-confidence; and, the season being winter, and the month for such things being no nearer than June, we are considering canoeing.

Cornelia Otis Skinner

———

Being a woman is of special interest only to aspiring male transsexuals. To actual women, it is merely a good excuse not to play football.

Fran Lebowitz

———

GENERAL REVIEW

OF THE SEX SITUATION

Amyntas led me to a grove,
Where all the trees did shade us;
The sun itself, though it had strove,
It could not have betrayed us:
The place secured from human eyes,
No other fear allows,
But when the winds that gently rise,
Do kiss the yielding boughs.

Down there we sat upon the moss,
And did begin to play
A thousand amorous tricks, to pass
The heat of all the day.
A many kisses he did give,
And I returned the same
Which made me willing to receive
That which I dare not name.

His charming eyes no aid required
To tell their softening tale:

On her that was already fired,
Twas easy to prevail.
He did but kiss and clasp me round,
Whilst those his thoughts expressed,
And layed me gently on the ground;
Ah, who can guess the rest?

Aphra Behn

———

Once sex rears its ugly 'ead it's time to steer clear.

Margery Allingham

———

[On her abortion,] It serves me right for putting all my
eggs in one bastard.

Dorothy Parker

———

'Sex,' she says, 'is a subject like any other subject. Every bit
as interesting as agriculture.'

Muriel Spark

———

from Court Intrigues

Mrs Wouldbe and Mrs Abigail were our perpetual companions, nay, we had
an additional spy, a friend of Mrs Wouldbe's that was received there upon
some misfortunes of her husband. This was a damsel that pretended to airs
and charms, would ogle my lover and, whether by their desires or her own
inclinations, attempted to have made a diversion of his kindness. She offered
at so many advances that my jealous eyes called 'em unpardonable. However
her charms were no way dangerous and I believe I need have given myself
no pain that way. This creature won upon my easy nature by her assiduities
and she used often to rally at Mrs Wouldbe's fears for her brother.

Thus we were interrupted in the full course of our amour and 'twas impossible to speak without being overheard. One or both of the sisters were perpetually upon the hearken.

It was not so when any other company was with me, for I had a ridiculous pretender or two out of the town, which, had not my heart been engaged, might perhaps served me to laugh at. But I was ever uneasy, as well as Worthy, out of each other's company and, though we could only steal a glance or sometimes the touch of the hand, fancy improved our pleasures and made them greater than any other satisfaction out of ourselves. My first fires were in their full force, the object only changed by an invisible transmutation. I loved to the height of all my formed disorder, but it was with a more pleasing pain, a secret satisfaction. I having made a conquest over that hitherto inexorable virgin heart.

I conceive their fears were least young Worthy should marry me. I was a widow with an encumbered jointure and his affairs required a wife with a fortune in ready money. However, our intelligence had proceeded no further than the word love and it seems to me that he had not formed, no more than myself, any designs towards the possession of what he loved.

Mrs Wouldbe and Mrs Marwould (the name of the other lady) were invited to an entertainment in the town that was like to hold till late. Mrs Abigail was diverted another way, so that I was left alone, the old husband being abroad upon his occasions. Young Worthy, ignorant of their designs, for they kept it from us, was likewise from home.

The weather was hot. I undressed myself to a loose night-gown and Marseilles petticoat and laid me down after dinner upon the bed to sleep.

Young Worthy returned by instinct, or the whispers of his good genius, as he calls it, and, hearing all were gone out, came as usual to my chamber. I cast my eyes to the door as it opened and saw him with so elevated a joy that scarce gave him time to shut it after him, for, running to me as I lay, he threw himself upon my mouth and eyes so transportedly kissed me that I could no longer doubt but his modesty was giving place to his desires.

When, hearing somebody come up the stairs, which answered directly to my chamber, I broke from his arms and, opening the door, was ready to swoon at the sight of Mrs Wouldbe, returned very ill, or pretendedly so. She would have gone in but I shut it after me and directed her into the dining-room.

She asked me who I had with me. I told her, in utmost confusion, a gentleman. She said, 'Why don't you then, madam, go to him?'

'So I must,' answered I and, returning, shut the door to after me, but the key was left on the outside.

Young Worthy saw my disorder and the guilty air which yet I could not recover. I told him, though we were never so innocent, all appearances were against us. My undress, the dishabille of the bed, the door shut upon us and my refusal to let her enter. So that, happen what would, for his sake, I was resolved his sister should not see him, who most diligently kept sentry in the dining-room to watch who should come out.

I ran the hazard and scandal of being suspected with any rather than being confirmed with him.

She goes down to the servants to enquire who was with me. They tell her none but her brother, who was come in two moments before her. She returned again to her post in the dining-room. Having not so far lost her respect to attempt my chamber door though, as I told you, the key was on the outside.

I was at my wits' end for my invention and would have him get out of my dressing-room window upon the leads that answered to a window in another part of the house and which, by chance, was then open, from whence he might descend the back stairs and possibly get off unseen. He objected some men that were working in the next neighbour's yard. I told him in a case like that something must be hazarded and therefore, removing with expedition the glass and toilet that was spread upon a table under that window, he shot in a moment from one to the other and, good fortune favouring him, got down the stairs and through the house without any of their people seeing him. This was a luck conveyance, successful legerdemain, and I, recovered from my fright, could not choose but laugh at the sick lady upon duty. She stirred not from her post (I wonder how her patience could hold from interrupting us?) till after three hours.

I calling for candles, she asked the servant who brought 'em who was with me and she, answering 'nobody', you must imagine what she could think! She had set one sentry at the street door, which, how they escaped Worthy go out I can't imagine. Herself had been upon the watch above. I had told her there was a gentleman in the chamber with me; one maid says 'tis her brother and, soon after, another tells her there was nobody there; my apparent confusion and dishabille – all these were what confounded even her cunning. I believe till that minute she suspected not that her brother had discovered to me his love, but the appearances were now strong and she imagined us to be really criminal. Why should I of a sudden be so undressed?

Why shut up alone with her brother, where she was refused entrance? Why so confused? There were indeed circumstantial evidences.

But what could I have said had she entered and found us as at first? It would certainly have condemned us and getting him off so was all that was left for us to do as making the best of a bad market.

'Twas at worst a moot point whether he was with me or no. Politic Mrs Wouldbe said nothing to her brother or me, but kept close, as well as Abigail, to their watch. We had not time to speak together for above a week after.

Delarivier Manley

It doesn't matter what you do in the bedroom as long as you don't do it in the street and frighten the horses.

Mrs Patrick Campbell

Lost in last July, behind the late Sir George Whitmore's, a maidenhead, the owner never having missed it till the person who since married her expected to have had it as part of her dowry. If the pastry cook in Fleet Street, who is supposed to have brought it away out of a frolic, will restore it again to Mrs Sarah Stroakings, at the Cow-House at Islington, he shall be treated with a syllabub.

The Female Tatler

One more drink and I'd have been under the host.

Dorothy Parker

[On being asked what she found to talk about with her new lover, a hussar:] Speech happens not to be his language.

Madame de Staël

Personally I know nothing about sex, because I've always
been married.

Zsa Zsa Gabor

―――

from The Female Spectator

Belinda is descended of a good family among the gentry, is agreeable without
being a beauty, and has somewhat of a sparkle in her conversation, which
with many people passes for wit; for as she never gives herself the trouble to
think what she is about to say, but speaks all that comes into her head, some
very smart things frequently fall from her, which being reported afterwards
in other companies, serve in this undistinguishing age, to establish her
character. She came very early into the great world, and her youth and a new
face were sufficient to make her be taken notice of by *Rinaldo*, as his quality
was to make her pleased and vain of his address; but that great person looks
upon it as derogatory to his dignity to attach himself to any particular
mistress, so that the amour between them continued no longer than just to
say there had been one. Some women would have been inconsolable to find
themselves no sooner gained than abandoned; their *pride*, if not their *love*,
would have made them regret the loss of so illustrious an admirer. But *Belinda*
was just the same laughing, rallying, romping creature as before; she seemed
no more affected by this change than she had been at the reproofs given to
her by her friends on the first rumour of her intimacy with *Rinaldo*; and
Lavallie, a man of no less gallantry and inconstancy succeeded to her affection,
if that kind of liking which serves only to amuse an idle hour, is worthy to be
called so.

Equally gay, inconsiderate and regardless of the censure of the world,
this intrigue was managed with so little circumspection, that it soon reached
the ears of *Manella*, the wife of *Lavallie*, a lady infinitely fond of her husband
and so tenacious of the rights of love, that even a tender glance to any other
woman seemed the most unpardonable injury to her. But though she had
been enough accustomed to vexations of that kind, to have inured a person
less vehement in her passions to have borne them with more patience, and
the little advantage she gained over him, by publishing all the discoveries
she made of his amours, it might have made her see that it would have been
greater prudence in her to be silent; yet the greatness of her spirit would not

suffer her to sit tamely down under the least indignity offered to her love or beauty. She reproached him on the score of *Belinda* with a bitterness, which perhaps to revenge, he persisted with his intrigue with that lady much longer than his inclinations, without having been thus provoked, would have prompted him to; and the rage she was in served (being reported to *Belinda*) to make that thoughtless creature triumph in the power of her own charms, and instead of giving her the least share of shame or remorse afforded her matter of merriment and ridicule.

Manella finding all she could say to her husband was far from working the effect she desired, was resolved to fly to any extremities to break off the intercourse between him and this hated rival. She knew very well that *Rinaldo* had once a liking to that young lady, and though he seemed at present entirely divested of his former inclinations, yet she imagined it might pique him to be told that one he had honoured with his address should condescend to receive those of a person so much his inferior; and therefore flattered herself that he would not fail to lay his commands on *Lavallie* to desist his visits to her, especially when he had so plausible pretence for it as the complaints of a wife.

She therefore threw herself at his feet, informed him of everything she had heard, and with a shower of tears beseeched him to exert the authority he had over her perfidious husband, to oblige him to return to his first vows, and not entirely break the heart of the woman who had married him more for love than interest, and had never swerved even in thought from the duties of her place.

The noble *Rinaldo* easily saw into the thing, but would not seem to do so; and would fain have persuaded *Manella* there was no foundation for her suspicions, but she was not to be so easily put off. She renewed her entreaties, she repeated the reasons which convinced her of the injustice done her, and became so importunate that he at last promised to speak with *Lavallie* to be at least more circumspect in his behaviour.

Whether this great person thought any farther on it is uncertain, but chance and the inadvertency of the parties concerned gave the jealous *Manella* a sufficient opportunity to vent all her enraged soul was full on the persons who had wronged her.

She happened one day to go to a milliner, where she was accustomed to buy some trifles belonging to her dress, and finding the mistress of the house not in the shop, ran directly upstairs, where was kept a kind of lace chamber. Though she had often been there before, and was perfectly acquainted with the room, by accident she pushed open the door of another, which being but just thrown to without being locked, easily gave her admittance and afforded a prospect she little expected: her husband and *Belinda* in a situation such as might have assured her of their guilt, had she not been so before.

Astonishment at finding them in that place for some moments kept her silent as shame and vexation to be thus caught did them; but the milliner who hearing she was come upstairs and fearing the consequence, came running into the room and was beginning to make some awkward excuses such as crying to *Lavallie* and *Belinda, good heaven how came you here! and you, madam*, to *Manella; Bless me! sure you have all mistaken the apartment! Nobody ever comes into this room but for – But for private purposes infamous woman!* cried *Manella*, in a voice quite hoarse with passion, which rose with so much vehemence in her throat as to render what she said scarce intelligible; then flew at her, at *Belinda* and her husband, railing, shrieking, scratching, and throwing promiscuously the patch, powder-boxes and everything that stood upon the toilet; till *Lavallie* recovered from the confusion which the surprise of her first entrance had thrown him in, ran to her, held her hands, and told her if she did not behave with more moderation, he would oblige her to it by worse usage.

This menace only served to give fresh addition to her fury, and that increasing her strength, she broke from him, and flying to the window where she perceived he had laid his sword, instantly drew it and made at *Belinda* with such precipitation that it was as much as *Lavallie* could do to save his mistress from feeling a fatal effect of her desperation.

By superior force, however, he disarmed this enraged amazon, though not without cutting his own hands in the struggle. All this time there was such a mingle of sound, of curses, shrieks, cries of murder and stamping on the floor, as must be very alarming to those who heard it.

As this milliner got infinitely more by her *private customers* than by her *publick*, and kept a house chiefly for the meeting of persons of condition, *Rinaldo*, who at the time had a new flame, and was come to gratify it with the beloved subject, heard this disturbance from an adjacent chamber; and wholly unable to guess the occasion, ran with his sword in his hand to inform himself of the truth where the noise directed.

He came into the room just as *Lavallie* had wrenched from his wife's hand that weapon of destruction, and seeing who was there, was no longer at a loss to know what had happened. His presence, however, obliged every-one to more moderation, and *Belinda* took this opportunity of running away, which before she could not do, the furious *Manella* being between her and the door. The milliner now began to account for this accident in a more plausible manner than she had done before. She said that *Belinda* being taken with a sudden faintness, she had desired to lie down on her bed in order to recover herself, and that she being afterwards busy with customers had not seen *Lavallie* enter, but imagined that being but little acquainted with the house, he had gone into that room by mistake.

Lavallie took the hint she had given and protested that being directed up to the lace chamber, he had opened this door as being the first he came to, and seeing a lady lie on the bed, he had the curiosity to approach in order to see if he knew her, and to rally her for trusting herself in that posture in an unlocked chamber. As I drew near, continued he, I found it was *Belinda*, and also by some groans that she was indisposed. Good manners, as well as good nature, obliged me to enquire how she did, and as I was stooping towards the bed, that she might hear what I had to say with the more ease, *Manella* came into the room with a rage little becoming her *character, and loaded that innocent lady and myself with the most opprobrious reflections malice could invent.*

All the time he was speaking, *Manella* shook her head and bit her lips till they even bled, with inward vexation, but the presence of *Rinaldo* forbidding her to continue her reproaches in the same manner she had done before his entrance, she only said that heaven who knew how greatly she was injured would one time or other defend her cause.

Belinda met with the most severe reproofs from all her friends for her ill conduct, yet so insensible was this unthinking lady, either of shame or the prejudice it might be to her interest to forfeit the love and esteem of her family, that, though she heard their admonitions with her sensual ears, those of her mind seemed wholly deaf; nor could all that was said to her make the least alteration in her deportment or prevail on her to give herself one moment's reflection. Thus with the same unmoved, unshaken indolence she had ever behaved, did she go on laughing, singing, dancing, coquetting among the gay world. The truth is whatever was reported of her so little concerned her that her carelessness blunted the edge of scandal.

Eliza Haywood

General Review of the Sex Situation

Woman wants monogamy;
Man delights in novelty.
Love is woman's moon and sun;
Man has other forms of fun.
Woman lives but in her lord;
Count to ten, and man is bored.
With this the gist and sum of it,
What earthly good can come of it?

Dorothy Parker

The Herpes Tango

Introduction

The place was by the river . . .
    Alone, and late at night;
A woman stood there weeping;
    A melancholy sight;
And as I moved to help her,
    She gave a shuddering sigh;
And as she plunged into the waters,
    I heard her shudd'ring sigh . . .

Refrain

Herpes!
I wish I'd never heard of herpes;
I must admit I'm far from chirpy
Since I discovered what I'd caught;
Herpes
Is very bad to catch at thirty;
Besides my mother thinks it's dirty;
I'll have to tell her it's a wart.

Verse

I used to dance
And dream of romance
On my hacienda;
Gay caballeros
Wearing sombreros –
Looks warm and tender;
  Steamy siestas with virile vaqueros
  Fiery fiestas with macho rancheros
  But one night bewitching
  And I got this itching
  On my pudenda.

Refrain

Painful;
And ev'rybody's so disdainful;
They seem to think it's all so shameful,
And yet it wasn't even fun;
I get this burning,
With bouts of nausea returning;
I should have been much more discerning;
I'd rather Herpes Simplex One.

Verse

A man named Fernandez
Came from the Andes
Full of allu-re;
Tried to say nada
To his enchillada –
I was so pu-re;
  But just a couple of beers and I got myself stewed,
  Now I'll have One Hundred Years of Solitude,
  And I'm down on my knees
  With this bloody disease
  For which there's no cu-re.

[8 BARS VAMP IN EVERY SENSE OF THE WORD]

What could be sweeter than to be with a gaucho?
But this chiquita, she just thinks 'ouch, oh!'
It's terrible when you're
Refusing a señor,
You just go home on your burro.

Final verse

So listen sisters;
Be careful when you kiss those misters,
Or else you'll end with nasty blisters,
And you will long for N.S.U.;
My story's done now;
I think I really better run now;
Because I'm off to be a nun now . . .
Well what else can I do
With Simplex Two?

**Dillie Keane, with Marilyn Cutts
and Lizzie Richardson**

———

Texan woman: Are you a homo? We don't have homos in
Texas – not live ones anyway.

Susan Harris

———

If you have a psychotic fixation and you go to the doctor
and you want these two fingers amputated he will not cut
them off. But he *will* remove your genitals. I have more
trouble getting a prescription for valium that I do having
my uterus lowered and made into a penis.

Lily Tomlin

———

If sex is such a natural phenomenon, how come there are so
many books on how to?

Bette Midler

EVEN IF YOU WIN,

YOU'RE STILL A RAT

English are obsessed with class. Even your letters travel first
and second class. Do the first class letters get a little in-flight
movie and paper-parasoled cocktail on route or what?

Kathy Lette

———

from The English Aristocracy

The English aristocracy may seem to be on the verge of decadence, but it is
the only real aristocracy left in the world today. It has real political power
through the House of Lords and a real social position through the Queen.
An aristocracy in a republic is like a chicken whose head has been cut off: it
may run about in a lively way, but in fact it is dead. There is nothing to stop
a Frenchman, German, or Italian from calling himself the Duke of Carabosse
if he wants to, and in fact the Continent abounds with invented titles.

*

The lords have never cared very much for London, and are, in this respect,
the exact opposite of their French counterparts who loathe the country. But

even where his country house is concerned, the English nobleman, whose forbears were such lovers of beauty, seems to have lost all aesthetic sense, and it is sad to see the havoc he often brings to his abode, both inside and out. His ancestors spent months abroad, buying pictures and statues, which he cheerfully sells in order to spend months abroad. Should one of his guests perceive that a blackened square of canvas in a spare bedroom is a genuine Caravaggio, that picture will appear at Christies before you can say Jack Robinson, though there is no necessity whatever for such a sale. The Caravaggio buyer planted his estate with avenues and copices and clumps of cedar trees. The Caravaggio seller fiddles about with herbaceous borders, one of the most hideous conceptions known to man. He never seems to plant anything larger than a flowering prunus, never builds ornamental bridges, or digs lakes, or adds wings to his house. The last nobleman to build a folly on his estate must have been Lord Berners and he was regarded as foolish indeed to do such a thing. The noble eccentric, alas, seems to be dying out. Lord Berners was one, another was the late Duke of Bedford, pacifist, zoologist, and a good man. One of the chapters of his autobiography, I seem to remember, was headed 'Spiders I have known', and he tells of one spider he knew whose favourite food was roast beef and Yorkshire pudding. The great days of patronage, too, are over, though there are country houses which still shelter some mild literary figure as librarian. The modern nobleman cannot, however, be blamed for no longer patronizing art, music, and letters. Artists, musicians, and writers are today among the very richest members of the community and even an English aristocrat could hardly afford to maintain Mr Somerset Maugham, M. Stravinsky, or M. Picasso as part of his establishment.

Nancy Mitford

Today I met Princess Di and I was shocked and appalled by my response. I'm an American. I thought I was free from being heightened to hysteria at the mere flicker of a Royal sighting. I have seen bright, well-educated adult English people catch a glimpse of the Queen 'Mum', jolt to rigid attention and break into involuntary song as tears of love stream down their faces and I'd pity them and smirk in superiority. So I'm asked to go and meet Princess Di at a charity event. (Take note they're mounting my knighthood

could be just around the corner.) They want me to be
'received' by her, meaning I stand in a queue with three other
women and wait to be touched. So out of curiosity, I go. I'm
very cool, amusing, thinking I'll just tell her how worried
I was we'd be in the same outfit. But by the time she arrived
I was a wreck. If you had an experimental rat stand in that
queue as long as I did, watching photographers prepare for a
feeding frenzy, it too would snap to a curtsey by the time
she showed up. When she finally took my hand, I said
something so insane if I could have sued my own mouth, I
would have – I told her I'd see her again next month at her
house. Her eyes drifted heavenwards for help. So I said it
louder. 'I'll be coming to your house.' I said, 'Buckingham
Palace and I hope you show up or I'll be arrested.' She smiled
patiently and inquired what I was talking about. I told her
that I'd been invited to come to the Palace in a month
(which is true, I swear to God), to meet the Princess Royal.
At that point someone tackled me to the floor and
whispered, 'She isn't the Princess Royal.' Well I know that
piece of information when my mind is still connected to me
but it had drifted off into its own orbit. I then argued loudly
that she could be a Princess Royal because she has both
those qualifications. I said she could be called lots of things
like Princess of Height as well. You could hear a pin drop.
Everyone moved away from me in disgust. I realised I made a
big mistake and curtsied my way backward out of the room.
Then I went home and beat myself. Yes, this country has
created something beyond fame, beyond something money
can buy. The people of this country have invested and
empowered these perfectly normal samples of homo sapiens
with such attention that you could literally surf off the
charisma that waves off of them. Like a piece of modern art
that can demand millions even if it's just some mustard
squirted on a blank canvas.

And who am I to argue? Di, if you're reading this, call
me. I love you.

Your humble servant,
Ruby.

Ruby Wax

So that's what hay looks like.

Queen Mary

———

Fat Aristocrats (Part I)

Two large old upper-class women. They are balding but headscarfed, with hairy old chins. Dressed in wellington boots or brogues, old jackets and droopy old dresses. They obviously drive old Land Rovers and live in run-down country houses surrounded by labradors. They are tough as nails.

    Large country kitchen. Run down. A stainless steel sink piled high with dog bowls and washing up. The room is full of old horse blankets, grooming kits, bottles of embrocation. Old hunting prints on the wall and a couple of old Formica covered units. Large old table. Old fridge.

    The two women are sitting at the table having tea. There is a bottle of whisky standing by the pot.

FAT WOMAN A (Jennifer) Bloody leg.

Hits her leg with a walking stick.

FAT WOMAN B (Dawn) What's that?
FAT WOMAN A This bloody leg o' mine, still causing me a bit of gyp.
FAT WOMAN B What happened there then?
FAT WOMAN A Hit by the bloody Land Rover.
FAT WOMAN B Some bloody bastard driving it?
FAT WOMAN A No, my bloody Land Rover, forgot to put the handbrake on, came hurtling down the hill, smashed into my bloody leg. Bones and blood everywhere.
FAT WOMAN B Out beagling?
FAT WOMAN A Yes, a lot of people wanted to see to it you know.
FAT WOMAN B A lot of bloody fuss and nonsense.
FAT WOMAN A Yes. I don't believe one should give in to these things. Sort themselves out.
FAT WOMAN B Leave well bloody alone.
FAT WOMAN A I'm not one for a lot of fuss and bother, and nonsense. Look after myself . . .
FAT WOMAN B . . . thank you very much.
FAT WOMAN A Quite right.

Dawn gets up. Goes to pick up whisky bottle from dresser.

FAT WOMAN B   Same thing happened to me the other day, out shooting. Some bloody young clot, came up behind me. 12-bore shotgun. Point-blank range. Blast my bloody back open. Everybody saying go to bloody hospital. I said 'Don't be stupid,' lot of fuss and nonsense.

FAT WOMAN A   Save it for someone who needs it, I say. Bloody National Health Service, rubbish, lot of mamby pamby nonsense.

Gets up and goes to cut bread on draining board.

FAT WOMAN B   Remember the time I sat on the bloody shooting stick – top came off and the stick went right up me jacksy.

FAT WOMAN A   Nothing wrong with that.

FAT WOMAN B   They all wanted me to get down to the hospital. I said, stop making such a bloody fuss and nonsense. I said let nature take his course. The bloody thing will be out by supper time. And it was!

Fat Woman A lets out a deep yell and puts down the knife. Clutches her hand.

FAT WOMAN A   Damnation, bloody bugger, blood and sand!! Cut me bloody finger off.

FAT WOMAN B   What completely off?

FAT WOMAN A   No, just dangling . . . Oh what the hell, just cut it off completely and be done with it.

FAT WOMAN B   Run it under the cold water tap.

She turns around, hand wrapped in bloodied towel, clutching the amputated finger.

FAT WOMAN A   No, that's a lot of fuss and nonsense. Just cut it off altogether and be done with it. Dogs can have it. (*Throws finger to dogs.*) Here you are, Durbain.

FAT WOMAN B   What about Tibs – she hasn't had one!

FAT WOMAN A   What, one each? OK . . . Come on . . . Come on . . .

Fat Woman A goes back to draining board, cuts fingers off and then throws them to dogs.

Dawn French and Jennifer Saunders

———

Towards people with whom they disagree the English
gentry, or at any rate that small cross-section of them
which I have seen, are tranquilly good-natured. It is not
comme il faut to establish the supremacy of an idea by
smashing in the faces of all the people who try to
contradict it. The English never smash in a face.
They merely refrain from asking it to dinner.

Margaret Halsey

————

Ruislip

The suburbs, it has been said, are one of the most brilliant inventions of the
twentieth century. The finger of urban squalor never pointed as far as Ruislip,
Pinner, Surbiton or East Sheen. Not for them the delinquent shadow of the
sixties' high rises, nor the left-over maze of the Victorian slum. Not for them
the feudal inequalities of the open countryside. In the suburbs each man
has his similar patch, each wife her child, each child its dog, each bird its
bath, each garden its rockery, each rockery its gnome. The suburbs are a
microcosm of perfection.

Fifty years after their planning, the almond avenues have blossomed,
the grass has matured, and generations of bluetits have learned to turn upside
down on generations of half coconuts; and the suburbs assault you with this
perfection. The pollen tickles the nostrils, the ozone spurs the step while the
spray-on Simoniz reflects the perfectly endless rows of perfectly identical
Tudorbethan three-ups and two-downs in perfect states of repair. Scarcely a
façade without its Snowcem, a lawn without its stripes, a border without its
slug pellets, a patio without its deckchair. Scarcely a garden *with* a vegetable
patch. The suburbs are against real life. All-caring, vigilante suburban man
is on the warpath against loud music, foul footpaths, rusty bodywork, copious
greenfly and garish gables – especially other people's. Only the slight disarray
of the whiter than white nylon net curtains points to the imperfections of
some human beings. The suburbs are as proper as the ambitions of average
man. On the surface, that is. Transplant a feminist to Ruislip and she will seem
like the perfect wife and mother. Transplant a spy and he will be the main-
spring of the commuter club. A ripper will take orders, a pederast run the
PTA, a lesbian the WI, a swinger will appoint himself marriage counsellor, an

alcoholic will serve behind the counter at the pub. People may wonder about them, speculate about them, hallucinate about them; they may stick their eyes to keyholes in pursuit of vicarious thrills, walk their dogs or post their letters at improbable hours, but suburban people will never ask questions of the people concerned. This is because they do not want to hear the answers. Metroland is the promised land and never must the fear be actually voiced that the milk and honey could actually dry up. Metroland was named for the Metropolitan Line, which was wrongly named since it appears to have something to do with town. Metroman would be carried away from the sins of the city upon it, together with his two and a fraction children, to a land of dreams as surely as if it were Disneyland, a place where the goldfish never turn into piranhas, the tea-roses to Venus fly-traps, nor the *Daily Mail* to the *Morning Star*, because the inhabitants never quite grow up.

In exchange for this perfection Metroman sacrificed his proper roots. Since he no longer knows where he comes from he is doubly uncertain about everyone else. This makes Metroman suspicious of everyone but uncertain quite what to do about it. Metroman is not action man except when it comes to moving someone else's car from his grass verge. In Ruislip, Pinner, Surbiton and East Sheen people never actually move their own cars if they can help it. Ruislip people know that the only good Honda is the Honda in a garage. In the garage the car may be preserved as long as possible as a symbol of their earning power rather than their mobility, which they have sacrificed by moving to the suburbs. You may get under a car and fiddle with it, or on top of the car and fiddle with it, you may drive it to the station once a month at a pinch, you may take it on Sunday as far as the end of the road. But you must never, never park it on the street in front of some alien privet no matter what emergency may prompt you. This leads to car wars. Car wars last for ever once they have been declared. Similarly dog wars and the wars of the roses. Alien dogs are for ever damned, or dogged, and woe betide the child that beheads your semi-standard, Peace. Since Ruislip people never ask questions they never get the explanations for any piece of behaviour even if it is accidental. Ruislip people make statements. 'That child will come to a sticky end,' they pronounce. 'He is pale, she is too thin, she is a lovely girl, he has let the side down. She is going to be a doctor. He should go on the stage. As good as anything I have seen on television any time.'

Most of these statements involve children. This is because children are the right size for Ruislip. Suburban people who live in Lilliputian houses have to cut everything down to size. Conifers are dwarves, poodles are miniatures, glasses are thimbles, books are digested and records highlighted. Small things are controllable and suburban people like to be in control at all times. Metroman only drinks in public at Christmas – and then only one glass – he never speaks of drugs, foreigners, foreign food, the Pope or party politics. He speaks about the weather and the Queen. Too much speaking is out in Metroland, but then so is too much silence. Should a benign silence once descend in Ruislip, someone is bound to say, quite unexpectedly, 'Isn't it nice and quiet?' This will be repeated by the budgie, granny and by mother, who will add, 'Shall we all have a nice cup of tea?' She will then turn on the television.

Television has naturally taken over the focal point of any room and will be placed in front of the artificial gas fire or in the centre of the bay window. Ruislip people do not make any attempt to follow any of the programmes, however. Anyone who looks too deeply into an apparent plot is immediately offered a fairy cake. Ruislip people never have any time to be hungry. They are always being offered a good square meal. No sooner have they finished breakfast than someone is peeling the sprouts for lunch. No sooner has everyone's plate been cleared than the tea trolley appears. No sooner has the trolley been emptied than on comes high tea. Ruislip people love eating because they love washing up. Town people hate washing up. In Chelsea, Islington and Hampstead no one ever washes up if they can help it. They like to be invited out. If they are not invited out they simply go out. Chelsea, Islington and Hampstead people would rather eat out all the time than ever do any washing up. They would rather go out to breakfast (or not come home in time for it) than ever wash up a coffee cup. In Ruislip, Pinner, Surbiton and East Sheen they start washing up before they have finished eating. When they have finished washing the dishes they take down the curtains. In between courses they do the hoovering. Ruislip people bring out the hoover in between every home-made sponge. They bring it out if you put on a record or dare to open a book. When they have finished hoovering around your ankles they queue up to show you their do-it-yourself carpet laying, their do-it-yourself developing and the kitten picture they bought for fivepence at the church bazaar. They show you the garden with the do-it-yourself workshop at the bottom. Or they show you the toilet. There is absolutely no need to show anyone in Ruislip the toilet since they can certainly find it themselves. Ruislip toilets are always marked by a ceramic tile in pink, blue or yellow which may or may not have a bullfighter on it saying something like, 'Penny for your thoughts', 'Smallest room', or 'Ancestral seat'.

Inside the toilet it will be very cosy. There will be a candlewick cosy on the seat and a matching candlewick cosy on the floor. The Airwick will be suction cupped behind the rosebud curtains and the water in the cistern will run baby blue. Do not be tempted to linger in this haven. In Clapham, Muswell Hill and Barnes you get a pine bookshelf next to the washbasin containing a few lewd books, magazines with the odd mention of the householder, and last week's Sunday papers. Woe betide you if you come back to the assembled company without having fathomed the point of the display. In Ruislip, Pinner, Surbiton and East Sheen, nothing of the sort. Any unexplained absence will be put down to undue curiosity about the upstairs décor. Ruislip people get very fidgety if you take an unreasonable amount of time over your ablutions. At which point they are liable to sprint stealthily upstairs and catch you appraising the candlewick bedspreads and the orange geometric bedroom wallpaper. Ruislip people know that this is what you will be doing because this is what they would be doing themselves rather than ask to see the bedroom wallpaper.

Ruislip people enjoy their silent sleuthing and they enjoy following other people in their attempts to do their own silent sleuthing. They put up huge fences around their property, or giant hollyhocks to encourage curiosity. Ruislip people always keep their telephones by the front door in the hall. This is so that every telephone conversation can be monitored without it actually going on record that it is being monitored. A telephone conversation in the living-room must either be overtly avoided or deliberately overheard. A telephone conversation in the bedroom is always bound to be discreet. But a telephone conversation in the hall offers the sort of challenge to subterfuge that Ruislip minds adore. The moment a Ruislip telephone rings, doors open all over the place in Ruislip semis. People who were previously perfectly happy reading the serial in *Woman's Own* will immediately cross the hallway, ostensibly to make a cup of tea. People washing the upstairs windows – and meanwhile taking a peek at the state of the next-door garden – will suddenly remember they have to bring in the milk or put out the cat. This entails passing the telephone on tiptoe. When they have heard what they have overheard Ruislip people will never mention it to the person who has said it, but they will wonder, speculate, hallucinate and quietly conclude the absolute worst. It is always the way in the suburbs. Concluding the worst is the natural reaction to living with permanent perfection. I wonder if the town planners ever realised that living with perfection would be such a strain?

Glenys Roberts

Economy was always 'elegant', and money-spending always
'vulgar' and ostentatious – a sort of sour-grapeism, which
made us very peaceful and satisfied.

Elizabeth Gaskell

Nervous Prostration

I married a man of the Croydon class
When I was twenty-two.
And I vex him, and he bores me
Till we don't know what to do!
It isn't good form in the Croydon class
To say you love your wife,
So I spend my days with the tradesmen's books
And pray for the end of life.

In green fields are blossoming trees
And a golden wealth of gorse,
And young birds sing for joy of worms:
It's perfectly clear, of course,
That it wouldn't be taste in the Croydon class
To sing over dinner or tea:
But I sometimes wish the gentleman
Would turn and talk to me!

But every man of the Croydon class
Lives in terror of joy and speech.
'Words are betrayers,' 'Joys are brief' –
The maxims their wise ones teach –
And for all my labour of love and life
I shall be clothed and fed,
And they'll give me an orderly funeral
When I'm still enough to be dead.

I married a man of the Croydon class
When I was twenty-two.

And I vex him, and he bores me
Till we don't know what to do!
And as I sit in his ordered house,
I feel I must sob or shriek,
To force a man of the Croydon class
To live, or to love, or to speak!

Anna Wickham

————

Come away; poverty's catching.

Aphra Behn

————

The trouble with being in the rat race is that even if you
win, you're still a rat.

Lily Tomlin

————

The most radical revolutionary will become a conservative
on the day after the revolution.

Hannah Arendt

————

Tories are not always wrong, but they are always wrong at
the right moment.

Lady Violet Bonham Carter

————

In an autocracy, one person has his way; in an aristocracy,
a few people have their way; in a democracy, no one has
his way.

Celia Green

————

Communism is the opiate of the intellectuals.

Clare Booth Luce

A diplomat . . . is a person who can tell you to go hell in such a way that you actually look forward to the trip.

Caskie Stinnett

———

If you can keep your head when all about you are losing theirs, it's just possible you haven't grasped the situation.

Jean Kerr

———

The vote, I thought, means nothing to women. We should be armed.

Edna O'Brien

———

'Tis hard we should be by the men despised,
Yet kept from knowing what would make us prized;
Debarred from knowledge, banished from the schools,
And with the utmost industry bred fools.

Lady Mary Chudleigh

———

But if God had wanted us to think just with our wombs, why did He give us a brain?

Clare Booth Luce

———

There is no female mind. The brain is not an organ of sex. As well speak of the female liver.

Charlotte Perkins Gilman

———

If all men are born free, how is it that all women are born slaves?

Mary Astell

I slept, and dreamed that life was beauty;
I woke, and found that life was duty.

Ellen Sturgis Hooper

———

Stop Miss World – we want to get off

Banner Outside Miss World Competition

———

I'm furious about the women's liberationists. They keep
getting up on soap-boxes and proclaiming that women are
brighter than men. That's true, but it should be kept very
quiet or it ruins the whole racket.

Anita Loos

———

When I burnt my bra it took the fire department four days
to put out the blaze.

Dolly Parton

———

Letters from a Faint-hearted Feminist

21 January

Dear Mary,

Sorry I haven't written for a while, but back here in Persil Country the festive season lasts from November 1 (make plum pudding) to January 31 (lose
hope and write husband's thank-you letters). I got some lovely presents. A
useful Spare Rib Diary. A book called *The Implications of Urban Women's Image in
Early American Literature*. A Marks and Sparks rape alarm. A canvas Backa-Pak
so that the baby can come with me wherever I go – a sort of DIY rape alarm.
And, of course, your bracing notelets, which will be boomeranging back to
you for the rest of the year. Things I did not get for Christmas: a Janet Reger
nightie, a feather boa, a pair of glittery tights.

Looking back, what with 'God Rest Ye Merry Gentlemen', 'Good King Wenceslas', 'Unto Us a Son is Born', 'We Three Kings', Father Christmas ho-hoing all over the place and the house full of tired and emotional males, I feel like I'm just tidying up after a marathon stag party. Our Lady popped up now and again but who remembers the words to *her* songs once they've left school? We learnt them but, then, ours was an all-girl school, in the business of turning out Virgin Mother replicas. If I ever get to heaven, I'll be stuck making manna in the Holy Kitchens and putti-sitting fat feathered babies quicker than I can say Saint Peter. Josh, on the other hand, will get a celestial club chair and a stiff drink. If God is a woman, why is She so short of thunderbolts?

I went to a fair number of parties dressed up as Wife of Josh but, to tell you the shameful truth, it was my Women's Collective beanfeast that finally broke my nerve. One wouldn't think one could work up a cold sweat about going as oneself to an all-woman party, would one? One can. I had six acute panic attacks about what to wear, for a start. Half my clothes are sackcloth, due to what Josh still calls my menopausal baby (come to me, my menopausal baby) and the other half are ashes, cold embers of the woman I once was. Fashion may well be a tool of women's oppression but having to guess is worse. In the end I went make-up-less in old flared jeans and saw, too late, that Liberation equals Calvin Klein and Lip Gloss or Swanky Modes and Toyah hair but not, repeat not, Conservative Association jumble. Misery brought on tunnel vision, I swooned like a Victorian lady and had to be woman-handled into a taxi home. Quelle fiasco.

That same evening, the blood back in my cheeks, I complained to Josh that I was cooking the three hundred and sixtieth meal of 1980 and he said move aside, I'll take over. Coming to, I found myself, family and carry-cot in a taxi driving to a posh restaurant. Very nice, too, but Josh was so smug afterwards that I felt it incumbent upon me, in the name of Wages for Housework, to point out that his solution to the domestic chore-sharing problem had just cost us fifty quid, and if he intended to keep that up, he'd have to apply for funding to the IMF. Bickered for the rest of the evening, Josh wittily intoning his Battle of Britain speech – you can please some of the women all of the time and all of the women . . . but you know the rest, ha ha.

I had hardly recovered from these two blows to the system when Mother arrived to administer her weekly dose of alarm and despondency. How can I *think*, she said eighteen times, of letting my Daughter drive van, alone, to Spain? Do I *want* her to be raped, mutilated and left for dead in foreign parts? It is my duty to insist that a *man* goes with her. I point out that Jane is a large, tough twenty-year-old rather more competent than me. Mother and Mother's Husband put together and Mother leaves room in huff. I then had a panic attack about Jane being raped, mutilated and left for dead in foreign parts and insisted she took a man with her. Like the Yorkshire Ripper, you mean, shouted Jane and left room in huff.

Myself, I blame British Rail. Does Sir Peter Parker realize the mayhem caused to family units all over Britain by pound-a-trip Grans intent on inject- ing overdue guilt into long-unvisited daughters? Josh's Ma trained over, too, apparently to make sure I wouldn't grass on Josh if he turned out to be the Yorkshire Ripper. Ma, I said, what alternative would I have? Even the sacred marriage bonds might snap, given that one's spouse was a mass murderer. Marriage bonds maybe, she said, but I am his Mother. Then she said would I inform on Ben, I said what else could I do, and she said you could stop his pocket money. She did. Ben, I said, glaring at the stick of celery that is my son, if I hear you've murdered one more woman, no sixpence for you next Friday. Well, now they've arrested someone who's got a wife and a mother. Keep your ears pinned back for the feminine connection.

Ben's friend Flanagan stayed most of the holiday. He explained that he had left home because his mother had this new boyfriend. How difficult it must be, I thought, for adolescent boys in the midst of the Oedipal Dilemma to have alien males vying for their love-object's favours. Flanagan said he couldn't stand the way his Mum bullied her boyfriends and now she had chucked them both out because of her women's meetings. You're as bad as the NFers, he told her. I can't help being a boy, can I, any more than if I was black? But you *are* black, Flanagan, I said, and Black is Beautiful. Yeah, except I'm white, he said. Flanagan's Dad is white, said Ben, so why shouldn't Flanagan choose? What am I, anyway, a racist or something? With that, they both pulled on jackets covered with swastikas and went out. At times like this, I am so grateful for the baby. Dear thing, he's hardly a boy yet at all.

You probably won't read this letter until mid-January – I read in the papers that your lot had gone to Rome to picket Nativity Scenes. My goings-on here on the home front must seem very trivial to you. Ah well, we also serve who only stand and whine.

Yours, from a hot stove,
Martha

Jill Tweedie

Lady Chapel

While Arthur was trying to get a proper night's sleep in Dallas, Sukie Smith was finding it all too easy to fill her chapel meeting in London. It was a Sunday and no one had anything better to do. This was the best entertainment around.

The feminist branch came in force. Even those women who had not been working for years were delighted to lend their support to a really important cause. Just for starters, everyone on maternity leave turned up. The room was full of suckling mothers, of fathers with babies strapped to their backs in aluminium frames, of crawling infants spread out on chainstore sheets decorated with teddy bears or flailing their chubby limbs with frustration in striped pushchairs. They were joined by everyone on sabbatical, and everyone on sick-leave who had miraculously risen from their beds.

Sukie's acne had flared up since this American sex-maniac dared to call her 'baby' in the kitchen. It was not just the insult, the man had also cost her money. She had had to call her alternative doctor and go on a vegan diet to counteract the collective poison released into the ether by all red-meat-eating males like this Frederick Fisher. The guy obviously ate half a cow for breakfast. He would follow that up, no doubt, with sausages, bacon and eggs sunny side up, the whole lot covered in maple syrup and washed down with a couple of pints of milk. It was the accumulative aggression of this macho diet that had led him to do the sinister thing of which he stood accused. He had tried to subvert the morals of an impeccable British thinking female by insinuating that both he and she were tarred with the same brush. Why else would he have called her sister?

This was just the beginning of Sukie Smith's long saga of woes. She thought something ought to be done about it. Fisher ought to do something about it. Fleet Street ought to do something about it. But most of all, the government ought to do something about it. The Prime Minister herself had a lot to answer for. Sukie went methodically through the agenda she had drawn up for the meeting of the feminist chapel, and when she had finished she received a standing ovation from all those who had somehow managed to stay awake. A vote was taken and carried unanimously that the complaint would be put before the Equal Opportunities Commission and the following recommendation made, subject to discussion.

1. The word 'baby' must not be used in the newspaper or in the building in which the paper was produced, no matter to what or whom it might refer.

Even the reference to a person smaller than adult could not be condoned since such reference was a form of discrimination against small people, implying, as it did, that the person had less experience than another person and therefore less competence and was somehow small of mind as well as body.

There was a bit of a problem over spin-off or compound words containing the suffix or prefix 'baby'. 'Tar-baby' was completely out on several counts, though mainly because of racism. The word 'babywalker' posed a completely different kind of problem. No other alternative readily came to mind to describe this method of infant locomotion, which was demonstrably popular at the meeting itself with several kamikaze kids careering round the floor in their plastic vehicles while their mothers wrangled against the din. The word 'infant' itself was a problem. You could, of course, indicate the passage of a being through life by mentioning his or her or rather its age at every juncture. In the old days, indeed, this would have been recommended to students of journalism as handily providing a thumb-nail sketch for the readers as to the subject's experience and appearance. Nowadays, however, this sort of pigeon-holing could give rise to the accusation of ageism.

It was therefore recommended that any concept giving rise to any such form of prejudice be radically avoided and another word be substituted altogether for the word 'baby'. Now all that remained was to decide which word. To use the word 'small' about a person was inevitably to belittle them, therefore small would not fit the bill. To use the word 'child' was to invite the adjective 'childish', which was a form of denigration. After much toing and froing it was decided that the only acceptable substitute was the word 'person' itself. The motion was carried unanimously.

2. The word 'sister' should henceforth be deleted from the vocabulary of Fisher employees and the style book of Fisher newspapers.

At first it was thought the obvious substitute would be 'female brother' until it was pointed out that any qualification of the word 'brother', especially through the addition of adjectives normally reserved for the distaff branch of humankind, would somehow imply a lesser or younger brother. For a while the term 'sororial person' seemed a possibility, yet again the sticking point was the diminution through qualification. A sororial person was not a fraternal person, and the distinction immediately invited some form of comparison and therefore discrimination.

The feminists were hopeful they had hit on a solution with the word 'sibling' since it could describe a sororial sibling or fraternal sibling, but after a while there were various factions who were unhappy with sibling since its most usual overtones were those of sibling rivalry. It was felt it was essential to indicate to this sheriff from Texas, who was in danger of mistaking the West End for the Wild West, that competitiveness of any sort was considered directly against the policy of this newspaper. No sort of excellence could be condoned unless everyone had some of it. Some trouble-maker was worried about the definition in this case of the word 'excellence', and this occasioned a popular move to accuse the word itself of élitism and have it banned from the dictionary. A discussion was launched about wordism at this point, but this discussion was wisely shelved till later because there were several people whose nappies needed changing.

So, after much discussion, it was decided that the only acceptable substitute for the word 'sister' was the word 'person' itself. Once again the motion was carried unanimously.

The motion having been debated to this conclusion, it was obvious that Fisher had been guilty of sexist discrimination in uttering the words 'baby' and 'sister'. These insults would never have been addressed to a male member of the staff, thus obviating the necessity for Sukie Smith's reaction.

It was further agreed, moreover, that Fisher would never have dared to insult any male employee by taking him into the kitchen and trying to humiliate him by firing him expressly in such domestic surroundings. At this point in the discussion, a most interesting dilemma arose. In order to eliminate any possibility of this sort of humiliation in the future, there would seem to be two obvious courses of action. One was to eliminate the word 'kitchen', the other was to eliminate the object kitchen. At first this second course of action seemed altogether preferable. But though the kitchen itself should be eliminated, provision could still be made for those endless cups of tea and coffee without which a newspaper would never make it to the presses. It was agreed that the kitchen could be eliminated by the provision of a vending machine in any open space with no specific designation.

On the other hand, it was pointed out, the end-result of the provision of such a vending machine was that some employee, usually female, would regularly be sent to said vending machine to bring back those polystyrene cups of beverage invented to save the humiliation of washing the dishes.

The fact that females tended to volunteer their services to perform these mundane tasks only served to underline their perennial exploitation activated by years of sociologically inspired masochism. It was decided that this masochism would always be perpetuated unless every employee had it written into their contract that they had equal, indeed compulsory (say, every half hour) access to the vending machine. It was important to make it compulsory, otherwise the more kind-hearted would offer their services and be exploited for the offer, and the betting was the kind-hearted would be female. To get round this, a secretary and an editor, any employee in whatever capacity and indeed a proprietor should all fetch their own coffee on the half hour.

At this point someone put their hand up and objected to the word 'employee' as a word that implied a form of formalized subjugation open to exploitation and discrimination. Someone else suggested the word 'personnel' rather than 'employee', but yet again it was agreed that a slight aura of inferiority attached to this word as well. It was therefore suggested that the only suitable word for use in these circumstances should be 'person' and the motion was carried unanimously.

Now the question remained from what source this person should fetch a cup of coffee. Even a vending machine had to be placed in some area, which, if it were not called 'kitchen', had otherwise to be defined and was likely to be defined as menial the moment it was put to practical use.

A good hour was spent summoning up all the associations of the word 'kitchen'. A kitchen, it was generally agreed, invoked by historical definition the image of a servile female busying herself with menial tasks. The feminist chapel asked themselves what synonyms they knew for the word 'kitchen'. Some idiot suggested 'scullery' and was cried down. A scullery was even worse, for it was the province of a poor lowly creature called a scullery maid. The word 'bar' was discussed for a while and then rejected because of certain overtones of heartiness which might encourage any lingering macho streak, if there was such a thing in any newspaper person.

Finally the chapel came up with the word which was irrefutably perfect because it had no overtones at all. The word was 'room'. A kitchen and any other division of space such as lavatory would henceforth be known as room. The motion was carried unanimously.

There remained one task. It was to get the objection down on paper, after which it could be sent to Frederick Fisher. Now it was important to describe precisely what had happened and between whom. The feminists, however, found it impossible to address Frederick Fisher as Frederick Fisher since the first name, with its exclusively masculine associations, immediately invited some contrast with the name Sukie, with its exclusively feminine associations. Even the reduction to the formal Mr or Ms invited the same comparison. A satisfactory solution was finally found in referring to Fisher as Fisher and Smith as Smith, whereupon the incident could be described to the satisfaction of everyone present. Until someone raised their hand with another sticking point. This was that, since Fisher was known to be the proprietor of the newspaper and Smith known to be his employee, even to use this basic nomenclature on top of this knowledge was to prejudice the issue. In order to reduce this to its barest unprejudiced bones, it was agreed that any such appellation was impossible. The only logical thing to do in the circumstances was to describe Fisher as person A and Smith as person B. Whoops, no, that would not do, since the one came alphabetically *after* the other. For a similar reason, in that the one came numerically after the other, person one and person two were no sort of a solution. Neither could there be any question of a person and another person, another being an adjunct and an afterthought and therefore inferior.

They decided to adjourn the hour of decision while they discussed the right and wrong of Frederick Fisher interfering with Sukie Smith's personal habits, namely, her right to smoke a cigarette when and where she wished. It was generally agreed that smoking a cigarette represented exactly the same sort of right as wearing your personal choice of clothes to work. If the right to smoke cigarettes was not preserved, then pretty soon Fisher would have them all in uniform. If, indeed, he was allowed to dictate any part of their daily intake, whether it be into their lungs, their stomachs or even their minds, this represented a form of manipulation that would very probably end up in something completely unacceptable namely, overt censorship. Frederick Fisher had tried to patronize Sukie Smith by telling her that smoking was bad for her health. It was Sukie Smith's opinion that she should be allowed to take strychnine in full view of everyone if she so wished.

She now expounded at length her theories of personal liberty. It was her view that the age of personal patronage had died because personal relations between people could be guaranteed to bring out the worst in them. Sukie Smith maintained that satisfactory relations could be forged only with a satisfactory ideology which must be reinforced by law. There was no law against cigarette smoking, even if it killed the lot of them. Sukie Smith felt that there was only one way this could be made quite clear, and that was by upholding right up front the right to kill oneself as one of the inalienable rights of any contracted person. Not only would they have the right to a

proper funeral and memorial service at the expense of the newspaper, but
their heirs should have the right of inheritance of the vacated job.

It was all becoming excessively complicated. People were having
temper tantrums, demanding toast and Marmite and clearly needed to be put
to bed. The feminist chapel decided to confine themselves for the time being
to the description of the main incident. This was how the incident, in which
Sukie Smith had been taken into the kitchen by Frederick Fisher and there
fired, was finally described to the satisfaction of all present:

'A person in a room had addressed a person and called this person a
person. He' – whoops, the 'he' was struck out and replaced by the gender
indeterminate word 'person' – 'This person had furthermore addressed
this other person as another person.' There was still some dithering to do
over those 'others', nevertheless the memorandum finished up triumphantly,
'What was the person going to do about it?'

Glenys Roberts

—————

There Was Once

— There was once a poor girl, as beautiful as she was good, who lived with
her wicked stepmother in a house in the forest.

— Forest? *Forest* is passé, I mean, I've had it with all this wilderness stuff. It's
not a right image of our society, today. Let's have some *urban* for a
change.

— There was once a poor girl, as beautiful as she was good, who lived with
her wicked stepmother in a house in the suburbs.

— That's better. But I have to seriously query this word *poor*.

— But she *was* poor!

— Poor is relative. She lived in a house, didn't she?

— Yes.

— Then socioeconomically speaking, she was not poor.

— But none of the money was *hers*! The whole point of the story is that
the wicked stepmother makes her wear old clothes and sleep in the fireplace –

— Aha! They had a *fireplace*! With *poor*, let me tell you, there's no fireplace.

Come down to the park, come to the subway stations after dark, come down to where they sleep in cardboard boxes, and I'll show you *poor!*

— There was once a middle-class girl, as beautiful as she was good –

— Stop right there. I think we can cut the *beautiful*, don't you? Women these days have to deal with too many intimidating physical role models as it is, what with those bimbos in the ads. Can't you make her, well, more average?

— There was once a girl who was a little overweight and whose front teeth stuck out, who –

— I don't think it's nice to make fun of people's appearances. Plus, you're encouraging anorexia.

— I wasn't making fun! I was just describing –

— Skip the description. Description oppresses. But you can say what color she was.

— What color?

— You know. Black, white, red, brown, yellow. Those are the choices. And I'm telling you right now, I've had enough of white. Dominant culture this, dominant culture that –

— I don't know what color.

— Well, it would probably be *your* color, wouldn't it?

— But this isn't *about* me! It's about this girl –

— Everything is about you.

— Sounds to me like you don't want to hear this story at all.

— Oh well, go on. You could make her ethnic. That might help.

— There was once a girl of indeterminate descent, as average-looking as she was good, who lived with her wicked –

— Another thing. *Good* and *wicked*. Don't you think you should transcend those puritanical judgmental moralistic epithets? I mean, so much of that is conditioning, isn't it?

— There was once a girl, as average-looking as she was well-adjusted, who lived with her stepmother, who was not a very open and loving person because she herself had been abused in childhood.

— Better. But I am so *tired* of negative female images! And stepmothers – they always get it in the neck! Change it to step*father*, why don't you?

That would make more sense anyway, considering the bad behavior you're about to describe. And throw in some whips and chains. We all know what those twisted, repressed, middle-aged men are like –

— *Hey, just a minute!* I'm *a middle-aged* –

— Stuff it, Mister Nosy Parker. Nobody asked you to stick in your oar, or whatever you want to call that thing. This is between the two of us. Go on.

— There was once a girl –

— How old was she?

— I don't know. She was young.

— This ends with a marriage, right?

— Well, not to blow the plot, but – yes.

— Then you can scratch the condescending paternalistic terminology. It's *woman*, pal. *Woman*.

— There was once –

— What's this *was, once?* Enough of the dead past. Tell me about *now*.

— There –

— So?

— So, what?

— So, why not *here?*

Margaret Atwood

DOWN THE
GARDEN PATH

[On being challenged to use 'horticulture' in a sentence:]
You can lead a horticulture, but you can't make her think.

Dorothy Parker

Showing The Garden

An English lady of somewhat advanced middle age guides her visitor into her country garden, and as she talks they move down the pathway from one bed of flowers to another, pausing at each as she explains.

Come, Mrs Guffer, do come. I am longing for you to see the garden. . . . Tea is not quite ready – and I'm so afraid you are going to run away the moment we've had our tea that I am determined you should have at least a *tiny* glimpse of the garden! I won't take you far. . . . Happily it's very near. . . . I always feel that I am most fortunate in having a part of my garden into which I can fairly *tumble*. . . . Here we are already!

Oh, do you? . . . How very sweet of you!

As a matter of fact, you know I am rather sorry you should see the garden now, because alas! it is not looking its best. . . . Oh, it doesn't *compare* to what it was last year. . . . . We've had a very poor season, I think. . . . Oh, it's been very much too dry. . . . I think everyone has suffered . . . .

For example, take my Pomonas – these are the *Pomona Grandigloras*. . . . The blossoms should be as large as a small saucer, and you see, mine are *tiny*. . . . And as for my poor *Glubjullas*, they never came up at all! . . . I can't think why, because I generally have great luck with my *Glubjullas*. I am particularly fond of them, and I have a *great* variety. . . . People come from far and wide, and they all agree they have *never* seen finer *Glubjullas* than mine. . . . I take no credit for my success, because I happen to have particularly fine *Glubjulla* soil, and I *do* think in the case of *Glubjullas* everything is in the *soil*! . . . I can't *think* what happened this year. . . .

Next week my *Funnifelosis* should be in bloom. . . . They will completely fill that corner that is all bare now with their huge foliage and tall blue blossoms. . . . They will make a most lovely mass just there – where it looks rather sad just now, I'm afraid!

I'm so sorry those wretched creepers are completely hiding my *Lummylosias*. It *is* a pity – because they are all out. . . . If only we could see them! . . . See – there *is* one! . . . Just at the top of the wall. . . . I must see if I can find the gardener and ask him to cut away the creepers. . . . There he is! You don't mind if I call? . . . I have a rather piercing voice, I'm afraid. . . . (*She shouts*) Diggum! Diggum! . . . He hears me! . . . Diggum – will you please cut the creepers? I am very anxious for my friend to see the *Lummylosias*. It is a pity they grow so fast – they smother everything. . . . Cut them well away, Diggum. . . . I think we shall see them before you go. . . .

(*She sees a dog*).

Oh! Where *did* that wretched dog come from? Chase him away, Diggum! . . . How did he get into the garden? . . . Oh! You nasty little dog! Go away! Go away! . . . (*She suddenly turns at an interruption from Mrs Guffer*)

Oh! I *beg* your pardon. . . . Is he *yours*? . . . I *am* sorry! . . . Will you forgive me! I'd no idea you'd brought your dog. But why didn't you bring him to the house? I'm *very* fond of dogs. . . . Come here, you sweet puppy – come here, you darling! . . . What's his name? . . . Brownie? Come along, Brownie! . . . A *dear* little dog! (*She strokes the dog's head*) And what a friendly creature, to run to me when I spoke to him so brutally! . . . You *are* a darling! . . . No, really, Mrs Guffer. . . . Please believe me. . . . I am really *very* fond of dogs, and am most happy to have him! . . . But you see, sometimes stray dogs manage to get into the garden. . . . And they do scratch rather. . . . Oh!

But he couldn't hurt anything – those soft little paws. . . . Oh, no! . . . He's most welcome in my garden. . . . And how pretty he looks – running in and out among the flowers!

(*They move along to another bed*)

Now, Mrs Guffer – I am longing to show you something which I propose to do. . . . And I want you to persuade my husband that it's a *very happy* plan! . . . My husband – like so many men – is hopelessly conservative. . . . He never wants to change *anything*. . . . Whereas *I* think that part of the fun of having a garden is to make some little change each year – some little improvement. And I am always full of ideas, which he regularly sits upon, I may say! . . . Now would you mind coming over here? I think we can see it from here. . . . No, I believe it would be better if we went over there. . . . Yes – now I think I can show you what I mean. . . . Do you see that group of cypress trees there – the dark Italian cypress? . . . Then, you see to the right a group of smaller, rather insignificant trees? . . . That's it! You're looking right. . . . Do you know what I propose to do? . . . Cut them down! . . . Yes – take them all out! . . . There are five, I think.

It *does* seem rather drastic. But really, do you know – I am rather sorry that I haven't done it before. . . . I think it is going to be an enormous improvement. . . . It's going to give me a little *vista*, which will be rather exciting, I think! . . . I shall see more sky – which is always desirable. And on a clear day I hope I shall see the horizon – which would be *very* jolly! . . . Then, I shall have a sense of space – of distance. . . . A little glimpse into the *beyond* – as it were. . . . I think a vista always gives one a feeling of mystery. . . . And I always think it's *very* exciting. . . . When one opens something up, one never knows what one may find. . . .

Then, it's going to solve another problem. When I was in Venice some fifteen years ago, I picked up the most enchanting little statue – a little marble boy on a pedestal. . . . And I have *never* been able to make up my mind where to put him. . . . So the poor darling has been in my garage for fifteen years, hid under a bit of tarpaulin. . . . And now, I know what to do! . . . I shall bring him out and put him in the gap, and I think he will be very *happy* there, don't you? . . . Standing on his pedestal. . . . With his little arms outstretched against the sky. . . . He should feel very much at home. It will seem like a little bit of Italy. . . . Creamy marble and a cypress tree – they suggest Sunny Italy! A very happy thought, I think – on our gloomy winter days!

Then, too, I am trying to induce my husband to let me cut down that tree, and put in a little marble pool! . . . I agree – it is a very nice tree, and I am very, *very* fond of trees. . . . But I want to break this mass of green. . . . And then, I think water is *so* enchanting – don't you? . . . The way it always reflects things. . . . It does – doesn't it? . . . And I think it would be so delicious suddenly to stumble on the crescent moon, just *there*. . . . Or a pink cloud drifting by. . . . Or a star. . . .

Then, on *this* side – (*She swings her arm to the right, pointing*) Oh! I *beg* your pardon! . . . hope I didn't hurt you! . . . I propose to extend my hardy border. . . . I feel I must have more colour, and I propose to put in a mass of perennials. . . . Which will give me colour all summer long! . . .

And on that side (*She points to the left*) I propose to continue my old brick wall, and cover it with ivy. . . . I think it makes a *very* happy background – don't you? . . .

(*They move along*)

Oh, look at my *Seccalikums* just coming up! . . . Diggum – have you seen the *Seccalikums*? They're all up – doing beautifully. . . . Oh! Don't you *know* them? They thrive in dry weather! You see. . . . They're pushing their way through the very dusty soil, and appear to be quite happy. . . . I hope they're going to be yellow. . . . (*She stoops over the flowers*) Are you going to be yellow, my pets? . . . I *mean* them to be yellow! . . .

But my poor *Dampfobias* are not doing well at all, alas! . . . They need continual rain and damp. . . . They never thrive unless it rains every day. . . . And one can hardly wish for that!

I am sorry my *Schimonas* are over. . . . They were particularly fine this year. . . . I think it was a very fine *Schimonas* year. . . . *Every*one was talking about their *Schimonas*. . . . They are great favourites of mine. . . . Strange to think that was a mass of pink a week ago! There is only one left. . . . That little brown bell. . . . What a pity to think we shan't see them for another year!

(*Again she moves along*)

And my *Nosellas*, too, alas, are just over. . . . I am *very* fond of *Nosellas*! They're perfect poppets – most accommodating little chaps – and all that they need is a little *blood*. I gave them a little this year, and they throve on it! . . .

Oh, I am sorry! I wanted to cut you a *Mrs Huntley Buncum*, but I'm afraid they are all about to fall! . . . There were five perfect buds last night – and now, alas, they are full blown! . . . Oh, I *do*! . . . I think *Mrs Huntley Buncum* is my very favourite rose. . . . But the pity of it is – she fades so soon!

Oh, do you? How very sweet of you. . . . That border was a dream in June, and it's going to be nice again in October. . . . Could you possibly come back in October? . . . June and October are *the* months for that border. . . . Just there, where it is rather bare now, I had a mass of *Marinbellas*. . . . One is told to plant them at least fourteen inches apart. . . . And do you know what I did? . . . I put them in very close together – and the result was a *pool* of blue! . . . You can't *think* how lovely it was! . . . And behind my *Marinbellas*, I put *Mloops*. . . . White *Mloops*! . . . Oh, no! I shouldn't put any but white, Mrs Guffer. *Mloops* come in very peculiar colours, not always desirable. . . . They're rather treacherous. . . . One can never be sure of a *Mloop*. But with white one is always safe, I think. . . . Blue and white are safe in everything!

Then, I had a mass of yellow *Glypsafantums* – then, some mauve *Bosanias*. A delicious combination! . . . And in and out and all along the entire length of my border, I had a carpet, Mrs Guffer – no exaggeration, a *carpet* – of those darling little pale pink *Punnyfunkums*. . . . You don't *know* the *Punnyfunkums*? . . . Oh, Mrs Guffer! . . . You will never know peace until you discover the *Punnyfunkum*! It is an annual – and *such* a comfort! Anyone can have it. . . . Do put it down. . . . You have your little book? . . . I always carry one. . . . And a pencil? . . . (*She dictates as she watches Mrs Guffer write*) Pale pink *Punnyfunkum*, penny a packet. . . . Sow them freely in your border, and you can't think what a happy result you'll have! . . . Because, I think, we've all had the experience that in a border, something *always* disappoints one. . . . *Something* fails! . . . And when you have your *Punnyfunkum*, it really doesn't matter. . . . Nothing matters! . . . Because wherever there is nothing else, the *Punnyfunkum* goes! It creeps in and out and fills all gaps. . . . And the *great* advantage of the *Punnyfunkum* is that it does well in *any* soil, and appears to bloom at *all* seasons! . . . I can't think why there are none out now. . . . I have never known it to fail before!

(*They move on*)

Here is rather an interesting plant, Mrs Guffer – something I am very proud of. . . . It's a great favourite of mine. . . . It's called *Missayearea Idowtans*. . . . It blooms every second year. This *was* to have been its year. . . . But, alas! – the wireworms have got it, and I am *afraid* there will be no flower. . . .

I am sorry my *Millasquiffaglorians* have not done as well as usual this year. . . . We had a touch of frost last Thursday, so I fear they will not recover! . . .

Oh, here's my Arthur to take us in to tea! . . . Arthur – Mrs Guffer highly approves of my plan of cutting down the trees and putting in the little pool. Now, Mrs Guffer – you *must* tell my husband what you said to me! . . .

Oh! I beg your pardon! . . . I see a caterpillar on your hair. May I pick him off? . . . He's caught in a curl. . . . I have him! . . . I can't think where he came from! (*She squashes the caterpillar with her foot*) We *never* have caterpillars – do we, Arthur? . . .

But you *must* come again, Mrs Guffer, and see the garden when it's really looking its best. . . . Because this is not our real Fairhill weather. . . . . No – indeed! . . . The sun should be shining and the sky should be blue. . . . And if you come in October, I shall be able to show you a second blooming of my *Mloops* . . . and possibly pick you a *Mrs Huntley Buncum*. . . .

Shall we go in to tea? . . . I think it's ready now!

Ruth Draper

——

They had a passion for getting something for nothing.
Every blackberry in the hedgerow was an agony to Lavinia
until she had bottled it.

Vita Sackville-West

——

A Wet Day

'How is your lettuce, Ma'am?' asked the old parish priest. 'I hear it's been bad everywhere this year.' He paused and blew his nose loudly, and then he looked around him. 'Slugs!' he said then, very sternly, and went on a few paces after my aunt. We hadn't room to walk abreast on the narrow garden path. We went in single file; the three of us. After a minute the old man turned around and looked back at me.

'Slugs,' he said again, and only the fact that he put the word in the plural kept me from feeling that this sturdy and blunt old man was calling me names.

'Our lettuce is very good this year,' said my aunt, as all three of us somewhat unconsciously turned down towards the sodden path that led to the kitchen garden, and she took a firm grip of my arm although it meant that both of us got our legs wet by the border grasses. Father Gogarty distrusted students and my aunt probably linked me in case I might take offence at some remark of his, although it is scarcely likely that this would have happened.

My aunt was always nervous when the local clergy called because we had had a couple of brisk arguments, she and I, about one thing and another, and she was beginning to realize that in my estimate of a man's worth I did not allow credit for round collars and tussore. I met some fine men who were in clerical clothes, but my respect for them had nothing to do with their dress. My aunt, however, had no use for anything I said on certain subjects. She banged the door against all my arguments. Sometimes she went as far as saying that she doubted the wisdom of my parents in sending me to the University at all. It was there that I got my ideas, she said; ideas she distrusted. When she wasn't too angry to listen, she kept interrupting so much that she couldn't hear half what I said. Cheap anti-clericalism was the phrase she used most often to batter a way through my remarks. But as a matter of fact I believe that secretly she enjoyed these encounters that we had, and that they gave her a feeling of satisfaction as if she were Fighting for the Faith. I could understand, of course, that she wouldn't care to have outsiders overhear my views. And she lived in terror of my offending the local clergy.

That was why she linked me so close as we went into the kitchen garden. She wanted to keep me near her so that she could squeeze my arm, and nudge me, and, in general, keep a guide over my conversation and demeanour.

We walked along the garden path.

Just inside the kitchen garden was a large ramshackle fuchsia bush that hung out, heavy with raindrops, over the gravel path. Our legs were sprinkled with wet.

'You ought to clip back those bushes, Ma'am,' said the parish priest. 'Nothing would give you a cold quicker than wet feet.'

'I know that, Father,' said my aunt, deferentially, 'but they look very pretty on a sunny day; so shaggy and unpretentious.'

'On a sunny day!' said the old man. 'And when do we get a sunny day in this country I'd like to know? As far as I can see it's rain, rain, rain.'

He shook the bush with petulant strokes of his walking stick, while he was talking, and we knew that his thoughts were back in the days before his ordination, when he wandered along the blistered roads in Rome, and wiped the sweat from his red young face.

He often told us stories about those days, and all his stories had flashes of sunlight in them, that made up for the absence of humour. We thought, involuntarily, of sun-pools lying on hot, city pavements, between the chill shadows of lime leaves. We thought of barrows of melons and pawpaws and giant vegetable marrows; huge, waxy growths of red and yellow. We thought of the young priest from Ireland in his shining black alpaca, laying his hands on them, and smiling to find them warm; for at home they were always chill to the touch, with a mist of moisture on them.

It was extraordinary the way we thought of his youth like that every time we saw him, because it was forty-five years, at the very least, since those days when he knelt to the Pope in Rome, and out of those forty-five years we, ourselves, had only known him for ten; the last ten. And those ten years were the years least likely to make us think of his hot, healthy youth, because during all that time he was delicate and suffering, and the duties of the parish put a great strain on him.

He always looked cold, and although his face was rosy-appled over with broken veins, it nevertheless looked blue and chilly to us as we sat watching him in the bleak, concrete church where he went through Mass perfunctorily, and gave out a hard dry sermon, with a blackened silver watch in his hand, and his eye darting from one side of the church to the other, from the back to the front, from the organ-stall to the gallery steps, according to wherever a cough or a sneeze escaped from some incautious person. There was always someone coughing, or stifling a cough. He used to say that he would like to preach a sermon some day on avoiding colds; he'd like to tell the ignorant people at the back of the church to close the door quickly when they came in, and not to hold it open for someone halfway down the outside path. There were more colds contracted by false politeness, he explained, than by any other way. He'd like to tell his congregation to cover their mouths when they sneezed. But he knew that a sermon of this kind would not be taken in the spirit in which it was meant, and so he had to content himself with stopping in the middle of a sentence, whenever any-one coughed, and staring at the offender till his stare became a glare. They probably thought that he was annoyed at the interruption, but they might have known, had they any wits awake at all at that hour of the morning, that nothing could interrupt the perfect machinery of his sentences. They ran smoothly in the tracks they had cut for themselves through dogma and doctrine, over forty years before, when he was a careful curate, working under a careful pastor.

It was very remarkable the way Father Gogarty could pause to glare around the church, or even pause for a longer while, to take out his handker-chief, shake it, blow his nose in it for a considerable time, and finally fold it carefully and tuck it back in the pleats of his surplice, before he finished a sentence. And yet he always went on at the exact place where he had stopped, and never repeated as much as a preposition of what he had already said.

Once in a while he dropped hints in his sermons about the damp of the church, hoping perhaps that some confraternity would get up a sub-scription for a heating apparatus. The confraternity members, however, thought that the cold of the chapel and the draught that came in under the badly hung door and, yes, even the fact that you might get a splinter in your knee any minute from the rotten wood of the kneelers, were all additional earthly endurances that enhanced the beauty of their souls in the eyes of the Lord. The last thing that would have occurred to them would have been the installation of any form of comfort into the concrete church, although there were large subscriptions raised every other year or so, for silk banners with gilt tassels, for brass candelabra, or for yards of confraternity ribbon with fringes and picot edging.

'It's a pity, you know,' the old priest used to say, 'that the Irish people make no effort to counteract the climate, because it's a most unhealthy climate. It's damp. It's heavy. It is, as I say, very unhealthy to live in.'

It may have been his constant talk of health that made us associate him with the pagans of southern Europe, and made us feel a certain sympathy for him, trapped in a land of mist, where most of the days were sunless and where the nights were never without their frost or rain. My aunt often looked out at the sky and sighed.

'It looks like rain,' she would say. 'Poor Father Gogarty. This kind of weather is very injurious to him.'

And when he came to call, the conversation was mainly about galoshes and leaking roofs and the value of wool next to the skin. He was a diabetic. My aunt, of course, had a great sympathy for him, but it would not have exceeded mine, had it not been for the fact that she deliberately exploited his delicacy to gain merit for her calling.

'He's a martyr!' she often said, when we were sitting down to a well-cooked dinner. 'Can you imagine having nothing for your meal but a soup-plate of cabbage?'

'Or rhubarb,' I'd say, because I did feel sorry for the old man.

'Rhubarb is not so bad,' my aunt would say, pouring the melted butter over her fish.

'Without sugar?' I would inquire.

'Without sugar?' my aunt would say, looking up. 'Are you sure?'

'Of course I'm sure. Diabetics can't have sugar in any form. They can't even have green peas, or beans.'

'You don't tell me! I thought they could eat any vegetable they liked as long as it was a vegetable.'

And while I was explaining the differences between certain vegetables she would listen carefully, and on these occasions she looked as if she was pleased that I was going to the University and getting such general knowledge.

'Let's not talk about the poor man,' she would say at last. 'He is a martyr, that is the truth. How the rest of us can expect to reach heaven, is more than I can tell!' And here, she would call back Ellen, the parlour-maid, before she retired behind the service-screen, to ask her if the cheese soufflé had been sent back to the kitchen. 'It hasn't?' she'd say. 'Good! I think I could manage a little more. It's so good today,' and then, as she scraped the sides of the silver dish, and looked sideways at me to ask if I was quite sure, absolutely sure, that I wouldn't have another spoonful, she would send a message to the kitchen. 'My compliments to the cook!' she would cry.

If the old parish priest happened to call, as he sometimes did, after a conversation like that, we would both go out to the garden with him and walk around the sodden paths, urging him to take another head of sea-kale, or prising open the green curls of the cauliflower plants to see if even the smallest head had formed there, that he could have, as a change from what he called the Eternal Cabbage. Father Gogarty was supplied with vegetables from every little plot in the parish, but my aunt tried to keep him supplied with the kinds that were more difficult of culture, and which he would be unlikely to get elsewhere.

On this particular day in September, when he showed such solicitude for our lettuce, the weather was at its dirtiest, and of all places on earth to feel the dismay of rain I think a garden is the worst. The asters alone would depress the most steadfast heart. They were logged to the ground with rain and their shaggy petals of blue and pink and purple trailed dismally in the mud that streaked them all over. As we went slowly round the garden, and printed the path with our footprints, we left in our wake great heaps of vegetables, lettuce here, spinach there, to be collected by the gardener and put into the priest's car.

The gardener shared our sympathy for the old man and when my aunt would be ordering seeds from the catalogue that was sent to her every year from the city, he would often throw in a suggestion for some vegetable that we ourselves did not particularly like.

'What do we want with that?' my aunt would cry, impulsively, but she nearly always checked herself, quickly, before the gardener had time to explain that the old man had a partiality for it. 'You are quite right, Mike. I'm glad you reminded me. Put down a large patch of that too. And I think we could put in more spinach this year. It ran out towards the end of last year.'

The gardener was very fond of Father Gogarty, and when the old man came they always had a chat.

'We must keep the old machine going, Mike. Isn't that right?' Father Gogarty would say.

'That's right, Father,' Mike used to say. 'Mind your health. It's the only thing that will stand to you at the finish.'

'Perhaps you'd better throw in a few more of those cabbages,' Father Gogarty would say. 'And, by the way! while I think of it, I have been trying to keep it in my mind for a long time, to ask you a question, Mike!'

'Certainly Father. Anything at all I can tell you.'

'It's about lettuce. I wonder, Mike, is there any way of keeping lettuce fresh? My housekeeper says it should be kept airtight, but it gets all dried up, I notice, if you do that. I heard other people say they put it in water, but when that is done, I find, it gets yellow and flabby. I thought maybe that you might know of some knack for keeping it fresh. Do you now?'

'I can't say I do, Father, but why do you bother trying to keep it, can't you always get a bit fresh from here any time you want? What is the need in trying to preserve it? There's always plenty here.'

Mike would speak from his own bounty, but he would look over the priest's shoulder as he spoke, and talk loudly for my aunt to hear. On these occasions she would nod her approval.

'You're working for a kind woman, Mike. There aren't many like her going the way nowadays. She spoils us all. She spoils us all.' The old man sighed. 'I suppose it isn't right for me to let her spoil me like this. Eh, Mike?'

'Ah! Why wouldn't you let her spoil you, Father? She loves giving you the few poor vegetables!'

'She does, indeed. She does. I know that, Mike. I can see that. Isn't it a grand thing the way the Irish women are so good to the clergy?'

'Why wouldn't they be, Father? Where would we be only for the priests?'

'I suppose you're right, Mike, but sometimes I say to myself that I shouldn't be taking such care of myself, an old man like me. "I'll sit down and eat a bit of steak tonight," I say to myself, sometimes – "What harm if it kills me, amn't I near the end, anyway!" But then I say to myself that it's everyone's duty to guard the bit of life that's left in him, no matter what happens, and to keep it from giving out till the very last minute.'

'You've no need to talk of dying, Father. I never saw you looking better.'

'None of your flattery now, Mike,' he'd say, to round off the conversation, turning out of the greenhouse to where my aunt and I would be waiting for him. My aunt felt that the few words the priest had with any of the men or women on the place was, in some way, a part of his priestly duty, and she never liked to interrupt.

'Let him have a few words with Mike,' she would say to me, and she would busy herself until he came out of the greenhouse, by shaking the clay off the lettuce heads, or flicking slugs off with her long forefinger.

The end of the conversations with Mike, all of which were of a remarkable similarity, took place halfway in and halfway out of the glasshouse.

'It's up to all of us to keep going up to the very last minute, isn't that right, Mike?'

'That's right, Father. We should try to guard the bit of health we have. I've always heard that said.'

'Is that so? I'm glad to hear that now, Mike. I must remember that, now.'

Yes, the conversations were all alike, almost word for word alike upon every visit he made. But on this particular day that I mention, the day of rain and draggled fuchsias, Father Gogarty stopped and turned back suddenly to Mike, who was picking up a watering-can and going back into the greenhouse.

'Aren't you from somewhere around Mullingar, Mike?' he said.

'I'm from three miles the other side, Father.'

'I thought that, mind you! Did you know a young farmer there by the name of Molloy?'

'I did, Father. I knew him well, Father.'

'I hear he's dead, the poor fellow,' said Father Gogarty.

'I'm sorry to hear that now,' said Mike. 'He was a fine strong fellow, if I remember rightly.'

'A big broad-shouldered fellow?' said the priest.

'Yes,' said Mike. 'A big broad-shouldered fellow is right.'

'Reddish hair?'

'Red hair would be right.'

'About twenty-five years of age?'

'That's him,' said Mike.

'Yes, that would be him, all right,' said Father Gogarty. 'Well, he's dead.'

'Is that so?' said Mike and he left the watering-can on the ground. 'It just shows you can never tell the day nor the hour. Isn't that so, Father?'

Mike shook his head. Father Gogarty came out of the greenhouse and joined us on the wet gravel.

'I heard you talking to Mike, Father,' said my aunt sympathetically. 'I heard you talking about some young man who died. I hope he wasn't a relative of yours?'

'No,' said Father Gogarty. 'No, but it was a very sad case.' He shook his head dolefully, and then he became more cheerful. 'Do you know!' he said, impulsively, 'I'm a lucky man that it's not me that is under the sod this minute, instead of him.'

'God between us and all harm!' said my aunt. 'Tell us about it, quick.'

'I suppose you often heard me speak of my niece Lottie?' said Father Gogarty. 'She's my sister's daughter, you know, and she comes to see me once in a while. Every six months or so. She's a nurse up in Dublin. Well, anyway, to tell you about the young fellow that's dead. Lottie got engaged a few weeks back to this young fellow from Mullingar. They were planning on getting married next month.'

'Oh, how tragic!' said my aunt.

'Wait till you hear!' said the priest, looking back to make sure that Mike was coming after us with the basket of vegetables to put in the car. 'As I was saying, anyway,' he continued, 'they were planning on getting married next month, and nothing would do Lottie but that I'd see him before they were married. She wrote to say she was bringing him down. I suppose she had an eye to the wedding present, too, you know, but, however it was anyway, I was expecting them last Thursday, and I told my housekeeper to fix up a bit of dinner for them, to get a bit of meat and the like, as well as the dirty old cabbage and rhubarb that I have to eat. I told her to think up a bit of a sweet for them too. She's a good woman, this housekeeper of mine, and she is a great cook; not that her cooking gets any great strain put on it with me in the state of health I'm in! But anyway, she put a nice dinner together. The smell of it nearly drove me out of the house. And when I saw her throwing it out in the pigs' bucket next morning, I could have cried. I could. That's a fact.'

'Didn't they come?'

They came all right, but wait till you hear. It appears he had a cold on him for a day or two past, and coming down in the car he must have got a chill, because the fellow wasn't able to speak when they drew up to the door. The car was a ramshackle affair. You wouldn't wonder at what would happen to anyone in it. I wouldn't ride down the drive in it much less the journey they had made. The niece was very upset and she was fussing over him like as if they were married for fifteen years. Tea, she wanted for him, if you please, right away.

'"Don't mind about dinner," she said, "he couldn't look at a bit of food." Pillows, she wanted for him, if you please. "Get him a pillow so, if you haven't any cushions!" she said to the housekeeper, pushing her out of the way and going over to the sideboard and opening it wide. "Is there a drop of brandy here?" she said, "or where will I look for it? I want to rub it on his chest." I was pretty well sick of the fussing by this time, Ma'am, as you can imagine, and I gave it as my opinion that the best thing she could do would be to take him back to Dublin as quick as ever she could, where he could be given the proper attention.

'"But the drive back?" said Lottie, and I saw in a flash what was in the back of her mind.

'"The harm is done now," I said, "another hour or so won't make any difference. A strange bed might be the death of him. Wrap him up warm," I said, "I'll lend you my overcoat." It was my big frieze coat, Ma'am, you know the one? It was a good warm coat. But Lottie was fidgeting about. She didn't know what was best to do, she said. I was getting pretty uneasy by this time, I need not tell you. What on earth would I have done if they insisted on staying. The whole house would have been upset. There's only one hot jar. Where would I get blankets enough to cover a big fellow like that? There's only the one woman to do everything and she has her hands full looking after me. I couldn't stand the excitement. There would be running up and down the stairs all the night. There'd be noise. There'd be talking till all hours. The doctor would be there. The doctor would have to have a meal. Oh, I could see it all! I could see it all! I have to be careful at my age, you know. I have to have everything regular. I have to have quiet. "If you know what is right," I said to Lottie, "you'll take that man right back where he came from, and get good medical care for him," and as I was saying it, I was thinking to myself that if anyone knew what was right and what was wrong it ought to be her, with her hospital training. And sure enough, there were no flies on her. "I'll tell you what I'll do," she said, "I'll take his temperature, and if he has no temperature I'll take him back to the city and telephone to the hospital. If he has a temperature, of course, it would be madness to undertake the journey back. I suppose the doctor here is passable?" She was pulling out the drawers of the desk while she was talking, looking for the thermometer, I suppose. "Where do you keep the thermometer?" she said, looking round at me.

"'I haven't one," I said, but she wasn't listening to me. "His forehead is very hot, isn't it?" she said. "Why wouldn't it be," said I, "with your hand on it." And the poor fellow himself didn't see the joke, any more than her, he was so sick. "Where did you say the thermometer was?" she said again. "I said I haven't got such a thing," said I, and she was so vexed she could hardly speak. "Every house should have a thermometer," she said, "it's a downright shame not to have one." But she began to gather up rugs and pillows while she was giving out to me. "As long as you haven't one, I suppose I'd better not waste any more time but start getting him back to the city." She went over to the poor fellow. "Do you feel able for the journey back?" she asked, feeling his pulse and frowning.

'"I'm all right," said he. He was a nice lad, not wanting to cause any commotion, and different from her altogether.

'"We'll come down another day, Father," said Lottie, "I hope you hadn't made a lot of preparations for us?"

'"I'll make greater preparations next time," I said, just in order to cheer the poor fellow she was wrapping up with rugs and blankets in the back of the car. I wanted to cheer him up because I had a kind of feeling that he was worse than she thought he was. "I'll send you down a thermometer," she shouted back at me, as they went down the drive. "Everyone should keep a thermometer."'

'That was true for her,' my aunt interposed impulsively at this point, and I could see she was wondering if we had a second one in the house that she could give him.

'I know it was true for her, Ma'am. All I can say is I hope she won't send me one though. You don't think that a man like me would be without such a necessary thing as a thermometer, do you?' He looked at us sternly.

'You had one all the time?' my aunt asked, falteringly.

'Three!' he said. 'I had three of them, no less than three, but I wasn't going to let on to her that I had.' His face was criss-crossed with lines of aged cunning. 'Didn't I know by the feel of the fellow's hand that he had a temperature, but I wasn't going to let myself in for having him laid up in the presbytery for a couple of weeks, as he would have been, you know, with pneumonia.'

'Pneumonia?'

'That's right, Ma'am. He had pneumonia. Double pneumonia, I should say. He was dead the following evening. I was very sorry for the poor fellow. He was a nice lad. I was extremely sorry for him. I can't say that I was so sorry for my niece. It was a very inconsiderate thing, I think you will agree, Ma'am, to come along and visit anyone and bring a man that wasn't able to stand on his feet with a cold? People nowadays have no consideration at all; that's the long and the short of it; no consideration. I sent down to the chemists and got him to send up a bottle of strong disinfectant to sprinkle on the carpets after they went out. You can't afford to take risks. I consider I am a very lucky man to be alive today, a man in my state of health would have been gone in the twinkling of an eye if I was burthened with a young fellow like that in the house, for maybe a month. He might even have died there in any case, even if he didn't have the journey back, and then think of the fuss! I'd be in the grave along with him. There is no doubt in my mind whatsoever on that score.' He stood up. 'Here is Mike with the vegetables,' he said. 'Put the lettuce on the front seat, Mike, I don't want it to get crushed. "Eat plenty of lettuce" the doctor says to me at every visit.' He shook hands with us. 'I'm getting too old to be gadding about in a car,' he said, smiling out the car window at us, before he swung the car around and went off down the drive.

'I'll go for a walk,' I said to my aunt. 'I'll be back in time for dinner.' I thought the least said the better.

And when I came back from my walk, I had indeed forgotten all about the incident. The evening had been very sweet and scented after the recent rain. You'd forget anything walking along the roads and hearing the heavy drops fall from the trees on to the dead leaves in the wood, while the sky over your head was bright and blue and cloudless. And when I came back I was hungry. I was looking forward to my dinner. When Ellen came in with a bowl of salad I hoped my aunt would not take too big a helping because I felt I could eat the whole bowlful. But what do you think? Before the girl had time to set the bowl before us, my aunt snapped at her and rapped the table with her wrist.

'Take away that lettuce,' she said. 'We don't want any tonight.'

I was going to protest when I caught her eye, and held my tongue. We didn't mention that story of the big red-haired farmer, either then, or since, but isn't it a funny thing, I have been on better terms with my aunt since that day. We get on better. And we have less fights about books and politics and one thing and another.

Mary Lavin

———

You may go into the fields or down the lane, but don't go into Mr McGregor's garden: your Father had an accident there; he was put in a pie by Mrs McGregor.

Beatrix Potter

———

I am a bunny rabbit,
Sitting in me hutch,
I like to sit up this end,
I don't care for that end, much,
I'm glad tomorrow's Thursday,
'Cause with a bit of luck,
As far as I remember,
That's the day they pass the buck.

Pam Ayres

———

Lone Dog

I'm a lean dog, a keen dog, a wild dog, and lone;
I'm a rough dog, a tough dog, hunting on my own;
I'm a bad dog, a mad dog, teasing silly sheep;
I love to sit and bay at the moon, to keep fat souls from sleep.

Irene Rutherford McLeod

———

from With One Lousy Free Packet of Seed

'The thing you've got to remember about Margaret,' said Trent Carmichael to Michelle, as they watched her walk past their coffee-shop window, smiling privately to herself about something, 'is that she is an absolute *cow*.'

Michelle nodded. She knew the type.

'I mean it. Whatever you do,' he warned her, showing his teeth, 'don't tell her anything personal.'

'I won't.' Michelle thought about it. 'You mean the rubberized gardening-glove fetish sort of thing?'

'Exactly. She'd make something of it.'

'I understand. She resembles that sinister patricidal girl in *S is for . . . Secateurs!*, then?'

'Yes. In fact you might say she's the very model.'

They continued to stare out of the window, until Michelle broke the silence.

'She knows something about *you*, does she?'

'Alas, yes.'

'Pillow talk, was it?'

'Sadly, you're right.'

Michelle stiffened. She hated the thought of sharing Trent with another woman, especially a *cow* like Margaret.

'Actually, my little dung beetle (if I may),' Trent continued, 'it does occur to me that you still haven't told *me* anything personal, either, yet, except that you've got a mother you have to phone twice a day who loves my books almost to the point of obsession, and who can't wait to meet me.'

He put a hand on her thigh. It thrilled her.

'Haven't I?' she said, attempting an airy manner, but feeling her face redden.

'No.'

'Mm.' He moved his hand. He was awfully good at this.

'I've guessed a lot, though. I can't help looking for clues, you know, being a crime writer. I think I've, you know, ratiocinated quite a lot about you.'

'Such as?'

'Well, you are clever, obviously. But you're pale, you stay indoors a lot, and you don't have a boyfriend, and you do your nails, but not very well.' He smiled apologetically. She smiled back, allowed him to continue.

'Now, your clothes are a bit old-fashioned, and you obviously don't know how to communicate with people, and you have a devotional air and know about gardening, and you've got this big gap in your life going back, ooh, fifteen years.'

'So?'

'So I reckon you're a lapsed nun.'

Michelle said nothing. She felt like laughing, but thought it would be rude.

'I'm right aren't I?' said Trent.

She took a long, thoughtful drink of coffee.

'Well, put it this way,' she said, at last. 'You're not exactly wrong.'

She looked out of the window and smiled to herself. Two days ago she'd been in the office, doing usual Tuesday things. A mere forty-eight hours later she was in a Devon teashop with a famous lover with sympathetic kinky ideas, a plate of free cream buns, and a mysterious past involving wimples. What did she usually do at 11 a.m. on a Thursday morning? Good heavens, she'd forgotten. She'd almost forgotten about Osborne, too; but not quite.

'Trent, you know, I'm a twinge angry with *you*, my darling Green Thumb (if I may). You still haven't told me what happened yesterday, at your friend Angela's. Did you find out what was wrong with this – who was it, um, I forget – this shed-journalist? Storm in a teacup, was it? I don't suppose he had a hatchet, did he? Just some silly mistake.'

'Well, actually, no.' Carmichael looked around, and moved his chair closer to hers. 'If you can keep a secret,' he virtually whispered. 'Actually, he's dead. The shed burned down with him – and the hatchet – inside it. Dreadful business.'

Michelle went white. Dead? Her lovely Osborne? Dead? Dead, in a shed?

'Where is this place? I want to see it,' she cried, getting up suddenly and knocking over a trolley of cakes.

Carmichael stared at her with surprise and admiration. This woman was a real dark horse.

'It's down the lane from the guest-house,' he said. 'Past the Chimneypot Garden Centre. You can't miss it, it's got a burned-out shed in the garden.'

Angela had been mortified to find Osborne gone. Not only had he scarpered without saying goodbye, he had also taken the blankets, the cakes, the book and the rabbit. Jesus, men were such lousy scumbags. She slung an empty gin bottle into the rubbish, where it clanked against all the other bottles she'd emptied since yesterday. Vodka, Bailey's, sangria, Tizer, Worcester sauce – it had been a very long night, and she had invented some deeply unusual cocktails. And now she was giddily propping herself up at the kitchen window, all the weight on her forearms, frowning against a swirling mental fog, and barking down the phone to Gordon ('Ah, a *proto*-scumbag,' she thought, viciously), who had innocently rung her, to ask to come round.

'Jesus' sakes,. Gordon, sure she's a *cow*.' Staggering, she looked around for a stool to sit on, but there wasn't one, so she just collapsed on the kitchen vinyl, pulling the phone down on top of her with a crash. 'You still there? OK. No, I'm fine. But don't sound so shocked about whatsername, yeah, Margaret. I've told you a million times she's a cow. I wouldn't trust her further than I can throw my own pancreas.'

Just next to her face on the floor she noticed a small drip of golden liquid (the last of the whisky, perhaps?) and realized that if she moved her body a couple of inches to the left, she could probably lick it.

She turned her attention to Gordon. 'A cow is what she always was, Gordon baby. Barney left me because of her, I know it.' Actually, she'd never thought of this before, but she was free-associating, and it sounded like sense. 'Yeah, sure. I always knew it. Something they did together. Sometimes I've even wondered whether that *S is for . . . Secateurs!* was all about her and Barney and Trent. All that spooky burial stuff, you know.'

The proto-scumbag asked to come round. She said Sure. He needed advice. He said he'd just discovered that the B&B was crawling with disaffected staff from *Come Into the Garden*, one of whom was the ex-boyfriend of Margaret.

'Small world,' said Angela bitterly, not very interested in *Come Into the Garden* any more. 'Sure, come.' She hung up the phone, and added glumly, 'I've got nobody else here.'

She lay on her back. Scumbags, she thought. Manderley, what a joke. She made a decision and licked up the drip of whisky. It had some dirt in it, but it was OK. Then, with her arms folded across her chest and her eyes tightly closed, she surrendered herself to the familiar round-and-round out-of-body sensation she fondly called the helicopters, only this time it made her think of Wagner's 'Ride of the Valkyries', she didn't know why.

Tim and Gordon walked along together to Angela's house.

'She's a *cow*,' muttered Tim.

'You're right,' said Gordon.

'I'm glad we burned it.'

'Me too.'

Tim kicked a stone.

'I still can't believe you're the bastard who's closed down the mag.'

'Sorry.'

'I mean, it meant such a lot to me.'

'I know.'

'It was the thing I could count on, you know. A sort of shelter. I feel really exposed without it. I'm not sure I can survive in the outside world. I'm too weedy.'

'But you can survive without Margaret?'

'That's true. She's a cow.'

'You're right.'

'I'm quite excited about meeting Angela Farmer. I'm a fan.'

'Oh, she's terrific, you'll love her.'

It was only when they arrived at the gate that they heard a woman scream, from the vicinity of the burned-out shed. It was Michelle. She was standing in the ashes, holding a blackened hand (somebody else's) up to her face and shrieking. But as they raced towards her, they realized she was shrieking with hysterical laughter, not fear. 'It's not a real one,' she yelled to them, more loudly than was necessary, as they reached her, panting. She seemed exhilarated by relief. Tim was confused, he had never seen her so animated. 'I've seen hundreds of these. Look, it's just latex or something. My mother buys them in job lots. She's obsessed with *S is for . . . Secateurs!* and the others, always trying to re-create great moments from it.'

They all looked at the hand.

'So Makepeace isn't dead, then?' gasped Gordon.

'Makepeace?' said Tim and Michelle, with a single voice.

'But what was a trick severed hand doing in Angela's shed?' asked Gordon, puzzled. 'It wasn't there before.'

Michelle shrugged. Now Trent Carmichael had appeared at the gate, as well as Gordon's dad and, separately, Lillian. What the hell was Lillian doing here? 'Hi, Lillian,' said Tim, whom nothing surprised any more. 'I thought it was you I saw. Everybody's here, then. I even saw Osborne last night. Although, come to think of it, he didn't look too happy in his role as the spoils of Britannia.'

But his voice faded on the air, and everyone looked at Michelle.

Somehow it seemed like a moment of truth. The hand wanted to tell them something! As they all stood still in Angela's garden, they surveyed the scene as though they had never seen it before (to be fair, some of them hadn't), and tried to comprehend the full meaning of it all. Here, beside the shed, was the small area of recently dug earth where Makepeace had uncovered the hand. All around them, the autumnal garden held its breath, keeping its secrets, the very image of life suspended. Wordlessly they were gathering at the shed, to see the hand. It was a moment of deadly solemnity.

Angela, with her gumboots on the wrong feet, staggered across the lawn to join them.

'I expect you're wondering why I've asked you all here,' she said, beaming. And then vomited copiously on Trent Carmichael's shoes.

Lynne Truss

———

HERE COMES

THE BRIDE

In olden time sacrifices were made at the altar – a custom
which is still continued.

Helen Rowland

Wedlock. A Satire

Thou tyrant, whom I will not name,
Whom heaven and hell alike disclaim;
Abhorred and shunned, for different ends,
By angels, Jesuits, beasts and fiends!
What terms to curse thee shall I find,
Thou plague peculiar to mankind?
O may my verse excel in spite
The wiliest, wittiest imps of night!
Then lend me for a while your rage,
You maidens old and matrons sage:
So may my terms in railing seem

As vile and hateful as my theme.
  Eternal foe to soft desires,
Inflamer of forbidden fires,
Thou source of discord, pain and care,
Thou sure forerunner of despair,
Thou scorpion with a double face,
Thou lawful plague of human race,
Thou bane of freedom, ease and mirth,
Thou deep damnation upon earth,
Thou serpent which the angels fly,
Thou monster whom the beasts defy,
Whom wily Jesuits sneer at too;
And Satan (let him have his due)
Was never so confirmed a dunce
To risk damnation more than once.
That wretch, if such a wretch there be,
Who hopes for happiness from thee,
May search successfully as well
For truth in whores and ease in hell.

Hetty Wright

———

As soon as our engagement appeared in *The Times* wedding
presents poured in . . . the majority were frightful, and they
came in cohorts – fifteen lamps of the same design, forty
trays, a hundred and more glass vases. They were
assembled at Grosvenor Place . . . When the presents were
all arranged Lady Evelyn looked at them reflectively.
  'The glass will be the easiest,' she said. 'It only needs a
good kick.' She said silver was more of a problem. 'Walter
and I were lucky, *all* ours was stolen while we were on
honeymoon.'

Diana Mosley

———

from Miss Slimmens' Window

Clara! Dora! come here both of you, this very minute! Where's my teeth? Where's my teeth, I say! You don't know? Yes, you do know, too – you must! They're gone, and I can't find them anywhere in this room. I jest took them out, a few minutes ago, to brush 'em, and stepped out in the back-yard for some water, and come in, and now they're nowhere to be seen. You needn't tell me they walk out of that tumbler without help. There's been nobody within gun-shot but you two, and you're playing a trick on me. I'll have you both arrested – I will – marched off to jail, and kept on bread and water for a year. I'll swear you took 'em; for who else could? I'll go for the sheriff now, this minute. Why don't I go? Yes, and meet Mr Wiggleby at the very door, perhaps. He was to be here at two o'clock, to take me out a-riding, and it lacks but ten minutes of the hour, and here I am with my teeth gone. A pretty figure I shall cut, in this plight. Oh, girls, do help me hunt! Perhaps they've dropped somewhere, and I'm so distracted I can't see 'em. Do your best, and the one that finds 'em shall have a new silk dress, if she finds 'em before Mr Wiggleby arrives. What's that? The tumbler was standing close to the window, and perhaps the cats got them, or some little boy has come into the yard and took 'em for fun? Oh-h-h! perhaps! I never was in such misery in my life. Them teeth cost me sixty dollars, hard cash! and to lose them – lose them *now*, of all times! I'd rather have lost my head. Hark! wasn't that the sound of the buggy wheels? Oh, I'm so glad it wasn't! I shouldn't wonder if that plaguey Peters's boy, Jim, had been hangin' around and seen 'em; he's up to all sorts of deviltry. Run over there, Dora, and inquire. Clara! have you searched under the bed? Dear! dear! dear! the clock has struck two. Oh, my teeth! my poor lost teeth!

What's that? my tears are washing all my paint off! Oh, you hideous girls! you'll be the death of me yet! How can you have the heart to make fun of me when I'm in such trouble? One thing is certain! if I ever do find out you've had a hand in this, I'll be revenged – yes revenged!

There! there's the sound of a carriage stopping! He's knocking at the door! Oh, dear, what shall I do? I'll throw myself on the bed, and pretend to be sick. I can not see him, much as I want to; I look too frightful. Run, Clara, tell him I've been taken suddenly very ill, but I hope to be better by to-morrow, and will ride out with him then.

Has she gone, Dora? Oh, I dare not steal a look! I must hide my face in the pillow to stifle my groans. What's that, Clara Brown? Mr Wiggleby regrets exceedingly his disappointment, but, since he has the carriage at the door, would ask permission to take *you* out a little while. You can't go Clara; do you hear? If the jade isn't actually tying on her bonnet, and pretending not to hear! If I dared to step out and tell her, but he's standing right there; and I can't even forbid her. I'll bet a hundred dollars she heard me; and she'll have the impudence to say she didn't.

They've gone, and I've nothing to do but be wretched. Who knows what impression that saucy girl may have a chance to make? And I can't even go out to make good my loss. Oh, my unhappy teeth! Bless me, if they ain't lying right here on the bed! I believe I put 'em there myself; or else them girls have been playing me a trick. How I wish I could find out! I'd never forgive them to the latest hour of my existence.

They're a mile away by this time, and I can set down to make buannits again, I suppose. And this was to have been the happiest day of my life! for I'm sure that I could have brought him to a positive declaration. I could kill that Clara Brown. The happiest day of my life, indeed! I could tear things, I'm so mad.

*

Rain! rain! rain! Do see how it drips down before the window, so a person can hardly tell who is who that goes by! though there's not many people out *this* morning. I don't believe I shall have a customer to-day.

If Mr Wiggleby gets along, it'll be more than I expect; though I do think he is the devotedest of all the suitors I ever had. He's been perfectly inter-mittent in his intentions ever since I was the means, under Providence, of saving his life, and that's two weeks yesterday. I don't think the most envious creature in Pennyville, even Sally Meyers herself can say *now* that I'm counting my chickens before they're hatched. If such civilities as Mr Wiggleby has extended to me ain't paramount to a declaration, then I never received one. Six serenades, two buggy rides – besides the one I lost on account of mislaying my teeth – eight calls in the daytime, and twelve in the evening, walking home by my side from church, in the presence of the whole congregation – why, any jury in the land, that had a spark of sentiment in its breast for the feminine sex, who had a wife, or a mother, or a daughter, or a sister whose heart it did not wish wontonly trifled with, would give me damages in case Mr Wiggleby should back out at this hour. But I'd rather have *him* than five thousand dollars without him; and I don't think he has the least idea of retreating. I think he grows more arduous at every interview. He squeezed my hand so respectfully when he lifted me out of the buggy yesterday. I looked into his eyes to see if he meant anything, and he gave me such a glance. I declare I could hardly walk to the door without his assistance. What expressive eyes he's got, as black as this piece of crape, and as bright as spangles, and such a pellucid smile in them. What convinces me more than anything else of the sincerity of his intentions, is the frankness with which he has told me all about himself. It seems he came to Pennyville to do some law business for his father, who owns property out here about six miles – he shoed it to me the last time we druv out together – and 'twas there he was going that time when Smith's baulky horse throwed him out, and he was borne into my shop, and recovered through my exertions – and he didn't expect to be retained mor'n three or four days when he came here, but *business*, you know, is so prognosticating. He's been unavoidably delayed, he assures me, by occurrences which he did not foresee. In short, he's found attractions in Pennyville that he had no idea existed there, and he don't know when he shall be able to tear himself away; he told me so himself. 'Tear himself away' was the very words he used, and his manner spoke columns.

Now, Clara Brown, what's your face so red for? and you're crumpling that lace all up with your carelessness. I never see a girl change as you have the last two weeks; you seem not to know whether you're standing on your head or your feet mor'n half the time, and I've had to rip out and do over full three-quarters of your work. I'm thankful my trials in the apprentice line are pretty much over; for you'd better believe I'll shet up shop the day that I give up the name of Slimmens. I expect he'll build, maybe, on his father's property, and I've imitated pretty plain to him that I should have nigh on to a thousand dollars to help build and furnish the house with.

I want you girls to take hold and manage things a little more – take some of the responsibility on your own shoulders. If you do well and behave yourselves, there's no knowing but I may be induced to rent you the shop, and let you go along for yourselves. 'Tennyrate, I want you to take hold, now, for I've got sewing of my own to do; I've sewed for other folks about long enough; I'm going to scollop the collars and cuffs of that night-gown I'm making, and put tape trimming all around the edge; then I've ruffles to hem for three new nightcaps, and some bands to stitch, and to sew that knit lace on, that I did last winter in the evenings; I've my green silk to turn the skirt of, and, as soon as I can make up my mind what it shall be, I've another dress to make – a party dress, you know – he! he! I can't decide which to choose; whether to have a sweet white muslin, low in the neck and tucked to the waist, with white satin ribbon run in the tucks, and a sash of the same, or to have a pearl-coloured silk and wear my bunnet. It's such an important moment of one's destination, it requires some reflection to decide upon so momentary a question. The bridal toilet is always the object of so much excruciating remark.

There goes Josh Stebbins out in the rain, with his umbrella over his head, and his wife following him to the door, to scold him for something he's forgotten I make no doubt, or to ask him for something new, to make him draw down his stingy old face. I can see already that she's going to be very extravagant. There's groceries went into that house three times within a week, and a paper that I know was sugar every time; and they use three-quarters of a pound of butter every day of their lives, for I asked old Mrs Grimes, that brings it to them, that day she was in here to see about having new strings to her black satin bunnet. I hope the children are well fed, since things must be wasted in such profusion. I don't believe the poor things are happy, and I've my reasons for it. The other day I see little Jimmy standing out by the gate, looking so forlorn, and crying, as if his heart was breaking; and I called him over, and gave him a cake with carraway-seeds and a lump of sugar, and asked him what was the matter with him – if he didn't like his new mother? You ought to have seen that child eat that cake! he never answered me till he'd swallowed it all down; and then he said he was crying because he lost the pretty new ball his mother made for him; but it's my opinion he was crying from hunger, and nothing else, though the poor little fellow didn't realise what was the matter with him. I asked him how he liked his new ma, and he said he liked her twenty bushels; and I asked him if she told him to say that, and that she'd shet him up in the closet if he didn't when people asked him, and he acted as if he was afraid to tell me, but stammered, 'He guessed so – he didn't know; his new ma had shet him up in the closet once when he was very naughty.' My heart bled for him. I spread him a thick slice of bread, but he run off and wouldn't eat it. I've no doubt his stepmother has forbid him to stay anywhere long enough for the neighbours to find out how things is going. If she keeps anything that Alvira Slimmens doesn't worm out, either one way or another, she'll be the first inhabitant of Pennyville that's been deep enough to do it.

Oh, my! wouldn't I like to catch the first glance of Josh Stebbins's face when he hears *the news*!

Rain! rain! rain! just a purpose to keep Mr Wiggleby away, and prevent Miss Grant from coming to settle for that hat. It'll give my window a good washing anyhow; and it needed it bad enough. Run, Dora, and get a towel, and tuck around the sash there where it's beating in.

Well, for the land sake, if there isn't Johnathan Grimes driving his ox-team in such a day as this! He's worn that old straw hat now going on five year. See how the water drips off, and runs down his back, and his long legs hanging down into the mud, and that red flannin' shirt on! It's a mercy I didn't have *him*, if he *is* worth three thousand dollars, besides a part of the farm when his father dies. Did you ever hear how near we came to making a match, I and Jonathan? O, dear, I shall expire with laughing to think of it! It all came of that very old straw hat. You see, about those days, he used to look pretty spruce; though his legs always was rather long, and seemed to be in the way when he was sitting down, or dancing, or standing still; though they was well enough in climbing fences and planting punkin-seeds; but he kept fixed up right smart, for he was paying attention to Joe Waters, and there was talk of their making a match. Most people called Joe very handsome; though *I* never could never see much beauty about her, except her bright eyes, and her cheeks as red as pinys. In my opinion, she was right-down bold-looking with that dimple in her chin, and laughing whenever she got a chance. One day he came into my shop, and he had that hat in his hand, which he had just given two bushels of wheat for; and he wanted me to put a green silk lining in it, and a good broad green ribbon around it. So I asked him to take a seat while I was doing the job; and he made himself very agreeable; and finally I laughed and said, said I: 'I suppose you'll have another person besides Miss Slimmens to put the next lining in this hat for ye, if report says true, Mr Grimes?'

And he blushed like a beet, and hemmed, and said, 'he didn't know; he guessed not.' And just that minute, as luck would have it, Josephine Waters appeared at the open door, with a bunnit in her hand, which she had brought for me to trim with white. She looked kind of curious at us, to see Jonathan blushing and me laughing; and says I: 'Oh, it's nothing Joe! only I was accusing Mr Grimes of being engaged to a certain somebody, and he was denying of it, as if everybody didn't know without being told. But la! he needn't have got so mad about it, seeing he's going to have the best-looking girl about Pennyville. It's no insult to couple that name with his'n, I reckon.'

'I didn't know I got mad,' said he: for he was a kind of bashful chap, and hadn't spunk enough to carry anything out.

'Well, maybe you didn't,' said I; and then, to turn the subject, I asked him if he had heard of the rise of property in Pennyville since the railroad was talked of. 'Why,' said I, 'four year ago I paid fifty dollars for this lot, and a hundred and fifty for the shop; and now I wouldn't take six hundred for 'em. I've a notion to draw my money from the bank, and spec'late in real estate.'

'If you do, you'll make a pretty fortinate match for some man,' said he, as he took his hat and waited for Joe to do her errand. I see she begun to look grave, and her eyes flashed a little, for Joe was as poor as Job's turkey, and his folks had twitted her of it, once or twice; but she told me what she wanted done with the bunnit, and then told me, very polite, that her mother was to have a quilting-bee to-morrow, and had told her to be sure and ask me. Then I laughed again, and said, 'I'd be happy to attend, if I'd any way of getting there; but, as it was, I didn't see how I could, unless Mr Grimes would volunteer to bring me in his father's new buggy;' and of course he couldn't get out of it, and said, 'With the greatest willingness.' And the two went away, looking daggers toward one another, with me laughing in my sleeve. I wanted to plague 'em, because I knew I was asked to the bee because I was the fastest quilter in Pennyville: and I'd heard of Joe saying that I painted; and I knew she stuck herself up on the strength of her good looks.

The next day I was rigged out in my best, and the new buggy come to the door in grand style; and I was in such a good humour that I got Jonathan to speaking out quite free, a thing even Joe couldn't do; and we was chatting away as merry as blackbirds when we drove up to Widow Waters's. Joe came out to the gate to show me in, and I spoke out just as she got within hearing, and says I: 'No, indeed, it's too late now to break with *her*,' just as if I didn't intend she should hear. Jonathan kinder looked confused, but wasn't quick enough to take, and let the matter slip. Joe got as white as a sheet, but smiled, and made herself agreeable to me, while Mr Grimes drove off to stay away till tea-time. We quilted all the afternoon; and I saw she felt bad, and couldn't hardly make herself sociable with the visitors, while I was talking and joking all the time. During the evening I stuck to her beau like a burr to a woollen stocking, and flattered him up so that his face shone like a punkin; and, when we went off together after that dashing horse in that new rockaway by moonlight, *I* knew that Joe was just ready to burst out a-crying; but *he* didn't, for she bid him good-night so gay, and laughed so loud, that the fool thought she was all right. It takes men a great while to learn how a woman will

'Let congealment, like a worm in the mud,
Prey on her damaged cheek.'

What happened after that, I don't know, except they kept up a coolness; and folks said the match was broken off. Jonathan began to call in at the shop occasionally; and I expect if I'd a had him, he'd have married me. But his legs were too long, and he hadn't none of that romantic air which Mr Wiggleby possesses in such an imminent degree. So one day, about six months after, when he came in to get a new ribbon, and said that he and Joe had made up, and was going to be married in two weeks, I told him 'I thought they was a very good match, though the girl *was* poor, and her mother would likely be a dependence on him; and, seeing her heart was so set on him, I was glad I hadn't given him any more encouragement.' I sent my most formidable compliments to the bride that was to be, and we've been on speaking terms ever since, though I don't think Mrs Grimes has any love to spare.

They've got two young ones now, and I dare say she finds a farmer's wife has more work 'an play, while I, thank goodness, am still an independent candidate. There ain't a rag of her wedding finery left, while Alvira Slimmens is just indulging in the contemplation of what will become her best. Which do you think, girls – white muslin, or pearl-coloured silk? Dear me! what a delectable delight it is to the feminine sex to be engaged in deciding upon their bridal tournure! White muslin and a vail, or pearl-coloured silk and a bonnet? What a diploma to be in! Come, girls, say which you think will become *my style* best.

*

Ten o'clock in the morning, and those girls not here yet! This is the last time I'll let that Clara go home with Dora to sleep. I wouldn't have let 'em gone last night, but I expected Mr Wiggleby was waiting for a chance to ask me to name the day; and if he'd wanted to stay and set up late, I didn't want them a-peeping through the keyhole! My plan was a complete failure, for he never come near me. Here I sot, fixed up to kill, till after ten o'clock, my heart vacillating wildly at every sound, and never a knock from nobody but them pestering Peterses, wanting to know if had any peppermint, for the baby had the colic, as if *I* might be expected to keep baby-fixins on hand! They'll be coming over to borrow 'Mother's Relief' next; and now I feel as cross as a bear. I'm tormented to know what kept him away; I never *did* feel so uneasy before, in all my experience. I shouldn't like to let anybody but him know how I have set my affections on that man. I've wanted to marry bad enough, though I've made a pint of pretending not to; but I haven't been *really in love* before, for years and years. The very squeak of his patent-leather boots, as he comes along the sidewalk, sets the blood a-flying into my face, and when he gets to the door, and smiles, and bows, and says, 'Good-morning, Miss Slimmens!' in that irreparable way of his, my sensations are inexpressible; actually, I haven't the strength, sometimes, to offer him a chair. He's my beau-ideal of a beautiful man. If he wasn't worth a cent, but was some nameless adventurer, or belonged to a band of fierce bandanas, or was a political exile with a price set on his head, or an unfortunate patriarch obliged to flee from his ancestral halls, it wouldn't make a bit of difference; there's something in the quirl of his mustache and the bituminous depths of his dark eyes that the soul of a romantic being of the softer sex cannot resist. I'd rather be his wife, and carry on the millinary business for ever, than any of these Pennyville chaps, and roll in luxury, and never be obliged to set a stitch nor look at a fashionable plate.

Oh-h my! what a sigh that was! It come right up out of the pit of my stomach. I should so like to know what kept him away last night. I laid awake two hours, by the clock, thinking how I wasn't more'n twenty or twenty-two, and had my own hair and teeth back again, and was a Mexican heiress, riding on a steed through a mountain pass, with only one servant for a protector, and a band of bandanas should rush out of the cave and seize me, and I'd struggle and pretend to want to get away, but should be overpowered, and my servant tied to a tree, and I shouldn't be able to help myself, but should be carried off in their arms into the interior of the cave, and should open my eyes, after fainting away in a graceful position, to find myself in a splendid chamber full of silver, and gold, and jewels, robbed from travellers, and find the chief of the bandanas kneeling before me, insuring me that if I would accept his heart and hand and marry him, I should come to no harm, and when I lifted my eyes to his face, behold it was Mr Wiggleby, and I was impelled to wed him, whether or no!

I declare it makes me sick, to get up this morning and find this same old shop, and these same old bunnits, and my old sign a-swinging out there in the wind, after such a beautiful revelry. The millinary business was never intended for my destination, I am convinced of that. If Mr Wiggleby should come in here this hour and ask me to elope with him, I'd pack up my duds, draw my money from the bank, and do it. I do wish he'd come to terms, if he's a-going to. I feel that I've no time to spare, and I'm mighty uneasy about losing him; there isn't a girl in the village but would jump at the chance of becoming Mrs Wiggleby. I've told him, point-blank, that I was worth three times what I am, for I knew it would be the only way to keep him, when there was plenty of 'sweet seventeens' a-sighing for him. But I wish he'd *come to terms*! If there's anybody in the world that has had reason to realise that a 'bird in the hand is worth two in the bush,' it's me; and I wish Mr Wiggleby was safe in my hand. I feel an unaccountable sinking of the spirits this morning.

Them girls aren't in sight yet. They won't find me in the best of humour; they'll have to have a better excuse than there's any danger of, if they escape my wrath this time. Half-past ten of a Monday, and they not here to begin work! Such conduct is unprecedental! The nearer they come to being of age, the more liberties they take. If I ever need their service, it's now. There's them eight Leghorns and three Dunstables to be hung in the bleach-barrel, and that bunnit I didn't get done Saturday, on account of going out a-riding with Mr Wiggleby, to be sent home, and them children's flats to be lined and trimmed to-day, and I wanted to set down peaceably to my own sewing. The tape work isn't sewed on to that nightgown yet, and there's no telling how soon it'll be required. If he would happen along to apologise for not coming to keep Sunday night, I shouldn't mind their tardiness so much; but he isn't coming. I've looked up and down till my eyes ache, and that's all the good it's done.

I think that girl Clara has got altogether more vanity and pride than is good for her. What does she do but buy one of my prettiest white bunnits – a velvet one, with a plume – Saturday night, and pay for it out of her own purse. I didn't know she had saved up so much. She's set her cap for somebody, or she wouldn't have been guilty of such extravagance.

I told her plainly I didn't think a velvit bunnit would be very suitable to her condition, and she said if she earned it and could pay for it, she didn't know who had a right to interfere; and then she tried it on and looked in the glass, and asked Dora if it wasn't sweet.

I knew that she was thinking all the time that a pretty bunnit made a certain pretty face look handsomer still; and when somebody knocked and Mr Wiggleby walked in, I could have scratched her eyes out, she turned to him so saucy, with her cheeks all in a glow, and asked him how *he* liked her selection.

She *did* look outrageously handsome just then; and I was on nettles till I'd thought of a way of taking her down by asking her how many week's wages, at two dollars a week, it would take for a vain girl to buy a nine-dollar bunnit, and that I thought it would be very correspondent with a certain coloured merino shawl.

'Leven o'clock! Well, this beats all! I'll put on my bunnit and go after them stay-aways in less than five minutes; and I'll tell Dora's mother if she doesn't keep 'em in better order, she needn't expect *I'll* do any more for 'em. That's Dora now – no, it isn't – yes, it is; Dora Adams coming along alone, as slow as if she was marching to a funeral, and not a sign to be seen of Clara. I wonder what's that she's got in her hand, wrapped up in paper; and how she *dares* to take her time in this manner.

*

So miss, you've got along, have you? Of course, you've got an excellent excuse, something entirely satisfactory, for staying away till this hour, and putting the work back of a Monday morning. Where's Clara? Sick, I suppose, with cutting up of a Sabbath evening. What's that? You needn't stammer so, Dora Adams! You ain't stammering? Well, speak out, then. WHAT?

'Clara was married to Mr Wiggleby at nine o'clock this morning, and hopes you'll forgive her for not finishing out her time, as her husband is willing to make it all right if there's any damages, and she sends her card and a piece of the wedding-cake, with their compliments!'

No. I never will forgive her – you know I never will, Dora Adams! Throw that wedding-cake out in the street – throw it out, I say! – and that card. I'll sue 'em both for damages! I'll sue her for her time, and him for a breach of promise. I'll break 'em up and ruin 'em that I will! the deceitful, ungrateful, sly, tricky – hard-heated – mendacious – outrageous – creatures! Hand me the camphire, quick! I'm swooning-oo-oon-ooning! The cam-phire.

Yes, I'm better now! Stand off! don't go to fussing over me with your pretence of being sorry! You've aided and abetted in this wicked conspiracy! I see it all now! No wonder I was overcome at the ingratitude of that serpent that I've nourished in my bosom, as it were, for the last three years! treated her as if she was my own sister, learnt her how to trim and do up bunnits in the best style, fitted her out to get her own living, and now she's rewarded my care and trouble by going off and getting married without so much as even asking my advice, and she with no mother to advise her, the bold, indelicate thing! to a perfect stranger, too. Flown from the protecting influences of my shop into the arms of a man! gone off with one of the male sex that she hasn't known over six weeks! How does she know but what he's got two or three wives already – but that he's a Brigham Young in disguise? I hope he is. I *hope* and *trust* she'll get come up with for her undecent behaviour.

'You don't know as it's anything so unpardonable for a girl to get married, especially a poor girl, when she has a good chance?' No doubt you'd like to try the experiment yourself. How do you, or she, or anybody, know that Mr Wiggleby *is* a good chance? How do you know but what he's a runaway forger – I see one advertised not a month ago – or a gambler, or a contraband malefactor?

'Your mother wrote and ascertained all about him – that he was a most excellent young man?' Pretty business for a mother to be in! get up matches for other people! If she's upheld Clara Brown in this step to deceive and defraud me, do you go home to her, and tell her I've seen enough of you. Never do you darken my doors again, Dora Adams! I've had enough of pretence-girls bringing disgrace on my shop. There! you needn't flash up in that style! Isn't it a disgrace to have a young girl running off, and eloping with a stranger from the roof that sheltered her and the shop that learned her to bleach and trim, and the woman that took her in when she was a parentless orphan, with neither father nor mother? What's that? 'I *did* take her in more ways than one!' Clear out, I say! go home to your mother, and run away with the first counterfeiter that comes along. I thank Heaven I've kept out of *such* scrapes, if I have had my own way to make in the world! Go along with you! you needn't stop to look for your thimble. I'll send it home on a dray to your ladyship – hire a horse and cart a purpose. Go along, I say, and take in washing for a living, as your mother had to, before you came to me to eat and drink at my expense, and learn the trade of the best milliner in Pennyville. Not a word! I *won't* listen!

She's gone, and I'm 'alone with my grief.' Oh, Alvira, Alvira Slimmens! you built your house upon a sandy foundation, and now it's tumbled down, and buried your heart in its ruins.

Didn't I *say* a bird in the hand was worth two in the bush? as I've proved to my own satisfaction long ago. I'll *never* forgive them! I'll ruin them, if it's in my power! I'll sue him for five thousand dollars, and bring his own wife in to prove his perjury. His *wife*! Oh, Wiggleby! Wiggleby! I allowed myself to lie awake, and dream that the term of endearment would be applied to me. I can't be so mad at you as I want to be. I ain't half so mad at you as I was at Joshua Stebbins; but I feel a good deal worse. I may jest as well give up, and be an old maid, and done with it. I'll never put my hair in papers again; and, if I didn't need 'em to eat with, I believe I'd sell my teeth. Crying? Yes, the tears is literally washing the paint all into streaks on my cheeks; and I stand here before the glass, and see it, and don't care a straw.

I never felt so completely used up before. I'm worse off than the old woman that was 'cutting and contriving all day to get a nightcap out of a sheet.' I've been cutting and contriving for twenty odd years to get a husband, and I hain't got one yet; and the materials is all used up; and this last is the unkindest cut of all.

> 'Oh, ever thus from childhood's hour,
>   I've seen my fondest hopes decay!
> I never loved a tree or flower,
>   But 'twas the first to fade away.
>
> I never nursed a nice young man
>   That from a runaway buggy fell,
> Binding his wounds as a woman can,
>   But left as soon as he got well.'

I'll shet and lock the door! There sha'n't a customer get in this day! I'll lock the door and put down the curtain before the window, and take off my back braid, and take out my teeth, and unlace my corset, and hang up my hoop, and go in my bedroom, and have a good, comfortable cry.

Metta Victoria Victor

> When a girl marries she exchanges the attention of many
> men for the inattention of one.

Helen Rowland

> I do not think you ever know you are happily married until
> you have been unhappily married, first.

Angela Carter

------

from Cranford

We were sitting – Miss Matty and I – much as usual, she in the blue chintz easy-chair, with her back to the light, and her knitting in her hand, I reading aloud the *St. James's Chronicle*. A few minutes more, and we should have

gone to make the little alterations in dress usual before calling-time (twelve
o'clock) in Cranford. I remember the scene and the date well. We had been
talking of the signor's rapid recovery since the warmer weather had set in,
and praising Mr Hoggins's skill, and lamenting his want of refinement and
manner (it seems a curious coincidence that this should have been our
subject, but so it was), when a knock was heard – a caller's knock – three
distinct taps – and we were flying (that is to say, Miss Matty could not walk
very fast, having had a touch of rheumatism) to our rooms, to change cap
and collars, when Miss Pole arrested us by calling out, as she came up the
stairs: 'Don't go – I can't wait – it is not twelve, I know – but never mind your
dress – I must speak to you.' We did our best to look as if it was not we who
had made the hurried movement, the sound of which she had heard; for, of
course, we did not like to have it supposed that we had any old clothes that
it was convenient to wear out in the 'sanctuary of home', as Miss Jenkyns
once prettily called the back parlour, where she was tying up preserves. So
we threw our gentility with double force into our manners, and very genteel
we were for two minutes while Miss Pole recovered breath, and excited our
curiosity strongly by lifting up her hands in amazement, and bringing them
down in silence, as if what she had to say was too big for words, and could
only be expressed by pantomime.

'What do you think, Miss Matty? What *do* you think? Lady Glenmire
is to marry – is to be married, I mean – Lady Glenmire – Mr Hoggins – Mr
Hoggins is going to marry Lady Glenmire!'

'Marry!' said we. 'Marry! Madness!'

'Marry!' said Miss Pole, with the decision that belonged to her
character. 'I said marry! as you do; and I also said: "What a fool my lady is
going to make of herself!" I could have said "Madness!" but I controlled
myself, for it was in a public shop that I heard of it. Where feminine delicacy
is gone to, I don't know! You and I, Miss Matty, would have been ashamed
to have known that our marriage was spoken of in a grocer's shop, in the
hearing of shopmen!'

'But,' said Miss Matty, sighing as one recovering from a blow, 'perhaps
it is not true. Perhaps we are doing her injustice.'

'No,' said Miss Pole. 'I have taken care to ascertain that. I went straight
to Mrs Fitz-Adam, to borrow a cookery-book which I knew she had; and I
introduced my congratulations apropos of the difficulty gentlemen must
have in housekeeping; and Mrs Fitz-Adam bridled up, and said that she
believed it was true, though how and where I could have heard it she did

not know. She said her brother and Lady Glenmire had come to an under-standing at last. "Understanding!" Such a coarse word! But my lady will have to come down to many a want of refinement. I have reason to believe Mr Hoggins sups on bread and cheese and beer every night.'

'Marry!' said Miss Matty once again. 'Well! I never thought of it. Two people that we know going to be married. It's coming very near!'

'So near that my heart stopped beating when I heard of it, while you might have counted twelve,' said Miss Pole.

'One does not know whose turn may come next. Here, in Cranford, poor Lady Glenmire might have thought herself safe,' said Miss Matty, with a gentle pity in her tones.

'Bah!' said Miss Pole, with a toss of her head. 'Don't you remember poor dear Captain Brown's song 'Tibbie and Fowler', and the line:

'Set her on the Tintock tap,
The wind will blaw a man till her.'

'That was because "Tibbie Fowler" was rich, I think.'

'Well! there was a kind of attraction about Lady Glenmire that I, for one, should be ashamed to have.'

I put in my wonder. 'But how can she have fancied Mr Hoggins? I am not surprised that Mr Hoggins has liked her.'

'Oh! I don't know. Mr Hoggins is rich, and very pleasant-looking,' said Miss Matty, 'and very good-tempered and kind-hearted.'

'She has married for an establishment, that's it. I suppose she takes the surgery with it,' said Miss Pole, with a little dry laugh at her own joke. But, like many people who think they have made a severe and sarcastic speech, which yet is clever of its kind, she began to relax in her grimness from the moment when she made this allusion to the surgery; and we turned to speculate on the way in which Mrs Jamieson would receive the news. The person whom she had left in charge of her house to keep off followers from her maids to set up a follower of her own! And that follower a man whom Mrs Jamieson had tabooed as vulgar, and inadmissible to Cranford society, not merely on account of his name, but because of his voice, his complexion, his boots, smelling of the stable, and himself, smelling of drugs. Had he ever been to see Lady Glenmire at Mrs Jamieson's? Chloride of lime would not purify the house in its owner's estimation if he had. Or had their interviews been confined to the occasional meetings in the chamber of the poor sick conjuror, to whom, with all our sense of the *mésalliance*, we could not help allowing that they had both been exceedingly kind? And now it turned out that a servant of Mrs Jamieson's had been ill, and Mr Hoggins had been attending her for some weeks. So the wolf had got into the fold, and now he was carrying off the shepherdess. What would Mrs Jamieson say? We looked into the darkness of futurity as a child gazes after a rocket up in the cloudy sky, full of wondering expectation of the rattle, the discharge, and the brilliant shower of sparks and light. Then we brought ourselves down to earth and the present time by questioning each other (being all equally ignorant, and all equally without the slightest data to build any conclusions upon) as to when IT would take place? Where? How much a year Mr Hoggins had? Whether she would drop her title? And how Martha and the other correct servants in Cranford would ever be brought to announce a married couple as Lady Glenmire and Mr Hoggins? But would they be visited? Would Mrs Jamieson let us? Or must we choose between the Honourable Mrs Jamieson and the degraded Lady Glenmire? We all liked Lady Glenmire the best. She was bright, and kind, and sociable, and agreeable; and Mrs Jamieson was dull, and inert, and pompous, and tiresome. But we had acknowledged the sway of the latter so long, that it seemed like a kind of disloyalty now even to meditate disobedience to the prohibition we anticipated.

Mrs Forrester surprised us in our darned caps and patched collars; and we forgot all about them in our eagerness to see how she would bear the information, which we honourably left to Miss Pole, to impart, although, if we had been inclined to take unfair advantage, we might have rushed in ourselves, for she had a most out-of-place fit of coughing for five minutes after Mrs Forrester entered the room. I shall never forget the imploring expression of her eyes, as she looked at us over her pocket-handkerchief. They said, as plain as words could speak: 'Don't let Nature deprive me of the treasure which is mine, although for a time I can make no use of it.' And we did not.

Mrs Forrester's surprise was equal to ours; and her sense of injury rather greater, because she had to feel for her Order, and saw more fully than we could do how such conduct brought stains on the aristocracy.

When she and Miss Pole left us we endeavoured to subside into calmness; but Miss Matty was really upset by the intelligence she had heard. She reckoned it up, and it was more than fifteen years since she had heard of any of her acquaintance going to be married, with the one exception of Miss Jessie Brown; and, as she said, it gave her quite a shock, and made her feel as if she could not think what would happen next.

I don't know whether it is a fancy of mine, or a real fact, but I have noticed that, just after the announcement of an engagement in any set, the unmarried ladies in that set flutter out in an unusual gaiety and newness of dress, as much as to say, in a tacit and unconscious manner: 'We also are spinsters.' Miss Matty and Miss Pole talked and thought more about bonnets, gowns, caps, and shawls, during the fortnight that succeeded this call, than I had known them do for years before. But it might be the spring weather, for it was a warm and pleasant March; and merinoes and beavers, and woollen materials of all sorts were but ungracious receptacles of the bright sun's glancing rays. It had not been Lady Glenmire's dress that had won Mr Hoggins's heart, for she went about on her errands of kindness more shabby than ever. Although in the hurried glimpses I caught of her at church or else-where she appeared rather to shun meeting any of her friends, her face seemed to have almost something of the flush of youth in it; her lips looked redder and more trembling full than in their old compressed state, and her eyes dwelt on all things with a lingering light, as if she was learning to love Cranford and its belongings. Mr Hoggins looked broad and radiant, and creaked up the middle aisle at church in a brand-new pair of top-boots – an audible, as well as visible, sign of his purposed change of state; for the tradition went, that the boots he had worn till now were the identical pair in which he first set out on his rounds in Cranford twenty-five years ago; only they had been new-pieced, high and low, top and bottom, heel and sole, black leather and brown leather, more times than any one could tell.

None of the ladies in Cranford chose to sanction the marriage by congratulating either of the parties. We wished to ignore the whole affair until our liege lady, Mrs Jamieson, returned. Till she came back to give us our cue, we felt that it would be better to consider the engagement in the same light as the Queen of Spain's legs – facts which certainly existed, but the less said about the better. This restraint upon our tongues – for you see if we did not speak about it to any of the parties concerned, how could we get answers to the questions that we longed to ask? – was beginning to be irksome; and our idea of the dignity of silence was paling before our curiosity, when another direction was given to our thoughts, by an announcement on the part of the principal shopkeeper of Cranford, who ranged the trades from grocer and cheesemonger to man-milliner, as occasion required, that the spring fashions were arrived, and would be exhibited on the following Tuesday at his rooms in High Street.

Elizabeth Gaskell

from The Pursuit of Love

Louisa was married in the spring. Her wedding dress, of tulle frills and sprays of orange blossom, was short to the knee and had a train, as was the hideous fashion then. Jassy got very worked up about it.

'So unsuitable.'

'Why, Jassy?'

'To be buried in, I mean. Women are always buried in their wedding dresses, aren't they? Think of your poor old dead legs sticking out.'

'Oh, Jassy, don't be such a ghoul. I'll wrap them up in my train.'

'Not very nice for the undertakers.'

Louisa refused to have bridesmaids. I think she felt that it would be agreeable, for once in her life, to be more looked at than Linda.

'You can't think how stupid you'll look from behind,' Linda said, 'without any. Still, have it your own way. I'm sure we don't want to be guyed up in blue chiffon, I'm only thinking what would be kinder for you.'

On Louisa's birthday John Fort William, an ardent antiquarian, gave her a replica of King Alfred's jewel. Linda, whose disagreeableness at this time knew no bounds, said that it simply looked like a chicken's mess. 'Same shape, same size, same colour. Not my idea of a jewel.'

'I think it's lovely,' said Aunt Sadie, but Linda's words had left their sting all the same.

Aunt Sadie had a canary then, which sang all day, rivalling even Galli Curci in the pureness and loudness of its trills. Whenever I hear a canary sing so immoderately it recalls that happy visit, the endless flow of wedding presents, unpacking them, arranging them in the ballroom with shrieks of admiration or of horror, the hustle, the bustle, and Uncle Matthew's good temper, which went on, as fine weather sometimes does, day after unbelievable day.

Louisa was to have two houses, one in London, Connaught Square, and one in Scotland. Her dress allowance would be three hundred a year, she would possess a diamond tiara, a pearl necklace, a motor-car of her own and a fur cape. In fact, granted that she could bear John Fort William, her lot was an enviable one. He was terribly dull.

*

The wedding day was fine and balmy, and, when we went in the morning to see how Mrs Wills and Mrs Josh were getting on with the decorations, we found the light little church bunchy with spring flowers. Later, its well-known outlines blurred with a most unaccustomed throng of human beings, it looked quite different. I thought that I personally should have liked better to be married in it when it was so empty and flowery and full of the Holy Ghost.

Neither Linda nor I had ever been to a wedding before, as Aunt Emily, most unfairly we thought at the time, had been married privately in the chapel at Davey's home in the North of England, and we were hardly prepared for the sudden transformation on this day of dear old Louisa, of terribly dull John, into eternal types of Bride and Bridegroom, Heroine and Hero of romance.

From the moment when we left Louisa alone at Alconleigh with Uncle Matthew, to follow us in the Daimler in exactly eleven minutes, the atmosphere became positively dramatic. Louisa, enveloped from head to knee in tulle, sat gingerly on the edge of a chair, while Uncle Matthew, watch in hand, strode up and down the hall. We walked, as we always did, to the church, and arranged ourselves in the family pew at the back of it, from which vantage point we were able to observe with fascination, the unusual appearance of our neighbours, all tricked out in their best. The only person in the whole congregation who looked exactly as usual was Lord Merlin.

Suddenly there was a stir. John and his best man, Lord Stromboli, appearing like two jack-in-the-box from nowhere, stood beside the altar steps. In their morning coats, their hair heavily brilliantined, they looked quite glamorous, but we hardly had time to notice this fact before Mrs Wills struck up 'Here comes the Bride', with all the stops out, and Louisa, her veil over her face, was being dragged up the aisle at double quick time by Uncle Matthew. At this moment I think Linda would gladly have changed places with Louisa, even at the cost – the heavy cost – of being happy for ever after with John Fort William. In what seemed no time at all Louisa was being dragged down the aisle again by John, with her veil back, while Mrs Wills nearly broke the windows, so loud and triumphant was her 'Wedding March'.

Everything had gone like clockwork, and there was only one small incident. Davey slipped out of the family pew almost unobserved, in the middle of 'As pants the hart' (Louisa's favourite hymn) and went straight to London, making one of the wedding cars take him to Merlinford station. That evening he telephoned to say that he had twisted his tonsil, singing, and had thought it better to go immediately to Sir Andrew Macpherson, the nose, throat, and ear man, who was keeping him in bed for a week. The most extraordinary accidents always seemed to overtake poor Davey.

Nancy Mitford

——

Personally, I think that if a woman hasn't met the right man by the time she's twenty-four, she may be lucky.

Deborah Kerr

——

No man is in love when he marries. He may have loved before; I have even heard he has sometimes loved after: but at the time never. There is something in the formalities of the matrimonial preparations that drive away all the little cupidons.

Fanny Burney

——

A man in love is incomplete until he has married. Then he's finished.

Zsa Zsa Gabor

——

[Of Humphrey Bogart:] He cried at all his own weddings – and with reason.

Lauren Bacall

——

I knew nothing about marriage when I went into it. On my wedding night, I had a nightgown with feet. I said that Edgar brought his ex-girlfriend over. She said, 'I've heard all about you' – and presented me with *The Joy of Sex*. I went on, 'I know nothing about sex. All my mother told me was that the man gets on top, the woman gets on the bottom. I bought bunk beds.'

Joan Rivers

Marriage is the grave or tomb of wit.
Margaret Cavendish, Duchess of Newcastle

————

When you see what some girls marry, you realize how they must hate to work for a living.
Helen Rowland

————

There is not one in a hundred of either sex who is not taken in when they marry. Look where I will, I see that it is so; and I feel that it must be so, when I consider that it is, of all transactions, the one in which people expect most from others, and are least honest themselves.
Jane Austen

————

I married beneath me, all women do.
Nancy Astor

————

It should be a very happy marriage – they are both so much in love with *him*.
Irene Thomas

————

It is true that I never should have married, but I didn't want to live without a man. Brought up to respect the conventions, love had to end in marriage. I'm afraid it did.
Bette Davis

————

One doesn't have to get anywhere in a marriage. It's not a
public conveyance.

Iris Murdoch

Never go to bed mad. Stay up and fight.

Phyllis Diller

> For he or she, who drags the marriage chain,
> And finds in spouse occasion to complain,
> Should hide their frailties with a lover's care,
> And let th'ill-judging world conclude 'em fair;
> Better th'offence ne'er reach the offender's ear.
> For they who sin with caution, whilst concealed,
> Grow impudently careless, when revealed.

Susanna Centlivre

----

from Lady Addle Remembers

It seems hopelessly inadequate to devote only two short chapters to Mipsie
when several volumes could be written about her enchanting loveliness, her
talents, and her strange vivid life. It was, above all, Life which she loved –
loved so passionately that it led her into paths which would, possibly, have
been better left untrodden. But 'tout comprendre est tout pardonner', and I hope in
this short space to throw a new and more intimate light on some of the
events in her life which made the world talk so much, and sometimes so
unkindly.

It was in spring of 1902 that I first began to realize that things were
not going right between her and Oxo, chiefly through his fault, I must say.
While he was fighting in South Africa, Mipsie had done the obviously
sensible thing which was to save the vast expense of Brisket Castle by
shutting it up and taking house in Paris instead. He raised no objection at
the time, yet on his return, although Mipsie came home within six months,

which was as soon as she could manage to wind up her affairs in France, he was furious and practically refused to pay her Paris debts. He actually seemed to expect her to have existed there on the same money as she would have lived on at Brisket, which was frankly ridiculous. That was the beginning of the rift. The next quarrel was over the children. There were two, a girl and a boy, whom Mipsie worshipped and made a point of seeing at least twice a week. But she was always adorably vague and one day when Soppy and her family of eight were staying there Mipsie lifted up little Archie Hogshead and said to a caller: 'This is my baby.' It was a very natural mistake to make – they were, after all, first cousins – but Oxo chose to take umbrage and accused her of not knowing which were her own children. Mipsie, with her flashing wit, tried to ease matters by a playful rejoinder: 'Well, how do you know which are yours?' but he was too angry to be soothed. The breach widened.

The end came over a stupid misunderstanding. Mipsie was expected back from Brussels, where she had been on a visit, to act as hostess to a large shooting party at Brisket, but was taken suddenly ill and telegraphed: 'Cannot return. In bed with *migraine*.' Oxo, who was always a very poor French scholar, had never heard of the word, so completely misconstruing the contents of the message rushed frantically to Brussels, where, as bad luck would have it, Mipsie's attack had suddenly subsided and she was trying to revive her strength for the journey by a quiet little dinner with an old friend in the private room of an hotel. Explanations were all in vain. After a distressing scene of violent recriminations on both sides Oxo left for England, and we learnt that they had separated.

Poor darling brave Mipsie! What she must have suffered during the divorce proceedings, losing not only her good name but her children and the famous Brisket pearls as well as having her allowance cut down to a beggarly £3,000 a year, I dread to think. She was always so sensitive and so proud – the pride of a thoroughbred – and hated to fall short of any standard or ideal she had set for herself. That was the reason why she accepted the offer of Fr. 50,000 a year as an allowance from another old friend, the Marquis de Pelouse. It was to enable her to live as Oxo, in the days when he had loved her, would have liked her to. It was amazing loyalty for a woman who had been treated as Mipsie had; yet the world said malicious and bitter things even about that.

She soon married again. She never could bear loneliness and plenty of men were only too willing. Her second husband was Sir Constant Standing, a baronet of good family and a nice fellow, but somewhat weak and easily persuaded and far from clever. He had a comfortable income but quite inadequate to keep up the beautiful villa which they – especially Mipsie – had set their hearts on at Monte Carlo. It would really have been wiser if he had said so straight away instead of struggling on and attempting to recover by gambling, for which he had no aptitude whatever, or even liking. In fact he had never played at all until Mipsie taught him to, as she taught him many other things.

However, they were happy enough for a time and people seeing them together have often said what a wonderful wife she was and how she would never put on even the smallest stake at the tables without asking him for the money first. She tried to do him good in many other ways too, encouraging him to take life more seriously and put his back into some regular occupation and as a result he worked so hard on a system at baccarat that he spent a great deal more money than he should in testing it, and the worry of it produced a bad nervous breakdown, which made life even harder for my poor sister.

But it was not until after his bankruptcy that Mipsie began to realize that Constant was not, somehow, the same man as she thought she had married. I think it all came as rather a shock to her. And then she found out that the vastly rich uncle who had been intending to leave all his money to him had changed his will when Constant had declared his intention of marrying Mipsie and that quite broke her up. The cruelty of the uncle in taking that line just because she had the misfortune to be badly treated by her first husband, and above all the deceit, the base dishonesty of Constant in marrying her without telling her of the changed will – he gave the paltry excuse that he 'Didn't want to worry her and thought the old boy would come round' – were too much for my sister, who was always the soul of honour. She felt she could no longer live with one who had wounded and disappointed her so greatly and in the summer of 1906 she left him. I am told he has gone sadly downhill since that date. He now lives at Cannes and is to be found every day in a not very reputable bar where he will say to the merest stranger: 'Have I ever told you about my wife?' He will then proceed to use such indecent language that even the visitors from Palm Beach cannot stand it.

But to return to my sister. After she had procured her divorce she passed through a time of great loneliness and hardship, struggling to live on the pittance allowed her by Brisket, augmented only by gifts from one or two friends, and without any real background to her life. There were happy times, of course, for she was always incurably gay, but sometimes she longed for security again – someone of solid worth to fall back upon in every necessity. It was, I think, this instinctive craving for safety that prompted her to decide to go to America. She was greatly attracted by what she heard of the satisfactory and solid nature of American home life at that date, and her always vivid imagination was caught by an exquisite diamond-studded vanity-box which she had been shown by a friend and told it was a favour given in a cotillion at Newport, which was picturesquely known as 'the Millionaires' playground'. The idea of such fairy godmother presents being given at a mere ball appealed to the childish, almost elfin element in her nature and she, of course, always adored beauty in any form. I remember how once during a house party at Coots Balder, when we were girls and shared a room, I woke three nights running to discover Mipsie's bed empty, and each time when she returned she told me she had been in the garden listening to the nightingales. I longed to share her joy and begged to go with her one night, but she said the nightingales sang a different song for her, which I thought a charming whimsy. She was, indeed, a child of nature.

Had she gone to America that autumn her life might have been very different, for with her birth and beauty and brilliance she would soon, I am convinced, have been queen of the Four Hundred and perhaps married happily, though, of course, an American husband would have been rather a shock to the family! But once again it was her very womanhood – those qualities of sweet unselfishness and generosity that made her what she was – which directed her destiny otherwise.

She was actually on the eve of departure. I had lent her the money for her ticket as some of her investments had been giving her trouble, when at a soirée given by the Russian Ambassador in London a very old man was introduced to her as Prince Fédor Ubetzkoi, and with her invariable charming courtesy to the aged – who as she rightly says are often worth so much more than the younger generation – she sat and conversed with him in an alcove for a while. As they talked she became more and more impressed by his courtly manner and distinguished bearing and found her eyes riveted by the beauty of his finely-modelled hands, their delicate tapering fingers set off to perfection by the simple severity of two uncut emeralds the size of pigeons' eggs. Gently she drew him out about himself in the winning way she knew so much better than anyone, and when she learnt that he owned the whole of Goulashia with its vast platinum mines, that he was seventy-nine and a widower with one of the most beautiful palaces in Europe full of world-famous treasures, her whole woman's heart went out to the poor old man; his loneliness amidst such great possessions, his helplessness, his very age appealed to something deep within her. She could not bear to think of him growing nearer the grave each day, perhaps without even the consolation of knowing that after his death his treasures would give joy to someone dear to him. With characteristic impulsiveness she threw all her previous plans to the winds. She saw her duty, her destiny, clearly before her. Within a week they were married and the Prince and Princess Fédor Ubetzkoi had left for the palace at Ekaterinbog.

Mary Dunn

———

[When asked how many husbands she had had:] You mean apart from my own?

Zsa Zsa Gabor

———

JOAN RIVERS   Besides your husband, who's the best man you've ever been in bed with?
JOAN COLLINS   Your husband.
JOAN RIVERS   Funny, he didn't say the same about you.

———

The wages of sin is alimony

Carolyn Wells

———

'Always be civil to the girls, you never know who they may marry' is an aphorism which has saved many an English spinster from being treated like an Indian widow.

Nancy Mitford

———

from Excellent Women

I dressed rather carefully in preparation for my lunch with Mrs Gray and my appearance called forth comments from Mrs Bonner, who assumed that I was going to have lunch with 'that good-looking man you spoke to after one of the Lent services'. She was disappointed when I was honest enough to admit that my companion was to be nobody more exciting than another woman.

'I did hope it was that young man,' she said. 'I took a liking to him – what I saw, that is.'

'Oh, he's not at all the kind of person I like,' I said quickly. 'And he doesn't like me either, which does make a difference, you know.'

Mrs Bonner nodded mysteriously over her card-index. She was a great reader of fiction and I could imagine what she was thinking.

I was punctual at the restaurant and I had been waiting nearly ten minutes before Mrs Gray arrived.

'I'm so sorry,' she smiled, and I heard myself murmuring politely that I had arrived too early, as if it were really my fault that she was late.

'Where do you usually have lunch?' she asked. 'Or perhaps you go home to lunch as you only work in the mornings?'

'Yes, I do sometimes – otherwise I go to Lyons or somewhere like that.'

'Oh, dear, Lyons – I don't think I could! *Far* too many people.' She shuddered and began looking at the menu. 'I think we should like a drink, don't you? Shall we have some sherry?'

We drank our sherry and made rather stilted conversation about parish matters. When the food came Mrs Gray ate very little, pushing it round her plate with her fork and then leaving it, which made me feel brutish, for I was hungry and had eaten everything.

'I'm like the young ladies in *Crome Yellow*,' she said, 'although it isn't so easy nowadays to go home and eat an enormous meal secretly. What was it they had? A huge ham, I know, but I don't remember the other things.'

I did not really know what she was talking about and could only ask if she would like to order something else.

'Oh, no, I'm afraid I have a very small appetite naturally. And then things haven't been too easy, you know.' She looked at me with a penetrating gaze that seemed to invite confidences.

It made me feel stiff and awkward as if I wanted to withdraw into my shell. But I felt that I had to say something, though I could produce nothing better than 'No, I suppose they haven't.'

At that moment the waiter came with some fruit salad.

'I don't suppose you have had an altogether easy life, either,' Mrs Gray continued.

'Oh, well,' I found myself saying in a brisk robust tone, 'who has, if it comes to that?' It began to seem a little absurd, two women in their early thirties, eating a good meal on a fine summer day and discussing the easiness or otherwise of their lives.

'I haven't been married, so perhaps that's one source of happiness or unhappiness removed straight away.'

Mrs Gray smiled. 'Ah, yes, it isn't always an unmixed blessing.'

'One sees so many broken marriages,' I began and then had to be honest with myself and add up the number of which I had a personal knowledge. I could not think of a single one, unless I counted the Napiers' rather unstable arrangement, and I hoped that Mrs Gray would not take me up on the point.

'Yes, I suppose you would see a good deal of that sort of thing in your work,' she agreed.

'In my work?' I asked, puzzled. 'But I work for the Care of Aged Gentlewomen.'

'Oh,' she smiled, 'I had an idea it was fallen women or something like that, though I suppose even a gentlewoman can fall. But now I come to think of it, Julian did tell me where you worked.'

She said the name casually but it was obvious that she had been waiting to bring it into the conversation. I imagined them talking about me and wondered what they had said.

'Julian has asked me to marry him,' she went on quickly. 'I wanted you to be the first to know.'

'Oh, but I think I *did* know, I mean I guessed,' I said rather quickly and brightly. 'I'm so glad.'

'You're glad? Oh, what a relief!' She laughed and lit another cigarette.

'Well, it seems a very good thing for both of you and I wish you every happiness,' I mumbled, not feeling capable of explaining any further a gladness I did not really feel.

'That really is sweet of you. I was so afraid . . . oh, but I know you're not that kind of person.'

'What were you afraid of?' I asked.

'Oh, that you'd disapprove . . . '

'A clergyman's widow?' I smiled. 'How could I possibly disapprove?'

She smiled too. It seemed wrong that we should be smiling about her being a clergyman's widow.

'You and Julian will be admirably suited to each other,' I said more seriously.

'I think you're marvellous,' she said. 'And you really don't mind?'

'Mind?' I said, laughing, but then I stopped laughing because I suddenly realized what it was that she was trying to say. She was trying to tell me how glad and relieved she was that I didn't mind too much when I must surely have wanted to marry Julian myself.

'Oh, no, of course I don't mind,' I said. 'We have always been good friends, but there's never been any question of anything else, anything more than friendship.'

'Julian thought perhaps. . . .' She hesitated.

'He thought that I loved him?' I exclaimed, in rather too loud a voice, I am afraid, for I noticed a woman at a near-by table making an amused comment to her companion. 'But what made him think that?'

'Oh, well, I suppose there would have been nothing extraordinary in it if you had,' said Mrs Gray slightly on the defensive.

'You mean it would be quite the usual thing? Yes, I suppose it might very well have been.'

How stupid I had been not to see it like that, for it had not occurred to me that anyone might think I was in love with Julian. But there it was, the old obvious situation, presentable unmarried clergyman and woman interested in good works – had everyone seen it like that? Julian himself? Winifred? Sister Blatt? Mr Mallett and Mr Conybeare? Of course, I thought, trying to be completely honest with myself, there had been a time when I first met him when I had wondered whether there might ever be anything between us, but I had so soon realized that it was impossible that I had never given it another thought.

'Oh, I hope you weren't worrying about that,' I said in a hearty sort of way to cover my confusion.

'No, not *worrying* exactly. I'm afraid people in love are rather selfish and perhaps don't consider other people's feelings as much as they ought.'

'Certainly not when they fall in love with other people's husbands and wives,' I said.

Mrs Gray laughed. 'There you are,' she said, 'one *does* see these broken marriages.'

'Winifred will be delighted at your news,' I said.

'Oh, yes, dear Winifred,' Mrs Gray sighed. 'There's a bit of a problem there.'

'A problem? How?'

'Well, where is she going to live when we're married, poor soul?'

'Oh, I'm sure Julian would want her to stay at the vicarage. They are devoted to each other. She could have the flat you've been living in,' I suggested, becoming practical.

'Poor dear, she *is* rather irritating, though. But I know you're very fond of her.'

Fond of her? Yes, of course I was, but I could see only too well that she might be a very irritating person to live with.

'That's why I was wondering,' Mrs Gray began and then hesitated. 'No, perhaps I couldn't ask it, really.'

'You mean you think that she might live with me?' I blurted out.

'Yes, don't you think it would be a splendid idea? You get on well, and she's so fond of you. Besides, you haven't any other ties, have you?'

The room seemed suddenly very hot and I saw Mrs Gray's face rather too close to mine, her eyes wide open and penetrating, her teeth small and pointed, her skin a smooth apricot colour.

'I don't think I could do that,' I said, gathering up my bag and gloves, for I felt trapped and longed to get away.

'Oh, do think about it, Mildred. There's a dear. I know you are one.'

'No, I'm not,' I said ungraciously, for nobody really likes to be called a dear. There is something so very faint and dull about it.

The waiter was hovering near us with a bill, which Mrs Gray picked up quickly from the table. I fumbled in my purse and handed her some silver, but she closed my hand firmly on it and I was forced to put it back.

'The very least I can do is to pay for your lunch,' she said.

'Does Julian know this? About Winifred, I mean?' I asked.

'Heavens, no. I think it's much better to keep men in the dark about one's plans, don't you?'

'Yes, I suppose it is,' I said uncertainly, feeling myself at a disadvantage in never having been in the position to keep a man in the dark about anything.

'I'm sure you and Winifred would get on *frightfully* well together,' said Mrs Gray persuasively.

'She could live with Father Greatorex,' I suggested frivolously.

'Poor dears, I can just imagine them together. I wonder if there *could* be anything in that, or would it be quite impossible? What do women *do* if they don't marry,' she mused, as if she had no idea what it could be, having been married once herself and being about to marry again.

'Oh, they stay at home with an aged parent and do the flowers, or they used to, but now perhaps they have jobs and careers and live in bed-sitting-rooms or hostels. And then of course they become indispensable in the parish and some of them even go into religious communities.'

'Oh, dear, you make it sound rather dreary.' Mrs Gray looked almost guilty. 'I suppose you have to get back to your work now?' she suggested, as if there were some connection, as indeed there may well have been, between me and dreariness.

'Yes,' I lied, 'I have to go back there for a while. Thank you very much for my lunch.'

'Oh, it was a pleasure. We must do it again some time.'

I walked away in the direction of my office and, when I had seen Mrs Gray get on to a bus, went into a shop. I had a feeling that I must escape and longed to be lost in a crowd of busy women shopping, which was why I followed blindly the crowd that surged in through the swinging doors of a large store. Some were hurrying, making for this or that department or counter, but others like myself seemed bewildered and aimless, pushed and buffeted as we stood not knowing which way to turn.

I strolled through a grove of dress materials and found myself at a counter piled high with jars of face-cream and lipsticks. I suddenly remem-bered Allegra Gray's smooth apricot-coloured face rather too close to mine and wondered what it was that she used to get such a striking effect. There was a mirror on the counter and I caught sight of my own face, colourless and worried-looking, the eyes large and rather frightened, the lips too pale. I did not feel that I could ever acquire a smooth apricot complexion but I could at least buy a new lipstick, I thought, consulting the shade-card. The colours had such peculiar names but at last I chose one that seemed right and began to turn over a pile of lipsticks in a bowl in an effort to find it. But the colour I had chosen was either very elusive or not there at all, and the girl behind the counter, who had been watching my scrabblings in a disinterested way, said at last, 'What shade was it you wanted, dear?'

I was a little annoyed at being called 'dear', though it was perhaps more friendly than 'madam', suggesting as it did that I lacked the years and poise to merit the more dignified title.

'It's called Hawaiian Fire,' I mumbled, feeling rather foolish, for it had not occurred to me that I should have to say it out loud.

'Oh, Hawaiian Fire. It's rather an orange red, dear,' she said doubtfully, scrutinizing my face. 'I shouldn't have thought it was quite your colour. Still, I think I've got one here.' She took a box from behind the counter and began to look in it.

'Oh, it doesn't matter really,' I said quickly. 'Perhaps another colour would be better. What would you recommend?'

'Well, dear, I don't know, really.' She looked at me blankly as if no shade could really do anything for me. 'Jungle Red is very popular – or Sea Coral, that's a pretty shade, quite pale, you know.'

'Thank you, but I think I will have Hawaiian Fire,' I said obstinately, savouring the ludicrous words and the full depths of my shame.

I hurried away and found myself on an escalator. Hawaiian Fire, indeed! Nothing more unsuitable could possibly be imagined. I began to smile and only just stopped myself from laughing out loud by suddenly remembering Mrs Gray and the engagement and the worry about poor Winifred. This made me proceed very soberly, floor by floor, stepping on and off the escalators until I reached the top floor where the Ladies' Room was.

Inside it was a sobering sight indeed and one to put us all in mind of the futility of material things and of our own mortality. *All flesh is but as grass* . . . I thought, watching the women working at their faces with savage concentration, opening their mouths wide, biting and licking their lips, stabbing at their noses and chins with powder-puffs. Some, who had abandoned the struggle to keep up, sat in chairs, their bodies slumped down, their hands resting on their parcels. One woman lay on a couch, her hat and shoes off, her eyes closed. I tiptoed past her with my penny in my hand.

Later I went into the restaurant to have tea, where the women, with an occasional man looking strangely out of place, seemed braced up, their faces newly done, their spirits revived by tea. Many had the satisfaction of having done a good day's shopping and would have something to gloat over when they got home. I had only my Hawaiian Fire and something not very interesting for supper.

Barbara Pym

Happy am I who out of danger sit,
Can see and pity them who wade thro it;
Need take no thought my treasure to dispose,
What I ne'er had I cannot fear to lose.

Mary Astell

---

from The Holiday

I like to see how the married ladies get along, and I sit and listen and watch, and I see how much they think about their husbands, even if they hate 'em like hell there is this thought, this attention.

How can you keep it up, Maria? I ask the women friends, I think you are absolutely marvellous to keep on thinking about them and listening to them and having the children and keeping the house going on turning round the men. I have never had such a thing heigh-ho.

And they are at first immensely pleased about this that I have been saying, but then they begin to wish not to stress how martyr-like wonderful it is, and they begin to say how much one is missing if one does not have it; so I have had trouble with my married women friends, and with those who are living free-like and unmarried with their darling chosen one, I have had trouble for two reasons, because sometimes I like the chosen-one too much, but mostly and the most trouble, because I do not like him enough, and because I think it is so wonderful of the women to be so unselfish and so kind. But I can see that they have to do it, if they are going to have a darling husband and a darling home of their own and darling children, they have to do it, there is no other way, and if you do not then you will live lonely and grow up to old solitude. Amen.

Stevie Smith

BITCHING AND

WISECRACKING

It's not true that life is one damn thing after another – it's one damn thing over and over.

Edna St Vincent Millay

___

Life is something to do when you can't get to sleep.

Fran Lebowitz

___

I learned that one can never go back, that one should not ever try to go back, that the essence of life is going forward. Life is really a One Way Street.

Agatha Christie

___

Reality is just a crutch for people who can't cope with drugs.

Lily Tomlin

Cocaine habit-forming? Of course not. I ought to know.
I've been using it for years.

Tallulah Bankhead

———

There is no such think as inner peace. There is only
nervousness or death. Any attempt to prove otherwise
constitutes unacceptable behaviour.

Fran Lebowitz

———

Success is counted sweetest
By those who ne'er succeed.
To comprehend a nectar
Requires sorest need.

Emily Dickinson

———

It's a delightful thing to think of perfection, but it's vastly
more amusing to talk of errors and absurdities.

Fanny Burney

———

Spreading the News

SCENE   *The outskirts of a Fair. An Apple Stall.* MRS TARPEY *sitting at it.* MAGISTRATE
and POLICEMAN *enter.*

MAGISTRATE   So that is the Fair Green. Cattle and sheep and mud. No
system. What a repulsive sight!

POLICEMAN   That is so, indeed.

MAGISTRATE   I suppose there is a good deal of disorder in this place?

POLICEMAN   There is.

MAGISTRATE   Common assault?

POLICEMAN   It's common enough.

MAGISTRATE	Agrarian crime, no doubt?
POLICEMAN	That is so.
MAGISTRATE	Boycotting? Maiming of cattle? Firing into houses?
POLICEMAN	There was one time, and there might be again.
MAGISTRATE	That is bad. Does it go any farther than that?
POLICEMAN	Far enough, indeed.
MAGISTRATE	Homicide, then! This district has been shamefully neglected! I will change all that. When I was in the Andaman Islands, my system never failed. Yes, yes, I will change all that. What has that woman on her stall?
POLICEMAN	Apples mostly – and sweets.
MAGISTRATE	Just see if there are any unlicensed goods underneath – spirits or the like. We had evasions of the salt tax in the Andaman Islands.
POLICEMAN	(*sniffing cautiously and upsetting a heap of apples*) I see no spirits here – or salt.
MAGISTRATE	(*to MRS TARPEY*) Do you know this town well, my good woman?
MRS TARPEY	(*holding out some apples*) A penny the half-dozen, your honour.
POLICEMAN	(*shouting*) The gentleman is asking do you know the town! He's the new magistrate!
MRS TARPEY	(*rising and ducking*) Do I know the town? I do, to be sure.
MAGISTRATE	(*shouting*) What is its chief business?
MRS TARPEY	Business, is it? What business would the people here have but to be minding one another's business?
MAGISTRATE	I mean what trade have they?
MRS TARPEY	Not a trade. No trade at all but to be talking.
MAGISTRATE	I shall learn nothing here.

(*JAMES RYAN comes in, pipe in mouth. Seeing MAGISTRATE he retreats quickly, taking pipe from mouth.*)

MAGISTRATE	The smoke from that man's pipe had a greenish look; he may be growing unlicensed tobacco at home. I wish I had brought my telescope to this district. Come to the post-office, I will telegraph for it. I found it very useful in the Andaman Islands.

(*MAGISTRATE and POLICEMAN go out left.*)

MRS TARPEY	Bad luck to Jo Muldoon, knocking my apples this way and that way. (*Begins arranging them*). Showing off he was to the new magistrate.

(*Enter BARTLEY FALLON and MRS FALLON.*)

BARTLEY   Indeed it's a poor country and a scarce country to be living in. But I'm thinking if I went to America it's long ago the day I'd be dead!

MRS FALLON   So you might, indeed.

(*She puts her basket on a barrel and begins putting parcels in it, taking them from under her cloak.*)

BARTLEY   And it's a great expense for a poor man to be buried in America.

MRS FALLON   Never fear, Bartley Fallon, but I'll give you a good burying the day you'll die.

BARTLEY   Maybe it's yourself will be buried in the graveyard of Cloonmara before me, Mary Fallon, and I myself that will be dying unbeknownst some night, and no one a-near me. And the cat itself may be gone straying through the country, and the mice squealing over the quilt.

MRS FALLON   Leave off talking of dying. It might be twenty years you'll be living yet.

BARTLEY   (*with a deep sigh*) I'm thinking if I'll be living at the end of twenty years, it's a very old man I'll be then!

MRS TARPEY   (*turns and sees them*) Good morrow, Bartley Fallon; good morrow, Mrs Fallon. Well, Bartley, you'll find no cause for complaining to-day; they are all saying it was a good fair.

BARTLEY   (*raising his voice*) It was not a good fair, Mrs Tarpey. It was a scattered sort of a fair. If we didn't expect more, we got less. That's the way with me always; whatever I have to sell goes down and whatever I have to buy goes up. If there's ever any misfortune coming to this world, it's on myself it pitches, like a flock of crows on seed potatoes.

MRS FALLON   Leave off talking of misfortunes, and listen to Jack Smith that is coming the way, and he singing.

(*Voice of JACK SMITH heard singing:*)

I thought, my first love,
    There'd be but one house between you and me,
And I thought I would find
    Yourself coaxing my child on your knee.
Over the tide

> I would leap with the leap of a swan,
> Till I came to the side
>   Of the wife of the Red-haired man!

(*JACK SMITH comes in; he is a red-haired man, and is carrying a hayfork.*)

MRS TARPEY   That should be a good song if I had my hearing.

MRS FALLON   (*shouting*) It's 'The Red-haired Man's Wife'.

MRS TARPEY   I know it well. That's the song that has a skin on it!

(*She turns her back to them and goes on arranging her apples.*)

MRS FALLON   Where's herself, Jack Smith?

JACK SMITH   She was delayed with her washing; bleaching the clothes on the hedge she is, and she daren't leave them, with all the tinkers that do be passing to the fair. It isn't to the fair I came myself, but up to the Five Acre Meadow I'm going, where I have a contract for the hay. We'll get a share of it into tramps to-day.

(*He lays down hayfork and lights his pipe.*)

BARTLEY   You will not get it into tramps to-day. The rain will be down on it by evening, and on myself too. It's seldom I ever started on a journey but the rain would come down on me before I'd find any place of shelter.

JACK SMITH   If it didn't itself, Bartley, it is my belief you would carry a leaky pail on your head in place of a hat, the way you'd not be without some cause of complaining.

(*A voice heard, 'Go on, now, go on out o' that. Go on I say.'*)

JACK SMITH   Look at that young mare of Pat Ryan's that is backing into Shaughnessy's bullocks with the dint of the crowd! Don't be daunted, Pat, I'll give you a hand with her.

(*He goes out, leaving his hayfork.*)

MRS FALLON   It's time for ourselves to be going home. I have all I bought put in the basket. Look at there, Jack Smith's hayfork he left after him! He'll be wanting it. (*Calls.*) Jack Smith! Jack Smith! – He's gone through the crowd – hurry after him, Bartley, he'll be wanting it.

BARTLEY   I'll do that. This is no safe place to be leaving it. (*He takes up fork awkwardly and upsets the basket.*) Look at that now! If

there is any basket in the fair upset, it must be our own
basket!

(*He goes out to right.*)

MRS FALLON   Get out of that! It is your own fault, it is. Talk of misfor-
                tunes and misfortunes will come. Glory be! Look at my
                new egg-cups rolling in every part – and my two pound of
                sugar with the paper broke –

MRS TARPEY   (*turning from stall*) God help us, Mrs Fallon, what happened
                to your basket?

MRS FALLON   It's himself that knocked it down, bad manners to him.
                (*Putting things up.*) My grand sugar that's destroyed, and he'll
                not drink his tea without it. I had best go back to the shop
                for more, much good may it do him!

(*Enter TIM CASEY.*)

TIM CASEY   Where is Bartley Fallon, Mrs Fallon? I want a word with
                him before he'll leave the fair. I was afraid he might have
                gone home by this, for he's a temperate man.

MRS FALLON   I wish he did go home! It'd be best for me if he went home
                straight from the fair green, or if he never came with me at
                all. Where is he, is it? He's gone up the road (*jerks elbow*)
                following Jack Smith with a hayfork.

(*She goes out to left.*)

TIM CASEY   Following Jack Smith with a hayfork! Did ever any one
                hear the like of that. (*Shouts.*) Did you hear that news,
                Mrs Tarpey?

MRS TARPEY   I heard no news at all.

TIM CASEY   Some dispute I suppose it was that rose between Jack
                Smith and Bartley Fallon, and it seems Jack made off, and
                Bartley is following him with a hayfork!

MRS TARPEY   Is he now? Well, that was quick work! It's not ten minutes
                since the two of them were here, Bartley going home and
                Jack going to the Five Acre Meadow; and I had my apples
                to settle up, that Jo Muldoon of the police had scattered,
                and when I looked round again Jack Smith was gone, and
                Bartley Fallon was gone, and Mrs Fallon's basket upset, and
                all in it strewed upon the ground – the tea here – the two
                pound of sugar there – the egg-cups there – Look, now,

what a great hardship the deafness puts upon me, that I didn't hear the commencement of the fight! Wait till I tell James Ryan that I see below; he is a neighbour of Bartley's, it would be a pity if he wouldn't hear the news!

(*She goes out. Enter SHAWN EARLY and MRS TULLY.*)

TIM CASEY   Listen, Shawn Early! Listen, Mrs Tully, to the news! Jack Smith and Bartley Fallon had a falling out, and Jack knocked Mrs Fallon's basket into the road, and Bartley made an attack on him with a hayfork, and away with Jack, and Bartley after him. Look at the sugar here yet on the road!

SHAWN EARLY   Do you tell me so? Well, that's a queer thing, and Bartley Fallon so quiet a man!

MRS TULLY   I wouldn't wonder at all. I would never think well of a man that would have that sort of a mouldering look. It's likely he has overtaken Jack by this.

(*Enter JAMES RYAN and MRS TARPEY.*)

JAMES RYAN   That is great news Mrs Tarpey was telling me! I suppose that's what brought the police and the magistrate up this way. I was wondering to see them in it a while ago.

SHAWN EARLY   The police after them? Bartley Fallon must have injured Jack so. They wouldn't meddle in a fight that was only for show!

MRS TULLY   Why wouldn't he injure him? There was many a man killed with no more of a weapon than a hayfork.

JAMES RYAN   Wait till I run north as far as Kelly's bar to spread the news! (*He goes out.*)

TIM CASEY   I'll go tell Jack Smith's first cousin that is standing there south of the church after selling his lambs. (*Goes out.*)

MRS TULLY   I'll go telling a few of the neighbours I see beyond to the west. (*Goes out.*)

SHAWN EARLY   I'll give word of it beyond at the east of the green.

(*Is going out when MRS TARPEY seizes hold of him.*)

MRS TARPEY   Stop a minute, Shawn Early, and tell me did you see red Jack Smith's wife, Kitty Keary, in any place?

SHAWN EARLY   I did. At her own house she was, drying clothes on the hedge as I passed.

MRS TARPEY	What did you say she was doing?
SHAWN EARLY	(*breaking away*) Laying out a sheet on the hedge. (*He goes.*)
MRS TARPEY	Laying out a sheet for the dead! The Lord have mercy on us! Jack Smith dead, and his wife laying out a sheet for his burying! (*Calls out.*) Why didn't you tell me that before, Shawn Early? Isn't the deafness the great hardship? Half the world might be dead without me knowing of it or getting word of it at all! (*She sits down and rocks herself.*) O my poor Jack Smith! To be going to his work so nice and so hearty, and to be left stretched on the ground in the full light of the day!

(*Enter TIM CASEY.*)

TIM CASEY	What is it, Mrs Tarpey? What happened since?
MRS TARPEY	O my poor Jack Smith!
TIM CASEY	Did Bartley overtake him?
MRS TARPEY	O the poor man!
TIM CASEY	Is it killed he is?
MRS TARPEY	Stretched in the Five Acre Meadow!
TIM CASEY	The Lord have mercy on us! Is that a fact?
MRS TARPEY	Without the rites of the Church or a ha'porth!
TIM CASEY	Who was telling you?
MRS TARPEY	And the wife laying out a sheet for his corpse. (*Sits up and wipes her eyes.*) I suppose they'll wake him the same as another?

(*Enter MRS TULLY, SHAWN EARLY, and JAMES RYAN.*)

MRS TULLY	There is great talk about this work in every quarter of the fair.
MRS TARPEY	Ochone! cold and dead. And myself maybe the last he was speaking to!
JAMES RYAN	The Lord save us! Is it dead he is?
TIM CASEY	Dead surely, and the wife getting provision for the wake.
SHAWN EARLY	Well, now, hadn't Bartley Fallon great venom in him?
MRS TULLY	You may be sure he had some cause. Why would he have made an end of him if he had not? (*To MRS TARPEY, raising her voice.*) What was it rose the dispute at all, Mrs Tarpey?
MRS TARPEY	Not a one of me knows. The last I saw of them, Jack Smith was standing there, and Bartley Fallon was standing there,

quiet and easy, and he listening to 'The Red-haired Man's Wife'.

MRS TULLY   Do you hear that, Tim Casey? Do you hear that, Shawn Early and James Ryan? Bartley Fallon was here this morning listening to red Jack Smith's wife, Kitty Keary that was! Listening to her and whispering with her! It was she started the fight so!

SHAWN EARLY   She must have followed him from her own house. It is likely some person roused him.

TIM CASEY   I never knew, before, Bartley Fallon was great with Jack Smith's wife.

MRS TULLY   How would you know it? Sure it's not in the streets they would be calling it. If Mrs Fallon didn't know of it, and if I that have the next house to them didn't know of it, and if Jack Smith himself didn't know of it, it is not likely you would know of it, Tim Casey.

SHAWN EARLY   Let Bartley Fallon take charge of her, and let him provide for her. It is little pity she will get from any person in this parish.

TIM CASEY   How can he take charge of her? Sure he has a wife of his own. Sure you don't think he'd turn souper and marry her in a Protestant church?

JAMES RYAN   It would be easy for him to marry her if he brought her to America.

SHAWN EARLY   With or without Kitty Keary, believe me it is for America he's making at this minute. I saw the new magistrate and Jo Muldoon of the police going into the post-office as I came up – there was hurry on them – you may be sure it was to telegraph they went, the way he'll be stopped in the docks at Queenstown!

MRS TULLY   It's likely Kitty Keary is gone with him, and not minding a sheet or a wake at all. The poor man, to be deserted by his own wife, and the breath hardly gone out yet from his body that is lying bloody in the field!

(*Enter MRS FALLON.*)

MRS FALLON   What is it the whole of the town is talking about? And what is it you yourselves are talking about? Is it about my man Bartley Fallon you are talking? Is it lies about him you

	are telling, saying that he went killing Jack Smith? My grief that ever he came into this place at all!
JAMES RYAN	Be easy now, Mrs Fallon. Sure there is no one at all in the whole fair but is sorry for you!
MRS FALLON	Sorry for me, is it? Why would any one be sorry for me? Let you be sorry for yourselves, and that there may be shame on you for ever and at the day of judgment, for the words you are saying and the lies you are telling to take away the character of my poor man, and to take the good name off of him, and to drive him to destruction! That is what you are doing!
SHAWN EARLY	Take comfort now, Mrs Fallon. The police are not so smart as they think. Sure he might give them the slip yet, the same as Lynchehaun.
MRS TULLY	If they do get him, and if they do put a rope around his neck, there is no one can say he does not deserve it!
MRS FALLON	Is that what you are saying, Bridget Tully, and is that what you think? I tell you it's too much talk you have, making yourself out to be such a great one, and to be running down every respectable person! A rope, is it? It isn't much of a rope was needed to tie up your own furniture the day you came into Martin Tully's house, and you never bringing as much as a blanket, or a penny, or a suit of clothes with you and I myself bringing seventy pounds and two feather beds. And now you are stiffer than a woman would have a hundred pounds! It is too much talk the whole of you have. A rope is it? I tell you the whole of this town is full of liars and schemers that would hang you up for half a glass of whiskey. (*Turning to go.*) People they are you wouldn't believe as much as daylight from without you'd get up to have a look at it yourself. Killing Jack Smith indeed! Where are you at all, Bartley, till I bring you out of this? My nice quiet little man! My decent comrade! He that is as kind and as harmless as an innocent beast of the field! He'll be doing no harm at all if he'll shed the blood of some of you after this day's work! That much would be no harm at all. (*Calls out*) Bartley! Bartley Fallon! Where are you? (*Going out.*) Did any one see Bartley Fallon?

(*All turn to look after her.*)

JAMES RYAN   It is hard for her to believe any such a thing, God help her!

(*Enter BARTLEY FALLON from right, carrying hayfork.*)

BARTLEY   It is what I often said to myself, if there is ever any misfortune coming to this world it is on myself it is sure to come!

(*All turn round and face him.*)

BARTLEY   To be going about with this fork and to find no one to take it, and no place to leave it down, and I wanting to be gone out of this – Is that you, Shawn Early? (*Holds out fork.*) It's well I met you. You have no call to be leaving the fair for a while the way I have, and how can I go till I'm rid of this fork? Will you take it and keep it until such time as Jack Smith –

SHAWN EARLY   (*backing*) I will not take it, Bartley Fallon, I'm very thankful to you!

BARTLEY   (*turning to apple stall*) Look at it now, Mrs Tarpey, it was here I got it; let me thrust it in under the stall. It will lie there safe enough, and no one will take notice of it until such time as Jack Smith –

MRS TARPEY   Take your fork out of that! Is it to put trouble on me and to destroy me you want? Putting it there for the police to be rooting it out maybe. (*Thrusts him back.*)

BARTLEY   That is a very unneighbourly thing for you to do, Mrs Tarpey. Hadn't I enough care on me with that fork before this, running up and down with it like the swinging of a clock, and afeard to lay it down in any place! I wish I never touched it or meddled with it at all!

JAMES RYAN   It is a pity, indeed, you ever did.

BARTLEY   Will you yourself take it, James Ryan? You were always a neighbourly man.

JAMES RYAN   (*backing*) There is many a thing I would do for you, Bartley Fallon, but I won't do that!

SHAWN EARLY   I tell you there is no man will give you any help or any encouragement for this day's work. If it was something agrarian now –

| BARTLEY | If no one at all will take it, maybe it's best to give it up to the police. |
| TIM CASEY | There'd be a welcome for it with them surely! |

(*Laughter.*)

MRS TULLY	And it is to the police Kitty Keary herself will be brought.
MRS TARPEY	(*rocking to and fro*) I wonder now who will take the expense of the wake for poor Jack Smith?
BARTLEY	The wake for Jack Smith!
TIM CASEY	Why wouldn't he get a wake as well as another? Would you begrudge him that much?
BARTLEY	Red Jack Smith dead! Who was telling you?
SHAWN EARLY	The whole town knows of it by this.
BARTLEY	Do they say what way did he die?
JAMES RYAN	You don't know that yourself, I suppose, Bartley Fallon? You don't know he was followed and that he was laid dead with the stab of a hayfork?
BARTLEY	The stab of a hayfork!
SHAWN EARLY	You don't know, I suppose, that the body was found in the Five Acre Meadow?
BARTLEY	The Five Acre Meadow!
TIM CASEY	It is likely you don't know that the police are after the man that did it?
BARTLEY	The man that did it!
MRS TULLY	You don't know, maybe, that he was made away with for the sake of Kitty Keary, his wife?
BARTLEY	Kitty Keary, his wife!

(*Sits down bewildered.*)

MRS TULLY	And what have you to say now, Bartley Fallon?
BARTLEY	(*crossing himself*) I to bring that fork here, and to find that news before me! It is much if I can ever stir from this place at all, or reach as far as the road!
TIM CASEY	Look, boys, at the new magistrate, and Jo Muldoon along with him! It's best for us to quit this.
SHAWN EARLY	That is so. It is best not to be mixed in this business at all.
JAMES RYAN	Bad as he is, I wouldn't like to be an informer against any man.

(All hurry away except MRS TARPEY, who remains behind her stall. Enter MAGISTRATE and POLICEMAN.)

MAGISTRATE   I knew the district was in a bad state, but I did not expect to be confronted with a murder at the first fair I came to.

POLICEMAN   I am sure you did not, indeed.

MAGISTRATE   It was well I had not gone home. I caught a few words here and there that roused my suspicions.

POLICEMAN   So they would, too.

MAGISTRATE   You heard the same story from everyone you asked?

POLICEMAN   The same story – or if it was not altogether the same, anyway it was no less than the first story.

MAGISTRATE   What is that man doing? He is sitting alone with a hayfork. He has a guilty look. The murder was done with a hayfork!

POLICEMAN   *(in a whisper)* That's the very man they say did the act; Bartley Fallon himself!

MAGISTRATE   He must have found escape difficult – he is trying to brazen it out. A convict in the Andaman Islands tried the same game, but he could not escape my system! Stand aside – Don't go far – have the handcuffs ready. *(He walks up to BARTLEY, folds his arms, and stands before him.)* Here, my man, do you know anything of John Smith?

BARTLEY   Of John Smith! Who is he, now?

POLICEMAN   Jack Smith, sir – Red Jack Smith!

MAGISTRATE   *(coming a step nearer and tapping him on the shoulder)* Where is Jack Smith?

BARTLEY   *(with a deep sigh, and shaking his head slowly)* Where is he, indeed?

MAGISTRATE   What have you to tell?

BARTLEY   It is where he was this morning, standing in this spot, singing his share of songs – no, but lighting his pipe – scraping a match on the sole of his shoes –

MAGISTRATE   I ask you, for the third time, where is he?

BARTLEY   I wouldn't like to say that. It is a great mystery, and it is hard to say of any man, did he earn hatred or love.

MAGISTRATE   Tell me all you know.

BARTLEY   All that I know – Well, there are the three estates; there is Limbo, and there is Purgatory, and there is –

MAGISTRATE	Nonsense! This is trifling! Get to the point.
BARTLEY	Maybe you don't hold with the clergy so? That is the teaching of the clergy. Maybe you hold with the old people. It is what they do be saying, that the shadow goes wandering, and the soul is tired, and the body is taking a rest – The shadow! (*Starts up.*) I was nearly sure I saw Jack Smith not ten minutes ago at the corner of the forge, and I lost him again – Was it his ghost I saw, do you think?
MAGISTRATE	(*to POLICEMAN*) Conscience-struck! He will confess all now!
BARTLEY	His ghost to come before me! It is likely it was on account of the fork! I to have it and he to have no way to defend himself the time he met with his death!
MAGISTRATE	(*to POLICEMAN*) I must note down his words. (*Takes out notebook.*) (*To BARTLEY*) I warn you that your words are being noted.
BARTLEY	If I had ha' run faster in the beginning, this terror would not be on me at the latter end! Maybe he will cast it up against me at the day of judgment – I wouldn't wonder at all at that.
MAGISTRATE	(*writing*) At the day of judgment –
BARTLEY	It was soon for his ghost to appear to me – is it coming after me always by day it will be, and stripping the clothes off in the night time? – I wouldn't wonder at all at that, being as I am an unfortunate man!
MAGISTRATE	(*sternly*) Tell me this truly. What was the motive of this crime?
BARTLEY	The motive, is it?
MAGISTRATE	Yes; the motive; the cause.
BARTLEY	I'd sooner not say that.
MAGISTRATE	You had better tell me truly. Was it money?
BARTLEY	Not at all! What did poor Jack Smith ever have in his pockets unless it might be his hands that would be in them?
MAGISTRATE	Any dispute about land?
BARTLEY	(*indignantly*). Not at all! He never was a grabber or grabbed from any one!
MAGISTRATE	You will find it better for you if you tell me at once.
BARTLEY	I tell you I wouldn't for the whole world wish to say what

	it was – it is a thing I would not like to be talking about.
MAGISTRATE	There is no use in hiding it. It will be discovered in the end.
BARTLEY	Well, I suppose it will, seeing that mostly everybody knows it before. Whisper here now. I will tell no lie; where would be the use? (*Puts his hand to his mouth, and* MAGISTRATE *stoops.*) Don't be putting the blame on the parish, for such a thing was never done in the parish before – it was done for the sake of Kitty Keary, Jack Smith's wife.
MAGISTRATE	(*to* POLICEMAN) Put on the handcuffs. We have been saved some trouble. I knew he would confess if taken in the right way.

(POLICEMAN *puts on handcuffs.*)

BARTLEY	Handcuffs now! Glory be! I always said, if there was ever any misfortune coming to this place it was on myself it would fall. I to be in handcuffs! There's no wonder at all in that.

(*Enter* MRS FALLON, *followed by the rest. She is looking back at them as she speaks.*)

MRS FALLON	Telling lies the whole of the people of this town are; telling lies, telling lies as fast as a dog will trot! Speaking against my poor respectable man! Saying he made an end of Jack Smith! My decent comrade! There is no better man and no kinder man in the whole of the five parishes! It's little annoyance he ever gave to any one! (*Turns and sees him.*) What in the earthly world do I see before me? Bartley Fallon in charge of the police! Handcuffs on him! O Bartley, what did you do at all at all?
BARTLEY	O Mary, there has a great misfortune come upon me! It is what I always said, that if there is ever any misfortune –
MRS FALLON	What did he do at all, or is it bewitched I am?
MAGISTRATE	This man has been arrested on a charge of murder.
MRS FALLON	Whose charge is that? Don't believe them! They are all liars in this place! Give me back my man!
MAGISTRATE	It is natural you should take his part, but you have no cause of complaint against your neighbours. He has been arrested for the murder of John Smith, on his own confession.

MRS FALLON	The saints of heaven protect us! And what did he want killing Jack Smith?
MAGISTRATE	It is best you should know all. He did it on account of a love affair with the murdered man's wife.
MRS FALLON	(*sitting down*). With Jack Smith's wife! With Kitty Keary – Ochone, the traitor!
THE CROWD	A great shame, indeed. He is a traitor indeed.
MRS TULLY	To America he was bringing her, Mrs Fallon.
BARTLEY	What are you saying, Mary? I tell you –
MRS FALLON	Don't say a word! I won't listen to any word you'll say! (*stops her ears*.) O, isn't he the treacherous villain? Ohone go deo!
BARTLEY	Be quiet till I speak! Listen to what I say!
MRS FALLON	Sitting beside me on the ass car coming to the town, so quiet and so respectable, and treachery like that in his heart!
BARTLEY	Is it your wits you have lost or is it I myself that have lost my wits?
MRS FALLON	And it's hard I earned you, slaving – and you grumbling, and sighing, and coughing, and discontented, and the priest wore out anointing you, with all the times you threatened to die!
BARTLEY	Let you be quiet till I tell you!
MRS FALLON	You to bring such a disgrace into the parish. A thing that was never heard of before!
BARTLEY	Will you shut your mouth and hear me speaking?
MRS FALLON	And if it was for any sort of a fine handsome woman, but for a little fistful of a woman like Kitty Keary, that's not four feet high hardly, and not three teeth in her head unless she got new ones! May God reward you, Bartley Fallon, for the black treachery in your heart and the wickedness in your mind, and the red blood of poor Jack Smith that is wet upon your hand!

(*Voice of JACK SMITH heard singing:*)

> The sea shall be dry,
> 　　The earth under mourning and ban!
> Then loud shall he cry
> 　　For the wife of the red-haired man!

BARTLEY	It's Jack Smith's voice – I never knew a ghost to sing before –. It is after myself and the fork he is coming! (*Goes back. Enter* JACK SMITH.) Let one of you give him the fork and I will be clear of him now and for eternity!
MRS TARPEY	The Lord have mercy on us! Red Jack Smith! The man that was going to be waked!
JAMES RYAN	Is it back from the grave you are come?
SHAWN EARLY	Is it alive you are, or is it dead you are?
TIM CASEY	Is it yourself at all that's in it?
MRS TULLY	Is it letting on you were to be dead?
MRS FALLON	Dead or alive, let you stop Kitty Keary, your wife, from bringing my man away with her to America!
JACK SMITH	It is what I think, the wits are gone astray on the whole of you. What would my wife want bringing Bartley Fallon to America?
MRS FALLON	To leave yourself, and to get quit of you she wants, Jack Smith, and to bring him away from myself. That's what the two of them had settled together.
JACK SMITH	I'll break the head of any man that says that! Who is it says it? (*To* TIM CASEY.) Was it you said it? (*To* SHAWN EARLY.) Was it you?
ALL TOGETHER	(*backing and shaking their heads*) It wasn't I said it!
JACK SMITH	Tell me the name of any man that said it!
ALL TOGETHER	(*pointing to* BARTLEY) It was *him* that said it!
JACK SMITH	Let me at him till I break his head!

(BARTLEY *backs in terror. Neighbours hold* JACK SMITH *back.*)

JACK SMITH	(*trying to free himself*) Let me at him! Isn't he the pleasant sort of a scarecrow for any woman to be crossing the ocean with! It's back from the docks of New York he'd be turned (*trying to rush at him again*), with a lie in his mouth and treachery in his heart, and another man's wife by his side, and he passing her off as his own! Let me at him can't you.

(*Makes another rush, but is held back.*)

MAGISTRATE	(*pointing to* JACK SMITH) Policeman, put the handcuffs on this man. I see it all now. A case of false impersonation, a conspiracy to defeat the ends of justice. There was a case

	in the Andaman Islands, a murderer of the Mopsa tribe, a religious enthusiast –
POLICEMAN	So he might be, too.
MAGISTRATE	We must take both these men to the scene of the murder. We must confront them with the body of the real Jack Smith.
JACK SMITH	I'll break the head of any man that will find my dead body!
MAGISTRATE	I'll call more help from the barracks. (*Blows POLICEMAN's whistle.*)
BARTLEY	It is what I am thinking, if myself and Jack Smith are put together in the one cell for the night, the handcuffs will be taken off him, and his hands will be free, and murder will be done that time surely!
MAGISTRATE	Come on! (*They turn to the right.*)

Curtain
Lady Augusta Gregory

—

Almost everybody in the neighbourhood had 'troubles', frankly localized and specified, but only the chosen had 'complications'. To have them was in itself a distinction, though it was also, in most cases, a death-warrant. People struggled on for years with 'troubles', but they almost always succumbed to 'complications'.

Edith Wharton

—

Civility costs nothing and buys everything.
Lady Mary Wortley Montagu

—

There are different kinds of wrong. The people sinned against are not always the best.
Ivy Compton-Burnett

I'll not listen to reason. Reason always means what someone
else has got to say.

Elizabeth Gaskell

_____

Nobody speaks the truth when there's something they must
have.

Elizabeth Bowen

_____

If someone tells you he is going to make a 'realistic
decision', you immediately understand that he has resolved
to do something bad.

Mary McCarthy

_____

You ask if they were happy. This is not a characteristic of a
European. To be contented – that's for the cows.

Coco Chanel

_____

A little alarm now and then keeps life from stagnation.

Fanny Burney

_____

My candle burns at both ends;
It will not last the night;
But ah, my foes, and oh, my friends –
It gives a lovely light.

Edna St Vincent Millay

_____

Millions long for immortality who do not know what to do
with themselves on a rainy Sunday afternoon.

Susan Ertz

from The Female Tatler

Chloe and Celia, two young gentlewomen that are cousins, of whose affairs I knew more than either of them imagined, coming to see me this afternoon, complained that *The Female Tatler* had left off taking notice of the scandal that was sent her. They talk of dullness, hackney writing, and several other things that displeased me, for which, having a mind to be revenged on them, I told them that I had received two true stories of scandal upon two ladies, whom I knew not, that if they would give themselves the trouble of hearing them, I should be glad of their opinions, whether they were worth publishing or not. They answered by all means, nothing of scandal could come amiss to them. So, whilst my maid set the tea-table, I unlocked my scrutore and took out a sheet of paper, writ in a small character. We had hardly drank two dishes each, but I saw that the ladies were impatient to hear what I had offered, and accordingly, looking on my paper under pretence of reading it, I began the first story.

Having described a certain merchant by his size and complexion, the place where he lived and the commodity he dealt in, so exactly, that any-body who was acquainted with him might know it was Chloe's father I meant, I continued thus: 'This gentleman,' said I, 'has a sprightly young lady to his daughter that takes abundance of care to appear unaffected and gay, behaves herself with a more than ordinary freedom in all manner and company and yet pretends to be strictly chaste, and is proud of her conduct. She is very censorious upon all young people that are not of the same temper, calls modesty slyness, and hardly allows any body to be virtuous that is more reserved than herself. They had a gentleman that boarded with them, whom their daughter treated very familiarly, played at romps with him, admitted him into her chamber, and sometimes scrupled not to enter his. The father had a good opinion of his daughter, the mother doted on her, and neither of them suspecting her virtue. She was never controlled in her actions.

'One morning she complained of having lost one of her garters. Search was made throughout her chamber, the mother looked in every corner of her own, the maid did the same in the parlour and the dining-room, but no garter was found. Some two hours after, the maid being come down from making the beds, held out the garter to her young mistress, where she sat with her father and mother, and smiled. The lady, snatching it away, asked her, where she had it, but being answered in Mr P—'s bed, which was the gentleman that boarded with them, she discovered so much astonishment, as well as the gentleman himself, who likewise happened to be present, that it was easily seen that whether the garter was found in his bed or not, the owner of it had certainly been there.'

I had observed that whilst as they thought I was reading history, Celia all along had been wonderfully pleased, and continually sniggering and nodding at her cousin, who for her part looked very grave and seemed as uneasy as if she had sat upon nettles, and when I had finished, as the one called it, a silly story, and wondered Celia could laugh at anything so dull and insipid, so the other, extolling it as extravagantly, said it was the best she ever heard, and earnestly preferred me go on with the second. I wanted not much entreaty, for as these two stories, which I had ready for 'em, the first touched Chloe to the quick, so this was to be as home upon her cousin, both being literally true. Celia was the reverse of Chloe, and seemed as affectedly cautious as the other was over free. She pretended to have a great aversion to men, was very circumspect in their company, and thought ill of all women that were not equally coy and retired as herself. When I made an end of Celia's character and had been particular enough in the description of her person and circumstances to make her known, I saw that her mirth was over, and that all her good humour vanished, but on the other side Chloe, by degrees recovering from her dumps, assumed a merrier countenance, and at last seemed to feel the same satisfaction that her cousin had experienced before.

Looking still steadfastly upon my paper, I went on in this manner.

'This reserved lady,' said I, 'persuaded by her mother and other relations, relented at last and vouchsafed a more favourable hearing to one of her suitors, whom we shall call Lysander, than hitherto she had done to any, and a match was in great forwardness, when the gallant's father, who lived a hundred miles off, falls sick, and in post-haste sends for his son, who, willing to obey his father, took short leave of his mistress and went down with a promise of a speedy return. The father, after two months' illness, dies, and leaves his son a large, but encumbered estate, the troubles of which detaining Lysander longer than willingly he would have stayed, almost half a year escaped before he came back from London, where he was sooner arrived, but received the unwelcome news of his mistress being very ill and likely to die. He heard that she was gone ten miles off to a little hamlet in Essex, where her mother had a small farm of twenty pound per annum, and that her distemper was a kind of dropsy, called the Tympany. He made what haste he could to see her, but, coming there, she happened to be very bad, that he could not be admitted. But when Lysander would not be denied by the servant that spoke to him, and made several instances to see her, comes down to him at last an elderly matron, who, by telling him that the lady had been lightheaded for some days, and was that minute dropped into a slumber, and giving him a specious account of the whole state of her illness, persuaded him, tho' much ado, to forbear his visit, and go as he came.

'After this Lysander expected every hour to hear she was dead, but the third day was joyfully revived with the unhoped for tidings of his mistress being on the mending hand. She now daily recovers apace, the swelling is gone, Lysander is allowed to see her, the chief of her distemper is weakness, and in a month's time she is happily restored to her former health. Everything now was got ready for the nuptials, when the day before they were to be celebrated, Lysander, just as he was entering a hosier's shop, saw an ancient gentlewoman that came out of it step into a coach. He remembered that he had seen her face, but could not presently think where, till recollecting himself he called to mind that it was the careful old lady that, with so much oratory and affection, had dissuaded him from disturbing his mistress when she was at the worst. "Do you know," said he, "that gentlewoman?", looking upon the master of the shop, who, smiling, answered, "Yes, Sir, she is a midwife, well approved for her skill, but more particularly noted for her faithfulness and discretion on all occasions where secrecy is required." At the sound of a midwife, Lysander turned pale, and, before the hosier had quite pronounced the word secrecy, looked like a man that was thunderstruck. He asked no more questions, but, without so much as thinking what he came for, left the shop and immediately went to a physician that was his intimate friend and, having communicated to him whatever he knew concerning his mistress's distemper, as well as her cure, upon his advice broke off the match.'

I took a great deal of delight to see the different working this relation had upon the two cousins, and when I had made an end, I found Chloe in the gayest humour imaginable, continually repeating 'Tympany' and 'Midwife', but Celia in almost as much amazement as we suppose Lysander to have been at the hosier's, till, at length her passion prevailing over her concern, she could contain herself no longer and casting her eyes full of spite and anger upon her cousin, asked her if she had laughed as much when the maid told her where she had found her garter? 'My garter!' said Chloe, 'why that upon me? I laughed at the lady that had the Tympany, what cousin is it you? I know you pretended once . . .' 'Pretended!' replied Celia, interrupting her. 'I scorn your words; it is well known that I had a dropsy, and what of that? There was no occasion to suspect me, cousin, unless my garter had been found in a gentleman's bed before I complained.' At this, Chloe, enraged in her turn, the conversation between the two cousins began to be very loud and full of quick repartee, and at last became so violent that I could understand nothing but 'garter' and 'gentleman's bed' on one side, and 'Tympany' and 'Midwife' on the other. Chloe thro' eagerness, forgetting the tea she had in her hand, her dish slipped from the saucer, and fell upon Celia's white petticoat, who, no doubting that it was done to affront her, took up her own which I had filled that moment, and flung it in her cousin's face. Then both got up, Chloe to attack Celia, and Celia to avoid Chloe. Celia being on my right, the first step she made threw down the boiling tea-kettle, spirits and all, and miserably scalded one of my dogs that lay by me, whilst the furbelow of Chloe's scarf in the pursuit took hold of the tea-table and overthrew it. The clatter of china, the screaming of one dog and the barking of another, joined to the loudness of the combatants, and the noise of my parrot, who upon occasions is used to join in the chorus, made such a hideous consort, that I was glad to quit the room and get up into my closet, to set down what had happened.

Lucinda

Perhaps the rare and simple pleasure of being seen for what one is compensates for the misery of being it.

Margaret Drabble

By six years of age I was a fatso who finished her midnight snack just in time for breakfast and ate so much she had stretch marks around her mouth. In high school my acne was so bad, blind people tried to read my face. In biology class a frog tried to dissect me. I sat out more dances than FDR. I was petting with a boy, and his hand went to sleep.

My father was a general practitioner – our family motto was 'A good epidemic means meat on the table.' My mother could make anybody feel guilty – she used to get letters of apology from people she didn't even know. She was desperate to get me married. She used to say, 'Sure he's a murderer. But he's a *single* murderer.' I was dating a transvestite, and she said, 'Marry him. You'll double your wardrobe.' She was a very elegant woman. When a flying saucer landed on the lawn, she turned it over to see if it was Wedgwood.

Joan Rivers

———

When I appear in public people expect me to neigh, grind my teeth, paw the ground and swish my tail – none of which is easy.

Princess Anne

———

I know two things about the horse
And one of them is rather coarse.

Naomi Royde-Smith

———

When I'm good, I'm very, very good, but when I'm bad, I'm better.

Mae West

———

I have often wished I had time to cultivate modesty. . . But I am too busy thinking about myself.

Edith Sitwell

———

I've been on a calendar but never on time.

Marilyn Monroe

———

I used to be Snow White . . . but I drifted.

Mae West

———

I'm as pure as the driven slush.

Tallulah Bankhead

———

Tallulah [Bankhead] is always skating on thin ice. Everyone
wants to be there when it breaks.

Mrs Patrick Campbell

———

Virginia Woolf, I enjoyed talking to her, but thought
nothing of her writing. I considered her 'a beautiful little
knitter'.

Edith Sitwell

———

Edith Sitwell looks like a high altar on the move.

Elizabeth Bowen

———

Princess Diana is always complaining, 'I'm not happy. I'm
not happy.' She married one of the richest men in the
world. His mother owns England, Ireland, Scotland,
Canada, New Zealand, Australia. By sleeping with Prince
Charles, one day she will own – listen to the verb, *own*
– England, Ireland, Scotland, Canada, New Zealand, and
Australia . . . Then I say, 'I would screw a duck for Rhode
Island. What does she want?'

Joan Rivers

———

Ettie [Lady Desborough] is an ox: she will be made into
Bovril when she dies. . . She tells enough white lies to ice a
wedding cake.

Margot Asquith

————

[Of another actress:] She's the original good time that was
had by all.

Bette Davis

————

[When Jean Harlow pronounced her name 'Margott':] No,
no, Jean. The t is silent, as in Harlow.

Margot Asquith

————

[Of Maureen O'Hara:] She looked as though butter
wouldn't melt in her mouth – or anywhere else.

Elsa Lanchester

————

[Of Lillian Hellman:] Every word she writes is a lie,
including 'and' and 'the'.

Mary McCarthy

————

[Of Katherine Hepburn at a Broadway first night:] She ran
the whole gamut of the emotions from A to B.

Dorothy Parker

————

[On Elizabeth Taylor:] Is she fat? She wore yellow and ten
schoolchildren got aboard. Her favourite food is seconds.

She's so fat she's my two best friends. She wears stretch kaftans. She's got more chins than the Chinese telephone directory.

Joan Rivers

———

I came across a woman at a party not very much later who was Mrs Nicodemus Bliss to the life, a crusader against some variety of reputed evil, though I couldn't remember which. Since it was my party, I stopped to chat for a moment and this quickie developed:

'I know I mustn't offer you a cocktail,' said I, making small talk. 'You're chairman of the Temperance League.'

The good lady glared. 'I am *not*. I am president of the Anti-Vice Committee.'

My service. 'I knew there was something we mustn't offer you.'

Beatrice Lillie

———

If all the young ladies who attended the Yale promenade dance were laid end to end, no one would be the least surprised.

Dorothy Parker

———

She does not understand the concept of Roman numerals. She thought we just fought World War Eleven.

Joan Rivers

———

People wish their enemies dead but I do not; I say give them the gout, give them the stone!

Lady Mary Wortley Montagu

———

It would be unfair to suggest that one of the most characteristic sounds of the English Sunday is the sound of
Harold Hobson barking up the wrong tree.

Penelope Gilliatt

———

David Frost has risen without trace.

Kitty Muggeridge

———

E.M. Forster never gets any further than warming the
teapot. He's a rare fine hand at that. Feel this teapot.
Is it not beautifully warm? Yes, but there ain't going
to be no tea.

Katherine Mansfield

———

The trouble with Ian [Fleming] is that he gets off with
women because he can't get on with them.

Rosamond Lehmann

———

[Of Lloyd George:] He can't see a belt without hitting
below it.

Margot Asquith

———

[Of Thomas Dewey:] He is just about the nastiest little
man I've ever known. He struts sitting down.

Lillian K. Dykestra

———

[Of Gladstone:] He speaks to Me as if I was a public meeting.

Queen Victoria

———

[During the 1963 trial of Stephen Ward]

MR BURGE   Do you know Lord Astor has made a statement to the police saying that these allegations of yours are absolutely untrue?

MANDY RICE-DAVIS   He would, wouldn't he?

———

Lord Birkenhead is very clever but sometimes his brains go to his head.

Margot Asquith

———

[Of Michael Arlen:] He is every other inch a gentleman.

Rebecca West

———

I'm still suffering from the big dénouement in [Jeffrey Archer's book] *Not A Penny More* when 'the three stood motionless like sheep in the stare of a python'. The whole thing keeps me awake at night. Here are these sheep, gambolling about in the Welsh jungle, when up pops a python. A python, what's more, who thinks he's a cobra.

Nancy Banks-Smith

———

ALL GOD'S

CHILDREN

All God's children are not beautiful. Most of God's
children are, in fact, barely presentable.

Fran Lebowitz

———

When I had my baby, I screamed and screamed. And that
was just during conception.

Joan Rivers

———

I cannot believe that women were intended to suffer as
much as they do, and be as helpless as they are, in
child-bearing. In spite of the third chapter of Genesis, I
cannot believe that all the agony and debility attendant
upon the entrance of a new creature into the world was
ordained, but rather that both are the consequence
of our many and various abuses of our constitutions and

infractions of God's natural laws. Tight stays, tight garters, tight waistbands and tight bodices must have a tendency to injure irreparably the compressed parts, to impede the circulation and respiration in many ways we are not aware of. Many women here, when they become mothers, seem to lose looks, health and strength and are mere wrecks. One is tempted to wish that the legislature would interfere and prevent the desperate injury which is thus done to the race.

Fanny Kemble

———

To simulate the birth experience, take one car jack, insert into rectum, pump to maximum height and replace with a jack-hammer. And that would be a good birth

Kathy Lette

———

I had a Jewish delivery: they knock you out with the first pain; they wake you up when the hairdresser shows.

Joan Rivers

———

When I was born, I was so surprised I couldn't talk for a year and a half.

Gracie Allen

———

from The Pursuit of Love

Linda's child, a girl, was born in May. She was ill for a long time before, and very ill indeed at her confinement. The doctors told her that she must never have another child, as it would almost certainly kill her if she did. This was a blow to the Kroesigs, as bankers, it seems, like kings, require many sons, but Linda did not appear to mind at all. She took no interest whatever in the baby she had got. I went to see her as soon as I was allowed to. She lay in a bower of blossom and pink roses, and looked like a corpse. I was expecting a baby myself, and naturally took a great interest in Linda's.

'What are you going to call her – where is she, anyway?'

'In Sister's room – it shrieks. Moira, I believe.'

'Not Moira, darling, you can't. I never heard such an awful name.'

'Tony likes it, he had a sister called Moira who died, and what d'you think I found out (not from him, but from their old nanny)? She died because Marjorie whacked her on the head with a hammer when she was four months old. Do you call that interesting? And then they say we are an uncontrolled family – why even Fa has never actually murdered anybody, or do you count that beater?'

'All the same, I don't see how you can saddle the poor little thing with a name like Moira, it's too unkind.'

'Not really, if you think. It'll have to grow up a Moira if the Kroesigs are to like it (people always grow up to their names I've noticed) and they might as well like it because frankly, I don't.'

'Linda, how can you be so naughty, and, anyway, you can't possibly tell whether you like her or not, yet.'

'Oh, yes I can. I can always tell if I like people from the start, and I don't like Moira, that's all. She's a fearful Counter-Hon, wait till you see her.'

At this point the Sister came in, and Linda introduced us.

'Oh, you are the cousin I hear so much about,' she said. 'You'll want to see the baby.'

She went away and presently returned carrying a Moses basket full of wails.

'Poor thing,' said Linda indifferently. 'It's really kinder not to look.'

'Don't pay any attention to her,' said the Sister. 'She pretends to be a wicked woman, but it's all put on.'

I did look, and, deep down among the frills and lace, there was the usual horrid sight of a howling orange in a fine black wig.

'Isn't she sweet,' said the Sister. 'Look at her little hands.'

I shuddered slightly, and said: 'Well, I know it's dreadful of me, but I don't much like them as small as that; I'm sure she'll be divine in a year or two.'

The wails now entered on a crescendo, and the whole room was filled with hideous noise.

'Poor soul,' said Linda. 'I think it must have caught sight of itself in a glass. Do take it away, Sister.'

Nancy Mitford

——

from A Narrative of the Life of Mrs Charlotte Charke

As I have promised to conceal nothing that might raise a laugh, I shall begin with a small specimen of my former madness, when I was but four years of age. Having, even then, a passionate fondness for a periwig, I crawled out of bed one summer's morning at Twickenham, where my father had part of a house and gardens for the season, and taking it into my small pate that by dint of a wig and a waistcoat I should be the perfect representative of my sire, I crept softly into the servants' hall, where I had the night before espied all things in order, to perpetrate the happy design I had framed for the next morning's expedition. Accordingly I paddled down stairs, taking with me my shoes, stockings, and little dimity coat, which I artfully contrived to pin up as well as I could to supply the want of a pair of breeches. By the help of a long broom I took down a waistcoat of my brother's and an enormous bushy tie-wig of my father's, which entirely enclosed my head and body, with the knots of the ties thumping my little heels as I marched along with slow and solemn pace. The covert of hair in which I was concealed, with the weight of a monstrous belt and large silver-hilted sword that I could scarce drag along, was a vast impediment in my procession, and what still added to the other inconveniences I laboured under was whelming myself under one of my father's large beaver hats, laden with lace as thick and as broad as a brickbat.

Being thus accoutred, I began to consider that it would be impossible for me to pass for Mr Cibber in girl's shoes, therefore took an opportunity to slip out of doors after the gardener, who went to his work, and rolled myself into a dry ditch, which was as deep as I was high, and in this grotesque pigmy state walked up and down the ditch bowing to all who came by me. But, behold, the oddity of my appearance soon assembled a crowd about me, which yielded me no small joy, as I conceived their risibility on this occasion to be marks of approbation and walked myself into a fever in the happy thought of being taken for the squire.

When the family arose, till which time I had employed myself in this regular march in my ditch, I was the first thing enquired after and missed, till Mrs Heron, the mother of the late celebrated actress of that name, happily espied me, and directly called forth the whole family to be witnessed of my state and dignity.

The drollery of my figure rendered it impossible, assisted by the fondness of both father and mother, to be angry with me, but, alas, I was borne off on the footman's shoulders, to my shame and disgrace, and forced into my proper habiliments.

The summer following our family resided at Hampton Town, near the Court. My mother being indisposed, at her first coming there, drank every morning and night asses' milk. I observed one of those little health-restoring animals was attended by its foal, which was about the height of a sizeable greyhound.

I immediately formed a resolution of following the fashion of taking the air early next morning, and fixed upon this young ass for a pad-nag [an easy-going horse], and, in order to bring this matter to bear, I communicated my design to a small troop of young gentlemen and ladies whose low births and adverse states rendered it entirely convenient for them to come into any scheme Miss Charlotte Cibber could possibly propose. Accordingly, my mother's bridle and saddle were secretly procured, but the riper judgements of some of my followers soon convinced me of the unnecessary trouble of carrying the saddle, as the little destined beast was too small and indeed too weak to bear the burden; upon which it was concluded to take the bridle only, and away went Miss and her attendants, who soon arrived at the happy field where the poor harmless creature was sucking. We soon seized and endeavoured to bridle it, but I remembered it was impossible to bring that point to bear, the head of the foal being so very small the trappings fell off as fast as they strove to put them on. One of the small crew, who was wiser than the rest, proposed their garters being converted to that use, which was soon effected, and I rode triumphantly into town astride, with a numerous retinue, whose huzzas were drowned by the dreadful braying of the tender dam, who pursued us with agonizing sounds of sorrow for her oppressed young one.

Upon making this grand entry into the town, I remember my father, from the violent acclamations of joy on so glorious an occasion, was excited to enquire into the meaning of what he perhaps imagined to be an insurrection; when, to his amazement, he beheld his daughter, mounted as before

described, preceded by a lad who scraped upon a twelve-penny fiddle of my
own to add to the dignity and grandeur of this extraordinary enterprise.

I perfectly remember, young as I was then, the strong mixture of
surprise, pleasure, pain, and shame in his countenance on his viewing me
seated on my infantical Rosinante, which, though I had not then sense
enough to distinguish, my memory has since afforded me the power to
describe, and also to repeat his very words, at his looking out of the window,
'Gad demme! An ass upon an ass!'

Charlotte Charke

———

I love children. Especially when they cry – for then
someone takes them away.

Nancy Mitford

———

Written for my son, and spoken by him at his first putting on breeches

What is it our mammas bewitches
To plague us little boys with breeches?

Mary Barber

———

from A Bad Boy's Diary

The gnu minister came to our house to tea to-nite. His name is Revrund
Nebneezer Slocum. He is 26 years ole, he said to hisself. He is pail, wares a
white choker, an' is fond of girls an' sweet-cake, so I juge. He patted me on
the head – I hate to be patted on the head, that will do for boys of three or
fore. I think he's sweet on Lil, but she won't have him. The only sole on earth
Lil cares for is Montagu De Jones. I carried a letter to him this fournoon. She
gave me a dime if Ide prommus not to tell ennybuddy. He wrote one back,
an' he give me anuther dime. Lil was out in the yard waiteing wen I got back.
She put his letter to her pocket an' went upstairs. Wot duz this mene?

When tea was et we all went in the parlor. Mr Slocum ast me was I fond of gum drops, 'cause I was eating some. We was by ourselfs in the winder; he wanted to be pleasant. I tole him yes, I liked 'em; when Mr De Jones give me money for bringin' letters to my sister Lilly I allers bought gum drops. What could a made him turn so green when I said that? At last he ast me how often do you buy 'em? and I said every day. He gave a little kind o' mone like he had et too much. Pritty soon he sed he must go back to his bording-house and write a sermon.

Oh, such a time! Fur oncst they didn't scold little Georgie, nor whip him, nor send him to bed by dalite. Pa says he's goin' to get me a velocipede next week. It seems I've bin of a good dele of use if I am only ait yeres old. Las' night wen I had writ in my diry I wasn't a bit sleepy, so I went into Lily's room to put on one of her rappers to scare Betty, an' I felt sunthin' in the pocket wich was a letter that I read. It said: 'The carridge will be at the corner at nine to-nite – slip out quitely, all will go well; do not fale, me deerest Lily.'

'Wot's up?' sez I; 'it's most nine now. I'll go and see.'

I hung the rapper back in the clost, krept down the back stares, an' reched the street. I dodged behind a ash barrel; sure enuff a carridge stoped at the corner. 'Bout a minit after I see my sister Lily come along rapped in a watter-proof, carrying a satchel. Mister De Jones jumped out of the carridge, helped her in, shut the door, un' off they went; the driver he licked the horses like he was in a allfired hurry. I run home with all my mite an' mane, burst in were the folks were sitting, an' gasped: 'You better hurry up if you want to catch 'em. I think somebuddy ought to arest that driver for lickin' his horses.'

'Wot are you talking about?' sez mamma.

'Oh, nuthing. Why, Lily's run away with him in a carridge. They're goin' to Plattville to get marrid. I see 'em start.'

Then papa said a very bad word. Bess she flue up to Lil's room to see if I tole the truth. I was whisked off to bed, like I allers am when there's fun goin' on, an' wen I woke up this mornin', an' come down to brekfast, there was Miss Lily at the table with the rest, an' after brekfast she sez to me: 'Oh, Geordie, how *could* you tell on us?' an' burst rite out a cryin'.

I wish I hadn't.

*

There has been a aksident to our house. It nede not take a proffit to tell who was in fault. I am a dredful boy. To the, my diry, I must aknolige all my sins. I did not mene to do it. Am I then too blame? I wish big folks would stop a calling me names. I am a dredful boy, but not on purpose, it jus' happens. Now the hull town is down on me. Pa sez he xpecks I'll have to go to prison. O, my dere diry, did you ever think your little oner would have to go to jale? O, it is fereful to have the decons, an' the sheruf, an' ole Miss Harkness a frowning at you as if you was a hartless criminal wen you didn't go to do it at all. This morning I was a very good child, I played over to Johnny Brown's an' nuthin' happened that didn't ought to 'cept I staid to dinner coz Johnny's mother didn't want me to, an' after that he came over to my house an' we had a good time all day. We was up in mamma's room wen she was gone a visiting. I put a chair on the table an' climbed up to the top shelf of the chimbly cupbord an' got down some medicine and give it to Johnny wich said it tasted good, but bimeby he turned quite pail, he was that sick to his stumak he didn't no wether he stood on his heles or his head. So Betty made him drink a cup full o' warm, nasty water with mustard stired into it, such horrid stuff it made him thro it up, wen he felt better. Wen Betty was gone for the mustard I looked in papa's furs an' I found such a funny pistol. Johnny he said it was a revolver, so I tole him not to say a word an' I run an' hid it under my piller.

'We'll have some fun wen you get over bean sick, Johnny,' sez I, but he had to go home he felt so bad after he throed up his headaked.

I let the pistol remane under my piller, fur I was afrade Betty would see it. I wanted to scare my sisters with it cos I did not 'spose 'twas loded, but they would shreke all the same. Girls allers holler like mad wen they see a gun or pistol. So Mister Slocum he come to tea agane. Ministers are the gratest hands to come to tea, it's haf thare work to go around an' take thare suppers with the ladys. I kep dark. Pa had to go to town-meeting, an' ma she went to see how Johnny was. Sue she went a walkin' with the docktor, Bess an' Lily they undertook to see the minister didn't get sleepy in the parlor. Lily she hadn't spoke to me since the nite she run away. She isn't like she used to be one bit, oncest she was equil to a boy for fun and gokes, now I would not be surprised if she settled down into a parson's wife she is that sober, I wisht I had not tole on her that night, she wood a taken me to live with her, she sez, if she had married Mister Jones. Thus one by one my prospects of bliss fade away, this is a sad world.

'Now,' sez I, 'I'll crepe up stairs an' get that pistol, enter the parlor an' stir 'em up. Tain't loded.' O what fun to here them holler. 'Betty,' sez I, 'lend me your blankit sholl a fu minits I want to be a Injun brave.'

She did not dreme about the revolver so she lend me the sholl. I rapped it about me, put a cane over my shoulder fur a gun, then I krept up, quite still, so they wouldn't kno Injuns was skirmushin around thare camp. I pushed the door open vary, vary softly, and glared in upon 'em. The minister an' Bess was at opsite ends o' the sofy, Lil she was croshaying a lamp-mat, all was still, the hour was at hand, the moment had arrived, so with an unearthly yell I rushed into the camp, gave three shrill hoops, and pointed my pistol at 'em, saying: 'Surrender or I shoot!'

Bess clapped her hands to her eyes an' uttered screme after screme. Lily gets up and sez soft-like: 'Geordie, O Geordie don't! it's loded.'

'Surrender, pail chefe,' I ansered, dancing round an' round, pointing my weppon at the minister.

'O Geordie!' Lily begged coming tords me, 'stop, do stop!'

'I'm goin' to shoot the pail chefe dead in his tracks,' I ansered.

Bad as I fele I almost laugh when I rekolec how Mister Slocum bounced over the back o' the sofy an' scrouched down behind it. Lily got hold of my arm. I shook her off and fired.

Alas dere diry need I tell the more? The ole thing was loded after all! That was the terribul mistake I made. Who would have thunk twas loded all reddy to go of as soon as I pulled the trigger? The ball went right through the back o' the sofy like there want no sofy thare an' hit Mr Slocum square in the forrid, the ball logged in the brane inflictin' a paneful an' dangerous wound, at leste so the docktor says.

He is lain up stairs now in the best spare room. The Docktor is in thare an' ever so many other folks. He don't say enny thing cos he can't speke, he's senseless. I'm sure no little boy could feel badder'n I do about it.

I wish I had never tuched the ole thing. Wot bisness had it to go and be loded? I'm shut up in my room; I'm not to be let out for a hull month. Ten to one if he dyes the'll be mene enuff not to let me go to the funeral. They nede not be so hard on little Georgie, I didn't know 'twas loded. O dere me! what for dose a little bit of a ball in his brane make so much trubble. I'm glad it was not Lily: she's a dere girl. She kissed an' soothed me when I cried so hard thare was a lump in my throte; I thought I should choke I was so fritened an' sorry. Everbuddy but her skowled at me like I was a demon. If I ever get to be a man I hope I shal kno better than to pizen little Johnny an' shoot the minister; but I never, never shal, 'cause if I'm put in jaile an' hung I shan't live to grow up. O, wot a thought.

I cried myself to slepe late las nite. This day has been a thousan' miles long. Bred an' woter for breakfas, bred an' woter for dinner, bred an' woter for supper, not a sole to speke to, the door locked; I must pore out my trubbles now for twilite is coming on, an' I will not be aloud a lamp – no, not even a candel or a match. I am left to bare my gilt in darkness an' silence all alone. O, Betty, Betty, come! Hark, I here a whisper at the kehole – who is there? It was my darlin' sister Lily.

'Georgie,' sez she, rite throu the kehole, 'poor boy, don't feel so bad; he's better.'

'Hurray!' sez I.

'It didn't reach his brane,' sez she, 'the sofy broke the force o' the ball. It stopped in the frontal bone, and Docktor Moore took it out. Why, he's a settin' up in bed a eting tea an' toste. He'll be able to go home in a day or two.'

'I wish I was eting tea an' toste. Lily, you a good girl. Don't you ever marry Mr Slocum, coz he didn't stand fire. Wen I get out o' this I'm goin' to help you marry Montagu, an' do evrything you ast me to. Lily, will you pleze go an' teze pa to let me have a lite? Tell him it's barbrus to let little boys smell waffles frying wen they ain't to get any therselves. Tell cook to kepe the kitchen door shut, so I won't kno there's ham an' egs for brekfast. Is my squirl fed reglar! I guess Towser thinks I'm dead.

'Tell mamma I'm afraid I'm sick I've got such a queer feeling in the pit of my stumak.'

I tell you Lil's a brik! She's got a key wot fits my dore, an' she's brot me a nue book, a hunk o' cake, an' a candel. The cake tasted awful good. If Robinson Crusoe was shut up in a room would he stay there? No, he would contrive to free hisself. If I had some sissors I'd cut up my blankets, tie 'em in a rope, an' let myself down from the winder.

I had no sissors, but the sheets tored esy. I made a long string, tied one end to the handel of the buro-drawer which stood near by, crawled out o' the window, got a good hold o' my rope, like the folks does when the house is afire, an' let her slide.

Wot happened afterwords I can't describe, 'cause when my hed struck on the brick ary I didn't know anything for a good while. Mebbe the buro-drawer come out – mebbe the sheets werint tide tite enuff, all I know is that I saw stars, an' then – all was dark as nite. Father sez, when I cum to: 'He is incorgible. I give him up, 'taint no use. O wot a pity he cum to at all!'

Pra, wot did they have me for? I didn't ast 'em too. Wy didn't they have a reglar good little boy sent to 'em by Mrs McCandish sted of such a bad, bad boy as me? I gess if papa was kep on bred an' woter, like he was a criminal in the penny ten sherry, he'd tare the sheets up worse'n I did. Folks are so unjust to childrun.

Metta Victoria Victor

I'm at that stage of motherhood where I'm putting the kids under the sink and the lethal household substances within reach.

Kathy Lette

---

from Period Piece

I had a solitary game of my own, played at bedtime; it was called 'Being Kind to Poor Pamela'. Pamela was a child with whom I sometimes played, but whom I rather despised. The game was played by getting out of bed and lying on the floor, until you were as cold as you could bear to be. During that time you were Poor Pamela, lying out in the snow in her nightgown, owing to the cruelty of her parents. She was starving and the wolves were howling in the woods all round. Then you became yourself again, and went out into the cold and rescued poor Pamela – the wolves were getting very near – and you put her into your own bed and warmed her, and fed her, and comforted her most tenderly. This made you feel frightfully good and kind; and you could do it over and over again, until you could keep awake no longer. On showing this passage to Margaret, she revealed that she had independently practised a variety of this sport, when put to bed with a hot-water bottle, because she had a cold; only it was not Pamela whom she impersonated by lying naked on the oil-cloth, but a mother with a baby (a doll). A good cure for a cold.

But when I met Pamela again in real life, I was just as nasty to her as ever. This fortunately was not very often, as she did not live in Cambridge. She was the sort of person one was always nasty to; because, however hard one tried to be nice to her, she always managed to give you a remorseful feeling that you had not really understood her. It was just a quality she had. Once when I went to tea with her alone, we were given a special little feast; and among the good things were some raspberries. They turned out to be full of maggots, but Pamela ate them all up, both hers and mine. Without saying anything, she implied that she so seldom had anything nice for tea, that she was glad even of maggotty raspberries; while no doubt I, lucky I, had delicious fruit every day of my life (which was not very far indeed from being true). I think now, that there was not the faintest reason to believe that her parents were at all unkind to her; but in a patient, tolerant, uncomplaining way, she certainly made me think so then; and all without a word being said on the subject.

Gwen Raverat

———

from The Visitors

It occurred to Wragg to wonder what it must be like to have children, not so much the process of procreation parturition, and so on, as actually *having* them, ever-present, under one's feet. He himself, in his rare and fleeting brushes with the species, was accustomed to treat them with the utmost circumspection as undersized but none the less formidable adults. In fact, they appeared to him to be both sub- and super-human. Brazen little hedonists with time on their hands, and irked, he supposed, by constant supervision, they seemed quite ruthless in exploiting their natural advantages, i.e. soundness of wind and limb, acuteness of eye and ear as yet unimpaired by depravities of habit, all of which made them more than a match for the old crocks with whom they came in daily conflict. Their sole disadvantage, so far as he could judge, lay in lack of experience, which, far from being a handicap, allowed them the broadest possible latitude in their behaviour, exacerbated an already overweening self-assurance, and encouraged an irresponsibility in word and deed which they knew damn' well could always be covered by the blanket-excuse of youth. Now as cautiously he took stock of first one young Purdoe then the other, he saw no grounds for any basic revision of these opinions.

Mary McMinnies

———

Mrs Bott's Hat

'I've always wanted to be something excitin',' said William, 'and that's what I'm goin' to be.'

'What?' said his Outlaws.

'I'm goin' to be like this man,' said William; 'this man in this book I've just been reading.'

'Yes, but what *about* him?' said Ginger.

'I keep tryin' to *tell* you, but you keep int'ruptin',' said William impatiently. 'I tell you I want to do like this man did. It'd be jolly excitin', an' it's ever so long since I did anythin' really excitin'.'

'You made your geyser explode last week,' Douglas gently reminded him.

'Well, I don't call that *really* excitin',' said William, 'not excitin' like the things this man in the book did. Well, I'm goin' to start doin' them to-day.'

'Doin' what ?' said his Outlaws.

William sighed.

'I keep tellin' you. You won't *listen*. You will keep int'ruptin'. I want to do somethin' excitin' same as this man in this book did.'

'Yes, but *what* did he do ?' shouted the Outlaws.

'If you'd stop int'ruptin' for one *minute*,' said William sternly, 'I'd tell you. You keep int'ruptin' and *int'ruptin'*. This man stole things.'

'It's wrong to steal things,' said Douglas piously.

'Yes, I know, but it's only wrong to steal things if you keep them for yourself.'

'Well, we tried stealing things for the poor, and it wasn't a success.'

'Well, this man in this book didn't steal things for the poor.'

'Who did he steal them for then?'

'He didn't steal them for anyone. He just got someone to bet him he wouldn't steal something, and then he stole it just for the daringness of it and then put it back. And putting the things back was just as dangerous as stealing them. Well, that's what I'm goin' to do. I'm sick of nothin' excitin' happenin' for days an' *days*. You've got to fix on somethin' to bet me I won't steal an' then I'm goin' to steal it an' bring it to show you an' put it back an' it's goin' to be jolly dangerous an' excitin' same as it was in this book. Now you think of somethin' to bet me I won't steal. . . . '

The Outlaws brightened. The Christmas holidays were dragging somewhat. The weather, while debarring them from the activities that made the summer holidays so enjoyable, failed to provide compensating winter occupation. It had rained incessantly till to-day. To-day was fine, but cold, dark, and vaguely depressing. Therefore the Outlaws brightened at the thought of William's new career.

'Yes,' said Ginger judicially. 'I think it's a jolly fine idea. Well, you go away a minute an' we'll think of somethin'.'

William wandered over to the other side of the field till a cry of 'Ready' recalled him. He returned to the three Outlaws.

'You're not to send me to steal anything miles and miles away like somethin' in the Tower of London or anythin' like that,' he said, 'because it's too far for me to go an' I'm not goin' to waste any money on train fares.'

'No, it isn't that,' Ginger reassured him. 'It isn't anythin' in the Tower of London.'

'What is it then?' asked William.

'It's Mrs Bott's Sunday hat,' said Ginger.

Mrs Bott's Sunday hat was a well-known feature of the local landscape. It was large and plentifully trimmed with ostrich feathers. Mrs Bott's husband had made a fortune by his sauce, and, while Mrs Bott had acquired many of the tastes of the class into which the fortune had raised her, in millinery her taste remained true to the immortal type of Hampstead Heath.

'Mrs —' began William indignantly. 'A big thing like *that*! Why, I couldn't put it in my pocket or – or anywhere. I nat'rally meant something I could put in my pocket.'

'Well, you didn't say so,' said Ginger triumphantly, 'an' we've chosen Mrs Bott's Sunday hat.'

'I *can't* steal Mrs Bott's Sunday hat.'

'You can't steal anythin', that's what it is.'

'I can. I can steal anythin' but *that*. A *hat*! I never heard of anyone stealin' a *hat*. How'm I goin' to get it back even if I steal it – a big thing like that? You dunno how to choose things to steal.'

'Well, we're not goin' to choose anythin' else,' retorted Ginger, 'we've chosen Mrs Bott's Sunday hat an' we're not goin' to change. You're frightened of Mrs Bott, that's what it is.'

'I'm not.'

'You are.'

'I'm not.'

'You are.'

'I'm not.'

'All right – steal her Sunday hat then if you aren't frightened of her.'

'All right,' said William, stung to valour by their taunts, 'I will. Just to *show* you. You stay here an' I'll steal it an' bring it to you an' put it back again. I'm not frightened of *anyone*.'

The Outlaws cheered enthusiastically, and William set off with his best swagger down the road.

His swagger died down as he reached the Hall gates, and he entered them furtively, keeping well in the shadow of the shrubs that bordered the drive. When he came in sight of the house, he betook himself entirely to cover, and did not emerge till he was exactly opposite the front door, when he cautiously raised his head from the middle of a rhododendron bush and surveyed the prospect. The large, balconied bedroom with the bay window must be Mrs Bott's. His quarry was presumably there in a wardrobe or drawer or hat box. There was no convenient drainpipe near the window, and, in any case, he could hardly have climbed it in broad daylight and in full view of the whole garden. He was just considering without much hope the plan of calling boldly at the front door and saying that he had come to look at the gas meter or tune the piano (a trick often played by the hero of his book), when the front door opened, and Mrs Bott came out wearing her best coat and the Sunday hat secured by a large veil. William was too much startled to withdraw his head immediately, and for a minute Mrs Bott and William stared at each other in silence. Then Mrs Bott moved off down the drive to a spot where her head gardener was engaged in superintending the planting of a display of bulbs.

'Binks,' she said majestically, 'I don't like carved bushes, so don't start doing it here.'

'I beg your pardon, madam,' said the bewildered Binks.

'I say I don't like carved bushes,' she said. 'I think it's unnatural. I like a bush to be a bush same as nature made it. You ought to have asked me before you started doing it.'

'Doing what, madam?'

'Carving bushes. I've just told you. You've started carving bushes opposite the house, and I don't like it.'

'I still don't understand you, madam,' said Binks with all the majesty of a gardener who commanded four under-gardeners.

'Well, surely to goodness you know what carved bushes are, Binks?' said Mrs Bott impatiently.

'Are you referring to topiary work, madam?' said Binks.

'You can call it what you like,' said Mrs Bott, 'I call it carved bushes.

Bushes carved into shapes – balls and animals and suchlike. And I won't have it. It's unnatural.'

'There is no topiary work in this garden, madam,' said Binks coldly.

'Well, I may be short-sighted,' said Mrs Bott with spirit, 'I know I *am* short-sighted, but I can see when a bush has got a big ball sticking out in the middle of it, and balls don't come into bushes by themselves. They've got to be carved. Someone's started carving those bushes, and it's got to be stopped, and that's all I've got to say, and I'm not going to argue over it any more.'

With that she swept off down the drive towards the gate, leaving Binks gazing after her motionless, his mouth wide open.

William, who, concealed now in a laurel bush, had listened to the conversation with a good deal of relief, followed her under cover to the gate, and then set off behind her down the road, his eyes fixed longingly on the erection of nodding plumes that crowned the small, stout figure. As he walked, various plans for the possession of the prize revolved in his mind, only to be dismissed one after another. He might demand it highwayman fashion, saying that he had a colleague in hiding, armed with a pistol, who would shoot at once if she did not give it up to him. He might approach her and beg it from her on behalf of some imaginary old woman who could not go out because she was too poor to buy a hat. He might hurry on before her in the ditch, climb a tree, and bend down to twitch it off her head as she passed. It was just as he was reluctantly dismissing the last plan as impracticable that he realised with surprise that Mrs Bott was entering the gate of his own house. She knocked at the door and was admitted, evidently as an expected guest. William did not take much interest in his mother's social engagements, but he suddenly remembered having heard his mother say that she was expecting a visitor to tea. The visitor, then, was Mrs Bott. He entered behind her and hovered about in the hall as his mother came forward.

'Would you like to come upstairs and take your hat off?' said his mother after greeting her guest.

'Well, dear,' replied Mrs Bott, 'it *would* be rather nice. I mean, I always find a hat makes one's head ache, don't you? So heavy, aren't they, always, hats. It's very nice of you to think of it. Some people don't. . . .'

William waited in the hall, pretending to be engaged in looking for something on the hat stand, till Mrs Bott and his mother came downstairs. Mrs Bott was drawing her fingers through her very golden hair.

'You've simply got to be all eyes,' Mrs Bott was saying. 'The minute you turn your back they're up to some tricks. Carving the bushes they started to-day. If I'd not put my foot down the place would have been full of birds and animals and set-outs like that by the time I got home. Unnatural I call it. I like a bush to be a bush same as nature made it.'

Still talking, she entered the drawing-room and the door was closed.

William slipped quickly upstairs to his mother's bedroom and stood frowning thoughtfully at the enormous erection that lay upon the bed. Mrs Bott's visit to his mother had seemed at first to make everything gloriously, miraculously simple, but suddenly he wasn't sure.

It would be impossible to carry this creation through the village street to the old barn. Someone would be sure to recognise it and stop him. Impossible even to wrap it in paper. It was too large and feathery. It would refuse in any circumstances to form a 'parcel'. His brow cleared as a bright idea struck him. He would slip on hat and coat and veil and walk to the barn in them. Anyone meeting him would think he was Mrs Bott and pass by without suspicion or surprise. He would return from the old barn long before it was time for Mrs Bott to go home, slip up to the bedroom again, and replace the hat and coat on the bed without anyone's having discovered their disappearance. It was all perfectly simple. William put on the coat and hat and tied the veil tightly round the hat and under his chin. He was, of course, a little shorter than Mrs Bott, and the coat came right down to his shoes. Still – the hat came low over his forehead and the veil was very thick so that little of his face could be seen, and to a very casual observer he would certainly suggest Mrs Bott. He crept cautiously downstairs to the hall, then stood still and listened intently. The drawing-room door was slightly ajar, and from it came the sound of Mrs Bott's voice sustaining its inevitable monologue. 'All right for shows and suchlike,' it was saying, 'but in an ordinary garden I like a bush to be a bush same a nature made it, an' I told him so straight.'

From the kitchen came the subdued sounds of tea preparations. He crept to the side door and looked out. There was no one in the road. He opened the door very silently and slipped out of the house.

It happened that, just as he opened the side door, the housemaid opened the door of the kitchen and caught sight of his retreating figure. Open mouthed, she went into the hall and, pressing her face to the glass panes, watched him disappear into the road. Then she put her eye to the hinge of the drawing-room door to gaze at the figure of Mrs Bott seated in an armchair talking expansively. She returned to the kitchen as if in a dream.

'Well,' said the cook, 'where's them silver spoons?'

'I've not got 'em,' said the housemaid. 'I've seen a vishun.'

'Well, never mind vishuns,' said the cook, 'it was the silver spoons you went for.'

'I've seen the hastral body of Mrs Bott walking out of the house while her earthly body sits in the drawing-room talking to the mistress.'

'Well, you'll be talking to the mistress soon,' said the cook, 'if you don't hurry up and get them spoons from the dining-room.'

'Aren't you interested in vishuns?' said the housemaid, stung by the cook's attitude.

'No, I'm not,' said the cook, 'but I'm interested in having this tea on time, and I want them silver spoons.'

The housemaid tossed her head, affronted.

'I can tell you my New Thought Circle'll take it a bit different,' she said.

'They can take it how they like,' said the cook, 'so long as you get them silver spoons.'

Meantime William had passed safely through the village street, which happened to be empty. He had now only a few yards to go to the stile that led to the old barn. The adventure was practically at an end. It had been, on the whole, a little tame and disappointing. It was just as he came to this conclusion that he saw the figure of Mr Bott walking down the road to meet him. In panic-stricken flight he plunged down a side lane and looked around for a place of hiding. A few yards down the lane stood an unattended trade lorry.

William climbed quickly into this and drew a piece of sacking over his head. After a few moments he heard steps coming down the lane and approaching the lorry. Mr Bott, of course, coming to investigate the strange and sudden flight of his wife . . . William crouched beneath the sack, hardly daring to breathe.

Suddenly there came the sound of an engine starting up, and, before William realised what had happened, the lorry set off with a jerk, and he found himself travelling down the road at thirty miles an hour. William cautiously emerged from his sack. The steps had belonged to the lorry driver. Mr Bott, who was even more short-sighted than his wife, was placidly continuing his way through the village. The back of the lorry driver was broad and muscular – so broad and muscular that William decided not to make his presence known at once, but to wait till the lorry stopped and then depart from it as unobtrusively as he had entered it. Meantime, he sat up and looked about him. On the lorry were several baskets of apples. William thought he might as well take whatever compensations the situation offered, so he lay back comfortably against the end of the lorry, raising his veil, and began to munch apples and watch the countryside flash by. The lorry seemed to be going rather a long way. William was already considering the possibility of it being on its way to Scotland, when it stopped suddenly at a small public-house.

William gathered himself together for flight, but it turned out that the lorry driver was not, after all, leaving his lorry. A man in his shirt-sleeves came out from the public-house carrying a glass of beer.

'Usual, I suppose, Jim?' he said, and stood talking to the lorry man while he drank it.

William, who was well out of their sight at the head of the lorry, continued to munch his apple. His attention soon wandered from their conversation – which was very dull and concerned the prospects of various horses in various races – and he began to survey the landscape, trying without success to discover any familiar features. Suddenly there was a lull in the conversation, and William turned round with a start to find that the man in shirt-sleeves had walked round to the side of the lorry and was staring at him with amazement

'What yer lookin' at?' said the driver.

'Brought yer misses along ter-day, I see,' said the man. 'Wouldn't she like a glass of somethin'?'

There was an abrupt movement on the driver's seat, and William looked up to find a large red face glaring down at him furiously. Without a moment's hesitation William leapt from the lorry, and, gathering his voluminous coat about him, set off at a quick run down the road. Once out of sight and finding that he was not pursued, he stopped running and again looked about him. The road forked at the point where he had stopped, and one fork seemed to lead to a village. William decided to follow this. In the village he could find out how far he was from home. He pulled down his veil, arranged his coat and hat, and set off jauntily towards the village. William's spirit was not one that yields easily to defeat, and he still had hopes of winning his bet. When he had walked some way down the road, he heard the sound of the lorry, and turned to see it taking the other fork of the road, The lorry driver shook his fist in William's direction as he vanished from sight, and William put out his tongue behind his veil. In the village he approached an old man who sat on a seat outside a public-house, and, adopting the shrill falsetto voice with which in their games he impersonated the damsel whom the other Outlaws had to rescue, asked him the name of the village and the means of getting back to his home. The old man, who was deaf and short-sighted, noticed nothing peculiar in William's voice or appearance, and readily gave the required information, adopting on his side a quavering voice, and intimating that he suffered from a chronic complaint for which the doctor had prescribed beer, but that he had spent his last penny on food for a sick friend. William, not being the rich old lady of the old man's hopes, merely grunted on receiving this information, and busied himself in drawing up his coat to get to his trouser pocket (a proceeding that shocked the old man inexpressibly) and count his money. Yes he had enough money to get home by the 'bus. . . There was, however, half an hour to wait. William hated waiting. He sat down on the seat by the old man (who was still glaring at him, outraged by his lack of womanly modesty) and drummed his heels in the dust.

He waited for what seemed to him quite half an hour and found, on looking at the church clock, that only two minutes had gone. He then amused himself for some time by throwing stones at a tree across the road, increasing the horror and disgust of the old man, finally practising a long jump in the middle of the road – a proceeding that sent the old man hobbling quickly homewards. ('Out of Bedlam, her is . . . out of Bedlam.') Having practised long jumps for what seemed half an hour, William again looked at the church clock and found that only two more minutes had passed. It was just then that the unmistakable sound of a country fair came to his ears. He stood still and listened. William could never resist a country fair. He hastily felt in his pockets again. Yes, he had a few coppers beyond what would be needed for his 'bus fare. He could have a ride on the roundabout, and still be back in time to catch the 'bus home. Adjusting his hat and veil (for it still seemed less conspicuous to be a lady in a hat and coat than to be a boy carrying a lady's hat and coat), he set off down the road in the direction of the sounds and soon reached the fair ground. Already a dense crowd was streaming into it. William joined the crowd and made his way quickly to the nearest roundabout. He climbed upon it (remembering to sustain his character by sitting sideways) and surrendered himself to bliss. So lost was he to the ecstasy of the up-and-down-and-round-and-round movement that he failed to notice that he was attracting a good deal of attention. The large crowd that surrounded the merry-go-round was in fact occupying itself solely with watching him. Interested smiles followed his circular progress and his frequent reappearance at every part of the circle. Fingers pointed at him and voices cried: 'Look, there she is. There – coming round again!'

Still unaware of this, William, having spent his last available penny, descended decorously from the roundabout, and began to make his way towards the gate again. It was then that he realised with surprise and horror that he was walking between serried ranks of interested spectators, who made way for him, pointing him out to each other. 'Look, there she is . . . she's just been on the roundabout.'

The way that the crowd made for him did not lead to the exit. It led to a tent – a tent that bore a large notice: 'Mr & Mrs Tom Thumb. Entrance 2d. 6 o'clock prompt'. William had no option but to take it. He walked slowly and with a sinking of the heart toward the tent . . .

'Well, I shan't pay 2d. to see her now,' a woman said loudly as he passed her, 'and I don't think much of her either.'

William hesitated at the tent door, but the crowd that lined his path had closed up behind him and was pressing him on. He entered the tent door apprehensively. What chiefly worried him was the 'Entrance 2d'. Should the entrance fee be demanded of him, he would not have enough money left for his 'bus fare. He had a vague idea of hiding just inside the tent door till the crowd had dispersed, but there was no room to hide inside the tent door. It opened immediately into a sawdust-covered interior with a small platform at one end. A mirror hung from the pole that supported the tent, and in front of this stood a little woman about William's size arranging a hat that was, like William's, large and feathered. She wheeled round as William appeared and stood staring at him in amazement. Then her amazement vanished, and she came across to him, smiling a coy, bright, affected smile and holding out a small hand.

'How are you, dear? From Belson's, aren't you?'

William realised that if he was from Belson's he would be welcomed as a friend and no entrance fee demanded, so he decided to be from Belson's.

'Yes,' he said in his shrill falsetto voice.

'Of course, dear. Just for a moment it gave me quite a start seeing you standing there, then I knew, of course, you must be from Belson's. Funny you an' me 've never met before, isn't it, dear? An' so often we've just followed each other. Last time we were at Marleigh you'd moved on the day before.

People said: Why, Belson's Mrs Tom Thumb was here only yesterday. And as like as two peas to you, dear.' Of course, our strong man knows Belson's strong man quite well. It was him I sent the message to you by. It was good of you to come over at once, dear. I suppose you don't open till to-night?'

'No,' said William in his shrill falsetto.

'We don't open till six. I tell you what, dear. Suppose I walk over to Belson's with you. I'd love to see it. It's so seldom that one can see any show except one's own, and it's apt to make one a bit narrow. It's in the glebe field over at Marston, isn't it? I could easily be back by six. How's things going with you, dear? Our strong man says that Belson's elastic woman is nothing compared to ours, but that his mermaid beats ours hollow. I told the boss ours ought to have a fresh tail *months* ago. It drops scales whenever she moves, and a thing like that lets the whole show down. Well, dear, what about it? Shall I walk back to Belson's with you?'

'Yes,' shrilled William, wondering helplessly where the adventure was going to end.

'My hubby's just gone to have a drink with the fire swallower,' continued Mrs Tom Thumb. 'I don't expect he'll be back till six. . . Well, shall we start, dear? Out this way behind the tent. So many crowds at the front. Living in the limelight has its drawbacks, as I'm sure you've found out, dear. Sometimes I get sick of crowds and admiration.' She preened her small figure complacently. 'But there – we've got to put up with it same as royalty. . . Here we are. Through this gate to the road. It's only a mile or two, dear, isn't it?'

'Yes,' squeaked William, who felt as if in the grip of a nightmare.

There seemed nothing for it but to walk down the road with the garrulous little lady. She was glancing at him critically as they walked.

'Now, you mustn't mind me saying it, dear, but I'm surprised to find you like you are. I was told you were as dainty and elegant as me, but – well, you seem a bit clumsy somehow. You mustn't be annoyed, dear, because we can't be all in the front rank, as it were, can we? Well, it stands to reason that we can't, doesn't it? To me you seem made a bit clumsy, though I'll grant you you're short. Perhaps I'm over particular. Of course, the *Mudbury Chronicle* called me "a gem of miniature perfection", so I've probably got higher standards than what some people have – '

She stopped suddenly, and gave a gasp, staring at William in indignant horror.

For William had unthinkingly drawn up the coat again to get his handkerchief from his trousers pocket, and had revealed the stalwart nether limbs of a schoolboy clad in grey tweed shorts.

Mrs Tom Thumb's small countenance turned to an angry purple. Her eyes blazed furiously. 'A *boy*!' she screamed. 'A fraud, a cheat, that's what you are. I'll show you up. I'll show Belson's up. I'll tell the whole place what you are. Cheating the public all these years! And people saying you were as good as me – me that's a gem of miniature perfection, you little hound, you!

With these words the enraged lady sprang at William as if to shake or scratch him. William dodged and set off at a brisk run down the road, pursued for some distance by the gem of miniature perfection.

At the end of the road he stopped and turned round. Mrs Thumb had given up the chase and was now contenting herself with shaking a small fist at him and screaming abuse from halfway down the road. William turned the corner and looked about him apprehensively. There was nothing to be seen, however, but the 'bus that was just on the point of starting. He slipped a finger into each side of his mouth, emitted a piercing whistle, then ran down the road and leapt upon the 'bus under the eyes of the amazed conductor.

*

William alighted from the 'bus at his own gate and stood for a moment in the shadow of the hedge, again looking cautiously around him. Through the drawing-room window he could see Mrs Bott's golden head and fat, smiling face. She had evidently not yet discovered the loss of her hat and coat. There was no one in the side path. The side door was ajar. He could see the hall with its rows of hooks. Most of them supported coats and hats belonging to his family, but one was empty. The temptation to relieve himself of his encumbrances without further ceremony was irresistible. He went quickly up the side walk and into the hall; there he slipped off hat, coat, and veil, and was just in the act of hanging them on to the hook, when the house was filled with a strange commotion. Cook ran out of the kitchen and pounded upstairs, her large bulk moving with incredible speed. With the same furious speed she pounded down again, crying: 'Oh, mam, the boiler's burst. . . The water's coming down through the ceiling in your bedroom. . . I heard a funny noise and went up to see and it was that. . . And it's all coming down through the ceiling. . . . Oh, mam, oh, mam!'

Mrs Brown, followed by Mrs Bott, emerged from the drawing-room and ran hastily upstairs. . . Soon they reappeared.

'Ring up the plumber, Cook,' called Mrs Brown, 'and put some pans on the floor to catch the water. . . .'

Suddenly she noticed William, who had been struck motionless by amazement in the act of hanging up Mrs Bott's hat and coat.

'Oh, *William*!' said Mrs Brown, 'how *thoughtful* of you. . . . I think it was *splendid* of you, dear. Look, Mrs Bott, he ran upstairs to rescue your hat and coat as soon as he heard the water. . . You should have given the alarm at once, dear, but never mind. You saved Mrs Bott's hat and coat, which is the main thing. I think it showed *great* thoughtfulness and presence of mind.'

William hastily assumed an expression of thoughtfulness and presence of mind and wisely refrained from any comment on the situation.

Mrs Bott, feeling that any extension of her visit would be an anti-climax, thanked William profusely, and took her leave. As soon as she had gone, Mr Brown came home, and Mrs Brown gave him a confused but excited account of what had happened.

'And, my dear, it was *pouring* through from the ceiling of our bedroom. The man's seeing to it now and Cook's put pots and things all over the floor, but it's *soaked* the bed, and, my dear, I can't think *what* would have happened if William hadn't had the presence of mind to slip up and rescue her coat and hat as soon as he heard the sound of the dripping. My dear, Heaven only knows what that dreadful hat cost, and it would have been *ruined* – *ruined*! *And* the coat! It would have cost us *pounds* to replace them. It was really *splendid* of William to think of rescuing them, don't you think so, dear?'

'It certainly showed a bit more sense than I gave him credit for,' said Mr Brown, handing William a shilling before going upstairs to inspect the damage.

William set off to join his Outlaws. He walked with the swagger of one who has just performed a noble rescue. As he walked, his artist's mind was busy with the exploit – adjusting its details, making it more worthy of him.

The Outlaws were awaiting him at the old barn.

'Well?' they said eagerly.

'Well, I rescued her,' said William. 'The place was flooded. Flooded from top to bottom. An' she was upstairs an' no one could get to her an' she'd have been drowned in two seconds if I hadn't swum upstairs an' rescued her an' then swum downstairs again holdin' her in my arms, an' I saved her life, an' by rights I ought to have a statue put up to me.'

'Yes, but what about the *hat*?' said the Outlaws, who had heard too many stories of William's heroic exploits to be deeply impressed.

'I rescued her hat, too,' said William, 'and my father gave me a shilling.'

'Yes, but you were going to *steal* it,' the Outlaws reminded him vociferously.

William's mind travelled over the past to the adventure preceding the burst boiler.

'Oh, yes,' he said, 'I did steal it. I've been all over England in it.'

'Never mind all over England,' said Ginger sternly, 'the bet was that you'd to bring it here for us to see.'

'Oh, yes,' said William, 'I remember now. Well, I did steal the hat, but I forgot about bringin' it here. When I got back I was so sick of it that I jus' saw a hook in the hall an' didn't think of anything but jus' gettin' it hung up on it. I tell you I've been all over England in it. I've been on lorries an' performin' in fairs in it – '

'Oh, shut *up*,' said Ginger, for William suffered from the drawback that attends a fertile imagination in that people seldom gave him credit for such details in his stories as happened to be true. 'Shut up about lorries and fairs an' rubbish like that. You said you'd steal her hat and you didn't.'

'I did.'

'You didn't.'

'I did, I tell you.'

'Why didn't you bring it here, then?'

'I keep *telling* you, only you won't listen. I started out to bring it here, but I got all messed up in lorries an' fairs an' rescuing people from drownin' an' things like that.'

'I don't believe you ever *did* steal it.'

'Are you callin' me a liar?' said William, adopting a pugnacious attitude.

'Yes,' said Ginger simply.

'All right,' said William, and began to go through an elaborate process of taking off his coat and rolling up his sleeves with a good many unnecessary flourishes. Ginger did the same. . . But just as they were squaring up to each other, Douglas, who was standing at the door of the barn, called out: '*Look!*'

They ran to the door of the barn.

From the dark sky small white flakes were beginning to fall, growing bigger and bigger.

'Snow!' shouted the Outlaws excitedly.

Forgetting everything else in the world, they leapt forth exultantly, holding out their hands to catch the falling flakes in eager competition as to which of them should make the first snowball.

Richmal Crompton

Cleaning your house while your kids are still growing is
like shovelling the walk before it stops snowing.

Phyllis Diller

———

Sex is the tabasco sauce which an adolescent national
palate sprinkles on every course in the menu.

Mary Day Winn

———

from The Growing Pains of
Adrian Mole

Sunday   April 4th

My father has sent a telegram to the War Office. He wants to take part in
the war with Argentina. His telegram read:

> QUALIFIED HEATING ENGINEER STOP A1 FITNESS STOP OFFERS HIM-
> SELF IN THE SERVICE OF HIS COUNTRY STOP READY FOR IMMEDIATE
> MOBILIZATION

My mother says that my father will do anything to avoid working for
Manpower Services as a canal bank renovator.

At tea-time I was looking at our world map, but I couldn't see the
Falkland Islands anywhere. My mother found them; they were hidden under
a crumb of fruitcake.

I feel guilty about mentioning a personal anguish at this time of
national crisis, but ever since last night when a model aeroplane became
stuck fast to my nose with glue, I have suffered torment. My nose has
swollen up so much that I am frantic with worry that it might burst and take
my brain with it.

I rang the Casualty Department and, after a lot of laughing, the nurse
who removed the plane came on the line. She said that I was 'probably
allergic to the glue', and that the swelling would go down in a few days. She
added, 'Perhaps it will teach you not to sniff glue again.' I tried to explain
but she put the phone down.

Pandora has been round but I declined to see her. She would go straight off me if she saw my repulsive nose.

Monday   April 5th

Just my luck! It is the first day of the school holidays and I can't go out because of my gigantic swollen nose. Even my mother is a bit worried about it now. She wanted to prick it with a sterilized needle, but I wouldn't let her. She can't sew an accurate patch on a pair of jeans with a needle, let alone do delicate medical procedures with one. I've begged her to take me to a private nose specialist, but she has refused. She says she needs the money for her 'Well Woman' test. She is having her primary and secondary sexual organs checked. Yuk!

The dog is in love with a cocker spaniel called Mitzi. The dog stands no change, though: (a) it isn't a pedigree, and (b) it doesn't keep itself looking smart like most dogs. I tried to explain these things to the dog, but it just looked sad and mournful and went back to lying outside Mitzi's gate. Being in love is no joke. I have the same problem with Pandora that the dog has with Mitzi. We are both in a lower social class than our loved ones.

Tuesday   April 6th

The nation has been told that Britain and Argentina are not at war, we are at conflict.

I am reading *Scoop* by a woman called Evelyn Waugh.

Wednesday   April 7th

Wrote and sent Pandora a love letter and a poem. The letter said:

Pandora my love,

Due to an unfortunate physical disability I am unable to see you in person, but every fibre of my being cries out for your immediate physical proximity. Be patient, my love, soon we will laugh again.

Yours with undying love,
Adrian

PS. What are your views on the Argentinian conflict, with particular reference to Lord Carrington's resignation?

The Discontented Tuna
I am a Tuna fish,
Swimming in the sea of discontent
Oh, when, when,
Will I find the spawning ground?

I hope Pandora sees through my poem and realizes the symbolism of 'spawning ground'. I am sick of being the only virgin in our class. Everybody but me is sexually experienced. Barry Kent boasts about how many housewives he makes love to on his father's milkround. He says they are the reason why he is always late for school.

Thursday   April 8th
MAUNDY THURSDAY. FULL MOON

Nose has gone down a bit.

My mother came home from her 'Well Woman' check in a bad mood.

I allowed Pandora to visit me in my darkened bedroom. We had a brilliant kissing session. Pandora was wearing her mother's Janet Reger full-length silk slip under her dress and she allowed me to touch the lace on the hem. I was more interested in the lace near the shoulder straps but Pandora said, 'No darling, we must wait until we've got our O levels.'

I pointed out to Pandora that all this sexual frustration is playing havoc with my skin. But she said, 'If you really love me you will wait.'

I said, 'If you really love me you *wouldn't* wait.'

She went then; she had to replace the Janet Reger slip before her mother got back from work.

I have got thirty-eight spots: twenty-eight on my face and the rest on my shoulders.

Friday   April 9th
GOOD FRIDAY

Barry Kent has been spreading malicious rumours that I am addicted to Bostik. His auntie is a cleaner in the hospital and heard about the nose-stuck-to-model-aeroplane incident. I think it is disgusting that cleaners are allowed to talk about patients' private medical secrets. They should be made to take the Hippocratic oath, like doctors and nurses.

My mother is fed up. She is just sitting around the house smoking and sighing. There was a programme on BBC2 about French babies being born into swimming pools; it was most interesting (and erotic) but my mother quickly switched over to ITV and watched BERNIE WINTERS!!! When I protested she screamed, 'Why don't you clear off and sulk in your room like other teenagers?'

My father is as baffled as I am as to why my mother is depressed. She's been like it since she came back from the 'Well Woman' clinic.

Perhaps she's not well.

The *Canberra* has gone to the Falklands and taken Barry Kent's older brother, Clive, with it.

Sue Townsend

———

from Memories of a Catholic Girlhood

It was just at this time, too, that I found myself in a perfectly absurd situation, a very private one, which made me live, from month to month, in horror of discovery. I had waked up one morning, in my convent room, to find a few small spots of blood on my sheet; I had somehow scratched a trifling cut on one of my legs and opened it during the night. I wondered what to do about this, for the nuns were fussy about bed-making, as they were about our white collars and cuffs, and if we had an inspection those spots might count against me. It was best, I decided, to ask the nun on dormitory duty, tall, stout Mother Slattery, for a clean bottom sheet, even though she might scold me for having scratched my leg in my sleep and order me to cut my toe-nails. You never know what you might be blamed for. But Mother Slattery, when she bustled in to look at the sheet, did not scold me at all; indeed, she hardly seemed to be listening as I explained to her about the cut. She told me to sit down: she would be back in a minute. 'You can be excused from athletics today,' she added, closing the door. As I waited, I considered this remark, which seemed to me strangely munificent, in view of the unimportance of the cut. In a moment, she returned, but without the sheet. Instead, she produced out of her big pocket a sort of cloth girdle and a peculiar flannel object which I first took to be a bandage, and I began to protest that I did not need or want a bandage; all I needed was a bottom sheet. 'The sheet can wait,' said Mother Slattery, succinctly, handing me two large safety pins. It was the pins that abruptly enlightened me; I saw Mother Slattery's mistake, even as she was instructing me as to how this flannel article, which I now understood to be a sanitary napkin, was to be put on.

'Oh, no, Mother,' I said, feeling somewhat embarrassed. 'You don't understand. It's just a little cut, on my leg.' But Mother, again, was not listening; she appeared to have grown deaf, as the nuns had a habit of doing when what you were saying did not fit in with their ideas. And now that I knew what was in her mind, I was conscious of a funny constraint; I did not feel it proper to name a natural process, in so many words, to a nun. It was like trying not to think of their going to the bathroom or trying not to see the straggling iron-grey hair coming out of their coifs (the common notion that they shaved their heads was false). On the whole, it seemed better just to show her my cut. But when I offered to do so and unfastened my black stocking, she only glanced at my leg, cursorily. 'That's only a scratch, dear,' she said. 'Now hurry up and put this on or you'll be late for chapel. Have you any pain?' 'No, no, Mother!' I cried. 'You don't understand!' 'Yes, yes, I understand,' she replied soothingly, 'and you will too, a little later. Mother Superior will tell you about it some time during the morning. There's nothing to be afraid of. You have become a woman.'

'I know all about that,' I persisted. 'Mother, please listen. I just cut my leg. On the athletic field. Yesterday afternoon.' But the more excited I grew, the more soothing, and yet firm, Mother Slattery became. There seemed to be nothing for it but to give up and do as I was bid. I was in the grip of a higher authority, which almost had the power to persuade me that it was right and I was wrong. But of course I was not wrong; that would have been too good to be true. While Mother Slattery waited, just outside my door, I miserably donned the equipment she had given me, for there was no place to hide it, on account of drawer inspection. She led me down the hall to where there was a chute and explained how I was to dispose of the flannel thing, by dropping it down the chute into the laundry. (The convent arrangements were very old-fashioned, dating back, no doubt, to the days of Louis Philippe.)

The Mother Superior, Madame MacIllvra, was a sensible woman, and all through my early morning classes, I was on pins and needles, chafing for the promised interview with her which I trusted would clear things up. 'Ma Mère,' I would begin, 'Mother Slattery thinks . . . ' Then I would tell her about the cut and the athletic field. But precisely the same impasse confronted me when I was summoned to her office at recess-time. I talked about my cut, and *she* talked about becoming a woman. It was rather like a round, in which she was singing 'Scotland's burning, Scotland's burning', and I was singing 'Pour on water, pour on water'. Neither of us could hear the other, or, rather, I could hear her, but she could not hear me. Owing to our different positions in the convent, she was free to interrupt me, whereas I was expected to remain silent until she had finished speaking. When I kept breaking in, she hushed me, gently, and took me on her lap. Exactly like Mother Slattery, she attributed all my references to the cut to a blind fear of this new, unexpected reality that had supposedly entered my life. Many young girls, she reassured me, were frightened if they had not been prepared. 'And you, Mary, have lost your dear mother, who could have made this easier for you.' Rocked on Madame MacIllvra's lap, I felt paralysis overtake me and I lay, mutely listening, against her bosom, my face being tickled by her white, starched, fluted wimple, while she explained to me how babies were born, all of which I had heard before.

There was no use fighting the convent. I had to pretend to have become a woman, just as, not long before, I had had to pretend to get my faith back – for the sake of peace. This pretence was decidedly awkward. For fear of being found out by the lay sisters downstairs in the laundry (no doubt an imaginary contingency, but the convent was so very thorough), I reopened the cut on my leg, so as to draw a little blood to stain the napkins, which were issued me regularly, not only on this occasion, but every twenty-eight days thereafter. Eventually, I abandoned this bloodletting, for fear of lockjaw, and trusted to fate. Yet I was in awful dread of detection; my only hope, as I saw it, was either to be released from the convent or to become a woman in reality, which might take a year, at least, since I was only twelve. Getting out of athletics once a month was not sufficient compensation for the farce I was going through. It was not my fault; they had forced me into it; nevertheless, it was I who would look silly – worse than silly; half mad – if the truth ever came to light.

Mary McCarthy

Against Youth

Two very pretty teenage girls with peace slogans across their bosoms rang my doorbell the other day. They made a terrible mistake, they said. Their friend was driving down from Clacton to meet them and she had given them my address as a meeting place. Could they possibly wait and see whether she would turn up.

I wavered. They had been walking since seven o'clock, they pleaded; they had huge rucksacks on their backs, they were almost in tears. I weakened and let them in. I felt smugly conscious of bridging the Generation Gap; the young are not the only ones who can practise universal brotherhood, I thought, as I gave them coffee and biscuits.

They were very sweet and grateful. They admired the children and the house, then asked if I would mind if they left their things in the drawing-room while they nipped out for cigarettes.

It was only an hour later – when worried they might have got lost – I discovered not only had they not left their things behind, they had also stolen £25 from my handbag. The person from Clacton predictably never turned up.

As a result I'm a bit off Youth at the moment – in fact, next time a deb accosts me outside Harrods and asks me for a contribution to National Youth Week, I shall be tempted to ram her slit tin down her throat.

What really irritated me about the whole incident was that I'd been conned rotten. I ought to have realized that in most instances universal brotherhood is only another name for the perpetual scrounging practised by the young. They continually attack my generation for being materialistic, but they'll bleed us white given the opportunity.

Another reason I'm not wild about Youth is they make me feel so guilty – for a start – when they're sourly nibbling away at their horrible health foods. Guilty, in fact, about eating anything, when they're all so thin.

They also make me feel guilty about drinking (none of them seems to touch alcohol) and for talking too much. I was brought up to believe it was polite when you were in a room with someone to attempt to engage them in conversation. But if the younger generation don't feel like it, they don't bother to talk at all. 'Perceiving people non-verbally,' they call it. They seem totally unembarrassed by long silences.

On these counts, I emerge as a portly, sottish, garrulous carnivore – hardly attractive, is it?

Another hang-up I have is not being able to dance the way Youth do. Born and bred on the fox-trot, the current orgiastic shiver defeats me completely. Occasionally I lock myself in my bedroom and gyrate and flail in front of the mirror. I know nothing a consenting adult does in the privacy of her own room can be wrong – but it just looks wrong – not a bit like *Top of the Pops*.

The young also make me feel guilty because I have no desire to go back to Nature and live off the fruits of the earth. I love the country, but it bores me silly after a week or so. I much prefer dreary old London, and I loathe the idea of breaking down the family unit and living in a commune.

I read the most chilling piece about young people in communes recently, under the somewhat ambiguous title 'Getting it Together', telling you how all the adults shared their possessions and the daily tasks and the responsibility for the children; how all decisions were put to the vote and how, to break down sexual inhibitions, members of the commune wrote up on a noticeboard the names of other members with whom they wanted to sleep. Unfortunately it always turned out that everyone wanted Samantha, and no one wanted Janet. But that, said the communards, was life.

Anyway, with three children in the house at the moment, a nanny, a husband, five cats and the bailiffs, I'm practically living in a commune. Even so I have a sneaking feeling I'm not helping everyone to 'recognize their own special excellence', and that the cats ought to be put in charge of hewing wood, my son should tend the mangel-wurzels, and the new baby we've acquired should supervise home-made wine.

I know I should try harder, but somehow I'm not really attracted to the life young people seem to lead today. It's far too spartan, and I'm afraid I have a private bathroom mentality. I loathe the idea of roughing it in sleeping bags and crash pads, and living out of rucksacks (I mean whatever was the point of getting myself sacked from the Brownies). I'm scared stiff of riding on the back of motorbikes and hitchhiking is absolutely anathema. Whoever wants to ride for miles and miles with someone they haven't been introduced to?

But I suppose it is in the sexual field that the Generation Gap yawns the widest. My generation have a feeling they've missed out on all the permissiveness. In retrospect I rather enjoyed my youth, the only thing I regret about it was that it wasn't sufficiently misspent. I wasn't kissed until I was seventeen and a half.

Last year I employed a girl of eighteen and the first weekend I was staggering downstairs when a naked sailor came out of her bedroom. It was so early in the day that I was too shattered to say anything except 'Good morning'. He wasn't remotely embarrassed. Later, I found him cooking breakfast and he asked me if I'd like one egg or two.

I grow old, I grow old. I shall wear the bottoms of my trousers sawn off and fraying at Bermuda length. All my friends – particularly the men – seem so much better at keeping up with youth. They emerge at parties having jettisoned their unsuccessful pinstripe in place of tasselled handbags and tee-shirts covered with stars. Beards sprout on their chins, and their receding hair is coaxed forward into tendrils to cover their furrowed foreheads.

'We're taking a trip, this weekend,' they say.

'Oh lovely,' say I, 'Brighton?'

And they look at me pitifully and disappear into the next room and start tearing cigarettes apart, and muttering about meaningful lifestyles.

The young today want to change the world, my generation only wanted to change their hairstyles. We were the generation of alcohol and abdication, they are the age of pot and participation. Our main pre-occupation was getting a nine-to-five job, they reject such monotony, but beef even more if the unemployment figures are high and there aren't any nine-to-five jobs to reject.

My mother made the classic comment on the situation the other day. She arrived in great excitement – she'd seen a naked girl at the window next door and a car outside with a sticker saying 'Rolling Stones – Sticky Fingers'.

'Who lives there?' she asked.

'Oh lots of hippies,' I said.

'Don't they work,' she said, 'don't they even play in a band?'

But what finally convinced me of the Generation Chasm was being in the Mall the other day, when a Royal Coach crammed with Real Live Royalty and all the trappings of coachmen and postillions came by. On one of the horses rode a youth who cannot have been more than seventeen: pink-eared, staring rigidly in front of him. Suddenly, out of the corner of his eye, he saw a pretty girl in the crowd.

'Hullo, darling,' he shouted.

Jilly Cooper

For The Birthday of a Middle-Aged Child

I'm sorry you are wiser,
I'm sorry you are taller;
I liked you better foolish
And I liked you better smaller.

Aline Kilmer

The greatest advantage of not having children must be that you can go on believing that you are a nice person: once you have children, you realise how wars start.

Fay Weldon

———

THE SINCEREST

FORM OF FLATTERY

from Macbird!
PROLOGUE

[Enter middle-aged man dressed in standard business attire, except for a plume in his hat and a toy sword at his waist.]

O, for a fireless muse, that could descend
From kingdoms, princes, monarchs and the like
To common themes of marital affairs,
Of young romance and adolescent strife;
Then should our war-like leaders not appear
Upon this stage in false resemblances
'Twixt princes of the present and the past.
O pardon, gentles, these bright-painted spirits,
That, drawn too clear, seem more than what they say.
Can costumed kings who sweep across this stage
With antique garb and flashing swords of old
Be likened to our sober-suited leaders,
Who plot in prose their laceless, graceless deeds?

And think you that within these wooden walls
Can be confined two warring dynasties,
With swelling hosts of hacks, and clerks and claques
Whose high uprearèd and abutting prides
Now rip a ruling monolith asunder?
Can these bare boards support the vast machines
That now sustain two modern monarchies?
No, this weak wood but holds the airy actors
Who here portray fantastic lords of yore.
O, don't employ your own imaginations
To piece out imperfections in our plot.
For things that seem, I beg you, know no seeming;
Your very lack of thoughts must cloak our kings.
For my sake, seek no silly suppositions;
Disdain to note what likenesses may show;
Accept our words, ignore your intuitions;
For *honi soit qui mal y pense*, you know.

*

ACT ONE

SCENE ONE

[*Hotel corridor at Democratic convention. THREE WITCHES slink in. The first witch is a girl dressed as a student demonstrator, beatnik stereotype. The second witch is a Negro with the impeccable grooming and attire of a 'Muhammed Speaks' salesman. The third witch is an old leftist, wearing a worker's cap and overalls. He carries a lunch pail and an old movie projector.*]

BEATNIK WITCH　When shall we three meet again?
MUSLIM WITCH　In riot!
WORKER WITCH　　　Strike!
BEATNIK WITCH　　　　　Or stopping train?
MUSLIM WITCH　When the hurly burly's done,
　　When the race is lost or won.
WORKER WITCH　Out on the convention floor.
　　Or in some hotel corridor.
BEATNIK WITCH　Where cheering throngs can still be heard,
　　There to meet with . . . MacBird!
　　　[*A cry offstage.*]

MUSLIM WITCH   I come, soul brothers!
WORKER WITCH   Comrades call!
BEATNIK WITCH   Away!
    [*WITCHES move off, chanting.*]
THREE WITCHES   Fair is foul and foul is fair.
    Hover through stale and smoke-filled air.

Barbara Garson
(after Shakespeare's Macbeth)

———

Full Fathom Five Thy Father Lies

Full fathom five thy father lies,
His aqualung was the wrong size.

June Mercer Langfield
(after Shakespeare)

———

As Someone Might Like It

BUXOM MAID   Pardon me, good sir, which is the way to Windsor?
TALL HEROINE   Which way is right? You have right of way, but find you
    are left to right yourself or find yourself lost. And as your
    right is your due, due east is your right.
BUXOM MAID   I beg your pardon.
TALL HEROINE   While thus I stand your route is right, and London, lately
    left, is left. But if my axis I revolve, the sinister rite which
    I perform rights my left and leaves my right wrong. So,
    starboard, larboard, my back faces south though my face
    is left north.
BUXOM MAID   Goodness me! I only want to know which way to point
    my horse.
TALL HEROINE   Mayn't I mount your paltry palfry? Sure 'tis the droit de
    senior, senora.
BUXOM MAID   You'll ride with me?
TALL HEROINE   Fair maid you are too gauche! If you were married, single
    or widdershins, 'twould not be right to take a lift. Though
    I were left, I'd be left rightly.

BUXOM MAID   Will you escort me?

TALL HEROINE   Escort? In the course of your sport, you sport a skirt, yet skirt the sport of our intercourse.

BUXOM MAID   D'you fancy me or something?

TALL HEROINE   Ah, madam, though the apparel oft proclaims the man; 'tis oft the opposite seems the same. The same, though apposite, opposite is. It is apparent my apparel misleads you, though it leads you to miss a miss, madam.

BUXOM MAID   (*who's seen it all before*) You mean you're really a woman dressed up as a man . . . ?

TALL HEROINE   No. I'm a man dressed up as a woman dressed up as a man . . . well, actually I'm a woman pretending to be a man dressed up as a woman dressed up as a man.

BUXOM MAID   (*doubtfully*) And I'm a woman dressed up as a man dressed up as a woman.

They look at each other, counting on fingers trying to work out what's what.

TALL HEROINE   (*mounting horse*) Oh, (*shrugs*) . . . what the hell!

They gallop off into the sunset.

Fidelis Morgan
(after Shakespeare's Tall Heroines)

————

Gertrude Talks Back

I always thought it was a mistake, calling you Hamlet. I mean, what kind of a name is that for a young boy? It was your father's idea. Nothing would do but that you had to be called after him. Selfish. The other kids at school used to tease the life out of you. The nicknames! And those terrible jokes about pork.

I wanted to call you George.

I am *not* wringing my hands. I'm drying my nails.

Darling, please stop fidgeting with my mirror. That'll be the third one you've broken.

Yes, I've seen those pictures, thank you very much.

I *know* your father was handsomer than Claudius. High brow, aquiline nose and so on, looked great in uniform. But handsome isn't everything, especially in a man, and far be it from me to speak ill of the dead, but I think it's about time I pointed out to you that your dad just wasn't a whole lot of fun. Noble, sure. I grant you. But Claudius, well, he likes a drink now and then. He appreciates a decent meal. He enjoys a laugh, know what I mean? You don't always have to be tiptoeing around because of some holier-than-thou principle or something.

By the way, darling, I wish you wouldn't call your stepdad *the bloat king*. He does have a slight weight problem, and it hurts his feelings.

The rank sweat of a *what*? My bed is certainly not *enseamed*, whatever that might be! A nasty sty, indeed! Not that it's any of your business, but I change those sheets twice a week, which is more than you do, judging from that student slum pigpen in Wittenberg. I'll certainly never visit you *there* again without prior warning! I see that laundry of yours when you bring it home, and not often enough either, by a long shot! Only when you run out of black socks.

And let me tell you, everyone sweats at a time like that, as you'd find out very soon if you ever gave it a try. A real girlfriend would do you a heap of good. Not like that pasty-faced what's-her-name, all trussed up like a prize turkey in those touch-me-not corsets of hers. If you ask me, there's something off about that girl. Borderline. Any little shock could push her right over the edge.

Go get yourself someone more down-to-earth. Have a nice roll in the hay. Then you can talk to me about nasty sties.

No, darling, I am not *mad* at you. But I must say you're an awful prig sometimes. Just like your dad. *The Flesh*, he'd say. You'd think it was dog dirt. You can excuse that in a young person, they are always so intolerant, but in someone his age it was getting, well, very hard to live with, and that's the understatement of the year.

Some days I think it would have been better for both of us if you hadn't been an only child. But you realize who you have to thank for *that*. You have no idea what I used to put up with. And every time I felt like a little, you know, just to warm up my ageing bones, it was like I'd suggested murder.

Oh! You think *what*? You think Claudius murdered your dad? Well, no wonder you've been so rude to him at the dinner table!

If I'd known *that*, I could have put you straight in no time flat.

It wasn't Claudius, darling.

It was me.

Margaret Atwood
(dealing with Hamlet)

Paradise Lost 2–0

Their tumult ceased awhile, th'encircling throng,
Agape with keen anticipation, see,
Like coloured marbles roll'd on' the green sward
By young Olympians, th'opposing Teams
Now scatter as the Contest starts, Flies now,
As if some insect were caught in the Game
The Gods play with mere men, a speckl'd sphere;
Nor does it come to rest in either net,
Though those who watch implore their several Gods
It should be; some one end, t'other some,
But wait awhile! When th'allotted Time's
Not half way done, Vict'ry attends one man:
Nor is't in vain! At last the argent Cup,
Spite foul attacks, is held up by his Chief.
Then, breaking loose, the herded hordes run free:
Relieve themselves, drink deep, and savage all
Who in their path might accident'ly stray.

Margaret Rogers
(after Milton)

———

When lovely woman wants a favour,
    And finds, too late, that man won't bend,
What earthly circumstance can save her
    From disappointment in the end?

The only way to bring him over,
    The last experiment to try,
Whether a husband or a lover,
    If he have feeling, is, to cry!

Phoebe Carey
(after Goldsmith)

———

When Lovely Woman Stoops to Folly

When lovely woman stoops to folly
The evening can be awfully jolly.

Mary Demetriadis
(after Goldsmith)

For A' That and A' That

A NEW VERSION, RESPECTFULLY RECOMMENDED TO SUNDRY
WHOM IT CONCERNS.

More luck to honest poverty,
  It claims respect, and a' that;
But honest wealth's a better thing,
  We dare be rich for a' that.
    For a' that, and a' that,
      And spooney cant and a' that,
    A man may have a ten-pun note,
      And be a brick for a' that.

What though on soup and fish we dine,
  Wear evening togs and a' that,
A man may like good meat and wine,
  Nor be a knave for a' that.
    For a' that, and a' that,
      Their fustian talk and a' that,
    A gentleman, however clean,
      May have a heart for a' that.

You see yon prater called a Beales,
  Who bawls and brays and a' that,
Tho' hundreds cheer his blatant bosh,
  He's but a goose for a' that.
    For a' that, and a' that,
      His Bubblyjocks, and a' that,

A prince can make a belted knight,
A marquis, duke, and a' that,
And if the title's earned, all right,
Old England's fond of a' that.
For a' that, and a' that,
Beales' balderdash, and a' that,
A name that tells of service done
Is worth the wear, for a' that.

Then let us pray that come it may
And come it will for a' that,
That common sense may take the place
Of common cant and a' that.
For a' that, and a' that,
Who cackles trash and a' that,
Or be he lord, or be he low,
The man's an ass for a' that.

Shirley Brooks
(after Burns)

———

Fragment in Imitation of Wordsworth

There is a river clear and fair,
'Tis neither broad nor narrow;
It winds a little here and there –
It winds about like any hare;
And then it holds as straight a course
As, on the turnpike road, a horse,
Or, through the air, an arrow.

The trees that grow upon the shore
Have grown a hundred years or more;
So long there is no knowing:
Old Daniel Dobson does not know
When first those trees began to grow;
But still they grew, and grew, and grew,
As if they'd nothing else to do,
But ever must be growing.

The impulses of air and sky
Have reared their stately heads so high,
And clothed their boughs with green;
Their leaves the dews of evening quaff, –
And when the wind blows loud and keen,
I've seen the jolly timbers laugh,
And shake their sides with merry glee –
Wagging their heads in mockery.

Fixed are their feet in solid earth
Where winds can never blow;
But visitings of deeper birth
Have reached their roots below.
For they have gained the river's brink,
And of the living waters drink.

There's little Will, a five years' child –
He is my youngest boy;
To look on eyes so fair and wild,
It is a very joy.
He hath conversed with sun and shower,
And dwelt with every idle flower,
As fresh and gay as them.
He loiters with the briar-rose, –
The blue-bells are his play-fellows,
That dance upon their slender stem.

And I have said, my little Will,
Why should he not continue still
A thing of Nature's rearing?
A thing beyond the world's control –
A living vegetable soul, –
No human sorrow fearing.

It were a blessed sight to see
That child become a willow-tree,
His brother trees among.
He'd be four times as tall as me,
And live three times as long.

                              Catherine M. Fanshawe
                              (after Wordsworth)

Pride and Punishment

'Are not you happy in Hertfordshire, Mr Raskolnikov?' said Elizabeth.

Raskolnikov looked into her beautiful dark eyes. His own shone with feverish brilliance.

'Would you be happy,' he said, 'if you had killed a miserable pawn-broker?'

Elizabeth turned away to hide a smile. 'I hope I am not so deficient in sense and feeling as either to be capable of the attempt, or to remain in spirits when the crime was accomplished,' said she. 'But they are not within the range of my acquaintance – pawnbrokers are safe from me.'

'She was only a louse, a miserable insect,' murmured Raskolnikov. 'But I was wrong to kill her – and to kill Lizaveta too.'

'How easily may a bad habit be formed!' cried Elizabeth; and with this in mind, though she hoped he was not in earnest, she very soon afterwards took leave of him.

Gwen Foyle
(after Jane Austen)

———

A Grecian Urn Reconsidered

Into my room of peaceful quietude,
Unwished-for and mistrusted Grecian gift,
Thou com'st, a pseudo-attic shape, whose crude
Cheap gaudiness Time's workings cannot shift
Since, hourly, thou dost more unlovely grow.
From what small gifte-shoppe by the sad sea shore
(O Devil's mass-produced!), what Churchly sale,
What bargain-counter in a chainèd store,
Or stall in dusty market did'st thou hail?
Alas! – thou must be seen to be believed,
A tablet marked 'reduced' clings yet to thee,
And on the side in letters gold-relieved
These words, 'A PRESENT FROM THERMOPYLAE',
Tell all we know of thee or need to know.

Nancy Gunter
(after Keats)

Little Liberated Women

'These are capital boots, so boyish and comfortable,' cried Jo. 'What did Marmee say about your new mini-dress, Meg?'

Meg's cheeks grew rosy as she answered thoughtfully, 'Mother said it was neat and well made, but she wondered if I was wise to use a kingsize crochet hook.'

'It would look nicely over my body stocking,' said Jo. 'You might have it, but it's laddered. Mercy, what are you painting, Amy?'

'A psychopathic experience I had at the party last night,' returned Amy with dignity.

'If you mean psychedelic, I'd say so,' advised Jo, laughing, while Meg looked at the little picture and said gently, 'If that's his beard, dear, it was auburn, not red.'

'Mercy, I must fly,' exclaimed Jo. 'I'm meeting Laurie for a demonstration.'

'Let me come too,' coaxed Amy. 'I'd dearly love to see him pull a policeman off a horse.'

'Stop bothering,' scolded Jo. 'You'll be frightened of the crowds, Laurie will have to put his arm round you and protect you, and that will spoil our fun. How happy Beth looks!'

'She's hearing heavenly music,' said Amy.

'Christopher Columbus, look at the cats!'

'She shares her LSD with them,' whispered Meg, 'the little saint.'

Gwen Foyle
(after Louisa May Alcott)

---

from By Henry James Cozened

Author Winner sat serenely contemplating his novel. His legs, not ill-formed for his years, yet concealing the faint cyanic marbling of incipient varicosity under grey socks of the finest lisle, were crossed. He was settled in the fine, solidly-built, cannily (yet never parsimoniously, never niggardly) bargained-for chair that had been his father's, a chair that Author Winner himself was only beginning to think that, in the fullness of time, hope he reasonably might that he would be able (be possessed of the breadth and the depth) to fill. Hitching up the trousers that had been made for his father (tailored from a fabric woven to endure, with a hundred and sixty threads to the inch), he felt a twinge of the sciatica that had been his father's and had come down to him through the jeans. Author Winner was grateful for any resemblance; his father had been a man of unusual qualities: loyal, helpful, friendly, courteous, kind, obedient, cheerful, thrifty, brave, clean and reverent; in the simplest of terms: a man of *dharma*.

Author Winner turned a page; his fingers, ten in number, and remarkably, even redundantly uniform (save for the inherent, ineluctable differences of size, shape and function), rested lightly on the margins of pages 458 and 459, having fallen, quite without advertence, into a composition not, as a whole, lacking in grace, yet with each of its separate parts (its distinct but not unconnected digits) pointedly emphasizing (indeed emphatically pointing to) one of the better phrases studding jewel-like, with multiprismatic refractions, the four great paragraphs spread out, deployed, splayed on the facing, the, in a sense, equal but opposite pages before him.

Author Winner said: 'Not undistinguished; nor, in all candor, *inconsiderable*. One might, in fact, go further: Tolstoi would, as a sentient man, have been forced, though not without a tinge of viridity, to cry: "XOPOWO!" And Joyce?' Author Winner shrugged, allowing the question to hang for a moment in the air (that brave o'erhanging firmament!) above his head. *Re* Joyce: could any reasonable man pretend (without hypocrisy) to know what Joyce would have thought, or indeed what, ultimately, or for that matter, penultimately, he, in his anfractuosity *did* think? The answer was pellucid: No! One could not profitably go one's way *re*-Joycing.

Hearing then the sound of a key in the latch, Author Winner, with not-unceremonious decorum, rose. Bouncing in on sturdy feet encased in fulgent shoes of the best cordovan leather was his wife, Clarifier, her arms, although long and well-muscled, encumbered with packages. Of her burdens, relieving her (an act he performed habitually, indeed, instinctively in all his personal relations), Author Winner, with eloquent simplicity, said: 'Hello.'

Clarifier, with a faint (leporine) vellication of her nose (a tic Author Winner found at once repellent and subtly attractive), removed her hat. She said: 'Darling, I'll venture to guess that you, with your probing intelligence, will deduce that I've been out.'

Author Winner nodded wordlessly.

Clarifier, removing her coat and turning to suspend it in the well-constructed wardrobe that had been her father's-in-law (himself defunct while this relationship was still uneventuate), revealing a nascent tendency toward steatopygia, permitted a paper to flutter from her pocket, the which Author Winner stooped (his inherent grace negating the implicit onus of the act), to retrieve.

Clarifier heartily said: 'Oh, the milk bill. I had intended to give it to you, darling, before I departed from our residence at 10:08 this A.M.'

Author Winner went to his desk; he was a man who liked to settle his accounts promptly, his ancestors on both sides having been early settlers.

Following him with springy steps Clarifier said: 'We have, darling, a new milkman. Noting that he appeared ignorant concerning us, I invited him in for a cup of instant coffee and ventured to inform him that you, although an Author born, had only recently become a in-the-fullest-sense Winner, that I, following a chance encounter at the home of your germane cousin, Claude (the son of your mother's elder sister), and a courtship of four and a half months, became your wife in an extremely high church ceremony, and that we were now, as we had been then, childless.'

Author Winner said: 'What manner of man is this purveyor of milk?'

Clarifier said: 'I'm glad, darling, that you asked that question; he is, as I myself discovered, a most-interesting combination. His mother was half Negro and half Jewish; his father, Catholic and Episcopalian in equal parts.'

Frowning, Author Winner said: 'I trust you entertained the Episcopal part only.'

It was then that the storm broke: the inevitable effect of the fortuitous concatenation of air currents and pressure areas. Raging electrically, symbolically, above and on the four sides of the house, it was nevertheless able to exercise (intent upon exercising!) a subtle penetration. Author Winner and his wife, responding to a common (deep-rooted) impulse, found themselves moving toward the living-room windows, left open (no! intentionally raised some hours before against the matutinal calidity), and now admitting the (inadmissible) humectation. Together closing, then standing for a moment in the resultant closeness, they found themselves (together still!) mounting, mounting! Then a fumbling to open (the distaff distrait), superseded by Author Winner's deft dexterity; a brief interval of exploration, and then – the moment of revelation: His, and then Hers, Hers, Hers, and again and again Hers! in rapid succession, until Clarifier, sensing her husband's discomfiture, shyly said: 'There was a white sale at Macy's; the Hers towels were half price.'

Felicia Lamport
(after Henry James)

Mummy

I went into the kitchen to get a cup o' tea
The boys they stopped their talking and their eyes all said to me
'Look, can't you see we've friends in?' and they 'eaved a pointed sigh.
I climbed the staircase back to bed and to myself sez I:

> Oh, it's Mummy this and Mummy that and 'Mummy, do you *mind*!'
> But it's 'Mummy, can you help me?' when your boots are hard to find.
> 'I've left my football kit at home, so could you bring it round?
> 'Oh thanks, that's grand – and by the way – you haven't got a
> pound?'

When kids start on their schooling, those darn teachers know it all,
'Could try harder . . . must write neater . . . keep your eye upon the ball.'
If *you* should try and teach your kids – 'that's not the way it's done';
But you bet they'll blame 'is background if the boy goes on the run.

> Oh it's 'Mums keep out' and 'Mums don't fuss' from teachers that
> *we*'ve paid;
> But it's 'Thank you Mrs Atkins' when they want the lemonade,
> The biscuits and the costumes for the fourth-form pantomime;
> They're dead keen on us mothers when they want *our* overtime.

We're Mums, so we're the cleaners too, the washers and the cooks;
An' they think that's all we're good for, once we've lost our dolly looks.
My 'usband doesn't mind to say I'm just a silly moo,
But 'e sees it all quite different when 'e wants my wages too.

> Oh it's 'Mum's too slow' and 'Mum's too fat' and 'Mum's a bleeding fool'
> But it's 'Mum could make some money' once the kids are off to school.
> They want us scrubbing saucepans and they think that's all we do –
> But they call us 'Superwoman' when they want our wages too.

We ain't no superwomen nor we ain't no numbskulls too,
But common thinking people most remarkable like you,
And sometimes if our tempers isn't all your fancy paints,
Well, women stuck with 'ousework don't grow into plaster saints.

> The 'Mum, come 'ere' and 'Mum, get lost' would make you go berserk;
> But it's 'motherhood is precious' when it's men that want the work.
> It's washing and it's ironing and it's food to feed their gobs,
> But it's 'sacred task of motherhood' when men want all the jobs.

You talk o' better terms for us, playgroups an' nursery schools,
And think such things will settle it; you must think we're all fools.

It's a job without a let-up, and just when we think we're through
We find that we're expected to 'mother' Uncle too.
    Oh it's Mummy this and Mummy that and Mummy up and down;
    – But sailors all call 'Mother!' when they know they're goin' to drown.
    We love our kids and lump it; but all we get for pay
    Is the thin red bunch o' roses that you bring on Mother's Day.

Katharine Whitehorn
(after Kipling)

———

Wilde's St Joan

DAUPHIN	Where do you come from?
JOAN	A little village.
DAUPHIN	All villages are little; that is why they are villages. And as everyone leaves them they can't grow any bigger. Why have you come?
JOAN	To help you.
DAUPHIN	When a woman says that she means that she will help herself.
JOAN	And if a man says it?
DAUPHIN	A man never declares his intentions unless a woman makes him. Are yours honourable?
JOAN	Yes. Will you give me what I ask?
DAUPHIN	That is what they all say.
JOAN	Who?
DAUPHIN	All the women who come to Court. My wife doesn't like it. It takes an exceptional woman to appreciate her husband's generosity to anyone else.
JOAN	Would your wife like to be a queen?
DAUPHIN	Of course. All wives think they should be queens; that is their illusion. Sometimes their husbands encourage it unwisely; that is their collusion.
JOAN	Give me a horse and a suit of armour.
DAUPHIN	The others are more simple. They only want a carriage and a new dress. But perhaps you are subtler.

Vera Telfer
(after Shaw, in the style of Wilde)

The Bore

A woman in black sits on a chair. There is a small table at her side. Another, empty, chair is placed some way behind her, out of her eyeline, but within earshot. The woman is cracking nuts with her teeth. Outside we can hear a dog bark, then tapping. She begins to whistle, as she reads a book, flicking the pages over before she can possibly have read them. After a while, she slams the book shut and puts it down. She sighs, then talks.

Three long winters since we moved from the country to Kversk, Natalia Mariarovitch Nankenchovinska. Three winters so long that summer hardly seems to visit us at all.

Pause.

Do you know, I was talking to the Doctor only the other day, and he said that last summer was the shortest in living memory! And he should know, his knowledge of meteorology is apparently quite famous among the local villeins holding their land on a ten year lease but still paying tithes to the landowners.

She reaches out towards the table, but sees her glass is empty.

Pour me another glass of tea, there's a dear.

Pause.

And what have we achieved? Tortsov Ovstrovski still goes round exhorting us all to revive Serbian folk dance. But does he *do* anything? Its been ages since he last gave us a turn around the samovar. And little Yelena Kirchovinchna (what a dear sweet creature she is) still keeps pressing us all to revive the old traditions; never goes anywhere without that primitive peasant weave rug.

The trouble is they're all so bored. They think that life, here in the country, is boring, and that just because we don't attend the opera and frequent the fashionable places that there is nothing to do. But then, I suppose I'm just not the sort of person who goes in for activities like that anyway. Notwithstanding, there is really no less to do in the country . . . if one sets out to find it.

There is an endless pause.

Do you know why they're bored Natella? It's because they're boring! They never talk about interesting things; they're all so obsessed with themselves. They seem to think that I'm unusual in some sort of way, because I haven't got an obsession about anything, and consequently I don't go round boring everyone to sleep.

She stretches.

Did you see that? The way the sun caught my arm? Sometimes, when I see things like that: the beauty of an arm, the grace of my fingers, the glint of my hair in the sun, I begin to understand. I can see that nature, having created life, wants to remind us all that we are part of it. Do you understand?
She sighs.

No. I'm not obsessed with anything. That's why I'm not boring. You don't think I'm boring, do you? Natella?
She looks around and sees the empty chair for the first time.
Natella? Oh, she's gone.

There is a shot off-stage.

Fidelis Morgan and Carla Stafford
(after Chekhov)

A Football-Pool Winner

But I didn't even *choose* them! shrieked Clara silently. A few random crosses on a piece of paper, and hey presto! a cheque for one hundred thousand pounds was pressed into her hand. ('No really – I must confess, I did it with my eyes shut!') Yet here it was, a real cheque, not to mention the fifty-three letters, the idiotic telegrams from people she hadn't spoken to for years, and heavens above! the newspapers – that awful, simpering photograph ripped out, of all things, from a *hockey* group! Surely the world had gone quite mad. She rushed into the window, fearing shattered houses and a people fled . . . A milk bottle squatted on every doorstep, and the black-and-white cat opposite was placidly laundering his chest. She felt it was all some terrible mistake. It's no use – her mouth opened – we must send it back! But before the words could escape, another thought winged out without so much as an excuse-me: Could we really, now, afford to buy a *whole* island? One hand, aghast, flew to her mouth, but she gazed enraptured across the breakfast table. Breathing a little heavily, totally absorbed, Bill had not heard her (perhaps she didn't really say it). He went on stroking the glossy pages of one of the seventeen television catalogues . . .

Margaret Tims
(after Katherine Mansfield)

Advertisement Copy

'Oh, thank you, dear.'

(*Thinks*) And now I must be kissed, must smile, his scowl, his grumpiness – how strange men are! – utterly vanished. And still one gropes, like a blind man with a stick, for the reason; the late-night malted drink – was that it? – the crispy breakfast cereal – was that it? How could they spirit away that monster, those hooves trampling the pale leaves of my content, that near hatred? This, then: the teeming suds; white sheets flapping (like great swans fighting to be free); Monday, and his dinner not scamped; his wife gracious with leisure. It is to Rinsil, then, my thanks should go!

Elaine Morgan
(after Virginia Woolf)

――――

Little Brothers and Sisters

'So we were heard and not seen,' said Hector, reaching the schoolroom.

'It is not what children are supposed to be.'

'It is the opposite,' said Lesbia. 'We must be heard occasionally, though. It is expected of us.'

The Caistor children had been given the Christian names of rich God-parents, the richest of whom, Lesbia Chaveling, had had parents whose respect for the classics was matched by their ignorance of them. Lady Caistor regarded objections to the name as frivolous. The Chaveling fortune was large.

'Miss Wates will not let us know she heard,' said Hector. 'It is a good thing we saw her.'

'Yes. Forewarned is forearmed. Servants always listen, and governesses tell parents.'

'This one will not do so,' said Hector, at the window. 'Miss Wates is floating face down in the lake.'

'She will be seen and not heard,' said Lesbia.

Margaret Rogers
(after Ivy Compton-Burnett)

――――

Lady Police Serial

Juliet and Wilberforce, the desk sergeant, chatting at the front desk. They both have their hats on.

JULIET   Wilberforce.

WILBERFORCE   Ma'am?

JULIET   Do you mind if I ask you something?

WILBERFORCE   I don't, no.

JULIET   Do you know how to make a cup of tea?

WILBERFORCE   No, I don't, ma'am.

JULIET   No, neither do I. (*Bangs on desk.*) And I should know! Wilberforce – I've just had a call from Harry Potter.

WILBERFORCE   Harry Potter the safebreaker? Little feller? Black 'tache, hangs round The Mop and Bucket, easily led but unexpectedly generous?

JULIET   That's him. Do you know him?

WILBERFORCE   No. What did he want, ma'am?

JULIET   I don't know, we were cut off before he could tell me. He might have been murdered – I'll pop round on my way home. What happened about the brick that went missing from the building site, Wilberforce?

WILBERFORCE   It's been found, ma'am. It's chipped along one corner, but they think it's going to be all right.

JULIET   That's good. Our Asian friends – are they still being racially harassed?

WILBERFORCE   No. Those National Front skinheads have completely changed their tune, thanks to you. In fact, they're throwing a party for the entire Asian community tomorrow.

JULIET   Right. I thought that new ping-pong table would do the trick.

I might go to the party, Wilberforce – I've got a serge sari – where is it being held?

WILBERFORCE   Kitchener Street, ma'am – five streets away from the old playground where someone who did some shoplifting's mother was found wandering in a confused state – do you know it?

JULIET   Yes, I do. It backs on to the Cut where old Barney the tramp drowned himself because his dog had been run over by a Bedford van – I forget the registration number.

WILBERFORCE We all had a whip-round, ma'am, as you suggested, and bought him a new puppy.

JULIET Did it work?

WILBERFORCE Yes, the old tramp's alive again now. In fact, he's thinking of doing social sciences at the Open University.

Message comes through on the radio.

VOICE Oscar Delta Tango Charlie Farnsbarns to base, over.

Juliet grabs the mike.

JULIET I'll deal with this, Wilberforce. You go and check on Garstang's Television and Video Rental shop in the High Street. I passed there this morning and some of those televisions looked like they were about to be stolen.

WILBERFORCE Right away, ma'am. (*Leaves.*) I've just got to get some after-dinner mints and change my library books.

JULIET Good lad.

WILBERFORCE (*stopping in doorway*) Where is the High Street, ma'am?

JULIET Not sure, Wilberforce. Ask when you get there.

He leaves. She speaks into mike.

Oscar Delta Tango Charlie Farnsbarns, come in please – this is Bippetty Boppetty Eggwhisk Goulash Pantiegirdle, over.

VOICE There's an incident taking place on the moors, ma'am.

JULIET Got that. Anything else I should know?

VOICE It's quite windy.

JULIET Will I need a poncho?

VOICE You might need a sheepskin coat.

JULIET I'm on my way. Don't do anything stupid, Constable.

VOICE Like what, ma'am?

JULIET Hot air ballooning. It can be very dangerous given bad weather conditions like those you've described. I'll be with you as soon as I've had a good cry, because I'm only a woman and from time to time the pressure gets to me, tough as I am. Over and out. Wah!

Victoria Wood
(after Lady Police Serials)

OCCUPATIONAL

HAZARDS

from Bitching

Interview Rituals. Job interviews require a woman to curb her impulses toward hilarity and give a convincing demonstration that she has mastered the game of Attrac, Gd Fig, Typ, which is a post-graduate version of Playing Dumb. Although the formula quickly becomes second nature, an applicant still must take care in checking the want ads to distinguish the right answers from the smartass answers. A flair for comic invention helps:

1. The Dead End Ad

COLL GRAD   SOCIAL SERVICE $6500
Attrac, well groomed, must like dealing w/people. Knl of typ, steno, stepping stone for greater things. 4 weeks vac.
Right answer: 'Yes, I do have a B.A. in sociology but my real interests are working with people and typing.'
Smartass answer: 'Stepping stone to *what* greater things?'

2. The Mother's Helper Ad

EXECUTIVE SECRETARY $7200
YOUR BOSS, THE MARKETING VICE PRESIDENT:

I need a poised person with executive secretarial background to assist me. As my right hand you will become involved in all phases of the business. You'll meet customers, many of them important business executives. You should be attractive, skilled, possess a professional attitude, and have an outgoing personality.

Right answer: 'I've always wanted to learn all about the alarm installation business.'

Smartass answer: 'Big deal.'

3.   The Doggie Bag Ad

GAL/GUY FRIDAY $75
TV PRODUCTION

Producer of children's TV shows needs right hand indiv to help keep his busy sched. Attrac, typ, steno. Attend premiere parties.

Right answer: 'Sure I can live on $75 a week. I have just myself to support.'

Smartass answer: 'Myself, my fur coat, and my therapist.'

Once she has successfully reassured an employer that her life's ambition is to straddle a Smith-Corona Secretarial 300 or wet-nurse a marketing vice-president and, moreover, that she gratefully accepts doggie bags from premiere parties as partial salary, then the next step is parrying his snooping into her sexual activities. Should she be single, Big Daddy feels justified in grilling her about her matrimonial plans 'because we invest a lot of money in training you gals and we like you to stick around for a while.' Never mind the male trainee who scuttles off at the first sniff of a job paying $5 a week more; he's an ambitious fellow on his way up.

If she's married and childless, it's a company's prerogative to know her reproduction timetable. If she has children, she must cite some dire reason for abandoning them. To answer these questions, which are phrased in dainty personnelese, of course, a woman must come up with just the right false face. In Sandy's experience: 'I learned very quickly that the first thing you do when you walk into an interview is lie.'

The particular lie is inconsequential, as long as she avoids such crass replies as:

'I don't plan to marry.' (*Company translation: lesbian*)
'I don't plan to have children.' (*Translation: freak*)
'Taking care of children all day drives me nuts.' (*Monster mother*)

In addition to Attrac, Gd Fig, Typ, she may throw in a few immortal classics such as Smiling and Keeping One's Legs Crossed – just in case. At long last, Little Darling finds herself in an office where she now discovers what Daddy was up to for all those years.

Marion Meade

———

Be a governess! Better be a slave at once!

Charlotte Brontë

———

Portrait of a Barmaid

Metallic waves of people jar
Through crackling green toward the bar

Where on the tables chattering white,
The sharp drinks quarrel with the light.

Those coloured muslin blinds the smiles
Shroud wooden faces; and at whiles

They splash like a thin water (you
Yourself reflected in their hue).

The conversation, loud and bright,
Seem spinal bars of shunting light

In firework-spirting greenery.
O complicate machinery

For building Babel! Iron crane
Beneath your hair, that blue-ribbed mane

In noise and murder like the sea
Without its mutability!

Outside the bar, where jangling heat
Seems out of time and off the beat,

A concertina's glycerine
Exudes and mirrors in the green

Your soul, pure glucose edged with hints
Of tentative and half-soiled tints.

Edith Sitwell

The most devilish thing is 8 times 8 and 7 times 7 it is
what nature itselfe cant endure.

Marjory Fleming

————

from The Basset Table

The scene opens, and discovers VALERIA with books upon a table, a microscope, putting a fish upon it, several animals lying by.

VALERIA   'Pshaw! Thou fluttering thing. So, now I've fixed it.

Enter ALPIEW

ALPIEW   Madam, here's Mr Lovely. I have introduced him as one of my Lady's visitors, and brought him down the back-stairs.

VALERIA   I'm obliged to you, he comes opportunely.

Enter LOVELY

VALERIA   Oh Mr Lovely! Come, come here, look through this glass, and see how the blood circulates in the tail of this fish.

ENSIGN LOVELY   Wonderful! But it circulates prettier in this fair neck.

VALERIA   'Pshaw, be quiet. I'll show you a curiosity, the greatest that ever nature made (*opens a box*). In opening a dog the other day, I found this worm.

ENSIGN LOVELY   Prodigious! 'Tis the joint worm, which the learned talk of so much.

VALERIA   Aye. The Lumbricus Laetus, or Faescia, as Hippocrates calls it, or vulgarly in English, the tape-worm. Thadaeus tells us of one of these worms found in a human body, two hundred feet long, without head or tail.

ENSIGN LOVELY   (*aside*) I wish they be not got into thy brain. Oh, you charm me with these discoveries.

VALERIA   Here's another sort of worm called Lumbricus Teres Intestinalis.

ENSIGN LOVELY   I think the first you showed me the greatest curiosity.

VALERIA   'Tis very odd, really, that there should be every inch a joint, and every joint a mouth. Oh, the profound secrets of Nature!

ENSIGN LOVELY	'Tis strangely surprising. But now let me be heard, for mine's the voice of Nature too. Methinks you neglect yourself, the most perfect piece of all her works.
VALERIA	Why, what fault do you find in me?
ENSIGN LOVELY	You have not love enough. That fire would consume and banish all studies but its own. Your eyes would sparkle and spread I know not what, of lively and touching, o'er the whole face. This hand when pressed by him you love would tremble to your heart.
VALERIA	Why so it does. Have I not told you twenty times I love you, for I hate disguise? Your temper being adapted to mine gave my soul the first impression. You know my father's positive, but do not believe he shall force me to anything that does not love philosophy.
ENSIGN LOVELY	But that sea-captain, Valeria.
VALERIA	If he was a whale he might give you pain, for I should long to dissect him. But as he is a man, you have no reason to fear him.
ENSIGN LOVELY	Consent then to fly with me.
VALERIA	What, and leave my microscope and all my things for my father to break in pieces?

Susanna Centlivre

Faith is a fine invention
When Gentlemen can *see* –
But *Microscopes* are prudent
In an Emergency.

Emily Dickinson

An unalterable and unquestioned law of the musical world required that the German text of French operas sung by Swedish artists should be translated into Italian for the clearer understanding of English-speaking audiences.

Edith Wharton

I can hold a note as long as the Chase National Bank.

Ethel Merman

———

I did everything Fred Astaire did – except backwards and in high heels.

Ginger Rogers

———

Monday, 7th. The play was *Romeo and Juliet*; the house was extremely full. They are a delightful audience. My Romeo had gotten on a pair of breeches that looked as if he had borrowed them from some worthy Dutchman of a hundred years ago. He looked like a magical figure growing out of a monstrous strange-coloured melon, beneath which descended his unfortunate legs, thrust into a pair of red slippers. The play went off pretty well, except they broke one man's collar-bone and nearly dislocated a woman's shoulder by flinging the scenery about. My bed was not made in time, and when the scene drew, half a dozen carpenters in patched trowsers and tattered shirt sleeves were discovered smoothing down my pillows and adjusting my draperies. The last scene is too good not to be given verbatim:

ROMEO	Tear not our heart strings thus! They crack! They break! – Juliet! Juliet! (*dies*)
JULIET (*to corpse*)	Am I smothering you?
CORPSE (*to Juliet*)	Not at all; could you be so kind, do you think, as to put my wig on again for me? – it has fallen off.
JULIET (*to corpse*)	I'm afraid I can't, but I'll throw my muslin veil over it. You've broken the phial, haven't you? (*corpse nodded*)
JULIET	Where's your dagger?
CORPSE	'Pon my soul, I don't know.

Fanny Kemble

Shakespeare is so tiring. You never get a chance to sit down unless you're a king.

Josephine Hull

———

For an actress to be a success, she must have the face of a Venus, the brains of a Minerva, the grace of Terpsichore, the memory of a Macaulay, the figure of Juno, and the hide of a rhinoceros.

Ethel Barrymore

———

[On having a theatre named after her:] An actress's life is so transitory; suddenly you're a building.

Helen Hayes

———

Scratch an actor – and you'll find an actress.

Dorothy Parker

———

[Describing a revival of Maeterlinck's play *Aglavaine and Selysette*:] There is less in this than meets the eye.

Tallulah Bankhead

———

'Do you come to the play without knowing what it is?'
'O yes, Sir, yes, very frequently; I have no time to read play-bills; one merely comes to meet one's friends, and show that one's alive.'

Fanny Burney

———

I wouldn't say when you've seen one Western you've seen the lot; but when you've seen the lot you get the feeling you've seen one.

Katharine Whitehorn

The Prologue

I am obnoxious to each carping tongue,
Who says my hand a needle better fits,
A poet's pen, all scorn, I should thus wrong;
For such despite they cast on female wits:
If what I do prove well, it won't advance,
They'll say it's stolne, or else, it was by chance.

Anne Bradstreet

———

A masquerade, a murdered peer,
His throat just cut from ear to ear –
A rake turned hermit – a fond maid
Run mad, by some false loon betrayed –
These stores supply the female pen,
Which writes them o'er and o'er again,
And readers likewise may be found
To circulate them round and round.

Mary Alcock

———

from Self-Help

First, try to be something, anything, else. A movie star/astronaut. A movie
star/missionary. A movie star/kindergarten teacher. President of the World.
Fail miserably. It is best if you fail at an early age – say, fourteen. Early,
critical disillusionment is necessary so that at fifteen you can write long
haiku sequences about thwarted desire. It is a pond, a cherry blossom, a wind
brushing against sparrow wing leaving for mountain. Count the syllables.
Show it to your mom. She is tough and practical. She has a son in Vietnam
and a husband who may be having an affair. She believes in wearing brown
because it hides spots. She'll look briefly at your writing, then back up at
you with a face blank as a donut. She'll say: 'How about emptying the
dishwasher?' Look away. Shove the forks in the fork drawer. Accidentally
break one of the freebie gas station glasses. This is the required pain and
suffering. This is only for starters.

In your high school English class look only at Mr Killian's face. Decide faces are important. Write a villanelle about pores. Struggle. Write a sonnet. Count the syllables: nine, ten, eleven, thirteen. Decide to experiment with fiction. Here you don't have to count syllables. Write a short story about an elderly man and woman who accidentally shoot each other in the head, the result of an inexplicable malfunction of a shotgun which appears mysteriously in their living-room one night. Give it to Mr Killian as your final project. When you get it back, he has written on it: 'Some of your images are quite nice, but you have no sense of plot.' When you are home, in the privacy of your own room, faintly scrawl in pencil beneath his black-inked comments: 'Plots are for dead people, pore-face.'

Take all the babysitting jobs you can get. You are great with kids. They love you. You tell them stories about old people who die idiot deaths. You sing them songs like 'Blue Bells of Scotland,' which is their favorite. And when they are in their pajamas and have finally stopped pinching each other, when they are fast asleep, you read every sex manual in the house, and wonder how on earth anyone could ever do those things with someone they truly loved. Fall asleep in a chair reading Mr McMurphy's *Playboy*. When the McMurphys come home, they will tap you on the shoulder, look at the magazine in your lap, and grin. You will want to die. They will ask you if Tracey took her medicine all right. Explain, yes, she did, that you promised her a story if she would take it like a big girl and that seemed to work out just fine. 'Oh, marvelous,' they will exclaim.

Try to smile proudly.

Apply to college as a child psychology major.

As a child psychology major, you have some electives. You've always liked birds. Sign up for something called 'The Ornithological Field Trip.' It meets Tuesdays and Thursdays at two. When you arrive at Room 134 on the first day of class, everyone is sitting around a seminar table talking about metaphors. You've heard of these. After a short, excruciating while, raise your hand and say diffidently, 'Excuse me, isn't this Birdwatching One-oh-one?' The class stops and turns to look at you. They seem to all have one face – giant and blank as a vandalized clock. Someone with a beard booms out, 'No, this is Creative Writing.' Say: 'Oh – right,' as if perhaps you knew all along. Look down at your schedule. Wonder how the hell you ended up here. The computer, apparently, has made an error. You start to get up to leave and then don't. The lines at the registrar this week are huge. Perhaps you should stick with this mistake. Perhaps your creative writing isn't all that bad. Perhaps it is fate. Perhaps this is what your dad meant when he said, 'It's the age of computers, Francie, it's the age of computers.'

Decide that you like college life. In your dorm you meet many nice people. Some are smarter than you. And some, you notice, are dumber than you. You will continue, unfortunately, to view the world in exactly these terms for the rest of your life.

The assignment this week in creative writing is to narrate a violent happening. Turn in a story about driving with your Uncle Gordon and another one about two old people who are accidentally electrocuted when they go to turn on a badly wired desk lamp. The teacher will hand them back to you with comments: 'Much of your writing is smooth and energetic. You have, however, a ludicrous notion of plot.' Write another story about a man and a woman who, in the very first paragraph, have their lower torsos accidentally blitzed away by dynamite. In the second paragraph, with the insurance money, they buy a frozen yogurt stand together. There are six more paragraphs. You read the whole thing out loud in class. No one likes it. They say your sense of plot is outrageous and incompetent. After class someone asks you if you are crazy.

Decide that perhaps you should stick to comedies. Start dating someone who is funny, someone who has what in high school you called a 'really great sense of humor' and what now your creative writing class calls 'self-contempt giving rise to comic form.' Write down all of his jokes, but don't tell him you are doing this. Make up anagrams of his old girlfriend's name and name all of your socially handicapped characters with them. Tell him his old girlfriend is in all of your stories and then watch how funny he can be, see what a really great sense of humor he can have.

Your child psychology advisor tells you you are neglecting courses in your major. What you spend the most time on should be what you're majoring in. Say yes, you understand.

In creative writing seminars over the next two years, everyone continues to smoke cigarettes and ask the same things: 'But does it work?' 'Why should we care about this character?' 'Have you earned this cliché?' These seem like important questions.

On days when it is your turn, you look at the class hopefully as they scour your mimeographs for a plot. They look back up at you, drag deeply, and then smile in a sweet sort of way.

You spend too much time slouched and demoralized. Your boyfriend suggests bicycling. Your room-mate suggests a new boyfriend. You are said to be self-mutilating and losing weight, but you continue writing. The only happiness you have is writing something new, in the middle of the night, armpits damp, heart pounding, something no one has yet seen. You have only those brief, fragile, untested moments of exhilaration when you know: you are a genius. Understand what you must do. Switch majors. The kids in your nursery project will be disappointed, but you have a calling, an urge, a delusion, an unfortunate habit. You have, as your mother would say, fallen in with a bad crowd.

Why write? Where does writing come from? These are questions to ask yourself. They are like: Where does dust come from? Or: Why is there war? Or: If there's a God, then why is my brother now a cripple?

These are questions that you keep in your wallet, like calling cards. These are questions, your creative writing teacher says, that are good to address in your journals but rarely in your fiction.

The writing professor this fall is stressing the Power of the Imagination. Which means he doesn't want long descriptive stories about your camping trip last July. He wants you to start in a realistic context but then to alter it. Like recombinant DNA. He wants you to let your imagination sail, to let it grow big-bellied in the wind. This is a quote from Shakespeare.

Tell your room-mate your great idea, your great exercise of imaginative power: a transformation of Melville to contemporary life. It will be about monomania and the fish-eat-fish world of life insurance in Rochester, New York. The first line will be 'Call me Fishmeal,' and it will feature a menopausal suburban husband named Richard, who because he is so depressed all the time is called 'Mopey Dick' by his witty wife Elaine. Say to your room-mate: 'Mopey Dick, get it?' Your room-mate looks at you, her face blank as a large Kleenex. She comes up to you, like a buddy, and puts an arm around your burdened shoulders. 'Listen, Francie,' she says, slow as speech therapy. 'Let's go out and get a big beer.'

The seminar doesn't like this one either. You suspect they are beginning to feel sorry for you. They say: 'You have to think about what is happening. Where is the story here?'

The next semester the writing professor is obsessed with writing from personal experience. You must write from what you know, from what has happened to you. He wants deaths, he wants camping trips. Think about what has happened to you. In three years there have been three things: you lost your virginity; your parents got divorced; and your brother came home from a forest ten miles from the Cambodian border with only half a thigh, a permanent smirk nestled into one corner of his mouth.

About the first you write: 'It created a new space, which hurt and cried in a voice that wasn't mine, "I'm not the same anymore, but I'll be OK."'

About the second you write an elaborate story of an old married couple who stumble upon an unknown land mine in their kitchen and accidentally blow themselves up. You call it: 'For Better or for Liverwurst.'

About the last you write nothing. There are no words for this. Your typewriter hums. You can find no words.

At undergraduate cocktail parties, people say, 'Oh, you write? What do you write about?' Your room-mate, who has consumed too much wine, too little cheese, and no crackers at all, blurts: 'Oh, my god, she always writes about her dumb boyfriend.'

Later on in life you will learn that writers are merely open, helpless texts with no real understanding of what they have written and therefore must half-believe anything and everything that is said of them. You, however, have not yet reached this stage of literary criticism. You stiffen and say, 'I do not,' the same way you said it when someone in the fourth grade accused you of really liking oboe lessons and your parents really weren't just making you take them.

Insist you are not very interested in any one subject at all, that you are interested in the music of language, that you are interested in – in – syllables, because they are the atoms of poetry, the cells of the mind, the breath of the soul. Begin to feel woozy. Stare into your plastic wine cup.

'Syllables?' you will hear someone ask, voice trailing off, as they glide slowly toward the reassuring white of the dip.

Begin to wonder what you do write about. Or if you have anything to say. Or if there even is such a thing as a thing to say. Limit these thoughts to no more than ten minutes a day; like sit-ups, they can make you thin.

You will read somewhere that all writing has to do with one's genitals. Don't dwell on this. It will make you nervous.

Your mother will come visit you. She will look at the circles under your eyes and hand you a brown book with a brown briefcase on the cover. It is entitled: *How to Become a Business Executive*. She has also brought the *Names for Baby* encyclopedia you asked for; one of your characters, the ageing clown–schoolteacher, needs a new name. Your mother will shake her head and say: 'Francie, Francie, remember when you were going to be a child psychology major?'

Say: 'Mom, I like to write.'

She'll say: 'Sure you like to write. Of course. Sure you like to write.'

Write a story about a confused music student and title it: 'Schubert Was the One with the Glasses, Right?' It's not a big hit, although your room-mate likes the part where the two violinists accidentally blow themselves up in a recital room. 'I went out with a violinist once,' she says, snapping her gum.

Thank god you are taking other courses. You can find sanctuary in nineteenth-century ontological snags and invertebrate courting rituals. Certain globular mollusks have what is called 'Sex by the Arm.' The male octopus, for instance, loses the end of one arm when placing it inside the female body during intercourse. Marine biologists call it 'Seven Heaven.' Be glad you know these things. Be glad you are not just a writer. Apply to law school.

From here on in, many things can happen. But the main one will be this: you decide not to go to law school after all, and, instead, you spend a good, big chunk of your adult life telling people how you decided not to go to law school after all. Somehow you end up writing again. Perhaps you go to graduate school. Perhaps you work odd jobs and take writing courses at night. Perhaps you are working on a novel and writing down all the clever remarks and intimate personal confessions you hear during the day. Perhaps you are losing your pals, your acquaintances, your balance.

Lorrie Moore

In my youth people talked about Ruskin; now they talk about drains.

Mrs Humphrey Ward

I always say, keep a diary and some day it'll keep you.

Mae West

———

It's the good girls who keep the diaries; the bad girls never have the time.

Tallulah Bankhead

———

Do you think it pleases a man when he looks into a woman's eyes and sees a reflection of the British Museum reading room?

Muriel Spark

———

Mrs Ballinger is one of the ladies who pursue Culture in bands, as though it were dangerous to meet it alone.

Edith Wharton

———

At an Art Exhibition in Boston

The lady who enters the exhibition hall of the Boston Museum wears glasses, a long grey coat of the 'duster' type, a scarf at her throat, and a flat 'sensible' hat. She carries a large roomy handbag. Accompanying her are several old friends – there is Kate, perhaps a cousin; there is Mrs Walker; there is a child, perhaps a niece, called Mary. She moves slowly along the walls of the exhibition, from picture to picture. She speaks in a New England voice.

Come on, girls – here we are. . . . Now, lets keep together. We'll enjoy them so much more! . . . Oh! – oh! Look at them all! I never *saw* so many pictures! . . . Now – wait a minute. . . . Let's find out which way we go. . . . Do we go from right to left, or left to right? . . . It's very confusing, if we don't follow the order in which they are hung. . . . Well, I think I'll ask that lady – she looks pleasant and she's probably been around. . . . (*Speaks to a strange woman*) I beg your pardon – would you kindly tell me which way the pictures are hung? Does one go from right to left, or left to right? . . . They start in *this* corner? . . . Thank you so much. I hope you've enjoyed the exhibition – it looks very interesting. . . . Come on, Kate, we start over here! . . . The lady was very nice and she didn't mind my asking at all!

Now, who has the catalogue? . . . Mrs Walker, won't you give little Mary the catalogue? She reads very nicely and this is her first picture exhibition – isn't it, Mary? . . . This is a catalogue, darling, and it will tell us the names of all the pictures. You see, the numbers on the pictures correspond to these numbers, and beside each number is the name of the picture – what the artist meant it to be. . . . One doesn't always know! . . .

Come on – let's keep together. . . . Now, everybody look for number one – look for a little brass disk, darling, with number one on it. . . . In the corner of the picture. . . . Don't look at the pictures until you've found the number. . . . Number one – number one – where are you? . . . *Here* we are! Oh! I've found it – and you needn't look it up! Easy to see what that is, isn't it! An 'Old Red Barn'. . . . Isn't that pretty? . . . Come on, Kate. . . . 'The Old Red Barn'. . . . Oh! I love that. . . . That's what I call *Art*, Mrs Walker. . . . It brings back nature, and represents a familiar scene – certainly to a New Englander there's nothing more familiar than an old red barn. See the green door and the old shingled roof – moss on it. Reminds me of Grandmother's barn in Vermont. . . .

When cousin Kate and I were little girls, darling, we used to go up and spend part of our holidays with our grandmother in Vermont. . . . We came from Salem, but our grandmother lived in Vermont, and she had a great big barn just like that, and on rainy days we used to play in the hay-loft. . . . Remember the time that Freddie Bruce pushed me out of the swing? . . . And I fell where there wasn't any hay? . . . And oh, what a bump I got! . . . Those were happy days. . . . See the clover field! That lovely mauve – one can almost smell that warm sweet air. . . . Oh! Don't you *love* it? . . . I hope they keep bees. . . . Oh! They must – they're very stupid if they don't. . . . Think of all the lovely honey they might have. . . . I imagine the beehives are behind the barn or maybe in the apple orchard to the left. . . . Wouldn't you think so, Mrs Walker? . . . Look for the hives, Mary. . . . Well, we can't *see* them, darling, because they're probably behind the barn and the artist couldn't see them either. Artists can't paint what they don't see. . . . That wouldn't be honest. . . . But I'm sure they're there! . . .

What a lovely June day! . . . See the clouds floating in the blue. . . . hmmmh. . . . You can just *smell* that sweet hot air and all the apple blossoms. . . . I wonder if Freddie Bruce ever married that fat Hickson girl? . . . I wonder what became of them? . . . Oh, Oh, there's a cow! We had a cow named

Daisy, and we used to ride on her back while she munched the grass. Why, they've tied that cow to the apple tree.... *We* never tied Daisy! ... Sweet – sweet – sweet! ... (*She moves on*)

Heavens! What's *that*? ... *That* one – up there! ... Well, it's one of those very modern things.... Sometimes if you get well away from them, something emerges (*Backs away*).... I beg your pardon! (*She speaks to another stranger*) Did I tread on your foot? I'm so sorry.... I hope I didn't hurt you! ... (*To her companions again*) And sometimes, if you creep up on them with half-closed eyes.... I can't make head or tail of it.... D'you know what it looks like to me? ... It looks to me as if the artist had accidentally sat down on his palette, and then sat down on the canvas! ... Well, my dear – there's no *form* to it.... Just a whirl of colour.... Have you ever *seen* such colour? ... Oh – look at that scarlet – right next to the magenta.... And then the shrimp pink.... And what do you suppose the purple spots signify? ... D'you know, those colours set my teeth on edge.... Heavens! That reminds me! I have a dentist appointment on Tuesday.... I'd forgotten all about it. ... Isn't it lucky I saw that picture? I go to Dr Parker and he charges you whether you go or not! ... Look it up, darling – see what it's called.... Number seven.... What's it *meant* to be, dear? ... A 'Study'? ... It doesn't say what of? ... Well – that's an easy way out for the artist.... (*She moves on*)

Oh! There's a picture of the ocean! ... What a marvellous picture! ... Look at the sea, darling.... That's a seascape.... A picture of the ocean. ... Oh! What a rough, rough sea! ... Yet it's painted so smoothly.... How *can* they do it? ... Oh! Those wild, tempestuous waves! ... Aren't the artists brave to go out and paint a sea as rough as that? ... I don't see how he kept his canvas dry.... But that *can't* be painted from the shore, Kate.... You don't see those giant waves unless you get well out to sea.... I suppose he had tarpaulins and umbrellas to keep the spray off. (*Starts to sway*) It's a remarkable picture ... almost too realistic! I can't help it, but pictures of the sea make me think of just one thing.... Oh, I'm the worst in the world. I've never found *any* remedy that helped me. (*Moves slowly on to the next picture*)

Look at that man up there! ... What a *face*! ... Why, I've never seen such an ugly man! He's not only ugly – he looks *evil*.... That's an *evil* face. ... He looks to me like a criminal – almost a degenerate. Poor thing – I wonder why the artist wanted to paint anyone who looked like *that*? ... He must have been a morbid man to choose such a type.... My dear – I just had the most dreadful thought! ... Don't you see a slight resemblance to somebody we know? ... I hate to say it – but to me it looks a little bit like our dear friend, Charlie Miller. . . . Don't ever tell him I said so! . . . Look it up, darling. . . . See who the poor thing is. . . . Three hundred and forty-four. . . . 'Portrait of Mr Charles B. Miller'. . . . Heavens! It *is* Charlie Miller! Why – it's a libel! . . . It's no more like Charlie. . . . I never would have known it in the world! . . . Charlie 's got such a frank, sweet face. . . . And he's got a heart of gold! . . . Oh! I think it's *dreadful* to hang such a picture – without consultation with the family or friends. . . . Poor old Charlie. . . . He's such a dear – I hope his mother never sees it. . . . It's not one bit like him! . . . (*Moves on*)

Oh! There's a lovely picture! . . . Look at the balloons, Mary – see the balloons? Aren't they adorable? . . . All those strange shapes. . . . I've always loved balloons. . . . See them floating in the blue! . . . Aren't they pretty? . . . What? . . . They're *not* balloons? . . . What *are* they? . . . 'A Bowl of Fruit'? . . . Oh, well. . . . I think I see what you mean . . . Maybe you're right. . . . How funny! . . . Yes – it could be . . . could be bananas and pears and peaches and cherries . . . in a large blue bowl. . . . I see what you mean. . . . But to me they still look like balloons. . . . Well – Mary will tell us. . . . Now, Mary – this is where we want the catalogue. . . . Tell us who is right and who is wrong. Cousin Kate says it's a bowl of fruit and Auntie says that it's balloons. . . . Number three twenty-four. . . . Three twenty-four. . . . 'Nymphs Bathing'? . . . *Well!* – did you ever? . . . Well, I can't tell dear, because I've never seen any nymphs. . . . And if that's what they look like, I don't *want* to see them. . . . *Most* peculiar! . . . (*Moves on*)

Oh! Look at that picture of the willow-ware tea-set! Isn't that pretty? . . . Did you ever know my old aunt Agatha, Mrs Walker? . . . She was my grandfather's sister – my great-aunt Agatha. . . . She lived with him in Salem, and when we were children, we used to go to tea on Sundays. . . . There were fourteen grandchildren. . . . Do you remember Aunt Agatha's cookies, Kate? . . . I was looking through the old family Bible last winter, and glancing through Elijah, when out fell Aunt Agatha's recipe for cookies – right out of the middle of Elijah! . . . My grandfather was a sea captain in the China trade, and he had brought back beautiful things from China, and he had a willow-ware tea-set with a huge platter – just like that one. . . . And there would be a mountain of cookies, which we demolished. . . . How we loved those Sunday afternoons in the old house! . . . (*Moves on farther*)

Oh! Here's a pretty picture of a forest! . . . Mary, see the forest, darling? . . . Well, it's just a forest. . . . Beautiful green trees – pine trees – birch trees – it's what they call a grove. . . . It must be near sunset – at dusk. . . . See the

golden light filtering through the trees? . . . Oh! What a peaceful, quiet place
. . . cool and lovely . . . deep – *deep* in the forest . . . a little secret grove. . . .
Wouldn't it be lovely to wander down the path? . . . What, dear?
. . . Something going on in the corner? . . . *Is* there? . . . (*Abruptly, taking the
child's hand*) Mary – come with Auntie! . . .

Come here – I want you to look at this picture. . . . *This* one. . . . This
is a picture they call 'Still Life'. . . . And it is a picture of a dead fish. . . . See!
. . . Isn't that funny? . . . Well, there's a dead fish, and an onion . . . and an
oyster, and a string of pearls . . . and a silver cup, and a bottle . . . and a big
piece of ice. . . . See all those lovely cool grey and silver tones. . . . (*Grasps
little Mary's hand more firmly, leading her on*) No, no – darling – *not* that one. . . .

See that picture of the little tiger cubs. . . . Oh! Don't they look sweet,
like kittens? . . . That must be in a zoo. . . . I don't suppose he could paint in
the jungle. . . . Isn't it pretty? . . . And, my! What a variety of things! . . .
There's a picture of a young girl reading a letter. . . . Oh! She's had bad news
– poor thing! . . . There's his picture on the table. . . . I believe he's forsaken
her, Mrs Walker. . . . He has a very weak face, hasn't he? . . . She's reading a
letter – see the tear? How well that tear is painted. . . . Isn't that a pretty way
to do her hair? . . . You know, Kate – I think you could do something with
Charlotte's hair like that . . . just run the ribbon through the curls and tie it
around. . . . And see her little slipper in the firelight. . . . Look it up, darling
– see what it's called. . . . Number twenty-nine. . . . What's it called?
. . . 'Forsaken'. . . . I was right! – it's called 'Forsaken'. . . . Poor child! Still
– she's young – she'll get over it. . . . And I don't believe he was good enough
for her! . . . I love those story-pictures. . . . They always appeal to me. . . .
(*Again she moves on to the next picture*)

Oh! That must be an eruption of Vesuvius! . . . Let's get well away from
it. . . . What a dramatic picture! . . . See that great band of red and the
wild black clouds. . . . It must be – that must be the lava. . . . Well, it was a
mountain, darling, and the mountain exploded, and out of the mountain
poured a material called lava – which was really a sort of molten metal . . .
and it buried a whole city. . . . It was a dreadful disaster! . . . How fierce and
terrible Nature can be! I hear it's still smoking. . . . I've always wanted to see
the Bay of Naples, but I don't believe it's safe. . . . Look it up, dear – see if it
isn't the eruption of Mount Vesuvius. . . . Number sixty-nine. . . . What is it?
. . . 'Sunset in Vermont'! . . . Well! – It's not like any *I've* ever seen. . . . But you
know, I think artists see things differently – don't you, Mrs Walker? . . . (*She
turns to her friends*)

I think we must go now. . . . I have to take the four-forty trolley back to Jamaica Plain. . . . Well – it's an interesting exhibition . . . all except those nudes. . . . Why, I think it's dreadful to hang pictures like that in rooms with people you know. . . . Look at poor Charlie Miller! . . . I think Art is wonderful – and artists are wonderful . . . but I think that artists, like everybody else these days, are going *too far!* . . . Come, Mary. (*Mary has apparently tried to go back to the forest scene*) . . . Didn't you hear Auntie say *no?* . . .

(*Seizing Mary firmly by the hand she leads the party out of the gallery*)

Ruth Draper

———

Interpretation is the revenge of the intellect upon art.

Susan Sontag

———

GOD IS LOVE, BUT

GET IT IN WRITING

The Bacchante

HERMIONE   Excuse me, sir, does the bus stop here for Chorley Wood?

GUY   Who is Chorley Wood?

HERMIONE   Sir Henry Wood's brother, I think! No, I mean Chorley Wood – the wood you can't see for the trees.

GUY   Oh, I see.

HERMIONE   I'm looking for a wood to spend the night in.

GUY   It's only a tuppenny ride to Shepherd's Bush.

HERMIONE   Bush? I'm afraid that wouldn't quite do.

GUY   Why do you want to spend the night in a wood? If it isn't a rude answer.

HERMIONE   Well, you see, I'm a Bacchante.

GUY   Good heavens, a real Bacchante? I say, how are you?

HERMIONE   I'm very well, thank you. How are you?

GUY   Pretty well.

HERMIONE   Nothing serious, I hope.

GUY   Just a touch of spring fever.

HERMIONE   Have a grape.

GUY   No, I'm afraid my friend wouldn't like me to. Can I lend you a comb?

HERMIONE   I'm sorry my hair's in such a mess. It's being out in all winds
           and weathers. And the birds! The eagles are flying very low
           this summer, don't you think?
GUY   Well, I . . .
HERMIONE   I suppose you're not troubled much with birds?
GUY   Well, no. That's an awfully jolly outfit you're wearing.
HERMIONE   Do you like it? I made it myself with a pattern out of *Homers'
           Chat.*
GUY   I say, do you have orgies? I'd love to go to one.
HERMIONE   As a matter of fact, we're having one in Battersea Park next
           Tuesday. And I was told I could bring a friend. Would you
           like to come?
GUY   In fancy dress?
HERMIONE   Optional.
GUY   I've got a lovely Pierrot costume I wore at the Vic-Wells ball.
HERMIONE   Will you call for me?
GUY   Well, I'd rather meet you there. I don't think my friend would
           like me to be seen out with a Bacchante.
HERMIONE   Why not?
GUY   Well, they do go about 360 times too far, don't they?
HERMIONE   I see.
GUY   Well, I must be getting along. I'm frightfully glad to have met
           you.
HERMIONE   Goodbye.
GUY   Goodbye. By the way, what's your name?
HERMIONE   I'm Bessie Bacchante.
GUY   See you next Tuesday, Bessie.
HERMIONE   It's always the same! No really nice young man ever wants to
           take me home and introduce me to his mother.

           Oh why was I born a Bacchante?
           I find all-night orgies a bore.
           I feel such a sick dilettante
           In the morning after every night before.
           I'm tired of the taste of Chianti,
           Falernian makes me feel queer,
           And as for that Asti Spumante
           Well, I'd rather have some Alka Seltzer, dear.

We lead the strangest life on tour with Bacchus,
You never know what's going to happen next.
Those fauns are always waiting to attack us
And nobody could call them undersexed.
The other girls just think that nothing matters
And never seem to know WHO crushed their grapes,
But I must say I have no use for satyrs
From whom I've had the narrowest escapes.

Oh why was I born a Bacchante?
I never had much of a head.
The clothes are a great deal too scanty,
And it's always three before you get to bed.
I think that it must have been Dante
Who said, 'If you need an excuse,
When caught *in delicto flagrante*,
You can always tell your mother it was Zeus!'

I'm always spilling claret on my chiton,
I really hate to have to show my knees,
A wood's not very nice to spend a night in,
With all those Hamadryads in the trees.
I've never had a chance to meet Apollo
I'm always getting followed round by Pan,
And he's too much for any girl to swallow,
He's such a very hairy little man.

Oh, why was I born a Bacchante?
I find that my throat's got so hoarse
With shouting 'Eureka Avanti!'
And other things considerably more coarse.
I'd make such a good Corybante,
But I'm in a furious rage,
The censor they say is so Anti
That he won't allow my act on any stage.

**Diana Morgan (with Robert MacDermot,
and additional dialogue from
Hermione Gingold)**

from Lolly Willowes

'Where are you taking me?' she said. Mrs Leak made no answer, but in the darkness she took hold of Laura's hand. There was no need for further explanation. They were going to the Witches' Sabbath. Mrs Leak was a witch too; a matronly witch like Agnes Sampson, she would be Laura's chaperone. The night was full of voices. Padding rustic footsteps went by them in the dark. When they had reached the brow of the hill a faint continuous sound, resembling music, was borne towards them by the light wind. Laura remembered how young Billy Thomas, suffering from toothache, had played all night upon his mouth-organ. She laughed. Mrs Leak squeezed her hand.

The meeting-place was some way off, by the time they reached it Laura's eyes had grown accustomed to the darkness. She could see a crowd of people walking about in a large field; lights of some sort were burning under a hedge, and one or two paper garlands were looped over the trees. When she first caught sight of them, the assembled witches and warlocks seemed to be dancing, but now the music had stopped and they were just walking about. There was something about their air of disconnected jollity which reminded Laura of a Primrose League gala and fête. A couple of bullocks watched the Sabbath from an adjoining field.

Laura was denied the social gift, she had never been good at enjoying parties. But this, she hoped, would be a different and more exhilarating affair. She entered the field in a most propitious frame of mind, which not even Mr Gurdon, wearing a large rosette like a steward's and staring rudely and searchingly at each comer before he allowed them to pass through the gate, was able to check.

'Old Goat!' exclaimed Mrs Leak in a voice of contemptuous amusement after they had passed out of Mr Gurdon's hearing. 'He thinks he can boss us here, just as he does in the village.'

'Is Mr Jones here?' inquired Laura.

Mrs Leak shook her head and laughed.

'Mr Gurdon doesn't allow him to come.'

'I suppose he doesn't think it suitable for a clergyman.'

Perhaps it was as well that Mr Gurdon had such strict views. In spite of the example of Mr Lowis, that old reading parson, it might be a little awkward if Mr Jones were allowed to attend the Sabbath.

But that apparently was not the reason. Mrs Leak was beginning to explain when she broke off abruptly, coughed in a respectful way, and dropped a deep curtsey. Before them stood an old lady, carrying herself like a queen, and wearing a mackintosh that would have disgraced a tinker's drab. She acknowledged Mrs Leak's curtsey with an inclination of the head, and turned to Laura.

'I am Miss Larpent. And you, I think, must be Miss Willowes.'

The voice that spoke was clear as a small bell and colourless as if time had bleached it of every human feeling save pride. The hand that rested in Laura's was light as a bird's claw; a fine glove encased it like a membrane, and through the glove Laura felt the slender bones and the sharp-faceted rings.

'Long ago,' continued Miss Larpent, 'I had the pleasure of meeting your great-uncle, Commodore Willowes.'

Good heavens, thought Laura in a momentary confusion, was Great-uncle Demetrius a warlock? For Miss Larpent was so perfectly witch-like that it seemed scarcely possible that she should condescend to ordinary gentlemen.

Apparently Miss Larpent could read Laura's thoughts.

'At Cowes,' she added, reassuringly.

Laura raised her eyes to answer, but Miss Larpent had disappeared. Where she had stood, stood Miss Carloe, mincing and bridling, as though she would usurp the other's gentility. Over her face she wore a spotted veil. Recognising Laura she put on an air of delighted surprise and squeaked like a bat, and immediately she too edged away and was lost in the darkness.

Then a young man whom she did not know came up to Laura and put his arm respectfully round her waist. She found herself expected to dance. She could not hear any music, but she danced as best she could, keeping time to the rhythm of his breath upon her cheek. Their dance was short, she supposed she had not acquitted herself to her partner's satisfaction, for after a few turns he released her, and left her standing by the hedge. Not a word had passed between them. Laura felt that she ought to say something, but she could not think of a suitable opening. It was scarcely possible to praise the floor.

A familiar discouragement began to settle upon her spirits. In spite of her hopes she was not going to enjoy herself. Even as a witch, it seemed, she was doomed to social failure, and her first Sabbath was not going to open livelier vistas than were opened by her first ball. She remembered her dancing days in Somerset, Hunt Balls, and County Balls in the draughty Assembly Rooms. With the best intentions she had never managed to enjoy them. The first hour was well enough, but after that came increasing listlessness and boredom; the effort, when one danced again with the same partner, not to say the same things, combined with the obligation to say something rather like them, the control of eyelids, the conversion of yawns into smiles, the humbling consciousness that there was nothing to look forward to except the drive home. That was pleasant, and so was the fillip of supper at the drive's end, and the relief of yielding at last to an unfeigned hunger and sleepiness. But these were by-blow joys, of the delights for which balls are ordained she knew nothing.

She watched the dancers go by and wondered what the enchantment was which they felt and she could not. What made them come out in the middle of the night, loop paper garlands over the trees, light a row of candles in the ditch, and then, friends and enemies and indifferents, go bumping round on the rough grass? That fatal comparison with the Primrose League recurred to her. She was not entertained, so she blamed the entertainment. But the fault lay with her, she had never been good at parties, she had not got the proper Sabbath-keeping spirit. Miss Larpent was enjoying herself; Laura saw the bonnet whisk past. But doubtless Miss Larpent had enjoyed herself at Cowes.

These depressing thoughts were interrupted by red-haired Emily, who came spinning from her partner's arms, seized hold of Laura and carried her back into the dance. Laura liked dancing with Emily; the pasty-faced and anaemic young slattern whom she had seen dawdling about the village danced with a fervour that annihilated every misgiving. They whirled faster and faster, fused together like two suns that whirl and blaze in a single destruction. A strand of the red hair came undone and brushed across Laura's face. The contact made her tingle from head to foot. She shut her eyes and dived into obliviousness – with Emily for a partner she could dance until the gunpowder ran out of the heels of her boots. Alas! this happy ending was not to be, for at the height of their performance Emily was snatched away by Mr Jowl, the horse-doctor. Laura opened her eyes and saw the pale face disappearing in the throng as the moon sinks into the clouds.

Emily was in great request, and no wonder. Like a torch she was handed on from one to another, and every mutation shook down some more hair. The Sabbath was warming up nicely now, every one was jigging it, even Laura. For a while Mrs Leak kept up a semblance of chaperonage. Suddenly appearing at Laura's elbow she would ask her if she were enjoying herself, and glancing at her would slip away before she could answer. Or with vague gestures she indicated some evasively bowing partner, male or female; and silently Laura would give her hand and be drawn into the dance, presently to be relinquished or carried off by some one else.

The etiquette of a Sabbath appeared to consist of one rule only: to do nothing for long. Partners came and went, figures and conformations were in a continual flux. Sometimes the dancers were coupled, sometimes they jigged in a circle round some specially agile performer, sometimes they all took hands and galloped about the field. Halfway through a very formal quadrille presided over by the Misses Larpent they fell abruptly to playing Fox and Geese. In spite of Mr Gurdon's rosette there was no Master of Ceremonies. A single mysterious impulse seemed to govern the company. They wheeled and manœuvred like a flock of starlings.

After an hour or two of this Laura felt dizzy and bewildered. Taking advantage of the general lack of formality she tore herself from Mr Gurdon's arms, not to dance with another, but to slip away and sit quietly in the hedge.

She wondered where the music came from. She had heard it quite clearly as she came over the hill, but upon entering the field she had lost it. Now as she watched the others she heard it once more. When they neared it grew louder, when they retreated into the darkness it faded with them, as though the sound issued from the dancers themselves, and hung, a droning exhalation, above their heads. It was an odd kind of music, a continuous high shapeless blurr of sound. It was something like mosquitoes in a hot bedroom, and something like a distant threshing machine. But beside this, it had a faintly human quality, a metallic breathing as of trombones marking the measure; and when the dancers took hands and revolved in a leaping circle the music leaped and pounded with them, so much like the steam-organ music of a merry-go-round that for a moment Laura thought that they were riding on horses and dragons, bobbing up and down on crested dragons with heads like cocks, and horses with blood-red nostrils.

The candles burnt on in the dry ditch. Though the boughs of the thorn-trees moved above them and grated in the night-wind, the candle flames flowed steadily upwards. Thus lit from below, the dancers seemed of more than human stature, their bodies extending into the darkness as if in emulation of their gigantic upcast shadows. The air was full of the smell of bruised grass.

Mrs Leak had forgotten Laura now. She was dancing the Highland Schottische with a lean young man whose sleeves were rolled up over his tattooed forearms. The nails in his boots shone in the candle-light, and a lock of hair hung over his eye. Mrs Leak danced very well. Her feet flickered to and fro as nimbly as a tongue. At the turn of the figure she tripped forward to be caught up and swung round on the young man's arm. Though her feet were off the ground they twitched with the movements of the dance, and set down again they took up the uninterrupted measure. Laura watched her with admiration. Even at a Witches' Sabbath Mrs Leak lost none of her respectability. Her white apron was scarcely crumpled, she was as self-contained as a cat watching a mouse, and her eyes dwelt upon the young man's face as though she were listening to a sermon.

She preserved her dignity better than some of the others did. Mr Gurdon stood by himself, stamping his foot and tossing his head, more like the farmer's bull than ever. Miss Carloe was begging people to look at the hole in her leg where the hedgehog sucked her; and red-haired Emily, half naked and holding a candle in either hand, danced round a tree, curtseying to it, her mouth fixed in a breathless corpse-like grin.

Miss Minnie and Miss Jane had also changed their demeanour for the worse. They sat a little retired from the dancers, tearing up a cold grouse and gossiping with Mrs Dewey the midwife. A horrible curiosity stretched their skinny old necks. Miss Minnie had forgotten to gnaw her grouse, she leant forward, her hand covered the lower half of her face to conceal the workings of her mouth. Miss Jane listened as eagerly, and questioned the midwife. But at the answers she turned away with coquettish shudders, pretending to stop her ears, or threatening to slap her sister with a bone.

Laura averted her eyes. She wriggled herself a little further into the hedge. Once again the dancers veered away to the further side of the field, their music retreating with them. She hoped they would stay away, for their proximity was disturbing. They aroused in her neither fear nor disgust, but when they came close, and she felt their shadows darkening above her head, a nameless excitement caught hold of her. As they departed, heaviness took its place. She was not in the least sleepy and yet several times she found herself astray from her thoughts, as though she were falling asleep in a train. She wondered what time it was and looked up to consult the stars. But a featureless cloud covered the sky.

Laura resigned herself. There was nothing to do but to wait, though what she waited for she did not know: whether at length Mrs Leak would come, like a chaperone from the supper-room, and say: 'Well, my dear, I really must take you home' – or if, suddenly, at the first cock-crow, all the company would rise up in the air, a darkening bevy, and disperse, and she with them.

She was roused by a shrill whistle. The others heard it too. Miss Minnie and Miss Jane scrambled up and hurried across the field, outdistancing Mrs Dewey, who followed them panting for breath and twitching her skirts over the rough ground. The music had stopped. Laura saw all the witches and warlocks jostling each other, and pressing into a circle. She wondered what was happening now. Whatever it was, it seemed to please and excite them a great deal, for she could hear them all laughing and talking at once. Some newcomer, she supposed – for their behaviour was that of welcome. Now the newcomer must be making a speech, for they all became silent: a successful speech, for the silence was broken by acclamations, and bursts of laughter.

'Of course!' said Laura. 'It must be Satan!'

As she spoke she saw the distant group turn and with one accord begin running towards where she sat. She got up; she felt frightened, for their advance was like a stampede of animals, and she feared that they would knock her down and trample her underfoot. The first runner had already swooped upon her, she felt herself encompassed, caught hold of, and carried forward. Voices addressed her, but she did not understand what was said. She gathered that she was being encouraged and congratulated, as though the neglectful assembly had suddenly decided to make much of the unsuccessful guest. Presently she found herself between Mrs Leak and red-haired Emily. Each held an arm. Mrs Leak patted her encouragingly, and Emily whispered rapidly, incoherently, in her ear. They were quite close to the newcomer, Satan, if it were he, who was talking to Miss Minnie and Miss Jane. Laura looked at him. She could see him quite clearly, for those who stood round had taken up the candles to light him. He was standing with his back to her, speaking with great animation to the old ladies, bowing, and fidgeting his feet. As he spoke he threw out his hands, and his whole lean, lithe body seemed to be scarcely withheld from breaking into a dance. Laura saw Miss Jane point at her, and the stranger turned sharply round.

She saw his face. For a moment she thought that he was a Chinaman; then she saw that he was wearing a mask. The candle-light shone full upon it, but so fine and slight was the modelling that scarcely a shadow marked the indentations of cheek and jaw. The narrow eyes, the slanting brows, the small smiling mouth had a vivid innocent inexpressiveness. It was like the face of a very young girl. Alert and immobile the mask regarded her. And she, entranced, stared back at this imitation face that outwitted all perfections of flesh and blood. It was lifeless, lifeless! But below it, in the hollow of the girlish throat, she saw a flicker of life, a small regular pulse, small and regular as though a pearl necklace slid by under the skin. Mincing like a girl, the masked young man approached her, and as he approached the others drew back and left her alone. With secretive and undulating movements he came to her side. The lifeless face was near her own and through the slits in the mask the unseen eyes surveyed her. Suddenly she felt upon her cheeks a cold darting touch. With a fine tongue like a serpent's he had licked her right cheek, close to the ear. She started back, but found his hands detaining her.

'How are you enjoying your first Sabbath, Miss Willowes?' he said.

'Not at all,' answered Laura, and turned her back on him.

Sylvia Townsend Warner

———

The one certain way for a woman to hold a man is to leave him for religion.

Muriel Spark

———

Blessed are the pure in heart for they have so much more to talk about.

Edith Wharton

———

Jesus was also well-known for his miracles, and probably would have formed a band if Smokey Robinson hadn't done it.

Jo Brand

———

Of late years an abundant shower of curates has fallen upon the North of England.

Charlotte Brontë

———

I was brought up in a clergyman's household so I am a first
class liar.

Sybil Thorndike

———

Moi, je serai autocrate: c'est mon métier. Et le bon Dieu me pardonnera:
c'est son métier.
I shall be an autocrat: that's my trade. And the good Lord
will forgive me: that's his.

Catherine The Great

———

from Black Baby

'Bless me, Father, for I have sinned.'

For some reason, Dinah actually did go to confession.

She pulled back purple curtains to see what kind of man she was to
confide in and saw red jowls and frightened blue eyes. Perhaps he was afraid
of the dark. The penitential drapes smelled of dust. The priest caught her
looking at him and covered the side of his face with his hand.

'It is thirty years,' she said, 'since my last confession.'

'How have you sinned, my child?'

'Oh, Lord knows, I could write a book. Fornication?'

'On one occasion or on a number of occasions?'

'Not a whole lot, now you come to mention it.'

'Did you take pleasure?'

'Where there was any to be taken. Why do you ask such a thing?'

'Are you truly sorry for your sins?'

'I don't know. I have yet to meet a person who was not more sorry at
the end of their days, for lost opportunity than for lost virtue.'

'Well, try to be good in future. Your sins are forgiven. For your penance
. . .'

'Wait a minute!' The wood creaked as Dinah's knees shifted in annoyance. 'You are not forgiving my sins. You are dismissing them. It is true that
all this is of no account in the large scheme of the earth's decline, but even
so. You don't really care, do you, if I end up in hell or Havana?'

'Patience, child,' he urged, and a slice of startled blue appeared between his fingers, like the sky viewed between skyscraper rooflines. 'We are simply trying to keep up with the times. There isn't much demand for this service any more. Confession is no longer a draw. Mass absolution is the thing. All I get in here nowadays are old ladies who like the dark and someone to talk to. I haven't had a fornication in, oh, a decade.'

'Ah,' Dinah said. 'It is a part of the materialistic revolution – the refusal to believe in God. Even the Church has become a conspirator. We will have to work this out for ourselves. You asked if I took pleasure. I'll make a bargain. I will fill you in on the nature of carnal bliss if you, as holy man and celibate, will exchange your experiences of mystical ecstacy.'

'Get out of that!' the priest snarled in embarrassment. 'Do you want absolution or not?'

Dinah thought about it. 'Confession was what I really wanted – an opportunity to discuss my imperfections. And you did ask if I took pleasure.'

The holy man sighed most mournfully. 'I have had little consolation. I read the lives of the saints with envy. The most I have experienced are fleeting feelings of happiness in the certainty of God. The rest of the time I live in doubt.'

'There you are!' Dinah paused to light two cigarettes and she poked one in through the wire grille to her new acquaintance. 'It is much the same for me with my fornications – occasional brief bliss but most of the time a feeling of "what-the-hell-am-I-doing-here?" This is most interesting. Now let us move on to the nature of forgiveness. Do you really believe that you can forgive sins? If you have such power then why, if I come in to you and say, "I owe ten thousand pounds," can you not say, "Your debts are forgiven you?" The sin cannot be undone even if you are truly sorry. The transgression must remain outstanding just as the debt would be.'

'Ah, yes,' the priest said, livening, 'but there is a penance attached to the forgiveness of sin. If you owed a debt I would tell you to pay. So I ask you to pay for your sins by performing a penance – which I was about to do before you interrupted me.'

'I am sorry, Father. Pass on to the penance.'

'Your sins are forgiven.' He blessed her with fingers too soft for a man's hand. 'For your penance say five decades of the rosary.'

He began to mutter the ancient formula of expiation.

'Excuse me, please!' Dinah interrupted again.

'Yes?' When he frowned, his smooth face was marked all over by the years of doubt and compromise, like paw prints on clean lino.

'If prayer was given to us as a means of consolation, a manner of conversing with our heavenly mother and father, why is it also employed as penance?'

'Oh, good God!' he appealed. 'What do I know? Perhaps the theory is the same as that which argues against the imprisonment of criminals. Maybe it is seen as a means of positive reform rather than punishment.'

'That is fairly satisfactory,' Dinah nodded. 'You are an interesting man, you know. Perhaps I will commit some small sin in the near future so that we may take up this conversation again.'

Dinah did not immediately leave the stifling box but rummaged in her handbag and then thrust a gurgling bag around her door and through the windowed front of the booth.

'What are you doing?' The priest defended himself nervously.

'It's a present. I brought you a bottle of whiskey.'

'Oh, no. I couldn't take it.' In the gloom she could perceive that his eye was already trying to identify, through brown paper, the brand and nationality of the refreshment.

'It's a ten-year-old Irish,' she enlightened him. 'Where I originate, a man might throw out his daughter if she committed a transgression that was called deadly – oh, poisoning her husband, perhaps. But you have been clement to me and, although I do not believe that a magic word can quite erase sin, all the same I am surprised by how new I feel. Please honour me by accepting my gift.'

He took the whiskey. 'Come and talk to me again. Come even if you haven't a sin. It's dull in here and I enjoyed your company.'

'Yes, I would like that.' She hesitated and then she said: 'I have a favour to ask of you. Would you say a prayer for a little old lady who called me her daughter? She is of no account and yet in a strange way I believe it was her influence that brought me here. In fact, you might say she has changed my life.'

'She sounds a remarkable woman.' For the first time the priest smiled and Dinah saw a handsome face which might have charmed out of a different kind of dark and she felt a deep compassion for his bondage to God's holy order.

'She is, in fact, a kind of miracle.' She grinned at him mischievously. 'She is pure white.'

'Well, now.' God's representative looked nervous again. 'That's not so unusual these days.'

'And she is a virgin.'

Clare Boylan

————

Protestant women may take the pill. Roman Catholic women must keep taking The Tablet.

Irene Thomas

————

The best way to get the better of temptation is just to yield to it.

Clementina Stirling Graham

————

God is love, but get it in writing.

Gypsy Rose Lee

————

TOTTERING TOWARDS

THE TOMB

When men reach their sixties and retire, they go to
pieces. Women just go right on cooking.

Gail Sheehy

———

from Loving and Giving

One morning, some months after Dada's death, Aunt Tossie sat up in her
bunk bed, quietly comfortable. Her velvet dressing-gown kept her beautifully
warm, and just one bar of the small electric fire was enough to maintain her
caravan at a proper temperature. She missed Dada's company sadly, of course;
but his loss had retired into a secondary place when Gigi fell sick one
morning and died the next. She still sat, superbly well stuffed, in her cage. In
her silent presence, Aunt Tossie missed the evening gossip and nibbling love
tokens more acutely than if Gigi had been quite a ghost. 'Giving you fondies'
William had called it when he brought her tray and found them together. It
was William who had taken the dead bird away and persuaded the Post
Mistress to carry Gigi to Cork to be stuffed. When Aunt Tossie saw her again,

wired to her swing in the most lifelike way, she screamed with pleasure, or horror, it was hard for her to know which; perhaps gratitude for William's misplaced thoughtfulness was her strongest feeling. Pretty soon, Gigi's corpse became much the same to her as Dada's photograph, placed reverently on the po cupboard.

A curious quiet coma possessed her days, uninterrupted by the creation of Dada's dinners, or by the bother of his latest extravaganza. She felt free now to indulge herself in any little privilege she fancied. Shan't live for ever, she thought cheerfully, so why not relax and enjoy the second drink before dinner? There was no longer a cuddle with Gigi to fill in the time until William arrived with her tray. It seemed an unnecessary nonsense, moving into the morning-room for meals, and the dignified vault of the dining-room was unthinkable; in any case, the descent from the caravan was slightly perilous when she was what William called 'a little tired'. Aunt Tossie didn't call her happy state 'a little tired', she knew she was a little drunk, and enjoyed the short euphoria.

Very soon her cooking had become a lost interest and excitement now that she had no man to please. Why should I exhaust myself, she thought, I don't entertain, and I never go out. William's four-minute boiled eggs, or a neat little heap of sardines, were quite enough for her. Her only trouble was constipation, but four Cascara tablets soon settled that; and if she was conscious of a slight gasp and shudder when struggling on the Elsan, whiskey was the cure for that too.

Naturally, Andrew's horrid behaviour did upset her. She was disappointed in him, and her loving sympathy for Nicandra's unhappiness was boundless, or would have been boundless if Nicandra had come to her with tears and confidences. But she had, too, the rare ability to accept her place as an outsider: she never thought her generosities gave her any rights to affection. Young people had their own lives to live, pore things . . . the muddles. . . . When young herself, she could never have envisaged the peace and comfort of old age in a caravan. Even her gros point had become too much of a business, contented selfishness possessed her – when she folded her soft, crumpled hands against the hot-water bottle on her stomach, she dozed away from all troubles and anxieties, her own or anybody else's.

On one of these quiet, prospectless days, when William had left her with her morning cup of coffee, she sighed her way back among her pillows, before leaning out from her nest to reach into the po cupboard. Some time soon, next Thursday probably, she was going to open and answer all those dreadfully kind letters about Dada, as well as some of the rather disturbing ones in neatly typed envelopes. Aunt Tossie thought of them as arnvelopes, and would have gone to the stake in defence of her pronunciation. Now she drank up her medicated coffee while she considered the next step in her morning ... perhaps a biscuit. She was delighted to hear a knock on her door.

'Oh, do come in,' she called. 'Push, it sticks.' In her stately velvet dressing-gown, she was ready to receive at any hour of the day.

It was the grotesquely embarrassed face of Robert that looked round the door. 'Oh, it's you!' Aunt Tossie cried out in welcome, wondering who he was.

Robert was accustomed to delayed recognition – he fathomed her doubt without hesitation: 'I'm Robert.'

'Of course, I'm so senile about names.'

'I wanted to tell you – I was so sorry I missed Sir Dermot's funeral – I wanted to say, if there was anything I can do. . . . '

What could he possibly think he could do, dear fellow? 'You *are* kind,' she said.

Robert had squeezed himself into the caravan. He sat upright on the only symbol for a chair. In the back of her mind, Aunt Tossie knew there was some subject where they had a common interest. In a flash it came to her: 'How were your mother's Christmas roses this year?'

'Not very good. Lots of black spots,' Robert refrained from reminding her that his mother had been dead for five years.

'I'm not sure if you know,' he said, 'I thought I'd like to tell you myself. It seems a funny thing to say, I know: I've bought Deer Forest.'

'Have you? Have you really? You don't mean I don't own my caravan?'

'Of course not. What an idea.'

'But where am I to put it?'

'Don't move it. I like it here.'

'Oh, you *are* kind . . . there was a rumour of a buyer, of course we never dreamed of you. Do you mean to live here?'

'Not yet – there's the dry rot to consider.'

'Dry rot? I never noticed any.'

'And I want to make one bedroom habitable.'

'Which?'

'The sunniest.'

She stared at him. This talk from a stranger of dry rot and habitable bedrooms was curiously hurtful. Well as she recognized the horrid truth of what he said, she felt herself to be some sort of aboriginal, and Robert a species of kind white settler. She found herself wishing that he had been a nice, thoughtful Church of Ireland parson, like his father, and had not made all this money she had heard about. A tycoon, that was the word. Rather a nasty word too. It was a word that didn't properly fit Robert, sitting there breathing audibly but quietly (he had always been asthmatic) in her caravan. 'Anyhow,' she said, 'I expect it's all in one of those awful arnvelopes that come for my poor brother-in-law, he hated letters,' she stretched out a hand to touch the pile on the po cupboard. She didn't seem to have anything more to say. She sat there, grinding her teeth together in an abstracted way. Behind her Gigi, so adroitly stuffed and poised, moved a little on her swing as Aunt Tossie heaved, on her heap of pillows. For Robert, the gaudy bird lived. Each old parrot has her cage, he thought, and his heart was full of pity.

Molly Keane

As I grow older and older,
And totter towards the tomb,
I find that I care less and less
Who goes to bed with whom.

Dorothy L. Sayers

Being an old maid is like death by drowning, a really delightful sensation after you cease to struggle.

Edna Ferber

Ma'dear (for Estelle Ragsdale)

Last year the cost of living crunched me and I got tired of begging from Peter to pay Paul, so I took in three roomers. Two of 'em is live-in nurses and only come around here on weekends. Even then they don't talk to me much, except when they hand me their money orders. One is from Trinidad and the other is from Jamaica. Every winter they quit their jobs, fill up two and three barrels with I don't know what, ship 'em home, and follow behind on an airplane. They come back in the spring and start all over. Then there's the little college girl, Juanita, who claims she's going for architecture. Seem like to me that was always men's work, but I don't say nothing. She grown.

I'm seventy-two. Been a widow for the past thirty-two years. Weren't like I asked for all this solitude, just that couldn't nobody else take Jessie's place is all. He knew it. And I knew it. He fell and hit his head real bad on the tracks going to fetch us some fresh picked corn and okra for me to make us some succotash, and never come to. I couldn't picture myself with no other man, even though I looked after a few years of being alone in this big old house, walking from room to room with nobody to talk to, cook or clean for, and not much company either.

I missed him for the longest time and I thought I could find a man just like him, sincerely like him, but I couldn't. Went out for a spell with Esther Davis's ex-husband, Whimpy, but he was crazy. Drank too much bootleg and then started memorizing on World War I and how hard he fought and didn't get no respect and not a ounce of recognition for his heroic deeds. The only war Whimpy been in is with me for not keeping him around. He bragged something fearless about how he coulda been the heavyweight champion of the world. Didn't weigh but 160 pounds and shorter than me.

Chester Rutledge almost worked 'ceptin' he was boring, never had nothing on his mind worth talking about; claimed he didn't think about nothing besides me. Said his mind was always clear and visible. He just moved around like a zombie and worked hard at the cement foundry. Insisted on giving me his paychecks, which I kindly took for a while, but when I didn't want to be bothered no more, I stopped taking his money. He got on my nerves too bad, so I had to tell him I'd rather have a man with no money and a busy mind, least I'd know he's active somewheres. His feelings was hurt bad and he cussed me out, but we still friends to this very day. He in the home, you know, and I visits him regular. Takes him magazines and cuts out his horoscope and the comic strips from the newspaper and lets him read 'em in correct order.

Big Bill Ronsonville tried to convince me that I shoulda married him instead of Jessie, but he couldn't make me a believer of it. All he wanted to do was put his big rusty hands all on me without asking and smile at me with that big gold tooth sparkling and glittering in my face and tell me how lavish I was, lavish being a new word he just learnt. He kept wanting to take me for night rides way out in the country, out there by Smith Creek where ain't nothing but deep black ditches, giant mosquitoes, loud crickets, lightning bugs, and loose pigs, and turn off his motor. His breath stank like whiskey though he claimed and swore on the Bible he didn't drank no liquor. Aside from that his hands were way too heavy and hard, hurt me, sometimes left red marks on me like I been sucked on. I told him finally that I was too light for him, that I needed a smaller, more gentle man, and he said he knew exactly what I meant.

If you want to know the truth, after him I didn't think much about men the way I used too. Lost track of the ones who upped and died or the ones who couldn't do nothing if they was alive nohow. So, since nobody else seemed to be able to wear Jessie's shoes, I just stuck to myself all these years.

My life ain't so bad now 'cause I'm used to being alone and takes good care of myself. Occasionally I still has a good time. I goes to the park and sits for hours in good weather, watch folks move and listen in on confidential conversations. I add up numbers on license plates to keep my mind alert unless they pass too fast. This gives me a clear idea of how many folks is visiting from out of town. I can about guess the color of every state now, too. Once or twice a month I go to the matinee on Wednesdays, providing ain't no long line of senior citizens 'cause they can be so slow; miss half the picture show waiting for them to count their change and get their popcorn.

Sometimes, when I'm sitting in the park, I feed the pigeons old corn-bread crumbs, and I wonders what it'll be like not looking at the snow falling from the sky, not seeing the leaves form on the trees, not hearing no car engines, no sirens, no babies crying, not brushing my hair at night, drinking my Lipton tea, and not being able to go to bed early.

But right now, to tell you the truth, it don't bother me all *that* much. What is bothering me is my case worker. She supposed to pay me a visit tomorrow because my nosy neighbor, Clarabelle, saw two big trucks outside, one come right after the other, and she wondered what I was getting so new and so big that I needed trucks. My mama used to tell me that sometimes you can't see for looking. Clarabelle's had it out to do me in ever since last spring when I had the siding put on the house. I used the last of Jessie's insurance money 'cause the roof had been leaking so bad and the wood rotted and the paint chipped so much that it looked like a wicked old witch lived here. The house looked brand-new, and she couldn't stand to see an old woman's house looking better than hers. She know I been had roomers, and now all of a sudden my case worker claim she just want to visit to see how I'm doing, when really what she want to know is what I'm up to. Clarabelle work in her office.

The truth is my boiler broke and they was here to put in a new one. We liked to froze to death in here for two days. Yeah, I had a little chump change in the bank, but when they told me it was gonna cost $2,000 to get some heat, I cried. I had $862 in the bank; $300 of it I had just spent on this couch I got on sale; it was in the other truck. After twenty years the springs finally broke, and I figured it was time to buy a new one 'cause I ain't one for living in poverty, even at my age. I figured $200 was for my church's cross-country bus trip this summer.

Jessie's sister, Willamae, took out a loan for me to get the boiler, and I don't know how long it's gonna take me to pay her back. She only charge me fifteen or twenty dollars a month, depending. I probably be dead by the time it get down to zero.

My bank wouldn't give me the loan for the boiler, but then they keep sending me letters almost every week trying to get me to refinance my house. They must think I'm senile or something. On they best stationery, they write me. They say I'm up in age and wouldn't I like to take that trip I've been putting off because of no extra money. What trip? They tell me if I refinance my house for more than what I owe, which is about $3,000, that I could have enough money left over to go anywhere. Why would I want to refinance my house at fourteen and a half percent when I'm paying four and a half now? I ain't that stupid. They say dream about clear blue water, palm trees, and orange suns. Last night I dreamt I was doing a backstroke between big blue waves and tipped my straw hat down over my forehead and fell asleep under an umbrella. They made me think about it. And they asked me what would I do if I was to die today? They're what got me to thinking about all this dying mess in the first place. It never would've layed in my mind so heavy if they hadn't kept reminding me of it. Who would pay off your house? Wouldn't I feel bad leaving this kind of a burden on my family? What family they talking about? I don't even know where my people is no more.

I ain't gonna lie. It ain't easy being old. But I ain't complaining neither, 'cause I learned how to stretch my social security check. My roomers pay the house note and I pay the taxes. Oil is sky-high. Medicaid pays my doctor bills. I got a letter what told me to apply for food stamps. That case worker come here and checked to see if I had a real kitchen. When she saw I had a stove and sink and refrigerator, she didn't like the idea that my house was almost paid for, and just knew I was lying about having roomers. 'Are you certain that you reside here alone?' she asked me. 'I'm certain,' I said. She searched every inch of my cabinets to make sure I didn't have two of the same kinds of food, which would've been a dead giveaway. I hid it all in the basement inside the washing machine and dryer. Luckily, both of the nurses was in the islands at the time, and Juanita was visiting some boy what live in DC.

After she come here and caused me so much eruptions, I had to make trip after trip down to that office. They had me filling out all kinds of forms and still held up my stamps. I got tired of answering the same questions over and over and finally told 'em to keep their old food stamps. I ain't got to beg nobody to eat. I know how to keep myself comfortable and clean and well fed. I manage to buy my staples and toiletries and once in a while a few extras, like potato chips, ice cream, and maybe a pork chop.

My mama taught me when I was young that, no matter how poor you are, always eat nourishing food and your body will last. Learn to conserve, she said. So I keeps all my empty margarine containers and stores white rice, peas and carrots (my favorites), or my turnips from the garden in there. I can manage a garden when my arthritis ain't acting up. And water is the key. I drinks plenty of it like the doctor told me, and I cheats, eats Oreo cookies and saltines. They fills me right up, too. And when I feels like it, rolls, home-made biscuits, eats them with Alga syrup if I can find it at the store, and that sticks with me most of the day.

Long time ago, used to be I'd worry like crazy about gaining weight and my face breaking out from too many sweets, and about cellulite forming all over my hips and thighs. Of course, I was trying to catch Jessie then, though I didn't know it at the time. I was really just being cute, flirting, trying to see if I could get attention. Just so happens I lucked up and got all of his. Caught him like he was a spider and I was the web.

Lord, I'd be trying to look all sassy and prim. Have my hair all did, it be curled tight in rows that I wouldn't comb out for hours till they cooled off after Connie Curtis did it for a dollar and a Budweiser. Would take that dollar out my special savings, which I kept hid under the record player in the front room. My hair used to be fine, too: long and thick and black, past my shoulders, and mens used to say, 'Girl, you sure got a head of hair on them shoulders there, don't it make your neck sweat?' But I didn't never bother answering, just blushed and smiled and kept on walking, trying hard not to switch 'cause mama told me my behind was too big for my age and to watch out or I'd be luring grown mens toward me. Humph! I loved it, though, made me feel pretty, special, like I had attraction.

Ain't quite the same no more, though. I looks in the mirror at myself and I sees wrinkles, lots of them, and my skin look like it all be trying to run down toward my toes but then it changed its mind and just stayed there, sagging and lagging, laying limp against my thick bones. Shoot, mens used to say how sexy I was with these high cheeks, tell me I looked swollen, like I was pregnant, but it was just me, being all healthy and everything. My teeth was even bright white and straight in a row then. They ain't so bad now, 'cause ain't none of 'em mine. But I only been to the dentist twice in my whole life and that was 'cause on Easter Sunday I was in so much pain he didn't have time to take no X-ray and yanked it right out 'cause my mama told him to do anything he had to to shut me up. Second time was the last time, and that was 'cause the whole top row and the fat ones way in the back on the bottom ached me so bad the dentist yanked 'em all out so I wouldn't have to be bothered no more.

Don't get me wrong, I don't miss being young. I did everything I wanted to do and then some. I loved hard. But you take Jessie's niece, Thelma. She pitiful. Only twenty-six, don't think she made it past the tenth grade, got three children by different men, no husband and on welfare. Let her tell it, ain't nothing out here but dogs. I know some of these men out here ain't worth a pot to piss in, but all of 'em ain't dogs. There's gotta be some young Jessies floating somewhere in this world. My mama always told me you gotta have something to give if you want to get something in return. Thelma got long fingernails.

Me, myself, I didn't have no kids. Not 'cause I didn't want none or couldn't have none, just that Jessie wasn't full and couldn't give me the juices I needed to make no babies. I accepted it 'cause I really wanted him all to myself, even if he couldn't give me no new bloodlines. He was satisfying enough for me, quite satisfying if you don't mind me repeating myself.

I don't understand Thelma, like a lot of these young peoples. I be watching 'em on the streets and on TV. I be hearing things they be doing to themselves when I'm under the dryer at the beauty shop. (I go to the beauty shop once a month 'cause it make me feel like thangs ain't over yet. She give me a henna so the silver have a gold tint to it.) I can't afford it, but there ain't too many luxuries I can. I let her put makeup on me, too, if it's a Saturday and I feel like doing some window shopping. I still know how to flirt and sometimes I get stares, too. It feel good to be looked at and admired at my age. I try hard to keep myself up. Every weekday morning at five-thirty I do exercises with the TV set, when it don't hurt to stretch.

But like I was saying, Thelma and these young people don't look healthy, and they spirits is always so low. I watch 'em on the streets, on the train, when I'm going to the doctor. I looks in their eyes and they be red or brown where they supposed to be milky white and got bags deeper and heavier than mine, and I been through some thangs. I hear they be using these drugs of variety, and I can't understand why they need to use all these thangs to get from day to day. From what I do hear, it's supposed to give 'em much pleasure and make their minds disappear or make 'em not feel the thangs they supposed to be feeling anyway.

Heck, when I was young, we drank sarsaparilla and couldn't even buy no wine or any kind of liquor in no store. These youngsters ain't but eighteen and twenty and buys anything with a bite to it. I've seen 'em sit in front of the store and drank a whole bottle in one sitting. Girls, too.

We didn't have no dreams of carrying on like that, and specially on no corner. We was young ladies and young men with respect for ourselfs. And we didn't smoke none of them funny cigarettes all twisted up with no filters that smell like burning dirt. I ask myself, I say Ma'Dear, what's wrong with these kids? They can read and write and do arithmetic, finish high school, go to college and get letters behind their names, but every day I hear the neighbors complain that one of they youngsters done dropped out.

Lord, what I wouldn'ta done to finish high school and been able to write a full sentence or even went to college. I reckon I'da been a room decorator. I know they calls it be that fancy name now, interior designer, but it boil down to the same thang. I guess it's 'cause I loves so to make my surroundings pleasant, even right pretty, so I feels like a invited guest in my own house. And I always did have a flair for color. Folks used to say, 'Hazel, for somebody as poor as a church mouse, you got better taste in thangs than them Rockefellers!' Used to sew up a storm, too. Covered my mama's raggedy duffold and chairs. Made her a bedspread with matching pillowcases. Didn't mix more than two different patterns either. Make you dizzy.

Wouldn't that be just fine, being an interior designer? Learning the proper names of thangs and recognizing labels in catalogs, giving peoples my business cards and wearing a two-piece with white gloves. 'Yes, I decorated the Hartleys' and Cunninghams' home. It was such a pleasant experience. And they're such lovely people, simply lovely,' I'da said. Coulda told those rich folks just what they needed in their bedrooms, front rooms, and specially in the kitchen. So many of 'em still don't know what to do in there.

But like I was saying before I got all off the track, some of these young people don't appreciate what they got. And they don't know thangs like we used to. We knew about eating fresh vegetables from the garden, growing and picking 'em ourselves. What going to church was, being honest and faithful. Trusting each other. Leaving our front door open. We knew what it was like to starve and get cheated yearly when our crops didn't add up the way we figured. We suffered together, not separately. These youngsters don't know about suffering for any stretch of time. I hear 'em on the train complaining 'cause they can't afford no Club Med, no new record playing albums, cowboy boots, or those Brooke Shields–Calvin Klein blue jeans I see on TV. They be complaining about nonsense. Do they ever read books since they been taught is what I want to know? Do they be learning things and trying to figure out what to do with it?

And these young girls with all this thick makeup caked on their faces, wearing these high heels they can't hardly walk in. Trying to be cute. I used to wear high heels, mind you, with silk stockings, but at least I could walk in 'em. Jessie had a car then. Would pick me up, and I'd walk real careful down the front steps like I just won the Miss America pageant, one step at a time, and slide into his shiny black Ford. All the neighbors peeked through the curtains 'cause I was sure enough riding in a real automobile with my legitimate boyfriend.

If Jessie was here now I'd have somebody to talk to. Somebody to touch my skin. He'd probably take his fingers and run 'em through my hair like he used to; kiss me on my nose and tickle me where it made me laugh. I just loved it when he kissed me. My mind be so light, and I felt tickled and precious. Have to sit down sometime just to get hold of myself.

If he was here, I probably woulda beat him in three games of checkers by now and he'd be trying to get even. But since today is Thursday, I'd be standing in that window over there waiting for him to get home from work, and when I got tired or the sun be in my eyes, I'd hear the taps on his wing tips coming up the front porch. Sometime, even now, I watch for him, but I know he ain't coming back. Not that he wouldn't if he could, mind you, 'cause he always told me I made him feel lightning lighting up his heart.

Don't get me wrong, I got friends, though a heap of 'em is dead or got tubes coming out of their noses or going all through their bodies every whicha-way. Some in the old folks' home. I thank the Lord I ain't stuck in one of them places. I ain't never gonna get that old. They might as well just bury me standing up if I do. I don't want to be no nuisance to nobody, and I can't stand being around a lot of sick people for too long.

I visits Gunther and Chester when I can, and Vivian who I grew up with, but no soon as I walk through them long hallways, I get depressed. They lay there all limp and helpless, staring at the ceiling like they're really looking at something, or sitting stiff in their rocking chairs, pitiful, watching TV and don't be knowing what they watching half the time. They laugh when ain't nothing funny. They wait for it to get dark so they know it's time to go to sleep. They relatives don't hardly come visit 'em, just folks like me. Whimpy don't understand a word I say, and it makes me grateful I ain't lost no more than I have.

Sometime we sits on the sun porch rocking like fools, don't say one word to each other for hours. But last time Gunther told me about his grandson what got accepted to Stanford University, and another one at a university in Michigan. I asked him where was Stanford and he said he didn't know. 'What difference do it make?' he asked. 'It's one of those uppity schools for rich smart white people,' he said. 'The important thang is that my black grandson won a scholarship there, which mean he don't have to pay a dime to go.' I told him I know what a scholarship is. I ain't stupid. Gunther said he was gonna be there for at least four years or so, and by that time he would be a professional. 'Professional what?' I asked. 'Who cares, Ma'Dear, he gonna be a professional at whatever it is he learnt.' Vivian started mumbling when she hears us talking, 'cause she still like to be the center of attention. When she was nineteen she was Miss Springfield Gardens. Now she can't stand the thought that she old and wrinkled. She started yakking about all the places she'd been to, even described the landscape like she was looking at a photograph. She ain't been but twenty-two miles north of here in her entire life, and that's right there in that home.

Like I said, and this is the last time I'm gonna mention it. I don't mind being old, it's just that sometime I don't need all this solitude. You can't do everything by yourself and expect to have as much fun if somebody was there doing it with you. That's why when I'm feeling jittery or melancholy for long stretches, I read the Bible, and it soothes me. I water my morning glories and amaryllis. I baby-sit for Thelma every now and then, 'cause she don't trust me with the kids for too long. She mainly call on holidays and my birthday. And she the only one who don't forget my birthday: August 19th. She tell me I'm a Leo, that I got fire in my blood. She may be right, 'cause once in a while I gets a churning desire to be smothered in Jessie's arms again.

Anyway, it's getting late, but I ain't tired. I feel pretty good. That old case worker think she gonna get the truth out of me. She don't scare me. It ain't none of her business that I got money coming in here besides my social security check. How they 'spect a human being to live off $369 a month in this day and age is what I wanna know. Every time I walk out my front door it cost me at least two dollars. I bet she making thousands and got credit cards galore. Probably got a summer house on the Island and goes to Florida every January. If she found out how much I was getting from my roomers, the government would make me pay back a dollar for every two I made. I best to get my tail on upstairs and clear everything off their bureaus. I can hide all the nurses' stuff in the attic; they won't be back till next month. Juanita been living out of trunks since she got here, so if the woman ask what's in 'em, I'll tell her, old sheets and pillowcases and memories.

On second thought, I think I'm gonna take me a bubble bath first, and dust my chest with talcum powder, then I'll make myself a hot cup of Lipton's and paint my fingernails clear 'cause my hands feel pretty steady. I can get up at five and do all that other mess; case worker is always late anyway. After she leave, if it ain't snowing too bad, I'll go to the museum and look at the new paintings in the left wing. By the time she get here, I'ma make out like I'm a lonely old widow stuck in a big old house just sitting here waiting to die.

Terry McMillan

————

In a dream you are never eighty.

Anne Sexton

————

Death and taxes and childbirth! There's never any
convenient time for any of them.

Margaret Mitchell

————

from Birds of Paradise

Ellen was wondering how she could excuse herself, when there was a drum-roll from the platform, and the master of ceremonies took the microphone. It was time for the fancy dress parade, he announced, and the awarding of prizes. He asked all the passengers to get into a line.

'We can't miss the parade,' Ellen said. 'Your costume is bound to win a prize. It wouldn't be fair. Besides, if we were to leave now, everybody would want to know why, and I don't want anyone else to know except you. After the parade we can slip out quietly.'

Mr Bowers bought her logic, though he would willingly have forgone the chances of a prize, for his rage on Ellen's behalf was monumental. 'As soon as it's over,' he said, gripping her arm.

Ellen looked at his face. It was blazing with the zeal of his mission, and did much to enhance the authenticity of his saintly role.

He guided her into the parade. The stewards were busy separating the men from the women. The panel of judges had taken their seats on the platform and were already making notes. Alice and her namesake joined Ellen who was standing alone. Alice Dove took her chained place between them, so that each Elizabeth stood an equal chance. Ellen felt a tap on her shoulder. She turned round to find Mr Bowers standing directly behind her in the man's line. 'As soon as it's over,' he whispered. 'We must lose no time.'

Ellen smiled at him. She was suffused with relief that her troubles were at last shared. And happiness, too, on account of the profound intimacy their recent exchanges of confidences had engendered. She knew instinctively that their relationship had achieved some kind of specialness. For a moment she dared to hope that there now existed between them the possibility of permanence. Then she shivered with the thought that the good Mr Bowers might well be deterred by the knowledge that she was not only third hand, but very soiled goods indeed. She began to fear Mrs Dove again. But Mrs Dove had no story like hers to share. She and Mr Bowers had given each other their deepest secret, and their exchange bound them together indissolubly. She looked forward to a night of calm in troubled sleep, and a future in which Mr Bowers was no longer a shadowy figure from the past. She could hardly contain her joy.

Wally Peters and Mrs Dove remained seated at the table, he still loath to risk movement. But a steward approached and playfully dragged them to their feet and ushered them into line. Ellen noticed their temporary parting, and the look in both their eyes. She was glad for them. Now I'll have to get

Alice fixed up, she said to herself, her Alice, she meant, her hedge-Alice, whom she thought she knew so well, and certainly not that other one, whose confusion she would never in a lifetime understand. She took Alice Dove's hand out of pity.

'Now we want the ladies first,' the master of ceremonies shouted from the platform. 'Would you be so kind as to parade around the floor?'

The music struck up a stately march, and the women obliged, the Mesdames de Pompadour, the Elizabeths, one and two, the single Golda Meir and a handful of Curies. An Amelia Earhardt suddenly came to light, complete with model aeroplane and flying boots. As did a trio of ladies in Victorian dress carrying leather-bound books who repeated over and over again that they were none other than the Brontë sisters. They were too proud to wear a label, and were happy to attribute non-recognition of their parts to sheer illiteracy. The women moved around the floor with a gait that matched their parts, mincing, proud or manly, Alice's chains clanking all the while to the rhythm of the marching song. Out of the corner of her eye, Ellen could see the judges scribbling their controversial notes. If she were a judge, she thought, she would award the prize to her friend Alice, as compensation for the lack of a partner.

The women did a double turn of the floor, and then the judges seemed satisfied. The music stopped and the master of ceremonies introduced the chairman of the panel of judges. That gentleman stood to attention, and promised his listeners that he would make his speech short and come to the point straight away. But his promise was as short-lived as his speech was long. He felt obliged to discourse on the judgement of almost every costume, insisting, time and time again, that judging had not been an easy task. Then he could not resist the usual platitudes about the ethics of winning and losing, by which time he had lost most of his audience who had wandered over to the buffet table for more food. The MC nodded to the drummer to bring the wayward back to the flock, and in a rare pause in the judge's speech, the drummer obliged and the black sheep returned to the fold.

The judge took the hint and prepared to divulge the panel's findings. The prize, he said, had been awarded to the costume that had shown the greatest originality, which remark, in the minds of most of the women, could have been personally applicable. The judge was giving nothing away. But there came a further clue. 'By originality,' he said, 'we mean something that is the contribution of the wearer herself, rather than what she has acquired at the costumiers.'

On hearing this, all the Marie Antoinettes, Mesdames de Pompadours and the two Elizabeths felt ashamed, and would have been happy to withdraw from the competition in deserved humiliation.

'With this criteria,' the judge bumbled on, 'we have decided that the chains have won the day.'

It was clear that nobody knew what he was talking about, so he was obliged to clarify. 'The prize for the best ladies' costume goes to Sylvia Pankhurst,' he said.

Alice Dove was stunned. She had never in her life won a prize for anything, not even a booby one. She did not know what look to use to accommodate it. All she felt was ashamed, embarrassed and undeserving. There must be a look for that, she thought, then she realised that that was the look she was most at home with, the look she had worn most of her life, her face's natural reaction to the many blows and the lesser bonuses she had experienced. It struck her as odd that both eventualities merited equally the same look. Yet she couldn't help giggling, a bonus to herself, for something that was so unexpected, so unlooked-for. She was no longer available to disappointment. After her Venice rinse, the smallest detail would stir her curiosity, the most trivial pleasure, her joy. She regarded her prize as one for survival. Her costume and chains were mere incidentals. More pleased even than herself was her mother and she rushed to her side with her untouching congratulations. Both the Elizabeths were happy for her, in the light of what the poor woman had undergone, and, like her mother, both looked upon the prize as divine compensation. Wally Peters added his congratulations, and Mr Bowers, too, though he was late in arriving. Ellen noticed with some alarm that his gait appeared rather slow. His voice, too, was faint and she could only suppose that his role had consumed his heart and his soul.

When the men were called upon to make their parade, he was seen to shuffle into line. Yet he managed to look back at Ellen, and in a frail voice, his eyes ablaze, he said again, 'As soon as this is over.' She smiled at him, and wished him luck and was stabbed with the fearful thought that her wishes were extended to rather more than his costume.

As the men sorted themselves out for the parade, the sundry Hitlers tried to separate themselves in a pathetic bid for individuality. But there were so many of them, they seemed like standard fare. Stuart Petty, still convinced that he had invented the role, now squeezed it for all it had and goose-stepped the parade, his arm in an outstretched salute. The other Hitlers had the taste to think that tasteless. It was, after all, only a role, and a losing one at that. The goose-step matched the marching rhythm, which did equally well for Stalin. When Churchill tried to match it, however, it was sadly out of time and season. Gandhi ignored it altogether, pacing his still quiet circle like a holy beetle.

It took the judges only one round of the parade to come to a unanimous decision. This time another judge was called upon to announce the result, and he was a man of few words. He came to the point straight away. 'Ladies and gentlemen,' he said, 'the outright winner of this round is the most original. The prize goes, with our greatest respect, to Mahatma Gandhi.'

Nobody was surprised, except perhaps Mr Bowers himself. Or rather, he was irritated, for the prize-giving ceremony would only delay his urgent mission on Ellen's behalf. Besides, he was suddenly feeling rather poorly, with a stabbing pain in his chest. He badly wanted to lie down.

His friends gathered round him with their felicitations. As a group, they felt especially privileged, and there were some in the ballroom who, having noted their inseparableness during the course of the cruise, thought that the prizes were possibly rigged.

The band started to play again as a steward placed two large gift-wrapped parcels on the judges' table and motioned the winners to come forward. Alice Dove waited for Mr Bowers to join her, but he seemed suddenly immoveable. He uttered a long and very polite sigh, then his knees buckled beneath him, his face twisted in pain, and he sank to the floor.

Ellen rushed towards him. 'I'm sorry,' he said, in general apology rather than in the particular, for his eyes were closed. 'No, no,' Ellen whispered. 'You mustn't be ill. Now now. We've got work to do.' And Mrs Dove, who'd seen that sort of thing before, and Ellen and Alice, who, God knows, had had their lessons with Walsh, Thomas and Pickering, turned their faces away. And so did many of the passengers, but for other reasons, and mainly of annoyance. What with the disgraceful shenanigans in Venice, and now this, that particular group was giving the cruise a bad name, and they all felt contaminated by it. They hovered on the fringe of the hall, apart, in the survivors' position, their faces masks of manufactured concern.

A steward ran out of the ballroom to fetch the ship's doctor, who had apparently made an early night. Ellen and Alice knelt by Mr Bowers' side, and rubbed his hands. Then into their shadow loomed the white surplice, ruby ring, and dangling cross of Pope John.

'But he's not a Catholic,' Ellen hissed, boiling with Protestant mistrust. It did not occur to her that the Pope was no Pope either, but he had the costume and he could have fooled anybody, even perhaps those on high. 'What's it matter?' Wally Peters said, turning away. 'It's too late anyway.' The doctor, panting in his pyjamas, gave one look at the prone Mr Bowers, and could only confirm Wally's diagnosis. He suggested a massive heart-attack, which, even under intensive care, would have stood no chance at all.

Bernice Rubens

———

Widows are accountable to none of their actions.

Susanna Centlivre

———

We met Dr Hall in such very deep mourning that either his mother, his wife, or himself must be dead.

Jane Austen

———

Well, it's all over and done with, Brinvilliers is in the air. Her poor little body was thrown after the execution into a very big fire and the ashes to the winds, so that we shall breathe her, and through the communication of the subtle spirits we shall develop some poisoning urge which will astonish us all. She was tried yesterday and this morning the sentence was read to her; it was to make a public confession at Notre-Dame and to have her head cut off, her body burnt and the ashes scattered to the winds. She was taken to the torture but she said there was no need and that she would tell all. And indeed until five in the evening she recounted her life, even more appalling than people thought. She poisoned her father ten times running (she couldn't finish it off), her brothers and several others, and always love and confidential matters mixed up with it. She said nothing against Pennautier. This confession notwithstanding, they put her to the torture first thing in the morning, both ordinary and extraordinary, but she said nothing more. She asked to speak to the Public Prosecutor and was with him for an hour, but so far nobody knows the subject of this conversation. At six o'clock she was taken, with only a shift on and a rope around her neck, to make the public confession at Notre-Dame. Then she was put back into the tumbril in which I saw her, thrown on her back on to the straw, wearing a low cornet and her shift, having on one side a priest and on the other the executioner; it really made me shudder. Those who saw the execution say that she mounted the scaffold with great courage. As for me, I was on the Pont Notre-Dame with the good d'Escars; never has such a crowd been seen, nor Paris so excited and attentive. If you ask me what I saw, it was nothing but a cornet, but the day was given up to this tragedy.

Madame de Sévigné

I have nothing against undertakers personally. It's just that I wouldn't want one to bury my sister.

Jessica Mitford

On Visiting Westminster Abbey

Holy Moses! Have a look!
Flesh decayed in every nook!
Some rare bits of brain be here
Mortal loads of beef and beer.

. . .

Famous some were – yet they died:
Poets – Statesmen – Rogues beside,
Kings – Queens, all of them do rot,
What about them? Now – they're not!

Amanda M. Ros

THE SERIOUS BIT
A MESSAGE FROM COMIC RELIEF

It all began in 1985 and now, ten years on, Comic Relief has raised over £110 million, every penny of which has gone to support projects in Africa and the UK. The face behind the big Red Nose is an organisation called Charity Projects, a charity committed to raising money in a fun way and making everyone aware of the serious side of giving grants. The money raised is allocated in a responsible and effective way, making sure that all fund-raising costs are covered by generous sponsorship from the business world.

This means that every penny *you* raise goes straight to help fund projects and none is soaked up by administration costs at Comic Relief.

Looking back over the past ten years from the first No. 1 hit single when Cliff Richard and the Young Ones got themselves a 'crying, talking, sleeping, walking, living doll' to the recent 'Love Can Build A Bridge' featur-ing Cher, Chrissie Hynde and Neneh Cherry, the red nose has captured the imagination of the public. The very first night of comedy at the Shaftesbury Theatre, along with the 'Living Doll' single raised over one million pounds. It was clear then that a phenomenon was in the making.

The roll call that night was amazing – Lenny Henry, Rowan Atkinson, French and Saunders, Smith and Jones, Fry and Laurie, Rik Mayall, Billy Connolly and many more. Since that night, they have remained committed to the cause and continued to help. No one, it seems, is unhappy to become involved when the call comes.

The germ of the idea that was Comic Relief went into hyperdrive with the *proboscis rubus* – the Red Nose. No one can quite remember who actually had the idea, although there is the theory that it involved Ade Edmonson, a rake, a fridge door and a house brick. Quite how all those elements came together, no one is really sure, but one thing which is absolutely certain is that the idea culminated in six TV hours of the very best of British Comedy combined with serious films from Africa and the UK. This gave a focus for the public's desire to do something which might make a difference. It also gave them the chance to go crazy, have fun, humiliate their friends and raise millions upon millions of pounds.

The first Red Nose Day saw an outbreak of city gents wearing the lovely little red things and gently saying hello to their fellow commuters. By Red Nose Day 2, no Mini or Rolls Royce was safe – the Car Nose was born. As Hale and Pace 'stonked' their way through Red Nose Day 3, the Noses had even attacked buildings. The invasion continued on Red Nose Day 4 when a new breed of Tomato Nose appeared in places you couldn't imagine. And finally Red Nose Day '95 went colour-changing crazy keeping up with the discovery of thermochromatic (or heat responsive) plastic.

The public have done some amazing things in the name of Comic Relief. They have jumped out of aeroplanes, sat in porridge, maggots or raw eggs, bathed in onion gravy, eaten dinner underwater, abseiled down town halls, auctioned off teachers and sixth formers, composed songs, gunked anything that moved and there have even been nude skiers wearing nothing but carefully attached Red Noses! No scout, guide or brownie has failed in their duty. No headmaster or teacher has suffered in vain. Millions of Red Noses have inspired hundreds of thousands of sponsored events.

The result is that Red Nose money in Africa has built wells, sown seeds, performed operations, immunised children, clothed refugees and transported food and blankets. Here in the UK it has housed young homeless people, provided emergency beds, sheltered vulnerable women, taught young people about the dangers of drugs and alcohol, made buildings, transport and jobs available to disabled people and stood up for their rights as well as those of the nation's pensioners.

So much work has been done and mothers, fathers, sons, daughters, uncles, aunts, friends and neighbours throughout the UK have made it all possible. There is still more work to do and while that is the case the Comic Relief team will work as hard as ever to get it done. The public support for the Red Nose has been staggering, their efforts have been inspirational. The money they have raised has made a lasting difference to some of the poorest people in Africa and the UK is a testimony to their commitment and energy.

ACKNOWLEDGEMENTS

Every effort has been made to trace copyright holders. We apologise for any omissions and would be grateful to be informed of corrections to be made in subsequent editions. Special thanks to Eleanor Bron for excerpt from *Life and Other Punctures and poems*; to Elaine Morgan for two delicious quotes; to Dillie Keane and partners for 'Herpes Tango'; 'Bunny Rabbit' by kind permission of Aitken, Stone and Wylie Ltd, on behalf of Pam Ayres; Victoria Wood for *Lady Police Series* from Barmy reproduced by permission The Richard Stone Partnership; French & Saunders for *Fat Aristocrats* and *Fashion Expert* published by William Heinemann Ltd; Joan Rivers for extracts from *Still Talking*; Maeve Binchy for *Warren Street from Victoria Line*; Barbara Pym for excerpt from *Excellent Women* © Edna O'Brien; Molly Keane for extract from *Loving and Giving* published by Andre Deutsch Ltd; Glenys Roberts for 'Ruislip', from *Metropolitan Myths*, by permission Libra Mundi and 'Lady Chapel' from *Hard Pressed* by kind permission Quartet; *Poisson d'Avril* © E. Œ. Somerville and Martin Ross, reproduced by permission of Curtis Brown Group Ltd, London; Sue Townsend for extract from *The Growing Pains of Adrian Mole*; *Tommy* (after Kipling) and other quotes by Katharine Whitehorn and Nancy Banks Smith © *Guardian*; poems by Stevie Smith, by kind permission James MacGibbon; poems by Anna Wickham by kind permission of Jim Hepburn; Elizabeth Taylor extract from *The Soul of Kindness* © the estate of Elizabeth Taylor; *New Statesman* for parodies by June Mercer Langfield, Vera Telfer, Mary Demetriadis; 'Ma' Dear' by Terry McMillan by permission of Abner Stein; Muriel Spark's 'You Should Have Seen the Mess' from *The Go-Away Bird and Other Stories*, reprinted by permission of David Higham Associates; 'Loss' by Wendy Cope from *Serious Concerns* published by Faber & Faber Ltd; Gwen Raverat extracts from *Period Piece* published by Faber & Faber Ltd; Patricia Highsmith's 'The Perfectionist' from *Little Tales of Misogyny* reproduced by permission Reed Consumer books; various pieces by Nancy Mitford reprinted by permission of the Peters Fraser and Dunlop Group Ltd; poems and quotes by Dorothy Parker reprinted by permission the Duckworth Group; Dorothy Fields' 'Big Spender' © 1965 Notable Music Co Inc in association with Lida Enterprises Inc USA, used by permission of Campbell Connelly & Co Ltd, London, all rights reserved; 'Notes on Black', from *If you can't live without me why aren't you dead yet* by Cynthia Heimel reprinted by permission of Fourth Estate; 'Gertrude Talks Back' and 'There Was Once' from *Good Bones* published by Virago reproduced with permission of Curtis Brown Ltd, London on behalf of Margaret Atwood, © Margaret Atwood 1992; Joyce Grenfell's 'The Committee' from *Turn Back the Clock* by permission Richard Scott Simon Ltd; Lynne Truss' an extract from *With One Lousy Free Packet of Seed*, published by Hamish Hamilton, by permission David Higham Associates; extracts from *Memories of a Catholic Girlhood* by Mary McCarthy © Mary McCarthy; excerpt from 'Gentlemen Prefer Blondes' by Anita Loos reprinted with the permission of Liveright Publishing Corporation © 1925 by Anita Loos, © 1925 by International Magazine Co, renewed by Anita Loos Emerson, all rights reserved; 'Mrs Bott's Hat' by Richmal Crompton reproduced by permission Macmillan Children's books; extract from *Letters from a Faint-hearted Feminist* by Jill Tweedie by permission Robson Books; extract from *The Visitors* by Mary McMinnies reprinted by permission David Higham Associates; to Jilly Cooper for 'Against Youth'; 'How To Talk to a Hunter' from *Cowboys Are My Weakness* by Pam Houston, published by Virago Press, reprinted by permission Tessa Sayle Agency; 'The Fat Black Woman Goes Shopping' from *The Fat Black Women's Poems* by Grace Nichols, reprinted by permission of Virago Press; 'Jade Junkies' from *We, the Dangerous* by Janice Mirkitani, reprinted by permission of Virago Press. I would also like to thank all other, untraceable women (many long dead or out of copyright) whose contributions have made this book possible.

AUTHOR INDEX
(by century)

16th Century
Elizabeth I 15

17th Century
Astell, Mary 14, 144, 212
Behn, Aphra 22, 53, 74, 121, 143
Bradstreet, Anne 306
Cavendish, Margaret, Duchess of
    Newcastle 114, 200
Chudleigh, Mary, Lady 144
Sévigné, Madame de 4, 350
Wroth, Mary, Lady 68

18th Century
Alcock, Mary 306
Austen, Jane 40, 68, 78, 200, 350
Barber, Mary 248
Burney, Fanny 40, 199, 214, 231, 305
Catherine the Great 329
Centlivre, Susanna 201, 302, 350
Charke, Charlotte 246
Cornuel, Madame 17
Cowley, Hannah 24
Fanshawe, Catherine M. 286
Female Tatler, The 27, 125, 232
Haywood, Eliza 27, 126
Manley, Delarivier 122
Montagu, Mary Wortley, Lady 230,
    239
Staël, Madame de 125
Wright, Hetty 179

19th Century
Barrett Browning, Elizabeth 14, 65
Brontë, Charlotte 301, 328
Brooks, Shirley 285
Carey, Phoebe 284
Carlyle, Jane 14
Colette 26
Dickinson, Emily 214, 303
Fleming, Marjorie 302
Gaskell, Elizabeth 30, 142, 192, 231
Graham, Clementina Sterling 332
Gilman, Charlotte Perkins 144
Kemble, Fanny 243, 304
Ros, Amanda M. 351
Sturgis, Ellen Hooper 145
Victor, Metta Victoria 181, 248
Victoria, Queen 241
Ward, Mrs Humphrey 311
Wells, Carolyn 18, 205

20th Century
Banner 145
Wife 17
Allen, Gracie 244
Allingham, Margery 122
Anne, Princess 236
Arendt, Hannah 143
Ashford, Daisy 65
Asquith, Margot 238, 240, 241
Astor, Nancy 200
Atwood, Margaret 153, 282

Ayres, Pam 173
Bacall, Lauren 199
Bankhead, Tallulah 24, 214, 237, 305, 312
Banks-Smith, Nancy 241
Barrymore, Ethel 305
Binchy, Maeve 30
Bombeck, Erma 109, 110
Bonham-Carter, Violet, Lady 143
Bowen, Elizabeth 231, 237
Boylan, Clare 329
Brand, Jo 82, 328
Bron, Eleanor 41, 64, 96
Brookner, Anita 1
Campbell, Mrs Patrick 109, 125, 237
Carter, Angela 192
Chanel, Coco 231
Cheek, Mavis 93
Christie, Agatha 16, 213
Collins, Joan 205
Compton-Burnett, Ivy 230
Cooper, Jilly 273
Cope, Wendy 74
Crompton, Richmal 255
Davis, Bette 200, 214, 238
Delafield, E. M. 82
Demetriadis, Mary 285
Dietrich, Marlene 16
Diller, Phyllis 201, 268
Drabble, Margaret 41, 235
Draper, Ruth 157, 312
Dunn, Mary 94, 201
Dykestra, Lillian K. 240
Eden, Clarissa, Lady 92
Ertz, Susan 231
Ferber, Edna 24, 336
Fields, Dorothy 16
Foyle, Gwen 288, 289
French, Dawn & Saunders, Jennifer 24, 136
Gabor, Zsa Zsa 19, 126, 199, 205
Garson, Barbara 279
Gilliat, Penelope 240
Gingold, Hermione 22, 319

Gregory, Augusta, Lady 214
Green, Celia 143
Grenfell, Joyce 2
Gunter, Nancy 288
Halsey, Margaret 26, 138
Harris, Susan 132
Hayes, Helen 305
Heimel, Cynthia 28
Highsmith, Patricia 5
Hooper, Ellen Sturgis 145
Houston, Pam 53
Hull, Josephine 305
Jameson, Storm 96
Jillson, Joyce 5
Jong, Erica 15
Keane, Dillie 130
Keane, Molly 333
Kennedy, Florynce 18
Kerr, Deborah 199
Kerr, Jean 22, 144
Kilmer, Aline 276
Lamarr, Hedy 24
Lamport, Felicia 289
Lanchester, Elsa 238
Langfield, June Mercer 281
Lavin, Mary 162
Lebowitz, Fran 26, 39, 120, 213, 214, 243
Lecoat, Jenny 21
Lee, Gypsy Rose 332
Lee-Potter, Linda 16
Lehmann, Rosamond 240
Lette, Kathy 133, 244, 253
Lillie, Beatrice 26, 30, 40, 239
Loos, Anita 45, 145
Lopokova, Lydia 39
Luce Booth, Clare 143, 144
Macaulay, Rose 39
Mansfield, Katherine 59, 240
Margoyles, Miriam 110
Mary, Queen 136
McCarthy, Mary 231, 238, 271
McKinney, Joyce 64
McLeod, Irene Rutherford 173

McMillan, Terry 336
McMinnies, Mary 254
Mead, Margaret 16
Meade, Marion 299
Melba, Nellie 41
Merman, Ethel 304
Midler, Bette 41, 132
Millay, Edna St Vincent 58, 74, 213, 231
Mirikitani, Janice 99
Mitchell, Margaret 345
Mitford, Jessica 351
Mitford, Nancy 133, 197, 205, 244, 248
Monroe, Marilyn 24, 236
Moore, Lorrie 306
Morgan, Elaine 17, 296
Morgan, Diana 319
Morgan, Fidelis & Stafford, Carla 294
Morgan, Fidelis 281
Mosley, Diana 180
Muggeridge, Kitty 240
Murdoch, Iris 201
Nichols, Grace 37
O'Brien, Edna 144
Parker, Dorothy 15, 19, 53, 64, 75, 82,
    122, 125, 130, 157, 238, 239, 305
Parton, Dolly 145
Potter, Beatrix 173
Pym, Barbara 206
Raverat, Gwen 111, 253
Reagan, Nancy 14
Rice-Davies, Mandy 241
Rivers, Joan 21, 110, 199, 205, 235, 237,
    238, 239, 243, 244
Roberts, Glenys 138, 148
Rogers, Ginger 304
Rogers, Margaret 284, 296
Rowland, Helen 18, 19, 22, 179, 192,
    200
Royde-Smith, Naomi 236
Rubens, Bernice 346

Sackville-West, Vita 162
Sayers, Dorothy L. 336
Scott-Maxwell, Florida 14
Sexton, Anne 345
Sheehy, Gail 333
Sitwell, Edith 236, 237, 301
Skinner, Cornelia Otis 14, 114
Smith, Stevie 17, 77, 212
Somerville & Ross 100
Sontag, Susan 92, 317
Spark, Muriel 9, 122, 312, 328
Stark, Freya 2
Steinem, Gloria 15
Stinnet, Caskie 144
Taylor, Elizabeth 97
Telfer, Vera 293
Thomas, Irene 200, 332
Thorndike, Sybil 329
Tims, Margaret 295
Tomlin, Lily 24, 75, 132, 143, 213
Townsend, Sue vii, 268
Truss, Lynne 174
Tucker, Sophie 1
Tweedie, Jill 145
Warner, Sylvia Townsend 322
Warrender, Maude, Lady 45
Wax, Ruby 134
Weldon, Fay 277
West, Mae 1, 15, 18, 236, 237,
    312
West, Rebecca 241
Wharton, Edith 230, 303, 312,
    328
Whitehorn, Katharine 2, 15, 18, 26, 77,
    292, 305
Whitton, Charlotte 2
Wickham, Anna 18, 142
Winn, Mary Day 268
Winters, Shelley 41
Wood, Victoria 297

Where an author's life crosses centuries, we have chosen the century during which she accomplished most of her work.

	Treasure	Gina Davidson	£5.99
☐	Treasure	Gina Davidson	£5.99
☐	The Handmaid's Tale	Margaret Atwood	£5.99
☐	The Robber Bride	Margaret Atwood	£5.99
☐	The Magic Toyshop	Angela Carter	£6.99
☐	Cowboys are my Weakness	Pam Houston	£5.99
☐	Flesh and Blood	Michèle Roberts	£6.99
☐	Frost in May	Antonia White	£6.99
☐	Orlando	Virginia Woolf	£4.99

Virago now offers an exciting range of quality titles by both established and new authors. All of the books in this series are available from:

Little, Brown and Company (UK),
P.O. Box 11,
Falmouth,
Cornwall TR10 9EN.

Alternatively you may fax your order to the above address. Fax No. 01326 317444.

Payments can be made as follows: cheque, postal order (payable to Little, Brown and Company) or by credit cards, Visa/Access. Do not send cash or currency. UK customers and B.F.P.O. please allow £1.00 for postage and packing for the first book, plus 50p for the second book, plus 30p for each additional book up to a maximum charge of £3.00 (7 books plus).

Overseas customers including Ireland, please allow £2.00 for the first book plus £1.00 for the second book, plus 50p for each additional book.

NAME (Block Letters) ....

....

ADDRESS ....

....

....

☐ I enclose my remittance for ....

☐ I wish to pay by Access/Visa Card

Number ☐☐☐☐☐☐☐☐☐☐☐☐☐☐☐☐☐

Card Expiry Date ☐☐☐☐